Dirr's Trees and Shrubs for Warm Climates

Dirr's Trees and Shrubs for Warm Climates

AN ILLUSTRATED ENCYCLOPEDIA

by Michael A. Dirr

Timber Press
Portland, Oregon

Previous pages: *Quercus virginiana*
All photographs are by Michael A. Dirr.

Published in 2002 by
Timber Press, Inc.
The Haseltine Building
133 S.W. Second Avenue, Suite 450
Portland, Oregon 97204 U.S.A.

Printed in Hong Kong through Colorcraft Ltd.
Designed by Susan Applegate

Library of Congress Cataloging-in-Publication Data

Dirr, Michael.
    Dirr's trees and shrubs for warm climates : an illustrated encyclopedia /
    by Michael A. Dirr
        p.   cm.
    ISBN 0-88192-525-X
    1. Ornamental trees—Sunbelt States—Encyclopedias. 2. Ornamental
shrubs—Sunbelt States—Encyclopedias. 3. Ornamental trees—Sunbelt
States—Pictorial works. 4. Ornamental shrubs—Sunbelt States—Pictorial
works. 5. Landscape plants—Sunbelt States—Encyclopedias. 6. Landscape
plants—Sunbelt States—Pictorial works. I. Title: Trees and shrubs for warm
climates. II. Title.

SB435.52.S86 D57 2002
635.9'76'097503—dc21
                                                                    2001035810

Bonnie and I have three great children:
Katherine, Matthew, and Suzanne.
We could not imagine life without them.
All three are gardeners in their own right.
May they prize and preserve nature
in its myriad forms
and continue to appreciate
the Little Things.

Contents

Acknowledgments

To the great Timber staff, Hillary Barber, and Vickie Waters-Oldham:

Working with Mike Dirr is, at times, akin to placing one's hand in a bag of Tasmanian devils. Fortunately, no one was bitten as we worked toward a common goal. To the Timber team: Franni Bertolino Farrell, Neal Maillet, Michael Fox, Darcel Warren—your attention to detail and caring nurtured the book to fruition. To Hillary and Vickie—your persistence, patience, organizational skills, and senses of humor make the process educational, rewarding, and enjoyable.

Preface

I did not fathom the universal appeal of the photographs in *Dirr's Hardy Trees and Shrubs* (Portland, OR: Timber Press, 1997) and am most gratified by the continuing enthusiasm and support from readers. When Richard Abel, former owner and publisher, and I first discussed the photographic essay approach in the 1980s, the goals were two books: one entitled *Hardy Trees and Shrubs* to include Zone 3 to 6 plants, the other Zone 7 to 9 woodies. In both books some plant crossover into higher or lower zones would naturally occur. The pragmatic approach to both would be to include a representative selection of photos depicting growth habit and ornamental characteristics of each plant, with the text providing sufficient verbiage for readers to make an educated decision about utilizing the plant in their gardens and designs. The reception of the first book by you, the reader, has been gratifying, and the reviews by amateurs and professionals across the country have been extremely positive. Check Amazon.com for a steady stream of reviews.

This new book, *Dirr's Trees and Shrubs for Warm Climates*, also with a smattering of vines and groundcovers, includes those woody plants with several subshrub and die-back (to ground) woody species that peacefully coexist in Zone 7 to 9 gardens, with some growing into Zone 11. For example, a few *Lantana camara* cultivars, like 'Miss Huff', overwinter in Zone 7b, grow into 5- to 6-ft.-high rounded woody shrubs by summer, and flower until hard frosts in October and November. The same species is a woody perennial in Zones 10 and 11. Bonnie and I consider 'Miss Huff' among the top five summer-flowering "woodies" in our garden. Additionally, several garden-worthy woody plants missing from *Dirr's Hardy Trees and Shrubs* are included herein.

Also, in genera such as *Lagerstroemia*, *Loropetalum*, and *Osmanthus*, I provide in-depth text and photographs of the species and cultivars. The new red loropetalums, *Loropetalum chinense* var. *rubrum*, "immigrated" to the United States from China in 1989–91. I brought 'Burgundy' and 'Blush' to my University of Georgia program in 1991. An additional 13 to 15, many simply renames, have been evaluated. The most common and best are presented in this book.

The cold hardy palms are also included. They are a wonderful group of woody plants that contribute beauty, texture, and color to Zone 7 to 11 gardens. In 22 years at the University, winter lows have ranged from –5 to –10°F (Athens and Atlanta, Georgia) in the early 1980s to seldom lower than +15°F in the late 1990s. I have observed the "hardy" palms survive, brown, recover, or die. Without arbitration, *Rhapidiophyllum hystrix*, Needle Palm, is the most cold hardy, with others discussed as to their degree of temperature tolerances.

This book is a blending: observations on the performance of the old and new woody plants, and text and photographs that bring them to symbiotic garden life.

Enjoy the book. May the reader find new and renewed inspiration in the featured plants.

Reflections on Garden-making in Georgia

Welcome to the Dirr home and garden. The plant combinations change annually;
here *Helianthus angustifolius*, Swamp Sunflower, *Aster oblongifolius*, Aster, and
Lantana camara 'New Gold' provide a magnificent October greeting.

The Dirr house in the summer of 1979 was a sea of red Georgia soil. Transforming this shabby canvas into a garden was a great journey for Bonnie and me.

Remarkable transformation in 14 years. Bonnie and I planted every tree, shrub, and perennial seen in this October 1993 photograph and loved them into being.

Introductions to this type of book provide minimal benefit, so instead I have penned a short essay of our experiences in developing gardens. For more than 30 years my wife, Bonnie, and I have made gardens in Massachusetts, Illinois, and now Georgia, almost always short on infrastructure (water features, bricks and mortar, sculpture, and pottery) but prominently endowed with plants—shared, purchased, and propagated in-house.

The great journey has provided tremendous satisfaction—nurturing, coercing (at times), and loving the gardens into being. The water and earth have been kind to the plants. We commented during April and May of 2000 that the garden looked about as mature, rich, and vibrant as in any of our 22 years at Georgia. Then nature cast a pall of drought that stole the beauty of spring. Bonnie and I questioned our resolve. It was akin to a test of one's faith. Watering bans forced us to focus on the shrub border and specimen plants. Grass and annuals could always be replanted; an 18-year-old *Stewartia monadelpha*, likely never, in our gardening lifetime.

As I pen this, fall looms with the flip of the calendar and cooler temperatures are discernible. Bonnie and I talk about formalizing new borders with granite edging and a central focal point (water feature). This area was a pool that for 20 years the family enjoyed and eventually outgrew. Removed and filled in, with the surrounding fence taken down, a view was opened to the rest of the garden. Friends admonished us for years about creating views and vistas, but it took the fence removal for us to

An April 2000 photograph with the various *Acer palmatum* and *Loropetalum chinense* var. *rubrum* cultivars providing the touches of red and purple. The following photograph shows the same area taken from a location by the tree in the upper left corner.

13

fully comprehend the advice. Numerous trees and shrubs were planted along the fence, which, when removed, still provided structure and enclosure. We limbed up many of the branches and added shrubs and annuals. The entire process started in January, and the photograph on page 15 was taken in June 2000.

Our Georgia garden is now 22 growing seasons mature. The builder cleared the existing vegetation with the exception of about eight small trees and left a sea of Georgia red soil (some would say dirt). Initially, we established grass and added a few trees. Leyland Cypress (50 ft. high), *Koelreuteria bipinnata* (40 ft. high), *Cedrus deodara* (45 ft. high), *Cedrus atlantica* 'Glauca' (40 ft. high), and *Lagerstroemia* 'Natchez' (25 ft. high) are between 15 and 21 years old. Plant growth in the South is fast, particularly with adequate water and fertilizer.

On either side of the entrance to the driveway are two planting beds that comprise annuals, perennials, and woodies. Neighbors and casual drivers-by have stopped and asked the identity of certain plants. *Helianthus angustifolius*, Swamp Sunflower, *Salvia leucantha*, Mexican Sage, *Aster oblongifolius*, Aster, *Lantana camara* cultivars in variety, *Salvia guaranitica*, *Rosa chinensis* 'Mutabilis', *Buddleia davidii*, *Viburnum macrocephalum*, Chinese Snowball Viburnum, and *Camellia sinensis*, Tea, spark the greatest interest.

These entrance plantings serve as models for the way we have approached the entire garden. Throughout, we planned and planted for an overstory (trees), an understory (smaller shrubs), and a ground plane (small shrubs, perennials, and annuals). A 30-ft.-high and -wide *Koelreuteria bipinnata* provides golden yellow flowers in late August and September. In the shadows below reside seedling native azaleas, *Rhododendron canescens*; 'G. G.

The garden exponentially consumed most of the one and three-quarter acres. The back garden area slopes to a creek, and stone walls were added for structure and erosion control. In this May photograph, *Buddleia davidii* 'Empire Blue', *Lavandula* sp., and grasses, like *Miscanthus sinensis* 'Gracillimus', make for a pleasing composition.

Gerbing' and 'George L. Taber' Southern Indica azaleas; *Aralia elata* 'Variegata'; *Acer palmatum* 'Glowing Embers'; *Carpinus betulus* 'Pendula', Weeping European Hornbeam; white-flowered *Cercis chinensis*; *Loropetalum chinense* var. *rubrum* 'Burgundy'; *Hydrangea quercifolia* 'Snow Queen', and, in the ground plane, aster, salvia, mums, lantanas, and shrubby spireas. Degrees of color, texture, and mystery are evident year-round.

I grew up in the Midwest, where rows of yews and junipers across the front of the house constituted the "foundation" planting. I vowed never to "green meatball" any personal garden. In the South, this concept is often exaggerated with masses of green balls, each pruned to a shell of foliage so tight that if a coin were bounced off it, the result would be similar to a rocket launching. The dwarf hollies, like *Ilex crenata* 'Helleri', *I. cornuta* 'Carissa' and 'Rotunda', and *I. vomitoria* 'Schil-lings', and *Rhaphiolepis umbellata*, Indian Hawthorn, are utilized by the millions in Zones 7 to 9. These types of planting designs are no-brainers, and the plants utilized are what the nursery industry calls commodity items. For gardens and landscapes, there is a palette of plants that allows us to move from the paradigm of the rounded, cubed, and otherwise frozen green elements to vibrancy of color, texture, and form.

Our "foundation" consists of *Acer palmatum*, Japanese Maple, *Stewartia monadelpha*, *Viburnum* 'Conoy', *Illicium parviflorum*, *Leucothoe* (*Agarista*) *populifolia*, *Hydrangea arborescens* 'Annabelle', *Cercis canadensis* 'Forest Pansy', *Sarcococca confusa*, *Edgeworthia papyrifera*, *Aesculus parviflora*, and 20 others. Admittedly, the composition is a degree higgedly-piggedly but has now meshed into a pretty tapestry. Certainly never boring and always metamorphosizing with the seasons.

A new area in 2000, following swimming pool and fence removal. The many trees and shrubs located on the inside of the fence were very linear in placement, a fact made more obvious by fence's absence. New beds were extended, and the shrubs added in March 2000. In this June 2000 photograph, the trees read like part of the composition.

About 13 years ago, a curvilinear line of 'Natchez' crapemyrtle was planted on the west side of the garden to partially screen and direct the eye to the back of the garden. A freeze injured the crapemyrtles, and they resprouted, producing multiple stems that are now one of the highlights. The plants needed a background, so 'Nellie R. Stevens' hollies, mixed with *Ilex ×koehneana* 'Wirt L. Winn' and *Ilex ×attenuata* 'Hume', were added. They now function as the ideal framework to highlight the rich cinnamon-brown exfoliating bark of the crapemyrtle.

Collections of plants are often difficult to blend harmoniously because of vast foliage and growth habit differences. A rather large infusion of *Illicium* species and cultivars were planted under *Pinus taeda*, Loblolly Pine, and *Quercus falcata*, Southern Red Oak. After ten years, the composition appears natural. When walking through this area, I grab and crush an *Illicium* leaf, enjoying the aromatic fragrance. Collections allow the gardener to assess the best performing plants and with *Illicium* taxa, *I. henryi* displays greater heat and drought tolerance than others. This horticultural nugget does not appear in discussions of *Illicium* environmental tolerances.

Trees, limbed up, provide great cover for native azaleas and tender broadleaf evergreens like *Michelia figo*. The cascading autumn leaves are used as mulch for such plantings, enriching the soil in decomposition, reduc-

An ice storm in late January 2000 produced this fairyland spectacle. The large *Cedrus deodara*, Deodar Cedar, in the center, although loaded with ice, did not lose a limb.

ing weeds, conserving moisture, and providing more even, cooler soil temperatures. Our favorite understory azaleas are *Rhododendron austrinum*, Florida Azalea, *R. canescens*, Piedmont Azalea, and *R. alabamense*, Alabama Azalea, all fragrant and flowering in April in yellow, pink, and white, respectively. In early August, the non-fragrant, rich red-flowered *R. prunifolium* opens and serves as a homing device for hummingbirds.

An area devoted to vegetables is enriched yearly with "green manure" (largely crimson clover) and a top dressing of composted horse manure. No pesticides are utilized, with the exception of Round-Up™, for weed control; the bugs eat well and leave plenty for us. Tomatoes, peppers, squash, cucumbers, lettuce, and beans are the typical standards. Nothing better than bacon, lettuce, and tomato sandwiches. Bonnie and I believe in "garden equilibrium" and have practiced the dogma since we started gardening. A few aphids do not justify nuclear pesticide applications.

I enjoy growing seedlings of various woody plants in 2 in. by 8 in., 4 ft. by 8 ft. raised planters. A loose, friable, compost-based soil, rich with organic matter, is utilized. Seeds are collected when physiologically mature, sown immediately, and protected with hardware cloth if necessary. Seeds of *Aesculus parviflora*, Bottlebrush Buckeye, are collected in late September and early October, when the capsules split on the shrub. At this time, the seeds are easily removed. About 100 seeds per

A favorite tree, *Cladrastis kentukea*, American Yellowwood, developing fall color, which is consistently beautiful yellow. Three yellowwoods, including two pink-flowering trees, are ensconced in the garden.

17

raised planter are planted in rows, and within three weeks a tap root develops. The shoot usually emerges above ground the following spring. Over the years, hundreds of these beautiful buckeyes have been given to friends and visitors. The gift is much more meaningful and appreciated than some bauble. In 2000, red and bottlebrush buckeye, fringe tree, oak, hickory, *Baptisia*, and iris filled the beds. Also, when emptied of contents, these beds are used for radishes, lettuce, and potatoes.

Our total garden acreage is one and three-quarters. An area in the floodplain has been cleared and will be planted in the future with spring wildflowers. Many of the trees are 60 to 80 ft. high and provide the ideal shade for such plants. Whether we complete this chapter in garden making is unknown, but the seed for the concept has been planted.

Knowing what I do now compared to 22 years ago provides an opportunity to reflect on the successes and near misses. I estimate more plants have been lost, removed, or given away than currently reside in the garden. People always ask my favorites. Obviously that depends on what part of the country or world I am stumbling about in. For a Zone 7b garden, in the middle of the South, I would always include native azaleas, green and red loropetalums, Japanese maples, southern magnolias, fothergillas, oakleaf hydrangeas, anise-trees, viburnums, crapemyrtles, buckeyes, stewartia, butterfly-bush, hollies, dogwoods, plum yews, bottlebrush buckeye, teaolives, and rosemary.

May this new reference provide education and inspiration as the reader plans and plants for his or her specific landscape desires. Gardening is one of life's great adventures.

Enjoy!

Our front entrance welcomes visitors (we hope) with a varied palette of color, texture, and form. Please note the lack of any green meatballs, a.k.a. dwarf hollies, yews, and junipers. Two beloved plants are the *Stewartia monadelpha*, Tall Stewartia, on the left and the *Fothergilla major* 'Mt. Airy' with white flowers on the right. The time period is early April. Note the underplantings in the ground plane. Our goal is to reduce the sea of pine needle or deciduous leaf mulch.

Can the reader imagine a visitor chiding us for too many plants? More than once, this refrain has been sung. Obviously, friends like these are expendable. How can this mishmash be adequately explained? It can't. We love the colors and textures, although Bonnie, in a fit of madness, has told me she would like to see the house. This is a May photograph.

A quiet area of the garden in June 2000, with, from left to right, *Ilex glabra* 'Nigra', *Viburnum* 'Conoy', *Illicium parviflorum, Leucothoe* (*Agarista*) *populifolia, Stewartia monadelpha,* and the underplanting of *Hydrangea arborescens* 'Annabelle', pink 'Shibori' spirea, and white impatiens. Almost too calm for the Dirr garden!

Bark—exfoliating, richly colored, musclelike in texture—is a year-round asset but always at its showman's best from leaf drop to leaf emergence. This allée of *Lagerstroemia* 'Natchez' is enhanced by the holly background.

Fall in our garden is never consistent. One year *Fothergilla major* 'Mt. Airy' is yellow, another red, and often yellow-orange-red, similar to that visible in the right side of the photograph. This is the west side of the garden, and we continue to add plants and tweak the composition. Obviously we have a way to go. Notice the crapemyrtles in the right-center, background.

Aah—fresh tomatoes, peppers, beans, squash, and cucumbers
provide food for the body; the ornamentals nourishment for the soul.
There is balance in nature that translates to the garden.

Our forever favorite fall combination, which we have never been able to duplicate: *Rudbeckia* (yellow), *Chrysanthemum* (pink), *Sedum* 'Autumn Joy', and *Pennisetum* 'Burgundy Giant' with an old-timey double white mum, which I rescued from an antebellum home, in bud.

Spring returns to the Dirr garden in March, with the dogwood just opening and the yellow spireas ('Gold Mound') and maples (*Acer palmatum* 'Seiryu' and *A. oliverianum*, far right) unfurling their spring greenery. The sense of renewal is in the air. The garden beckons. A wonderful quote—"Show me your garden, and I shall tell you who you are"—defines and distinguishes those who love gardens and practice the art and science of garden-making.

A–Z Illustrated Guide
to Trees and Shrubs for Warm Climates

Abelia chinensis
CHINESE ABELIA

The Chinese Abelia is a great biological butterfly magnet. In the Dirr garden (Zone 7b), flowers open in June, continuing until frost. Small white fragrant flowers are borne in rounded panicles on the new growth of the season. The ¾- to 1½-in.-long, lustrous dark green leaves provide background to the flowers. Habit is rounded, spreading, loose. Prospers in moist, acid, well-drained soil. Full sun to half shade. Makes a great shrub border plant combined with butterfly-bushes and lantana. Prune in late winter, and by June and July, flowering is in high gear. Grows 5 to 7 ft. high and wide. Zones 6 to 9. China.

Abelia chinensis flowers

Abelia chinensis sepals

Abelia chinensis foliage and flowers

Abelia chinensis, Chinese Abelia
Overleaf: *Sabal palmetto*

Abelia ×*grandiflora*
GLOSSY ABELIA

No other flowering evergreen shrub displays the resiliency of this hybrid species (*Abelia chinensis* × *A. uniflora*). Originated in Italy before 1866 and in cultivation for over 100 years, it is still one of the most popular shrubs for southern gardens. White, flushed pink, ¾- to 1-in.-long tubular flowers open on new growth from May to frost. Individual flowers do not overwhelm, but a shrub in full flower is quite effective. The five sepals that subtend the flower age gracefully from green to rose-purple and literally smother the foliage canopy by late summer. Habit is rounded to spreading, densely foliated with ½- to 1½- in.-long lustrous dark green leaves that color bronze-red-purple in cold weather. Wonderfully serviceable shrub that prospers in sun and shade and in acid, well-drained soil. Three consecutive years of drought and heat, 1998 to 2000, showed *A.* ×*grandiflora* to be one of the most durable shrubs for southern gardens. Effective as border plant, mass, hedge, and butterfly attractant. One of my favorite shrubs. Our program, at the University of Georgia, is breeding abelias for unique flower colors (rose, yellow, and purple), increased flower size, improved evergreen foliage, compact habit, and increased cold hardiness. Grows 3 to 6 ft. high and wide; plants to 8 ft. occur. Zones 6 to 9.

Cultivars and Varieties. Confetti™ ('Conti') is a compact form to 2½ ft. high with cream-margined leaves that turn rose in winter; flowers (sparse) are white. Not a particularly vigorous plant.

'Edward Goucher', a hybrid between *Abelia* ×*grandiflora* and *A. schumannii*, produces lavender-pink flowers and is less cold hardy than *A.* ×*grandiflora*. Grows 4 to 5 ft. high and wide.

MORE ➤

Abelia ×*grandiflora* foliage

Abelia ×*grandiflora* flowers

Abelia 'Edward Goucher'

Abelia ×*grandiflora*, Glossy Abelia

Abelia ×grandiflora **continued**

'Francis Mason' produces copper-colored new shoots that mature yellow to yellow-green; pink to white flowers. Grows 5 to 7 ft. high.

'John Creech' (best), 'Little Richard' (middle), and 'Sherwoodii' (worst) are compact forms, 3 to 4 ft. high or less; I have observed reversion shoots on all.

'Rose Creek' is the first compact form from the Georgia breeding program. Grows 2 to 3 ft. high and wide, with broad-ovate lustrous dark green leaves and copious fragrant white flowers.

'Sunrise' is a yellow-margined branch sport of *Abelia ×grandiflora* discovered at Taylor's Nursery, Raleigh, North Carolina. Foliage, at its best, is quite attractive but has shown a tendency to revert to the species type, i.e., green shoots.

Abelia ×grandiflora Confetti™

Abelia ×grandiflora 'Rose Creek'

Abelia ×grandiflora 'Francis Mason'

Abelia ×grandiflora 'Sunrise'

Abies firma
MOMI FIR

Firs and heat are akin to cats and dogs; they simply do not socialize well. However, the Momi Fir is succeeding in Athens, Georgia, and Mobile, Alabama. Habit is pyramidal-conical in youth and maturity. The lustrous dark green needles are sharply notched at their ends. Cones are 3½ to 5 in. long, 1½ to 2 in. wide, and brown at maturity. Slight foliage yellowing may result from the winter sun. A plant in the Dirr garden, sited on the north side of deciduous woods, has prospered. Best performance occurs in moist, well-drained, acid soils. Slow to initiate strong growth—kind of stares at the gardener for several years, then decides to leap. Worthy specimen fir and, to my knowledge, the only viable candidate for the South. Grows 40 to 50 ft. high, 10 to 15 ft. wide. Zones 6 to 9. Japan.

Abutilon pictum
FLOWERING MAPLE, CHINESE BELL FLOWER, CHINESE LANTERN

Almost better known for container culture and bedding schemes, particularly in European gardens, than as a flowering shrub in the United States. Typically a dieback shrub that rejuvenates from the roots with accelerated growth and flowers in summer. Leaves are maplelike, typically three-lobed, yellow-green, and assume a slightly reflexed, graceful posture. The flowers develop from the leaf axils and are semi-pendulous, bell-shaped, 2 in. long with crepe-papery petals. Colors of the numerous cultivars are kaleidoscopic and range from white and yellow to pink, orange, and red, opening from summer until frost. Adaptable, but requires well-drained soil. Do not overfertilize, as this results in rampant vegetative

MORE ➤

Abutilon pictum, Flowering Maple, flower

Abies firma undersides of needles

Abies firma, Momi Fir

Abutilon pictum continued

growth at the expense of flower production. About four to six hours of sun suit plants best, yet they flower reasonably in partial shade. Wonderful plant for summer flowers. Useful as a filler in borders and containers. Foliage on the variegated types, like 'Thompsonii' (yellow-streaked and -flecked), adds sparkle. Expect 3 to 4 ft. of growth in Zone 7, larger in warmer areas. Zones 8 to 11. Brazil.

The related species *Abutilon megapotamicum*, Trailing Abutilon, is a finely branched shrub with leaves to 3 in. long, rarely lobed, and pendulous, 1-in.-long, red flowers on 1- to 2-in.-long, red stalks. Refined and delicate in flower. Fine container or bedding plant. Zones 8 to 9. Brazil.

Acacia dealbata
SILVER WATTLE, MIMOSA

I have chased *Acacia* species throughout my travels and have yet to fully understand this diverse genus, with estimates of 700 to 1200 species. Silver Wattle is one of the more common species in English gardens and also one of the hardiest (to 14°F). Typically an evergreen tree, loose and architectural in habit, with bipinnate leaves ranging from blue-green to medium green. Each leaf is 3 to 5 in. long, with eight to twenty pinnae (branches), each with 20 to 40 pairs of ⅛-in.-long, ¹⁄₂₄-in.-wide leaves. Fragrant, ball-shaped clusters of yellow flowers are borne in large racemes in late winter to early spring. Outside the library window at the Hillier Arboretum, England, a large *Acacia dealbata* provided great botanical

Abutilon megapotamicum, Trailing Abutilon

Acacia dealbata flowers and foliage

Acacia dealbata, Silver Wattle

intrigue during my 1999 sabbatical. Green and reticent upon my arrival in February, it blossomed in March and April, settling down by May, retreating to green. Provide well-drained, acid soil in sun or partial shade. Flowers develop from previous season's wood so prune after flowering. Reliable only in warmer West Coast gardens and south Florida, otherwise a conservatory plant. Grows 20 to 30 ft. high, although listed to 100 ft. Zones 8 to 10(11). Tasmania, Australia.

Acer barbatum fall color

Acer barbatum (right) and *A. leucoderme* (left) leaf undersides

Acer barbatum
(*A. saccharum* subsp. *barbatum*)
SOUTHERN SUGAR MAPLE

The true Sugar Maple, *Acer saccharum*, often struggles in the heat of Zone 7 and south. This southern native is a worthy alternative. I have observed thriving specimens in coastal South Carolina and near Nacadoches, Texas, that attest to its heat tolerance. The habit is oval-rounded, densely branched, and foliated with dark green leaves. One of the best ways to separate this species from the closely allied *Acer leucoderme* is by the grayish underside of the leaf, compared to green for *A. leucoderme*. Fall color varies from yellow to orange-red. No serious insects or diseases. A terrific candidate for bringing rich fall color to warm climates. Grows 20 to 30 ft. high, similar spread. Have observed trees over 60 ft. high in Texas. Zones (6)7 to 9. Virginia to Florida, southeastern Missouri, Arkansas, eastern Oklahoma, and Texas.

Acer barbatum, Southern Sugar Maple, in fall

Acer leucoderme
(*A. saccharum* subsp. *leucoderme*)
CHALKBARK MAPLE

In the Piedmont forests of Georgia, this wonderful maple resides in anonymity until autumn, when its flamboyant yellows, oranges, and reds vie for attention. Almost always an understory plant, usually single-stemmed, low-branched, or multi-stemmed, it develops a roundish outline. The leaves are lighter green than those of *Acer barbatum*. Several Georgia nurserymen have tried to commercialize the species, but the growth rate is slower than *A. barbatum* and the variation in fall color maddening. Found as an understory plant in drier, upland woods throughout its native range. Worthy of consideration in the South, but selections for desirable characteristics (habit, fall color) are necessary to bring the plant to everyday commerce. Grows 20 to 30 ft. high and wide. Zones 5 to 9. Native to Georgia, the panhandle of Florida, Louisiana, eastern Oklahoma, and Texas.

Acer leucoderme fall color

Acer leucoderme, Chalkbark Maple, in fall

Actinidia deliciosa
(*A. chinensis*)
KIWI, CHINESE GOOSEBERRY

Unique, rapid-growing, twining vine producing edible hairy brownish green "berry" fruit. The New Zealanders were the first to successfully commercialize the plant and make it a household word worldwide. The fuzzy young leaves emerge bronze to purplish green changing to dark green. The 1½-in.-diameter creamy white fragrant flowers open in April and May. The famous brownish green, hairy, 1- to 2-in.-long fruit ripen in fall. Susceptible to late spring frosts in Zone 7, and the emerging foliage is often killed. Provide full sun, moist, well-drained soils. Male ('Chico Male') and female ('Hayward') vines are required for effective fruit set. Grows 40 to 50 ft. or limited by structure. Zones (7)8 to 10. China.

Actinidia deliciosa flowers

Actinidia deliciosa new foliage

Actinidia deliciosa mature foliage

Actinidia deliciosa, Kiwi

Adina rubella
CHINESE BUTTONBUSH

Beautiful shiny-leaved shrub that, for foliage alone, is recommended for warm-climate gardens. The habit is loose, arching-spreading, and refreshingly fine-textured. The 1- to 2-in.-long, lustrous dark green leaves provide mirrorlike reflections. Leaves hold late; in Athens they are still a pristine green in late December. Flowers, akin to miniature sputniks, ½ to ¾ in. in diameter, initiate in June and July and continue into October in Zone 7b. Soft and creamy in color, they spew a slight fragrance. Unique and almost unknown plant for shady nooks and crannies. Worthy filler in the shady border, north and east side of structures. Any well-drained, acidic soil is suitable. Grows 8 to 10 ft. high and wide. Plant was killed to the ground after exposure to –24°F in Bernheim Arboretum, Clermont, Kentucky, and produced 3 to 4 ft. of new growth in a single season. Zones (6)7 to 9. China.

Adina rubella, Chinese Buttonbush

Adina rubella foliage

Adina rubella flowers

Aesculus californica flowers and foliage

Adina rubella flower-*cum*-sputnik

Aesculus californica fruit

Aesculus californica
CALIFORNIA BUCKEYE

Rather crafty buckeye, prospering in the warm, moist California spring, then shedding its leaves in the dry summer season. In Europe, leaves persist into fall. The leaves are composed of five lustrous green leaflets, each 3 to 6 in. long. Bark is beautiful light to pale silver, reminiscent of the bark of *Fagus grandifolia*, American Beech. Small, rounded to broad-rounded, low-branched tree of stunning elegance in flower. Numerous 4- to 8-in.-long, 2-in.-wide, cylindrical panicles of fragrant white flowers open in June. The smooth, pear-shaped capsule contains one to two, 1½- to 2-in.-diameter, pale orange-brown seeds. Have observed on dry hillsides in California and the moist soils of the English landscape. A collector's trophy plant, not for everyone. Grows 15 to 20 ft. high and wide. Zones 7 to 9(10). California.

Aesculus californica displaying its habit in the winter landscape

Aesculus californica, California Buckeye

Aesculus indica
INDIAN HORSECHESTNUT

A rarity in the United Sates and easily cultured only along the West Coast into Vancouver and elsewhere in coastal British Columbia. Large, rounded, densely foliated tree with seven (occasionally five or nine) lustrous dark green leaflets and a distinct, wavy leaf margin. In fall, leaves may develop auburn to orange-red coloration. Smooth gray bark develops on old specimens, and trunk becomes platy with unique puzzlelike pieces and patterns. Flowers, which appear in late May and June, are eyepoppers, 12 to 16 in. long, 4 to 5 in. wide, pinkish white to pinkish rose. The magnificent specimen trees at Kew Gardens, England, inspire casual and serious visitors. Fruit are 2- to 3-in.-diameter, rounded, roughened capsules. Grows to full genetic potential, 50 to 60 ft. high and wide, in moist soil, cool climate, and full sun. Zones 7 to 10 on the West Coast, not suitable for warm southeastern United States. Northwestern Himalayas.

Aesculus indica flowers

Aesculus indica, Indian Horsechestnut

Aesculus indica bark

Aesculus sylvatica seeds

Aesculus sylvatica
PAINTED BUCKEYE

Imagine northern slopes of southern woodlands covered with the bronze, brown, and red-purple early maturing leaves. What a great native plant for those understory situations in the garden. Almost always small, shrubby, wide-spreading, it occasionally reaches small tree status. My observations provide concrete data that this is a favorite landscape plant of squirrels—willy-nilly it emerges from the forest duff with the same pattern as a squirrel crossing the road. The five dark green leaflets produce a sprinkle of yellow fall color. Leaves may abscise early if summers are hot and dry. Yellow-green flowers, in 4- to 8-in.-long panicles, crown the foliage in April and May. Fruit, smooth, 1 to 2 in. in diameter, contain one to three shiny brown-black seeds. Wonderful for naturalizing in the understory. Grows 6 to 15 ft. high and wide. Zones 6 to 9. Virginia to Georgia, west to Tennessee and Alabama.

Aesculus sylvatica, Painted Buckeye

Aesculus sylvatica new foliage

Aesculus sylvatica flowers

Agave americana
CENTURY PLANT

Certainly not a woody plant in the classical definition but a collection of rosetted, large, fleshy (rawhide), spiny-margined leaves that adds impact to any garden. Forms a rounded outline, the large leaves splaying in all directions from the center. Leaves are blue-green, with hooked spines along the margin and a sharp spine at the tip. Leaves are formidable, so use with discretion. Flowers occur in an elongated stalk (variable length) in paniculate fashion, each about 3 in. long and yellow-green. Called the Century Plant because it supposedly flowers only once every hundred years. Actually flowers when physiologically mature at variable intervals. Have ob-

served in a garden in Wrightsville, Georgia, in dry, sandy soil. Any well-drained soil in sun is suitable. Excellent drought and salt tolerance. Makes a rather striking container plant, particularly the variegated forms. Margin leaf spines are dangerous, so site with some thought to safety. Individual leaves to 6 ft. long; entire plant grows 3 to 6 ft. high, 10 to 12 ft. wide. Zones (8b)9 to 10. Mexico.

Cultivars and Varieties. The literature mentions at least four variegated leaf forms; the most common is 'Marginata', with yellow-white margins and a more restrained habit.

Agave americana, Century Plant

Alangium platanifolium

Although a relative newcomer to the gardens of the United States, the species offers large textured leaves, yellow fall color, yellow-white flowers, and small tree/large shrub habit. The 4- to 8-in.-long, dark green leaves are thick-textured and meld to soft yellow in fall. Cream-yellow flowers appear in May and June in a loose pendent inflorescence. Soils should be moist and well-drained, although a specimen in the Dirr garden has prospered in the heat and drought of the 1998, 1999, and 2000 summers. When grown as a small tree the habit is pyramidal-rounded; as a shrub, more spreading and vase-shaped. Among the most unrecognized plants in our garden. Grows 6 to 10 (to 15) ft. high and wide. Zones (6)7 to 9. China.

Alangium platanifolium flowers and foliage

Alangium platanifolium

Aleurites fordii
TUNG-OIL TREE

Twenty-five years past, on the campus of Louisiana State University, Baton Rouge, I spied a completely unknown (to me) small tree with the glossiest dark green, deeply veined leaves. Detective work coupled with a worthy reference text pointed to Tung-oil Tree. Once experienced, it is impossible to forget. The habit is pyramidal to rounded with a dense canopy of foliage. Leaves may remain evergreen in warmer climates but turn brown and abscise where freezes occur. The flowers are beautiful, white changing to rose in center, bell-shaped, and borne in 6- to 8-in.-long panicles during mid- to late spring. Fruit are 2- to 3-in.-diameter globular drupes, each with three to five seeds. Seeds are the source of tung oil, which is used in the paint and varnish industry. Grows in any well-drained soil. Sun to partial shade. Grows 10 to 20 ft. high, as wide at maturity. Zones 8 to 10. China.

Aleurites fordii, Tung-oil Tree

Aleurites fordii foliage

Aleurites fordii flowers

Allamanda cathartica
GOLDEN TRUMPET or YELLOW ALLAMANDA

A fence, trellis, and mailbox broadleaf evergreen plant, vining in character, that is hardy only in the deep coastal South but is widely available North and South for color in the summer landscape. The glossy, leathery, broadleaf evergreen leaves, 4 to 6 in. long, occur in twos (up to three to five) at each node. Flowers develop on new growth over the entire growing season. Each five-lobed flower is shaped like a morning glory, 3 to 6 in. long and wide; red-brown buds open golden yellow. Best flowering in full sun in fertile, well-drained soil. Prune to keep tidy, and since flowers are formed on new growth, greater production will occur. Wonderful color element around pools and high traffic areas; requires support to climb. Grows 10 ft. high or more. Zones 9 to 11. South America.

Cultivars and Varieties. 'Hendersonii' has attractive, large, orange-yellow flowers.

Allamanda cathartica, Golden Trumpet Allamanda

Alnus serrulata
TAG or HAZEL ALDER

Considered the southern counterpart of *Alnus rugosa*, Speckled Alder, and common along watercourses throughout the South. I find this a most attractive, large spreading shrub or small pyramidal tree. The dark green, 2- to 4-in.-long leaves die off green to brown in autumn. The male flowers open in February and March and dangle like worms from the branches. On the same plant, in ovoid conelike structures, the reddish purple female flowers open at the same time. The female flowers produce fruit that mature in fall and are ½ in. long, resembling brownish pinecones in shape. Adaptable to drier soils as well as flooding, it is a great plant for naturalizing along stream banks, rivers, and troublesome erosion areas. Grows 10 to 20 ft. high and wide. Zones (4)5 to 9. Maine, south to Florida and Louisiana.

Alnus serrulata foliage

Alnus serrulata male and female flowers

MORE ➤

Alnus serrulata continued

Alnus serrulata, Tag Alder

Alnus serrulata fruit

Alnus serrulata in flower

Antigonon leptopus
CORAL VINE

Jogging around Brownsville, Texas, in October, I kept passing this rich pink-flowered vine. I tracked its identity and did the necessary taxonomic homework. The next time I witnessed it was in Charleston, South Carolina. A rampant twining deciduous vine, climbing by tendrils and requiring support. The bright green, heart- to arrow-shaped leaves, 3 to 4 in. long, are coarsely veined with wavy margins. The flowers open in summer; their showy portion, the reddish pink sepals, literally hides the foliage. As long as new growth continues, flowers will be produced. Prefers full sun and warm temperatures, well-drained soil, and low to moderate fertility. I have observed it draped over walls and fences to the degree the structures are hidden. The floral effect is overwhelming. Use with caution. Can become weedy and invasive. Fast growing to 20 (to 40) ft. or more. Zones 8 to 10. Mexico.

Cultivars and Varieties. 'Alba' is a white-flowered form.

Antigonon leptopus, Coral Vine

Araucaria araucana
MONKEY PUZZLE

A wild and rather "scary" tree with open splaying branches and spirally arranged, 1- to 2-in.-long, sharp-pointed, dark green leaves that cover the branches like armor plates. The habit is pyramidal-oval in youth, later with a slender bole and ascending branches near the top. The tree is associated with the Victorian era in England, where it was planted in great numbers. Male flowers occur in 3- to 5-in.-long cylindrical catkins; female in 5- to 8-in.-diameter, pineapple-shaped cones that take two years to mature. Cones are about twice the size of hand grenades and hurt even worse. Tolerates extremes of soil, except permanently moist. Useful as a specimen, or for groupings or accent. Have observed in California in reasonable numbers; seldom grown in southeastern United States. Grows 50 to 80 ft. high. Zones (7)8 to 11. Chile, Argentina.

Araucaria araucana, Monkey Puzzle

MORE ➤

46

Araucaria araucana continued

Araucaria araucana branches

Araucaria araucana

Arbutus menziesii foliage

Araucaria araucana bark

Arbutus menziesii bark

Arbutus menziesii
MADRONE

At its most beautiful, a one-of-a-kind evergreen tree with striking cinnamon-brown bark. The habit varies from cloudlike and low-branched to tall, slender trees. I have observed both types on Vancouver Island, British Columbia. The younger branches shed the brown bark in scales and sheets, exposing the red-brown to red inner bark. The tree would almost be more beautiful without leaves. The foliage is lustrous dark green, 2 to 6 in. long. Flowers, urn-shaped, ¼ to ⅓ in. long, white, occur in 3- to 9-in.-long, 6-in.-wide terminal panicles in May. The ½-in.-wide red fruit color in fall and persist into winter. Transplant from containers into well-drained, dryish soils. Excessive irrigation may prove lethal. Have noticed leaf spot susceptibility, particularly on plants in English gardens. Remarkable for the beauty of its bark. Grows 20 to 50 ft. high, 15 to 30 ft. wide in gardens; 75 to 100 ft. in native habitat. Zones 7 to 10. British Columbia to San Francisco area.

Arbutus menziesii, Madrone

Arbutus menziesii flowers

Arbutus unedo

STRAWBERRY TREE

I was privileged to experience the species in the Killarny National Park, Ireland, where it exists as a large shrub to small tree. The evergreen foliage is 2 to 4 in. long and provides a dark green contrast to the ¼-in.-long, urn-shaped white flowers that open from October through December. The ¾-in.-diameter, orange-shaped fruit ripen the year following flowering. Fruit are orange-red, almost fluorescent, and will definitely turn heads. Moist, well-drained soil, in sun or shade is suitable. Once established, will tolerate drier soils. Great accent or novelty plant and certainly a plant for the collector. Grows 10 to 15 ft. high, 8 to 12 ft. wide; to 30 ft. high in the wild. Zones 7 to 10. Southwestern Ireland to the Mediterranean region.

Arbutus ×*andrachnoides*, a hybrid between *A. unedo* and *A. andrachne*, is more common in cultivation than the latter parent. Unique for its rich reddish brown bark, smaller size, and easier culture. Zones 7 to 10.

Cultivars and Varieties. Several cultivars of garden interest, including 'Compacta' with contorted, picturesque, branching and 5 ft. by 5 ft. size.

'Elfin King' bears abundant flowers and fruit and grows 5 to 10 ft. high.

'Rubra' produces red-budded, dark pink flowers.

Arbutus unedo 'Elfin King' fruit

Arbutus unedo, Strawberry Tree

Arbutus unedo flowers

Arbutus unedo 'Compacta'

Arbutus ×*andrachnoides*

Ardisia japonica, Japanese Ardisia

Ardisia japonica
JAPANESE ARDISIA, MARLBERRY

An evergreen groundcover planting of this species under a massive Live Oak, *Quercus virginiana*, at Live Oak Gardens, New Iberia, Louisiana, made a believer out of me. Beautiful lustrous dark green leaves blanket the ground as thoroughly as *Pachysandra terminalis*. The 1½- to 3½-in.-long leaves, tapered at their ends, are crowded at the end of the stems and appear whorled. The white to pink, star-shaped, ½-in.-diameter flowers are borne two to six together in July and August and sporadically thereafter. Fruit, ¼-in.-diameter red drupes, mature in fall and persist through winter. Culturally, acid, organic, moist, well-drained soils are ideal. Site in partial to full shade. Have tried the species and cultivars in our Zone 7b garden; only 'Chirimen' is still alive. Foliage is often injured by late spring frosts. Grows 8 to 12 (to 16) in. high and spreads indefinitely by rhizomes. Zones 8 to 9(10). Japan, China.

The related species *Ardisia crenata*, Coralberry, Spiceberry, has shiny, dark green, toothed, evergreen leaves to 8 in. long, white to pink flowers, and bright red fruit. Requires well-drained soils and partial to full shade. Grows 2 to 4 (to 6) ft. high. Zones 8b to 10. Japan to northern India.

Ardisia japonica fruit

Ardisia japonica flowers

Ardisia crenata, Coralberry

Ardisia crenata fruit

Aucuba japonica
JAPANESE AUCUBA

Considered old-fashioned, dated, tired, and dinosauristic, but the infusion of new cultivars has brought a rejuvenated lease on landscape life to the species. Typically, haystack to rounded evergreen shrub, consisting of a thicket of erect or arching, limitedly branched shoots. The species type has lustrous leathery dark green leaves, 3 to 8 in. long and either entire or coarsely toothed. Leaves hold their color throughout the seasons when sited in shade. Flowers, male and female, open in March and April on separate plants, lurid purple on both, the former in large terminal panicles, the latter in clusters from the axils of the leaves. Female flowers yield shiny scarlet ellipsoidal drupes, ½ in. or longer, that ripen in fall and persist into winter. Grows in almost any well-drained soil, but should be sited in shade. Young leaves will blacken (burn) when exposed to full sun. Good choice for the shadowy area of the garden. The variegated leaf cultivars provide color to heavily shaded areas. Grows 6 to 10 ft. high and wide. Zones 7 to 10. Japan.

Aucuba japonica, Japanese Aucuba

Aucuba japonica fruit

Aucuba japonica male flowers

Aucuba japonica **continued**

Cultivars and Varieties. 'Crotonifolia' (female) and 'Marmorita' (female) are the best gold-variegated leaf forms, each richly endowed with vibrant gold markings consuming 70 percent of the leaf surface.

'Mr. Goldstrike' (male) and 'Golden King' (male) are beautiful gold-speckled leaf forms that serve as pollinators for the female forms.

'Rozannie' (female) is a compact, 3- to 4-ft.-high and -wide form with lustrous dark green foliage.

'Variegata' (female), the common form in cultivation, is less gold-speckled.

Aucuba japonica 'Mr. Goldstrike'

Aucuba japonica 'Crotonifolia'

Aucuba japonica 'Golden King'

Aucuba japonica 'Marmorita'

Aucuba japonica 'Rozannie'

Aucuba japonica 'Rozannie' foliage and fruit

Aucuba japonica 'Variegata'

Baccharis halimifolia
GROUNDSEL-BUSH

So nondescript that its existence is unknown until the female plants develop their white, cottony fruit, akin to dandelion seed heads, in late summer and fall. I have observed entire fields and marshy areas in Georgia and Louisiana literally invaded by the species. The habit is loose, lax, and arching, with occasional compact, oval to rounded forms evident. The bright to soft-green foliage is attractive and may remain evergreen in the South; deciduous in the North. Species is dioecious, sexes separate, with flowering and fruiting occurring in summer and fall, respectively. In Georgia, fruit persist into December. Grows in dry and moist soils; extremely salt-tolerant and easily maintained by cutting to the ground in late winter. Best as a filler in the border for foliage contrast. Aggressive and has taken over abandoned fields and dump sites. Plant a male to avoid seed production. Grows 5 to 12 ft. high and wide. Zones 5 to 9. Massachusetts to Florida and Texas.

MORE ➤

Baccharis halimifolia foliage

Baccharis halimifolia continued

Baccharis halimifolia, Groundsel-bush, in fruit

Bauhinia variegata foliage

Bauhinia variegata flower

Bauhinia blakeana flower

Bauhinia variegata
ORCHID TREE

None of the *Bauhinia* species are truly hardy below 20°F, but during travels to Orlando, Florida, I see *Bauhinia variegata* (pale purple to white flowers) and *B. blakeana* (pink to pinkish purple flowers) more than any other. Although treelike in habit, most grow as large shrubs. Leaves are light green and deeply cleft at the apex and base, producing a twin-leaf effect. Leaves may drop in fall or persist into winter. The great beauty is allocated to the orchidlike flowers with five unequal petals, each narrowed to a claw. The 2- to 3-in.-diameter, light pink to orchid-purple flowers open in January and February. The 1-in.-long, flat, sharp-beaked pods form after flowering. Place in full sun, well-drained soil, and stake for tree habit. Flowers on old wood, so reserve pruners until after flowering. Beautiful specimen shrub or tree, best located in a border. Grows 15 to 25 ft. high, more often 10 to 15 ft. as a shrub. Zones (9)10 to 11. India, China.

Bauhinia blakeana, Hong Kong Orchid Tree, has larger flowers, 5 to 6 in. across, in a range of colors from reddish to orchid-pink in late fall to spring. The gray-green foliage is tardily deciduous. Grows 20 ft. high. Zones 10 to 11. China.

Cultivars and Varieties. 'Candida' has white flowers.

Bougainvillea glabra (*B. spectabilis*)
BOUGAINVILLEA, TISSUE PAPER PLANT

Every gardener who witnesses the plant in flower—bright, vivid, vibrant, and fluorescent—hopes to grow one of the many cultivars. A wicked, spiny, scandent shrub or vine that has scissored my arms on several occasions; handle with leather gloves, for it requires a structure to climb and occasional nipping to keep it in check. The lustrous medium to dark green, 1- to 3-in.-long leaves are little more than the "food" factory that supports the overindulgent floral production engine. The showy portions of the flowers are the paperlike bracts, three together, 1 to 2 in. long, that surround the true flowers. Colors span the rainbow, and in late March, I stopped at a nursery in the Florida Keys to buy red and coppery salmon forms while salivating over 30 other cultivars. Requires sun, heat, and well-drained, acid soil. Typically, flowers in summer and fall in Zone 7b when grown as a container plant. Refrain from overfertilizing, as this leads to excessive vegetative growth. Great trellis, wall, fence, and container plant. A trip to Disney in Florida will make a Minnesotan a believer. Grows willy-nilly, 40 ft. or more. Zones 9 to 11. South America.

Cultivars and Varieties. Counted over 30 in one publication. 'Barbara Karst' is often listed as one of the hardiest with red flowers over a long period. 'Sanderiana' with magenta bracts, is common.

Bauhinia variegata, Orchid Tree

Bougainvillea glabra, Tissue Paper Plant

Broussonetia papyrifera
PAPER MULBERRY

An aggressive, intimidating, invasive species that colonizes waste areas and never lets go. In Athens, it is the biological glue that keeps the railroad embankment from eroding. In its best manifestation, however, the species develops into a round-headed tree of respectable attractiveness. The dull dark green leaves, 4 to 8 in. long, are covered with soft "furry" hairs on the lower leaf surfaces; the upper surfaces have the consistency of sandpaper. Leaves are variously lobed to entire with coarsely dentate teeth along the margins. Male and female flowers are borne on separate plants, the female producing ¾- to 1-in.-diameter orange-red drupes. Certainly not a tree for the average garden but perhaps for impossible sites. Full sun locations in well-drained, acid soils are best. Grows 30 to 50 ft. high and wide. Zones 6 to 10. China, Japan.

Cultivars and Varieties. 'Aurea', with rich yellow to yellow-gold leaves, holds the color through the growing season. Introduced by Don Shadow, Winchester, Tennessee.

Broussonetia papyrifera bark

Broussonetia papyrifera, Paper Mulberry

Broussonetia papyrifera fruit

Broussonetia papyrifera 'Aurea'

Brugmansia ×candida
(*B. suaveolens, Datura* spp.)
ANGEL'S TRUMPET

Mild weather over the past ten years has produced many surprises relative to outdoor plant survival. In August, I spied an 8-ft.-high, yellow-flowered Angel's Trumpet in the front garden of an Atlanta residence. Driving (by myself), I tend to verbalize to the imaginary garden friend in the passenger's seat: "Is this possible?" A die-back shrub into coastal Florida and Louisiana, rounded plants with thickish stems reach (6 to) 10 to 15 ft. high and wide. Leaves are large, 6 to 12 in. long, irregularly lobed with entire to coarsely serrated margins, and bright green. Flowers are head-knockers, 6 to 9 in. long, fragrant, trumpet-shaped, arching-pendulous in summer and fall. Well-drained soil in sun to light shade is acceptable. Provide supplemental water in droughts, fertilize lightly. Most often a die-back shrub at temperatures of 20 to 25°F and below. Regenerates quickly. Used in borders and containers. Plant parts are poisonous. Have observed 15-ft.-high, freestanding shrubs in St. Francisville, Louisiana. Grows 10 to 15 ft. high and wide. Zones (8)9 to 11. Peru, Ecuador, Chile.

Brugmansia ×candida, Angel's Trumpet

Brugmansia ×candida flowers

Brunfelsia pauciflora
YESTERDAY-TODAY-AND-TOMORROW

In coastal Georgia, occasionally used as a container plant for the beautiful violet (on the outside) flowers that open to a white, flat disk in the center. With time, flowers age to pale violet or white. Has an irregular shrublike habit and requires pruning. The oval to obovate, evergreen leaves are 3 to 6 in. long and dull dark green. Flowers change color from violet (purple) to white over a three-day period in spring and summer. Not winter hardy in most of the Southeast, where it is best grown as a container plant. Prefers full sun and fertile, well-drained soil high in organic matter. Use as a massing shrub in Zones 10 to 11. Grows 4 to 5 ft. high and wide. Zones (9)10 to 11. Brazil, Paraguay.

Buddleia lindleyana
LINDLEY BUTTERFLYBUSH

An anomaly among typical *Buddleia* species in that the flowers are *not fragrant*, yet *attract* copious quantities of butterflies. I was introduced to the species over 20 years ago when a specimen was brought to me for identification. Perusal of the literature indicated that it, like *Buddleia davidii*, had escaped from cultivation in the South. The evergreen, rounded-arching, suckering habit is not everyone's cup of tea. The lustrous dark green, 2- to 4-in.-long leaves are handsome year-round. From late May and June until frost, flowers are produced on new growth. Each flower is 1 to 1½ in. long, tubular, four-lobed at the mouth, dusty lavender on the outside, deep violet on the interior, and borne in 3- to 8-in.-long pani-

Brunfelsia pauciflora, Yesterday-Today-and-Tomorrow

Buddleia lindleyana 'Gloster' flowers

Buddleia lindleyana, Lindley Butterflybush

cles. The inflorescence is indeterminate, meaning it continues to elongate while the basal flowers are opening, resulting in structures 2 ft. or longer by summer's end. A tough, durable plant that requires full sun. Grows 4 to 6 ft. high, wider at maturity. Have observed a 10- to 12-ft.-high plant. Zones 7 to 9. Eastern China.

Cultivars and Varieties. 'Gloster' is a 6-ft.-high, strong-growing form with larger foliage and 2-ft.-long inflorescences.

'Miss Vicie' is smaller in stature (4 ft.) with smaller leaves and inflorescences.

Buddleia loricata

Another remarkable evergreen species from South Africa that is virtually unknown in American gardens but worthy of consideration. Like *Buddleia salvifolia*, this has become a foliage favorite of visitors to the University's *Buddleia* trials. The dense rounded habit and noninvasive nature make it one of the tidiest garden species. The narrow, 3- to 5-in.-long, lustrous dark green leaves are covered on the lower surface with cottony pubescence. The fragrant white flowers open in June and July from last year's wood. This and *B. salvifolia* should be pruned after flowering; any earlier pruning results in flower bud removal. Superb performer in the heat, drought, and blanketing humidity of Zone 7b, requiring full sun and well-drained soil. Terrific foliage in the border or when utilized in groupings and masses. Grows 4 to 5 ft. high and wide. Zones 7 to 9. South Africa.

Buddleia lindleyana 'Gloster' foliage

Buddleia loricata

Buddleia loricata flowers

Buddleia loricata foliage and foliage undersides

Buddleia salvifolia
SOUTH AFRICAN SAGE WOOD,
SOUTH AFRICAN SAGE BUTTER-
FLYBUSH

Who would have thought a butter-flybush from South Africa could prosper in the heat and humidity of the South? For starters, not this author, but over six seasons from 1995 to 2000, this evergreen shrub has grown over 10 ft. high and is configured into an upright-arching, densely foliaged shrub. The leaves are the most beautiful asset, 2 to 5 in. long, wavy-surfaced, sage-textured, gray-green above, gray-brown below. The flowers, pale lavender-lilac, open on last season's wood in April. They are not particularly showy and have only a slight fragrance. The species prospers in full sun, heat, and drought. Wonderful foliage plant for the borders, especially when pruned to the ground to force new shoots. Best thought of as a structural foliage plant for garden making. All visitors to our *Buddleia* trials have become enamored with the foliage. Grows 10 ft. high, 8 ft. wide. Zones 7 to 9. South Africa.

Buxus harlandii
HARLAND BOXWOOD

Although not well known in southern landscapes, this broad, vase-shaped, densely branched form is unique because of its larger leaves, to 2 in. long. The lustrous dark green leaves are broadest above the middle, almost spatulate, with distinct notches at their apices. The foliage color is a richer, brighter green than *Buxus sempervirens*. In the Dirr garden, the plant prospers in full sun and well-drained soil. Leafs out early; late spring frosts occasionally nip the foliage. Excellent for evergreen effect in the border or in groupings. One of my favorite plants in the winter landscape—always vibrant, rich green, and reassuring. Grows 6 ft. high and wide. Requires minimal pruning to keep it garden-worthy. Zones 7b to 9. China.

Buxus harlandii, Harland Boxwood

Buddleia salvifolia flowers

Buddleia salvifolia, South African Sage Wood, foliage

Callistemon citrinus
LEMON BOTTLEBRUSH

As a group, the bottlebrushes cause me more confusion in identification than about any other genus. This species is a large, evergreen shrub or small tree with coppery new growth, maturing to bright green. The leaves have a lemon odor when bruised. Leaves are 1 to 3 (to 4) in. long, ¼ to ⅝ in. wide, with a prominent ribbed midvein. The garden beauty resides in the bright crimson flowers, which develop on new growth in 4- to 5-in.-long, 2- to 2½-in.-wide, erect, terminal inflorescences. I have observed flowers in December, March, and summer in Orlando, Florida. Supposedly develops flowers at the base of each new growth flush. Grow in a well-drained soil, provide supplemental moisture and full sun. Makes a great container plant in northern areas. Excellent for flower color in the border or as an accent plant. Grows 10 to 15 ft. high and wide; 20 to 25 ft. high if staked and grown as a tree. Zones 8b to 11. Australia, New South Wales, Victoria, and Queensland.

Related species *Callistemon linearis*, Narrow-leaved Bottlebrush; *C. rigidus*, Stiff Bottlebrush; *C. speciosus*; and *C. viminalis*, Weeping Bottlebrush, produce red flowers. *Callistemon salignus* and *C. sieberi* have light yellow to pink, and cream to yellow flowers, respectively.

Callistemon citrinus, Lemon Bottlebrush

Callistemon citrinus flowers and foliage

Callistemon salignus flowers and foliage

Camellia japonica
JAPANESE CAMELLIA

Over the centuries, this woody species has probably had more cultivar selections, numbering some 3000, than any other broadleaf evergreen shrub or tree. The habit is a dense-pyramid, some selections almost columnar-pyramidal, rather stiff, stodgy, and formal. The 2- to 4-in.-long, leathery, lustrous dark green serrated leaves serve as the perfect foil for the flowers, 3 to 5 (to 6) in. in diameter, which span the rainbow in coloration. Flowers open in November and December (Zone 7b) with selected cultivars flowering in April. Provide moisture-retentive acidic soil and partial shade (pine shade is ideal), and protect from sweeping winds. Flowers are frost sensitive, and the petals turn to brown mush after cold nights. At one time, I totally rejected the species in the garden, but when scattered about and mingled with other shrubs, it provides beauty and flowers for the home. Ask the local garden center about the best cultivars for your area; in Athens, one garden center stocks 40 to 60 cultivars, a daunting number. Grows 10 to 15 ft. high, 6 to 10 ft. wide. Zones 7 to 9, 10 on the West Coast. China, Japan.

Cultivars and Varieties. The Camellia Society is located in Fort Valley, Georgia. The collections and displays are extensive. A visit indicates that too many similar cultivars have been introduced.

Camellia japonica, Japanese Camellia

Camellia japonica espaliered

Camellia japonica flowers

Camellia oleifera

TEA-OIL CAMELLIA

First time I spied the species, the beautiful golden brown bark was forever etched in my mind. The uniqueness of the species resides in its cold hardiness (Zone 6) and use as a breeding parent. The lustrous dark green leaves, 1 to 3 in. long, are serrated from the middle to apex. The 2- to 2½-in.-wide, five-petaled white flowers open from October through January. Flowers are not spectacular. In China, seeds are processed for the oil. Culture is the same as for *Camellia sasanqua*. Most notable aspect is its use as a breeding partner with *C. hiemalis* and *C. sasanqua* by Dr. William Ackerman, U.S. National Arboretum, to produce the October- and November-flowering, cold hardy cultivars like 'Frost Prince', 'Frost Princess', 'Polar Ice', and 'Snow Flurry'. I grew the latter two cultivars in our Georgia garden and found them not as satisfactory as *C. sasanqua* types. Grows 12 to 15 ft. high and wide. Zones 6 to 9. China.

Cultivars and Varieties. 'Lu Shan Snow' is the original plant of *Camellia oleifera* at the U.S. National Arboretum that was described and released. Beautiful bark as described above and average white flowers.

Camellia oleifera, Tea-oil Camellia

Camellia oleifera fruit

Camellia reticulata

Flowers the size of salad plates are part of the genetic soup of this species. Even at the Camellia Society headquarters in Fort Valley, Georgia, plants are protected in a greenhouse. My observations have been of a rather loose, open broadleaf evergreen shrub, the leaves to 4 in. long, leathery dark green, and net-veined (hence, *reticulata*). The flowers are 6 to 10 in. across with curly, wavy petals. Most are semidouble and literally weight the stem to an arching disposition. Flowers open in winter to early spring. Culture is similar to other species, except protect *Camellia reticulata* under pines or a large broadleaf evergreen tree, like Live Oak. Beautiful for large flowers and a worthy conservatory plant in the North. Grows 8 to 12 ft. high and wide. Zones 9b to 10(11). China

Camellia reticulata flowers and foliage

Camellia sasanqua
SASANQUA

For the everyday gardener, this evergreen species offers more aesthetic growth habit, finer texture, and reliable flowers (because of earlier fall flowering). Typically, less formal in habit than *Camellia japonica*, but still dense and oval-rounded to rounded with looser, arching branches. The 1½- to 3-in.-long, lustrous dark green, finely serrated leaves are beautiful through the seasons. The young shoots are covered with fine hairs, which distinguishes the species from the nonhairy *C. japonica*. The 2- to 4-in.-diameter flowers (singles, doubles, whites to reds) appear from September (Zone 7b) into early December. Petals abscise (fall) individually rather than as the entire floral tube in *C. japonica*. Culture is similar to *C. japonica*; however, *C. sasanqua* is more sun-tolerant and in field nurseries is grown in full sun for four to six years before being sold. Used in groupings, masses, and espaliers. In the Dirr garden, the plant is liberally sprinkled throughout the shady borders. Scale is the major insect problem on all camellias. Grows 6 to 10 ft. high and wide. Zones 7 to 9, 10 on the West Coast. China, Japan.

Camellia sasanqua flowers and foliage

Camellia sasanqua, Sasanqua

Camellia sinensis
TEA

Tea as an ornamental, who would have thought?! For over 20 years, Bonnie and I have grown the species in our Georgia garden. Remarkably resilient, it rewards us with 1- to 1½-in.-diameter, five-petaled, white, fragrant flowers with a mass of yellow stamens in late summer to fall. Bees love the nectar and provide a regular stage-show. The lustrous dark green, serrated, reticulate-veined leaves, 2 to 4½ in. long, are beautiful. Requires a modicum of shade, well-drained soil, and occasional pruning to keep it in bounds. Scale, as is true for all *Camellia* species, may occur. Mix with other broadleaf evergreens for foliage color and textural effects. Grows 4 to 6 (to 10) ft. high and wide. Zones 6 to 9. China.

Cultivars and Varieties. 'Rosea' ('Rubra') has pink flowers and rich reddish purple new growth. It is not as vigorous as the species.

Camellia sinensis foliage

Camellia sinensis flower and buds

Camellia sinensis, Tea

Camellia sinensis 'Rosea'

Campsis grandiflora
CHINESE TRUMPETCREEPER

In its own right, a spectacular apricot-orange flowered vine, but commercially outdistanced by one of its hybrids, 'Mme. Galen'. The late Dr. J. C. Raulston often touted this species, and a fine specimen at the J. C. Raulston Arboretum, Raleigh, North Carolina, when in flower, does justice to his beliefs. The foliage is lustrous dark green, each leaf consisting of seven to nine, 1½- to 3-in.-long, serrated leaflets. The 2- to 3-in.-long and -wide flowers open in June (Zone 7b) and do not reflower like *Campsis radicans*. Will tolerate any soil except permanently wet. Vigorous, requires pruning to keep it in check. Great for hiding unsightly structures, fences, or rusting automobiles. Grows 15 to 25 ft. or more. Zones (6)7 to 9. Japan, China.

Cultivars and Varieties. 'Morning Calm', a selection from the J. C. Raulston Arboretum, has apricot flowers.

Campsis grandiflora, Chinese Trumpet-creeper

Carissa macrocarpa (*C. grandiflora*)
NATAL PLUM

Broadleaf evergreen shrub, usually rounded, densely branched, with two- to four-pronged spines, and impenetrable. The opposite, leathery dark green leaves are 3 in. long and 2 in. wide. At the petiole base, sharp-branched stipular spines develop, giving the entire shrub a porcupine-like countenance. The five-petaled, star-shaped, fragrant white flowers, each 1½ to 3 in. across, open from spring into summer and thereafter. Red, plum-shaped fruit, 1 to 1½ in. long, ripen in late summer to fall and are utilized for jams and jellies. Adaptable, requires well-drained soil in sun to partial shade. Good mass or barrier plant, also used for hedges, foundations, and screens. Tolerant of salt spray and wind. Grows 5 to 10 ft. high and wide. Zones 9 to 11. South Africa.

Cultivars and Varieties. Several low-spreading and compact forms grow less than 5 ft. high. 'Boxwood Beauty' grows 2 ft. high and wide with deep green leaves and no thorns.

'Prostrata' grows 2 ft. high, wider in spread. Makes a good groundcover.

Carissa macrocarpa, Natal Plum

Carissa macrocarpa flowers

Carissa macrocarpa fruit on small-leaf form

Cassia

SENNA

Try as I have to grow the various species for their summer and fall yellow flowers, most have proven minimally hardy with the exception of *Cassia marilandica* (now *Senna marilandica*), Wild Senna, which still dies to the ground during winter and regrows 4 to 6 ft. each year. The habit is bushy, rounded, with compound pinnate, bright green leaves and clusters of yellow flowers in summer. All species prefer well-drained soil, moderate fertility, and full sun. Great plants for the border and late season flowering. On August 10, 2000, a 6- to 8-ft. specimen at the Atlanta Botanical Garden was just entering the flower cycle. Zones 7 to 10 (die-back shrub). Midwest and southeastern United States.

Cassia bicapsularis produces spectacular brown-yellow to golden yellow flowers in October in the Dirr garden. Unfortunately, it is killed to the ground each winter but regrows 6 to 8 ft. In Charleston, South Carolina, specimens over 10 ft. high are common. Great for late season color. Zones 9 to 11. Tropic regions worldwide.

Cassia marilandica, Wild Senna

Cassia marilandica foliage and flowers

Cassia bicapsularis flowers and foliage

Cassia bicapsularis in flower

68

Castanea pumila
ALLEGHENY CHINKAPIN

The southeastern mountains are rich with this smaller cousin of the more famous *Castanea dentata*, American Chestnut. During my hikes in Rabun County, Georgia, the tree, sometimes shrub, is a common sight. The telltale identification feature is the lustrous dark green leaf with the silver underside. The cream flowers occur in terminal panicles in June. The 1½-in.-diameter prickly-fruit covering houses one or two, ¾- to 1-in.-long, dark brown, sweet edible nuts. Requires full sun for best growth and tolerates drier soils. I often see it growing in the shade of the understory. Resistant to chestnut blight. Grows 20 to 25 ft. high, usually smaller. Zones 5 to 9. Pennsylvania to Florida, west to Oklahoma and Texas.

Ceanothus ×*delilianus*
FRENCH HYBRID CEANOTHUS

This hybrid, a cross between the tender *Ceanothus coeruleus* of Mexico and *C. americanus*, has given rise to beautiful blue-flowered forms. Habit is variable; some grow as mounding shrubs, others as tall, upright shrubs. The lustrous dark green leaves are evergreen to semi-evergreen. Flowers are light blue to deep blue and mask the foliage during May and June. Perhaps the bluest flower range of all woody shrubs is inherent in this group. Prefers drier conditions; thrives in California and for some reason most of Europe. Not happy in the Southeast. Grows 3 to 5 (to 15) ft. high; often espaliered on walls. Zones 8 to 10.

Castanea pumila, Allegheny Chinkapin, in fall

Ceanothus ×*delilianus* flowers

Castanea pumila foliage and new fruit

Castanea pumila fruit in fall

Ceanothus ×delilianus, French Hybrid Ceanothus

Ceanothus ×pallidus

The *Ceanothus* species and cultivars receive limited attention in the Southeast but are mainstays in West Coast gardens. I have observed and grown the cultivars 'Roseus' and 'Marie Simon' from Boston to Athens. Both are loosely branched shrubs with soft pink flowers developing on new growth of the season. The foliage is lustrous dark green and holds late in fall, with no appreciable fall color. Requires full sun and well-drained soil, erring toward the drier side. Works well as a filler in herbaceous and woody borders. Beautiful in flower. Grows 3 to 4 ft. high and wide. Zones 6 to 8.

Ceanothus ×pallidus 'Roseus'

Ceanothus ×pallidus 'Marie Simon'

Cephalotaxus fortunei, Fortune's Plum Yew

Cephalotaxus fortunei
FORTUNE'S PLUM YEW

Certainly not as well known as *Cephalotaxus harringtonia* but worthy of consideration in the warm-climate garden. Habit is more loose and open, with significantly longer needles, to 3½ in. long. The undersides of the needles are streaked with two prominent silver bands. The reproductive structures are similar to those of *C. harringtonia*, only larger. Requires shade and moist, well-drained soil. Useful for needle texture and accent but not preferable to *C. harringtonia* for everyday garden use. Grows 15 to 20 ft. high and wide. Zones 7 to 9. Eastern and central China.

Cultivars and Varieties. 'Grandis' has longer needles and graceful arching habit.

'Prostrate Spreader' is a wide-spreading, long-needled, densely branched form, 5 ft. high, 8 to 10 ft. wide.

Cephalotaxus fortunei needles and female flowers

Cephalotaxus fortunei 'Prostrate Spreader'

Cephalotaxus harringtonia

JAPANESE PLUM YEW

What a wonderful needle evergreen, in many respects resembling *Taxus*, yew, yet offering deer resistance and heat tolerance. The variation is phenomenal; 45 clones have been collected for testing at the University of Georgia. Prostrate, shrubby, and tree-type forms are included. The lustrous dark green needles are 1 to 2 in. long with two grayish bands on the lower side. Male and female flowers occur on separate plants in March and April with the female producing ¾- to 1-in.-long, olivelike seeds. Provide moist, well-drained soil in partial to heavy shade. The short-needled forms are acceptable in sun once established. Excellent for massing, grouping, and foundation plantings. Maintenance-free and one of the most serviceable needle evergreens for the South. Grows 5 to 10 ft. high and wide. Zones 6 to 9. Japan.

Cultivars and Varieties. 'Duke Gardens' is a short-needled, shrubby form

Cephalotaxus harringtonia, Japanese Plum Yew

Cephalotaxus harringtonia needles and male flowers

Cephalotaxus harringtonia seeds

Cephalotaxus harringtonia 'Fastigiata'

Cephalotaxus harringtonia 'Duke Gardens'

MORE ➤

Cephalotaxus harringtonia continued

with wide, vase-shaped growth habit. Grows 3 to 5 ft. high, wider at maturity.

'Fastigiata' is distinctly upright-columnar, broadening with age to 10 ft. high, 6 to 8 ft. wide. Needles are whorled around the stem, creating a bottlebrushlike composition.

'Prostrata' in its best form is low-growing and long-needled, 1½ to 2 ft. high, 4 to 6 ft. wide.

'Norris Johnson' is among my favorites. Shrubby spreading habit like 'Duke Gardens', but the needles whorl around the stems. Growing in full sun and full shade exposures, it has not flinched.

Cephalotaxus harringtonia 'Prostrata'

Cephalotaxus harringtonia 'Norris Johnson'

Chilopsis linearis
DESERT WILLOW

Great expectations in the Southeast for this southwestern species; unfortunately mildew and minimal tolerance for wet soil equated with miserable garden performance. In Texas, where I witnessed flowering plants, the habit was upright, loose, open, and lax. Since it flowers on new growth, the possibility of a cut-back shrub would offer promise. The rich green, willowlike leaves are 6 to 12 in. long, only ¼ to ½ in. wide. In June and into summer, the fragrant flowers, 1 to 1½ in. long and wide, funnelform-campanulate, with two upper and three lower lobes, open in shades of white, pink, rose, and lavender with interior purple markings. In Nagodoches, Texas, plants were still flowering in October. Fruit are 6- to 12-in.-long, ¼-in.-wide, two-valved capsules. Trunks are often twisted with shaggy bark. Full sun, well-drained, higher pH soils. Excellent heat tolerance. Not the easiest plant to incorporate into the landscape. Back of the border plant for airy texture. Cut back to promote new growth and flowers. Grows 15 to 25 ft. high, 10 to 15 ft. wide. Zones 7 to 9. Southern California to Texas, south to Mexico.

Cultivars and Varieties. A number were introduced by Texas A&M University; 'Alpine' (white-amaranth), 'Burgundy' (burgundy), 'Marfa Lace' (semidouble, blush pink-rose), 'Regal' (pale lavender to deep burgundy), and 'Tejas' (rose to pink to amaranth) are the best known.

Chilopsis linearis, Desert Willow

Chilopsis linearis flowers

×Chitalpa tashkentensis foliage

×Chitalpa tashkentensis flowers

×*Chitalpa tashkentensis*

A most rare intergeneric hybrid that I knew the Dirr garden could not live without. Well, after about five years serving as a mildew farm, it was removed. In that time, it grew 15 ft. high and formed a loose, open, rounded outline. The medium green leaves are 4 to 6 in. long, 1 to 2 in. wide. Lavender flowers, which developed in summer, were less than exciting. This hybrid is sterile; I never witnessed a single fruit. Requires full

MORE ➤

×Chitalpa tashkentensis

×*Chitalpa tashkentensis* continued

sun and well-drained soil. Responds to water and fertility and quickly overgrows its allotted boundaries. Use as a cut-back shrub in the border. Too many better deciduous shrubs to justify (like I did) chasing it down. A hybrid between *Catalpa bignonioides* and *Chilopsis linearis*; initial crosses were made in the former U.S.S.R. Have observed it in the vicinity of Portland, Oregon, in late August, where it was mildew-free and still producing a few flowers. Greater than 20 ft. high and wide at maturity. Zones 6 to 9.

Cultivars and Varieties. 'Morning Cloud' produces white to pale pink flowers with rich purple streaks in the interior.

'Pink Dawn' has light pink flowers with a pale yellow throat.

Choisya ternata foliage

Choisya ternata flowers

Choisya ternata
MEXICAN-ORANGE

A Mexican species that is a common shrub in England and Europe but almost absent in Zones 7 to 10, although with some attention to culture, it can be successfully grown. About as perfect in habit as a prescription for same could read—broad rounded, dense but not bulletproof, with lustrous dark green foliage. The opposite, trifoliate leaves, 3 to 6 in. long, are composed of 1½- to 3-in.-long, almost as wide, lustrous dark green leaflets. The flowers, white, fragrant, 1 to 1¼ in. wide, appear in three- to six-flowered corymbs at the ends of the shoots in May and June. The combination of glistening white flowers against the dark green foliage is spectacular. Partial shade to shade, well-drained, acid to neutral soils suit it best. I suspect high night temperatures in the South diminish performance. Excellent border, foundation, or grouping plant. Grows 6 to 8 ft. high and wide. Zones 7 to 9, robust on the West Coast.

Cultivars and Varieties. 'Aztec Pearl' (*Choisya arizonica × C. ternata*) is a finer-textured shrub than *C. ternata*, with narrow leaflets and pink flushed to white (open), fragrant flowers. Grows 3 to 4 ft. high, slightly wider at maturity.

'Sundance', a golden yellow leaf form with white flowers, is one of the most popular selections. Almost as vigorous as the species. Kind of like spackling mustard on the landscape.

'Goldfingers' represents a breakthrough in color and texture, with the gold of 'Sundance' and the fine foliage of 'Aztec Pearl' commingled into a single genotype.

Choisya ternata, Mexican-orange

Choisya ternata 'Aztec Pearl'

Cinnamomum camphora
CAMPHOR TREE

Beautiful broadleaf evergreen tree that from the coast of Georgia to south Florida makes a successful shade tree. In its finest form, a rounded to broad-rounded broadleaf evergreen with fine branches and a thick, stout, gray-brown trunk. The new leaves emerge bronze, finally lustrous dark green, 3 to 4 in. long, with three to four prominent veins. Inconspicuous, greenish white flowers yield copious amounts of shiny black, ⅓-in.-diameter fruit in fall and winter. At Leu Gardens in Orlando, Florida, the ground was covered with fruit in December. Full sun to partial shade in moist, well-drained soil. The aggressive root system competes with surrounding vegetation. Handsome tree when well grown. Grows 40 to 60 ft. high and wide. Zones (8)9 to 11. Japan, China, Taiwan.

Choisya ternata 'Sundance' foliage

Cinnamomum camphora foliage

Cinnamomum camphora, Camphor Tree

MORE ➤

Cinnamomum camphora continued

Cinnamomum camphora bark

Cistus ×purpureus, Orchid Rock Rose

Cistus ×purpureus flowers

Cistus
ROCK ROSE

Many species are known and are common garden fixtures in European gardens, but, with a Mediterranean heritage, they are best reserved for San Francisco–type climates into Vancouver, British Columbia. Have tried to grow _Cistus laurifolius_, with white, yellow-spotted fragrant flowers, but excessive moisture derailed the effort. Typically, broadleaf evergreen groundcovers to 3- to 6-ft.-high shrubs with dark green leaves that are sticky on both surfaces. Leaves are 1 to 3 in. long, dark green above, gray-tomentose below. Flowers occur in great profusion in June and July (and occasionally August), each five-petaled, 1 to 3 (to 4) in. wide, in shades of white, pink, reddish, often with a deeper colored spot at the base of the petal. Locate in full sun in well-drained, reasonably dry, limy soils. Transplant as container-grown plants, since they do not move readily bare root. In flower, they are knockouts; during our European garden tours, fellow travelers ask the inevitable: "Will it grow in South Carolina?" For groupings, borders, masses, simply terrific choices. Grows 1 to 3 (to 6) ft. high and wide. Zones 8 to 10. Mediterranean region.

Cistus ×purpureus, Orchid Rock Rose, produces reddish purple flowers, 3 in. and wider in diameter, with a darker spot at the petal base, on a 3- to 4-ft.-high and -wide, rounded, evergreen shrub.

Cistus laurifolius, Rock Rose

Clethra arborea

LILY OF THE VALLEY TREE, EVERGREEN CLETHRA

One of my most significant dreams (after, of course, two pieces of chocolate cake, a glass of milk, and a double cheeseburger at 11:30 p.m.) conjured the possibility of hybridizing this magnificent evergreen species with the native *Clethra alnifolia*, a deciduous species, and producing cold hardy, evergreen, large-flowered progeny. Still only a dream, but I am growing *C. arborea*, a large shrub/small tree, in a greenhouse in Athens. The emerging leaves are bronze-red-green, maturing to lustrous dark green, and 4 to 6 in. long. Flowers, summer to fall, occur in large panicles at the end of the shoots. Each flower is cup-shaped, pure white, ⅓ in. long, and slightly fragrant. Requires moist, well-drained soils and at least partial shade. Even in England, the plant grows well only in the mild southwest (Devon and Cornwall). Grows 10 to 20 ft. high. Zones 9 to 11. Madeira Islands.

Clethra arborea, Lily of the Valley Tree

Clethra arborea foliage

Clethra barbinervis

JAPANESE CLETHRA

Seldom available in nursery commerce but remarkable for the large panicles of white flowers in July and August and the richly colored exfoliating bark. Most commonly grown as a large shrub but also makes a handsome small tree. Bark is a beautiful, smooth, polished, rich gray-brown to cinnamon-brown, and displays an exfoliating character. Dark green leaves are 2 to 6 in. long and turn bronze-red to maroon in fall. The slightly fragrant white flowers occur in 4- to 6-in.-long and -wide, terminal, racemose panicles. I have grown and killed the species numerous times in our Zone 7b garden, ultimately concluding that shade and moisture-retentive soil are prerequisites for success. The lone plant in the garden, located in a shady, moist border, told me the secret. Beautiful in a mixed shrub border. Great plants at the Arnold Arboretum, Smith College Botanic Garden, and Barnes Foundation. Grows 10 to 20 ft. high. Zones 5 to 7. Japan.

Clethra barbinervis, Japanese Clethra

MORE ➤

Clethra barbinervis continued

Clethra barbinervis fall color

Clethra barbinervis flowers

Clethra barbinervis bark

Cleyera japonica
JAPANESE CLEYERA

Terribly confused with *Ternstroemia gymnanthera* and often marketed as that species. An easy way to separate this species is by the extended apex of the leaf and the terminal bud, which is crooked like a little finger. Habit can be dense and wide-spreading or loose and open, like a small tree. Plants grown in full sun tend toward the former. Leaves are 1 to 3 in. long, lustrous dark green in summer maintaining the color through winter. The ½-in.-wide, cream-white flowers, borne one to five from the leaf axils and underneath the leaves, open in June. The fruit are globose and black. Easy to culture but not well known. Two established plantings in Athens lend credence to heat and soil adaptability. Requires occasional pruning to maintain respectable shape. Worthy hedge, screening, and buffer plant but suffers from second cousin status to *T. gymnanthera*. Grows 10 to 15 ft. high. Zones 6b to 8(9). Japan, Korea, China.

Cultivars and Varieties. Two variegated selections are in cultivation: 'Fortunei' with thin, bright green leaves, cream, golden yellow, and rose along the margins, and 'Tricolor' with bronze-purple new growth, changing to gray-green center with cream-yellow margin, rose-pink in winter. The latter is more potent.

Cleyera japonica, Japanese Cleyera

Cleyera japonica flowers and foliage

Cleyera japonica 'Fortunei'

Cleyera japonica 'Tricolor'

Cliftonia monophylla foliage

Cliftonia monophylla flowers

Cliftonia monophylla
BUCKWHEAT-TREE, TITI

A relatively unknown southern native shrub or tree that produces 2½- to 3½-in.-long racemes of fragrant white flowers in March and April. The habit is loose and open with evergreen, 1- to 2-in.-long, lustrous dark green leaves. Fruit are three- to four-winged and similar to the buckwheat fruit in shape, hence, the common name. Grows in the same habitats as *Cyrilla racemiflora*. Tolerates full sun to partial shade. I have not found it as garden-worthy or adaptable as *C. racemiflora*. Grows 6 to 12 (to 18) ft. high, slightly less in spread. Zones 7 to 9. Georgia, Florida to Louisiana.

Cliftonia monophylla, Buckwheat-tree

Cocculus carolinus, Carolina Moonseed

Cocculus carolinus fruit

Cocculus laurifolius foliage

Cocculus laurifolius, Laurel-leaved Snailseed

Cocculus carolinus
CAROLINA MOONSEED

Sprinkled liberally with red fruit in September through November, this viney member of the moonseed family is frequently brought to my office for identification. A twining vine, not as thuggy as *Wisteria* species, for example; dovetails neatly with chain-link fences and trellises, and scrambles among shrubs. The 2- to 4-in.-long, lustrous dark green leaves turn yellowish in fall. The dioecious flowers are an inconspicuous yellow-green in spring. Gradually the greenish fruit turn to red, and soon the entire length of the vine appears decorated. Fruit are ¼-in.-wide, rounded drupes that occur in 2- to 4-in.-long racemes. Each fruit contains a single crescent moon–shaped seed. Adaptable to both sun and shade, and to moist or dry, acid soils. Occurs in the wild in sandy soils. Respectable, quick, chain-link fence eliminator. Grows 10 to 15 ft. Zones 6 to 9. Virginia to Illinois and Kansas to Florida and Texas.

The related species *Cocculus laurifolius*, Laurel-leaved Snailseed, is a broadleaf evergreen, rounded-arching shrub with shiny, leathery leaves, up to 6 in. long, each with three deeply impressed veins running from the base to the apex. Have observed in Mobile, Alabama, as a 4- to 6-ft.-high shrub, but best in central Florida and South. Grows 6 to 10 ft. high; further south to 20 ft. high. Zones (8)9 to 11. Himalayas to southern Japan.

Cornus capitata

BENTHAM'S CORNEL

Little-known evergreen dogwood that is suited only for the mildest areas of the United States. Small rounded tree with typical dogwood leaves and beautiful cream-yellow flowers arching upward at their middle, forming a cuplike composite. Have only observed flowering trees in Europe, particularly at the great Hillier Arboretum in Hampshire. Too beautiful to describe. The fleshy, rounded, 1-in.-diameter fruit turn brilliant red in fall.

Have tried to grow the species in our Zone 7b garden with no success. Grows 20 ft. high and wide. Zones 7 to 10 on the West Coast. China.

Cultivars and Varieties. Hybrids between *Cornus kousa* and *C. capitata*, notably 'Norman Hadden' and 'Porlock', are noteworthy for the cream-white bracts that age to rose and pink.

MORE ➤

Cornus capitata, Bentham's Cornel

Cornus capitata flowers and foliage

Cornus capitata fruit

Cornus capitata continued

Cornus 'Porlock'

Cornus 'Norman Hadden' flowers and foliage

Cotoneaster lacteus foliage and foliage undersides

Cotoneaster lacteus flowers

Cotoneaster lacteus
PARNEY COTONEASTER

Cotoneasters in the southeastern United States are decimated by fireblight, lace bug, and mites. All have been trialed and grown, and none, except for *Cotoneaster lacteus*, display staying power. Parney Cotoneaster is a lax, loose, upright-spreading evergreen shrub. The 1- to 2-in.-long, dark green leaves are cloaked with woolly pubescence on the undersides. White flowers, somewhat ill-scented, occur in 2- to 3-in.-wide corymbs in May. The red, football-shaped fruit are ¼ to ⅓ in. long and persist through winter. Grow in full sun or partial shade in average soil. Not a "fussy" cotoneaster and definitively more resistant than the typical commercial species. Excellent choice for large mass plantings to screen areas of the garden and define property boundaries, and for single plant use in the border. Grows 6 to 10 ft. high and wide. Zones 6 to 8. Western China.

Cotoneaster lacteus fruit

Cotoneaster lacteus, Parney Cotoneaster

Crataegus
MAYHAW, HAWTHORN

Difficult to discuss a genus so vaguely defined yet so similar in characteristics. Various references list as many as 100 species, others 35, for the Southeast. The three principal fruit-producing species (i.e., mayhaws) are *Crataegus aestivalis*, *C. opaca*, and *C. rufula*. All are small, oval to round-headed trees with dark green leaves, white flowers, and red fruit. Bark is often mottled, exfoliating, in gray, green, orange, and brown. Fruit are utilized to make a rich amber-orange jelly. The species occur in many habitats from river bottoms to thin soils of rock outcrops. Extremely important food source for wildlife, particularly birds. Thorns are irritating and dangerous. All mayhaws are susceptible to quince rust. Grows 20 to 30 ft. high and wide. Zones 7 to 9. Southeastern United States.

Crataegus sp. fruit

Crataegus sp., Mayhaw, bark

Crataegus sp. flowers

Croton alabamensis, Alabama Croton

Croton alabamensis
ALABAMA CROTON

Quite a captivating species—the crushed leaves emit the fragrance of apples, grapes, or a banana-apple compote. As I have observed the species, it is a loose, open, flopsy, mopsy shrub. The leaves, semi-evergreen to deciduous, 2 to 4 in. long, are rich green with silver scales above, silvery and shiny beneath. The senescent leaves turn brilliant orange in fall. Flowers are yellow-green and appear in 1- to 1½-in.-long racemes in March and April. Best sited in partial shade in moist, well-drained root run laden with organic matter. At its best, a collector's plant and nifty native that will taxonomically confound even the best plantspeople. Grows 6 to 8 ft. high, wider at maturity. Zones 6 to 8. Alabama.

Croton alabamensis leaf in fall color

Croton alabamensis foliage undersides

Croton alabamensis flowers

Cunninghamia lanceolata needles

Cunninghamia lanceolata cones

Cunninghamia lanceolata
COMMON CHINAFIR

Throughout the Southeast, in the remotest locations, one is apt to chance upon this prehistoric-appearing needle evergreen. Often broad-pyramidal in outline, the branches are cloaked with 1- to 2½-in.-long, sharp-pointed needles. The dead needles persist and contribute to the disheveled appearance. Needles range from lustrous dark green to blue-green and in their finest manifestations are quite handsome. The globose, pendent cones, 1½ in. across, look like artichokes. Bark is rich reddish brown, stringy, and seldom seen, since the lower branches remain into old age. Tolerates excessive heat and drought, full sun to partial shade. When cut back, regenerates by developing numerous shoots. Strictly a specimen plant and seldom available in modern commerce. Grows 30 to 75 ft. high, 10 to 30 ft. wide. Zones 7 to 9. China.

Cultivars and Varieties. 'Glauca' is unique because of the waxy deposits on the needles resulting in bluish coloration.

Cunninghamia lanceolata, Common Chinafir

Cunninghamia lanceolata 'Glauca'

Cunninghamia lanceolata bark

86

Cupressus glabra
SMOOTH CYPRESS

The delineation of this species, with its exfoliating, papery, purple to red bark and bright blue-green needles, from *Cupressus arizonica* (coarsely shredding, gray-brown bark and dull gray-green needles) is not clear-cut. What I meet in the Southeast favors *C. glabra*. Typically, habit is pyramidal becoming more open and feathery with age. Near Tucson, Arizona, as I ascended Mount Lemon, the variation in this species from green to bright blue needled forms was a feast for the collector's eyes. Instead of the flat, planar foliage common to arborvitae and false-cypress, the stems form dendritic (treelike) configurations, like stereoisomers from your college chemistry days. The oblong, 1- to 1¼-in.-diameter cones are six- to eight-scaled, each scale with a sharp point. Transplant from containers into well-drained, dryish soils in full sun. Several canker diseases are troublesome. Makes an unusual container plant. The rich blue needles provide contrast in southern and western gardens; do not expect long life in the Southeast, where it is now grown as a Christmas tree. More amenable for the Southwest and California. Grows 40 to 50 ft. high, 25 to 30 ft. wide. Zones 7 to 9, 10 on the West Coast. Central and southern Arizona.

Cultivars and Varieties. 'Blue Ice' has icy-blue foliage, mahogany-red stems, and tight, conical-pyramidal outline, particularly in youth.

'Blue Pyramid' appears similar to 'Blue Ice', and both, growing side by side in my Georgia trials, look like blue rockets on the launching pad.

'Carolina Sapphire' is loose and airy even as a young plant, with silver-blue, closer to silver-gray, needles.

Cupressus glabra, Smooth Cypress

Cupressus glabra cones

Cupressus glabra bark

Cupressus glabra 'Blue Ice'

Cupressus glabra 'Carolina Sapphire'

Cupressus macrocarpa
MONTEREY CYPRESS

Leaning, literally, along the Monterey Peninsula, over the Pacific Ocean, is this most famous needle evergreen, celebrated for being one of the parents of Leyland Cypress, ×*Cupressocyparis leylandii*. Habit is narrow and pyramidal in youth, becoming picturesque with age. Massive trees, 100 ft. high, grow in the moist atmosphere of Ireland. At Powerscourt and Emo Court, the trunks alone captivate the passerby. Foliage is rich dark green through the seasons. The eight- to fourteen-scaled cones are 1 in. or more in diameter. Relishes the moisture-laden atmosphere of the California coast around the Monterey Peninsula. *Seridium* canker has killed many trees in California, especially those planted away from the coast. Coastal plants I witnessed were 30 to 40 (to 50) ft. high and broad, sculpted by the wind. Zones 7 to 9, 10 on the West Coast. California.

Cultivars and Varieties. Several yellow- to gold-foliaged selections, 'Golden Cone', 'Donard Gold', and 'Goldcrest', are available. Often sold for container use in the eastern United States.

MORE ➤

Cupressus macrocarpa bark

Cupressus macrocarpa, Monterey Cypress

Cupressus macrocarpa continued

Cupressus macrocarpa on the Monterey Peninsula, "picturesque with age"

Cupressus macrocarpa 'Goldcrest'

Cupressus sempervirens
ITALIAN CYPRESS

Both the species and 'Stricta' in particular have been a part of garden-making since time immemorial. A Mediterranean species that is variable in habit but usually upright, with green to bluish needles. The cones are ovoid, 1 to 1½ in. long. Prefers hot, dry climates and well-drained soils but survives in the heat and humidity of the Southeast. Use as an accent plant, in formal planting, allées, and planters. Grows 20 to 30 ft. high, 5 to 10 ft. wide. Zones 7 to 9, 10 in California. Southern Europe, western Asia.

Cultivars and Varieties. 'Glauca' has rich blue-green foliage and columnar habit.

'Stricta' is narrow columnar with dark green foliage.

'Swain's Gold' is a slow-growing, narrow columnar form with golden needles.

Cupressus sempervirens, Italian Cypress

Cupressus sempervirens foliage

Cupressus sempervirens 'Stricta' cones

Cupressus sempervirens 'Swain's Gold'

Cupressus sempervirens 'Stricta'

Cycas revoluta
SAGO PALM

Not a true palm but a gymnosperm, with naked seeds produced on female plants and conelike structures on the male. Single-stemmed initially, side shoots (offsets) develop with age creating a multi-stemmed effect. Leaves occur in a pseudo-whorl and produce a feathery texture. Each leaf is 4 to 5 ft. long, with fernlike, lustrous dark green pinnae, each up to 6 in. long, with a sharp apex. Seeds are plum-shaped, 1 to 1½ in. wide, hard-shelled, with a fleshy, brownish orange outer covering. Provide well-drained soil and full sun to partial shade. On the Georgia coast, plants grow in pure sand and pine shade. Beautiful architectural plant, particularly in containers. Grows 4 to 6 (to 8) ft. high and wide. Zones 8 to 11. Temperature of 11°F defoliated plants in coastal Georgia but did not injure buds, and regrowth was normal. Southern Japan.

Cyrilla racemiflora
SWAMP CYRILLA, LEATHERWOOD

In June, frothy white flowers cover the previous season's growth and, in composite with the lustrous dark green leaves, are effective for a month and longer. The wet areas of the Coastal Plain of Georgia are rich with the species, and the spectacular flowers make one question the lack of garden use. Habit is sprawling-spreading, loose, and open, with branches bent, gnarled, and contorted. Plants sucker from roots to form large colonies. Leaves, 1½ to 4

Cycas revoluta, Sago Palm

Cycas revoluta foliage

Cycas revoluta seeds

Cyrilla racemiflora flowers

Cyrilla racemiflora fall foliage

in. long, are evergreen in the Deep South to deciduous further north, lustrous dark green, turning orange and scarlet upon aging. The white fragrant flowers are borne in 3- to 6-in.-long racemes in a horizontal whorl at the base of the current season's growth. The ½-in.-long, roundish, two-celled capsular fruit mature in August and September and persist into winter. Grows wild in swamps but will succeed in moist, well-drained, drier soils. Full sun to partial shade. Good native plant for the wild look. Tolerant of prolonged flooding and therefore ideal for wet areas in the landscape. Utilized it in the Dirr garden, but it grew too large. Seven years after removal, shoots were still developing from roots. Grows 10 to 15 ft. high and wide. Zones 6 to 11. Virginia to Florida.

Cyrilla arida is a microcosm of *C. racemiflora*, smaller in all its parts and growing only 6 ft. high and wide. Requires well-drained soils, preferably sandy. Zones 8 to 9(10). Central Florida.

Cyrilla racemiflora, Swamp Cyrilla

Cyrilla arida in flower

Cyrilla arida fruit

Cyrtomium falcatum
JAPANESE HOLLY FERN

One of the best evergreen, heat-tolerant ferns for use in Zones 8 and 9, with protection into Zone 7. Common in commercial landscapes throughout the region, particularly in shady nooks and crannies where few other plants survive. Habit is leafy, like a fine dark green leaf lettuce, somewhat rhizomatous, forming dense clumps. Leaves, 20 to 30 in. long, 8 in. wide, emerge the softest yellow-green, settling down to lustrous dark green. Leaves have wavy margins, a feature that imparts a rich texture to large plantings. Provide shade and moist, acid soils rich in organic matter. Fertilize with all-purpose (i.e., 8-8-8) fertilizer in late winter. Remove old fronds. Terrific filler, tall groundcover, and massing plant. Largely insect- and disease-free. Grows 2 ft. high, 3 ft. wide. Zones (7)8 to 9. China, Malaysia, Taiwan, India, eastern and southern Africa, Hawaii.

Danae racemosa
ALEXANDRIAN-LAUREL

A striking amalgamation of gracefully arching evergreen shoots with shimmering, shiny green leaves that brighten shady areas of the garden. Seldom available in commercial quantities, it is most often passed from gardener to gardener. It is a member of the lily family, and the leaves are actually modified stems. Typically, it must be propagated by division or seed. The orange-red, $\frac{3}{8}$- to $\frac{1}{2}$-in.-diameter, rounded berries are attractive but occur only on female plants. Seeds are tricky to germinate. Magnificent shade plant that requires preferably moist, well-drained soils laden with organic matter. In sunny locations, leaves become yellowish and appear nitrogen deficient. Grows 2 to 4 ft. high, wider at maturity. Zones 7b to 9. Northern Iran and Asia Minor.

Cyrtomium falcatum, Japanese Holly Fern

Danae racemosa foliage

Danae racemosa, Alexandrian-laurel

Danae racemosa fruit

Daphne odora
FRAGRANT or WINTER DAPHNE

A southern landscape without Fragrant Daphne is really not a garden. Over our 22 years in Athens, probably 30 have been planted with three large, magnificent specimens extant. In our garden, the alluring fragrance is released in January and is often still wafting in early March. Truly a sign from the Head Gardener that all is right with the world, certainly the gardening world. Typical mature habit approaches a broad mound with dense, lustrous dark green ever-green foliage, each leaf 1½ to 3½ in. long. Flowers occur at the end of the shoots, nestled in the pseudo-whorl of foliage. The rose-purple buds open to rose-pink, 1- to 1½-in.-diameter inflorescences. *Remarkable* for fragrance! Plant in well-drained soil in shade; do not disturb after planting. I have observed healthy plants on one day turn up their root tips and die the next. Biological truth is stranger than fiction. Spot plants throughout shady borders and woods, almost like bread-crumbs. The nose knows and will follow the scent. Grows 3 to 4 ft. high, slightly wider. Zones 7 to 9. China.

Cultivars and Varieties. 'Alba' has fragrant cream-white flowers and polished dark green leaves.

'Aureomarginata' is slightly hardier than the species with yellow-margined leaves and reddish purple flowers.

Daphne odora, Fragrant Daphne

Daphne odora flowers and foliage

Daphne odora 'Alba'

Daphne odora 'Aureomarginata'

Daphne odora 'Aureomarginata' foliage

Daphniphyllum macropodum

I listened to garden lecturers tout this Asiatic species for its wonderful rhododendron-like, lustrous dark green foliage and refused to buy into its uniqueness. Since 1990, a 15-ft.-high, haystack-shaped specimen has prospered at the University's Botanical Garden. The 5- to 6-in.-long leaves have red petioles with the color extending to the midrib of the leaf blade. The plant is unbelievably sun-tolerant and exhibits no discoloration. Pale green flowers are not particularly showy, and the 1/3-in.-long bluish black drupes occur on female plants. Difficult to root from cuttings and, to my knowledge, only seedling material is offered. In the South, a wonderful substitute for large-leaf rhododendrons for textural qualities. Tolerates shade and sun, provide only well-drained soil. Grows 10 to 15 ft. high and wide. Zones 7 to 9. China, Japan, Korea.

Daphniphyllum macropodum

Daphniphyllum macropodum foliage

Daphniphyllum macropodum flower buds

Decumaria barbara
WILD HYDRANGEAVINE, WOOD VAMP

A common southeastern native, true-clinging vine, found growing in flood plains and banks along watercourses. Climbs trees with the root-like holdfasts that originate from the stems. Beautiful lustrous dark green leaves, 3 to 5 in. long, up to 3 in. wide, turn pale cream-yellow in autumn. The fragrant white flowers are borne in 2- to 3-in.-high and -wide terminal corymbs in May and June. Flowers are attractive but do not overwhelm like those of *Hydrangea anomala* subsp. *petiolaris*, Climbing Hydrangea. Site in shade, provide moisture in dry periods. Trouble-free vine that offers beautiful foliage and fragrant flowers. Grows 30 to 40 ft. or limited by structure. Zones 5 to 9. Virginia to Florida to Louisiana.

Cultivars and Varieties. 'Barbara Ann' is a superior selection from the wilds of Madison County, Georgia, discovered by former University of Georgia football coach Vincent J. Dooley, Dr. Dongling Zhang, and me, and named after Coach Dooley's wife. Leathery, thickish, lustrous dark green leaves outshine all seedling-grown plants. Spectacular for foliage and flower.

Decumaria barbara, Wild Hydrangeavine

Decumaria barbara in flower

Decumaria barbara 'Barbara Ann'

Decumaria barbara in bud

Desfontainia spinosa

On a miserable, cold, and damp March day in Younger Botanic Garden, Scotland, I circled, stalked, mused, meditated, and attempted to identify the shrub with oppositely arranged, spiny, lustrous dark green leaves. A weird *Osmanthus* species I opined; the label said *Desfontainia* . . . I will never forget. The funnel-shaped, waxy corolla is orange-scarlet with five rounded lobes.

Flowers are spectacular and open from June and July into fall. Requires well-drained, moist soil and relatively cool climate. Only for the collector but is reported as satisfactory in Oregon. Grows 6 to 8 (to 10) ft. high with greater spread. A plant 10 ft. high and 32 ft. wide grew in Rowallane Garden, Ireland. Zones 7 to 9. Found in cool mountain cloud forests of the Andes, South America.

Desfontainia spinosa

Dicksonia antarctica
AUSTRALIAN TREE FERN

This genuine arborescent fern is a common occurrence in conservatories in the North and grows, typically, 15 to 20 ft. under outdoor cultivation in warmer climates. In Irish gardens, Dureen most remembered, this species grew like a shade tree. A stout trunk is topped by a uniform head of evergreen fronds, often 4 ft. long or more. Leaves dark green; the trunk is covered with brown fibrous roots. Reproduces by spores in moist climates. Requires shade and a moist environment. Unique architectural plant or container plant; groupings create a mini-forest. Zones 9 to 11. Australia, Tasmania.

Desfontainia spinosa foliage

Desfontainia spinosa flowers

Dicksonia antarctica, Australian Tree Fern

Dicksonia antarctica

Diospyros kaki
JAPANESE PERSIMMON

Twenty years past, traveling through south Georgia, I spied a small round-headed tree dripping with peaches, or so I thought. The tree was actually a *Diospyros kaki* laden with 3- to 4-in.-diameter orange fruit. Habit is rounded with thick-textured, lustrous dark green, 3- to 7-in.-long leaves, changing to vibrant shades of yellow, orange, and red. Fruit are edible; cultivars often require complete maturity to lose astringency. Prefers moist, well-drained soils, full sun but grows, once established, in droughty, heavy-textured soils. Always thought the male trees would make good drought-tolerant street trees. Good plant for the backyard fruit garden. Fruit are beautiful, ripening in fall and persisting into December in the Piedmont of Georgia. Grows 15 to 20 (to 30) ft. high and wide. Zones 7 to 9. China.

Diospyros kaki foliage in fall

Diospyros kaki, Japanese Persimmon, fall color

Diospyros kaki foliage

Diospyros kaki fruit

Diospyros kaki bark

Distylium racemosum

ISU TREE

An evergreen member of the witchhazel family (Hamamelidaceae) that, in leaf, appears totally unrelated; however, flowers and fruit do not lie. In Athens and Savannah, Georgia, and Asheville, North Carolina, old plants are upright and shrubby. The 1- to 1½-in.-long leaves are shiny dark green. The subdued reddish maroon flowers open in May, somewhat inconspicu-ously, and are followed by two-beaked woody capsules. Moist, acidic soils, laden with organic matter, are best; however, a plant in full sun and heavy soil at the Horticulture Farm in Athens has performed at the highest level over a ten-year period. At best, 10 to 15 ft. high, although the literature mentions 60-ft.-high plants in the wild. Zones 6b to 9. Southern Japan.

Distylium racemosum, Isu Tree

Distylium racemosum foliage

Distylium racemosum flowers

Duranta erecta
(*D. repens*)
PIGEON BERRY,
GOLDEN DEWDROP

H. P. Leu Gardens, Orlando, Florida, displayed fruiting specimens that had me checking identity. The ⅜- to ½-in.-diameter, yellow globose drupes ripen in late summer to fall. Excellent for fruit effect! Typically a die-back shrub, broad-spreading, on the Coastal Plain of Georgia but growing up to 18 ft. in central and south Florida gardens. Shiny rich green leaves (evergreen in Deep South) are quite handsome. Bluish flowers develop on new growth of the season in 6-in.-long panicles. Full sun and loose, well-drained soils are suitable. Grows 4 to 6 ft. high and wide. Zones 8 to 11. Tropical America.

Cultivars and Varieties. 'Golden Edge' is similar to 'Variegata' but with flashy gold patterns.

'Variegata' has leaves margined and irregularly splashed with cream and white.

Duranta erecta, Pigeon Berry

Duranta erecta fruit

Edgeworthia papyrifera foliage

Duranta erecta flowers

Edgeworthia papyrifera flowers

Edgeworthia papyrifera 'Rubra'

Edgeworthia papyrifera
PAPERBUSH

During our daily walks through the garden, Bonnie and I *always* remark about the oversized, beautiful bluish green leaves that combine so seamlessly with the leaves and flowers of *Hydrangea arborescens* 'Annabelle'. This unique plant is reserved for the shady nooks and crannies of the garden, where ample moisture is available. It is a suckering shrub, growing 3 to 4 ft. high. The lithe, spotted, and stippled stems, lustrous red-brown with permanent light gray crescent-shaped leaf scars, are handsome in winter. The dark blue-green leaves are typically 6 in. long, although leaves from the plant in our garden measured 10 in. long. Flowers are unique, opening on naked stems in March and April, fragrant, silky white and yellow, in 1- to 2-in.-wide umbels. Flowers open over long periods, at least four to six weeks. Wonderful plant to combine with shade-tolerant broadleaf evergreens and wildflowers. Becoming available in nursery commerce. Grows 3 to 4 (to 7) ft. high, spreads by rhizomes. Zones 7 to 9. China.

Cultivars and Varieties. 'Grandiflora' has large flowers and leaves; *Edgeworthia chrysantha* is bandied about as a larger-leaved species but looks like 'Grandiflora'.

'Jitsu Red', 'Red Dragon', and 'Rubra'—probably all the same—have reddish tinted flowers.

Ehretia dicksonii

Little-known small flowering tree with broad-spreading habit; leaves are shining dark green, 4 to 8 in. long, with no appreciable fall color. The white fragrant flowers occur in 2- to 4-in.-wide, flattish terminal panicles in May and June. Fruit are small blackish drupes. The gray-brown bark is deeply ridged and furrowed. Prospers in full sun and well-drained soil. Only for the obsessed collector. Grows 20 to 25 ft. high and wide. Zones (7)8 to 9. China, Taiwan, Japan.

Ehretia dicksonii foliage

Ehretia dicksonii flowers

MORE ➤

Edgeworthia papyrifera, Paperbush

Ehretia dicksonii **continued**

Ehretia dicksonii

Ehretia dicksonii bark

Elaeagnus ×ebbingei

A hybrid evergreen species, similar to *Elaeagnus pungens* and often difficult to distinguish. In general, a better garden plant with larger leaves and less rampant growth. In truth, still quite vigorous and requires pruning to remove the extraneous shoots. Leaves, flowers, and fruit similar to *E. pungens*. The differences are most manifest in the cultivars described below. Grows 8 to 10 ft. high and wide. Zones 7 to 9.

Cultivars and Varieties. 'Gilt Edge' has soft yellow-gold margins and light green center.

'Limelight' is the reverse, with pale gold to gold centers and green margins.

Elaeagnus ×ebbingei foliage

Elaeagnus ×ebbingei 'Limelight'

Elaeagnus ×ebbingei

Elaeagnus ×ebbingei 'Gilt Edge'

Elaeagnus ×ebbingei 'Gilt Edge' foliage

Elaeagnus macrophylla

One of the parents, along with *Elae-agnus pungens*, of *E. ×ebbingei*. As I witnessed the species in Europe, a robust rounded shrub not as wild as *E. pungens*. Leaves lustrous dark green above, silvery below. Flowers and fruit similar to *E. pungens*. Same uses as *E. pungens*. The new leaves appear coated with silver fur. When the leaves first emerge in spring the entire plant is attractive. Grows 8 to 12 ft. high and wide. Zones 8 to 9. Korea, Japan.

Elaeagnus macrophylla

Elaeagnus macrophylla new foliage

Elaeagnus pungens, Thorny Elaeagnus

Elaeagnus pungens foliage

Elaeagnus pungens foliage undersides

Elaeagnus pungens
THORNY ELAEAGNUS

Truly the cowboy of evergreen shrubs—wild, woolly, unkempt, and tough as rawhide. Grows anywhere and a remarkable plant for the location where nothing else prospers. Rounded, more or less, in outline with long, supple, buggy-whip shoots that wander in disarray. Silver leaves emerge in spring, the upper surface becoming lustrous dark green, the lower silver-brown. Stems, buds, and all other plant parts are covered with brownish scales. Flowers, tubular-flaring, white with brownish scales, fragrant, ½ in. long, open from September through November and are lost among the leaves. Often the only indication of flowering is the gardenia-esque fragrance saturating the autumn air. The ½- to ¾-in.-long, oval drupes are red with brownish scales and ripen in April of the year following flowering. They serve as bird food, for I see many seedlings in places that only birds travel. Grows in any soil except wet, in sun or in shade. Fixes atmospheric nitrogen and is apt to grow in the most infertile soils. Significant barrier or massing plant because of the density of the branches and thorns. Almost impenetrable even to a porcupine. Grows 10 to 15 ft. high and wide. Zones 6b to 9(10). Japan.

Cultivars and Varieties. Many selections, with 'Fruitlandii' more compact and not as wild.

'Maculata' has leaves with deep yellow blotches and staining in their centers; unstable and may revert to all green or gold leaves.

Elaeagnus pungens flowers

Elaeagnus pungens fruit

Elaeagnus pungens 'Maculata'

Elaeagnus pungens

Elliottia racemosa
GEORGIA PLUME

The more fickle the plant, the greater the desire to grow it in the garden. This Georgia native certainly fits the bill as it is nowhere common in gardens. Found wild in the sandy soils of Georgia and South Carolina, the species suckers and forms 8- to 12-ft.-high colonies. Isolated specimens make small trees; the national champion is 48 ft. high, 21 ft. wide. The 2- to 5-in.-long, dark blue-green leaves may develop bronze-red shades in November. The fragrant white flowers occur in 4- to 10-in.-long terminal racemes (panicles) in mid-June and early July. Well-drained soil, full sun to partial shade, and possibly mycorrhizae (fungal associations with roots) are necessary for good growth. The Arnold Arboretum germinated many seedlings, but subsequent growth was poor. Not for the once-a-year putterer, and a challenge to the embattled gardener. Zones 6 (once established) to 8(9).

Emmenopterys henryi

E. H. Wilson, the great plant explorer, described it as one of the most strikingly beautiful trees of the Chinese forests, reaching heights of 80 ft. Typically, in cultivation, it forms a rounded, spreading canopy. The oppositely arranged leaves, 6 to 9 in. long, lustrous dark green, with red to red-purple petioles, are beautiful. The leaves are red-bronze when first emerging. The exquisite flowers appear in corymbose panicles, 6 to 8 in. long, up to 10 in. wide, in June and July. The individual 1-in.-wide flowers are long funnel-shaped, with spreading, rounded lobes. The urn-shaped calyx (collection of sepals) has five rounded, hairy lobes, occasionally one lobe enlarging into a 2-in.-long, 1½-in.-wide white "bract." Provide deep, moist soils laden with organic matter, in sun, although partial shade in the South is advisable. One-of-a-kind specimen tree. Grows 30 to 50 ft. high and wide. Zones (6)7 to 8. China.

Emmenopterys henryi new foliage

Elliottia racemosa flowers

Emmenopterys henryi foliage

Elliottia racemosa, Georgia Plume

Emmenopterys henryi

Epigaea repens
TRAILING ARBUTUS

Somewhat of a stretch to include this evergreen groundcover, but its understated, subtle beauty provides legitimacy. The plant has followed Bonnie and me from our graduate student days at the University of Massachusetts, Amherst, to Athens, Georgia. Always evident during walks in Massachusetts; similarly so in north Georgia, where it is abundant. Almost have to look and see to discover. The glossy dark green leaves are covered with persistent stiff hairs on both surfaces. Flowers, which open in March and April in Georgia, are $5/8$ in. long, $1/2$ in. wide, fragrant, white to deep pink. Several deeper pink-flowered cultivars are described, but one can find the deeper colored forms in almost any native population. Fruit are whitish, berrylike, $1/2$-in.-diameter capsules that I have yet to observe. Best sited in acid, sandy, gravelly soil, mulched with decayed oak leaves or pine needles. Locate in wildflower garden. A true gardener's plant, not for the Wal-Mart crowd. Grows 2 to 4 (to 6) in. high, spreading along the ground. Zones 4 to 9. Massachusetts to Florida, west to Ohio and Tennessee.

Epigaea repens, Trailing Arbutus

Epigaea repens foliage and flowers

Eriobotrya japonica
LOQUAT

Great architectural plant for the warm-climate garden, with "cabbagy," leathery-textured, dark green leaves that are covered on the lower surface with grayish brown indumentum. Typically a die-back shrub in Athens, it develops into a large shrub to small rounded tree along the coast and further south. Bark is a beautiful cinnamon-brown on older trunks. Leaves, particularly on vigorous shoots, are up to 12 in. long and 5 in. wide. Flowers, which open in fall, September through January, are off-white, fragrant, and five-petaled, borne in 3- to 6-in.-long, stiff, terminal panicles. The edible yellow to orange, oblong to pear-shaped, 1- to 2-in.-long pome ripens from April through June. Tolerates extremes of soils, sun, and shade. Requires well-drained situation. Makes a great espalier against a wall or structure. Because of drought tolerance, makes a great container plant. Grows 15 to 25 ft. high and wide. Zones 8 to 10. China, Japan.

Cultivars and Varieties. 'Variegata', a pretty form with cream-margined leaves, would be useful for brightening dark shadowy areas of the garden.

Eriobotrya japonica, Loquat

Eriobotrya japonica espaliered

Eriobotrya japonica foliage

Eriobotrya japonica flowers

Eriobotrya japonica fruit

Erythrina ×bidwellii

CORAL-BEAN

Cardinal-red flowers in immense, elongated spires crown the foliage of this evergreen hybrid species. Terrific, almost epiphanic, surprise in the shrub or perennial border. Typically, in Zones 7 and 8, the species is a die-back shrub, growing into a large shrub in central and south Florida. Leaves have sharp prickles on the midrib and are as nasty as blackberry prickles. Flowers occur in 16- to 24-in.-long racemes on new growth of the season. Spectacular and almost always greeted by "Wow! What is it?" Full sun and drier soils suit it best. A hybrid between the southeastern United States native *Erythrina herbacea*, Cherokee-bean or Coral-bean, 3 to 5 ft. high in a single growing season with 1½-ft.-long racemes laden with deep scarlet flowers, and *E. crista-gallii*, Cockspur Coral-tree, an evergreen tree species with cardinal-red flowers from Brazil. Zones 9 to 11 for woody structures above ground, 7 to 8 for die-back shrubs.

Eriobotrya japonica bark

Erythrina ×bidwellii, Coral-bean

Erythrina herbacea, Cherokee-bean

Erythrina herbacea flowers and foliage

Erythrina crista-gallii, Cockspur Coral-tree

Erythrina crista-gallii flowers and foliage

Escallonia rubra

Terrific evergreen shrub with beautiful lustrous dark green leaves and red flowers in June. However, I have yet to observe any of the 50 to 60 *Escallonia* species thriving in the Southeast. Typically a large, rounded shrub, the red flowers appearing in 1- to 4-in.-long, leafy panicles. Best suited to a climate with less humidity and cooler nights. Full sun to partial shade in moist, well-drained, fertile soils are best. Excellent salt tolerance. Useful as large screen or hedge or combined in a shrub border. Grows 10 to 15 ft. high and wide; less in the Southeast. Zones 8 to 10, ideally utilized on the West Coast. Chile.

Escallonia rubra

Escallonia rubra flowers

Escallonia rubra foliage

Eucalyptus
EUCALYPTUS

Enormous group of trees (500 to 600 species most often listed), none completely cold hardy in Zone 7 but common in Florida and the West, Zones 8 to 10. Large trees (shrubs also) have juvenile leaves that are paired, rounded; mature leaves alternate in shades of gray, glaucous blue to dark green. Leaves contain high levels of oils (volatiles) and burn quite quickly. Flowers range from cream to red, often spectacular. Bark often exfoliates to expose white, gray-green, rich brown inner bark. Spectacular in their best forms. Prospers in heat and drought. Early fall freezes or late spring freezes may injure tissues. Handsome specimen tree, common in California. In the Southeast, often grown as a cut-back plant for the beautiful foliage. Grows 60 to 100 ft. high in the West; 8- to 10-ft.-high shrub in Atlanta to medium-sized tree in Orlando, Florida. The best garden choices for Zones 7 to 9 of the Southeast include *Eucalyptus gunnii*, *E. niphophila*, and *E. urnigera*. Do not believe nursery catalogs, as ratings for the cold hardiness of *E. gunnii* were listed as +10°F, 0°F, and −10°F by various nurseries. Australia, Tasmania, Malaysia, Philippines.

Eucalyptus gunnii juvenile foliage

Eucalyptus urnigera

Eucalyptus gunnii

Eucalyptus urnigera bark

Eucalyptus niphophila branches and bark

Eucryphia glutinosa
NIRRHE

To my knowledge, nowhere in evidence in the Southeast, but a large shrub to small tree that prospers in the Pacific Northwest into British Columbia. The July and August flowering period brings color when most trees and shrubs are green. Flowers, four-petaled, white, with numerous yellow stamens, fragrant, 1½ to 2 in. across, occur singly or in pairs from the leaf axils. During sabbatical at the Sir Harold Hillier Gardens and Arboretum, I was privileged to photograph and observe most of the common species and hybrids. All prefer a cool, moist climate and thrive in shade to full sun. Utilized in shrub borders and mixed tree and shrub plantings. Grows 10 to 25 ft. high, 5 to 15 ft. wide. Zones 8 to 10, West Coast. Chile.

Euonymus americanus
AMERICAN EUONYMUS, STRAWBERRY-BUSH, HEARTS-A-BURSTIN'

Obviously a schizophrenic shrub when burdened with such a ragamuffin litany of common names. Missed by most individuals until the red fruit and red seeds ripen in September and October. A loose (not all-together), suckering, fine-textured, green-stemmed shrub that grows in woods over much of the eastern United States. Leaves are medium green, 1½ to 3½ in. long, finely serrated, turning yellow-green (occasionally reddish purple) in fall. The ⅓-in.-diameter, greenish, five-petaled flowers open in May and June. The ½- to ¾-in.-diameter, three- to five-lobed, warty, red capsule opens to expose the bright red seeds that hang from the interior. Grows best in a degree of shade in dry soil. Scale is a major pest; mildew is common in extended, late season, rainy weather. Good naturalizing plant that should be left to its own foibles. Grows 4 to 6 ft. high and wide. Zones (5)6 to 9. New York, south to Florida, west to Texas.

Euonymus americanus, American Euonymus

Eucryphia glutinosa, Nirrhe, in bud

Eucryphia glutinosa flowers

Euonymus americanus fruit and seeds

Euonymus americanus flower

Euonymus japonicus
JAPANESE EUONYMUS

A much-overutilized evergreen shrub, particularly the variegated leaf selections. Has become synonymous with fast-food establishment landscaping and "Big Box" garden centers. Upright-oval in outline, densely branched and foliated. Sheeny, polished leaves are indeed beautiful, but the true species is seldom planted. Creamy, four-petaled, vinegary smelling flowers emerge in June, followed by ⅓-in.-diameter, four-valved, pinkish capsules with orange seeds. Grows anywhere except in wet soils. Astoundingly salt-tolerant and is a common hedge plant in English seaside gardens. Mildew and scale are serious problems. Grows 5 to 10 ft. high, less in spread. Zones (6)7 to 8, 9 and 10 on the West Coast. Japan.

Cultivars and Varieties. Cultivars with colored foliage flood the market.

'Aureomarginatus' has yellow margins, green center.

'Aureus' has a bright yellow center bordered with green but tends to revert.

'Microphyllus' has smaller leaves, ½ to 1 in. long, and is fashionably outfitted in green, yellow-margined, and cream-margined forms. It and variegated forms are less hardy than the species. Grows 1 to 3 ft. high, one-half as wide. A scale's best friend.

'Silver King', with cream-white margins and pale green large leaves, is common.

Euonymus japonicus, Japanese Euonymus

Euonymus japonicus foliage

Euonymus japonicus flowers

Euonymus japonicus 'Aureomarginatus'

Euonymus japonicus 'Aureus'

MORE ➤

Euonymus japonicus continued

Euonymus japonicus 'Silver King'

Euonymus japonicus 'Microphyllus Variegatus'

Eurya japonica

Rare broadleaf evergreen member of the tea family that is represented in select arboreta and botanical gardens but seldom ventures into commerce. A small spreading shrub with lustrous dark green leaves that turn bronze to purple-green in winter. Each leaf is 1 to 3 in. long and ½ to 1 in. wide. The axillary, ¼-in.-diameter, white flowers open in winter. In fact, I witnessed them fully open in late February at the Hillier Arboretum. The ⅕-in.-diameter, globose, black fruit ripen in late summer to fall. Tolerates full sun and heavy shade. Best performance in moist, acid, well-drained soils. Could be utilized for hedges, groupings, mixed borders. Grows 4

Eurya japonica

Eurya japonica foliage

Eurya emarginata foliage

Eurya emarginata

Eurya japonica flowers

to 6 ft. high and wide (my observations), although literature mentions to 30 ft. high. Zones (7)8 to 9. Japan.

The related species *Eurya emarginata* has 1- to 1½-in.-long, ½-in.-wide, lustrous dark green, crenate-serrate leaves, blackish, malodorous flowers, and ⅕-in.-diameter, globose, purple-black fruit. Forms a small mound, 2 to 3 ft. high. Zones 7 to 8. Japan.

Cultivars and Varieties. 'Winter Wine' is smaller, slower growing, more spreading than *Eurya japonica*, with burgundy winter foliage.

Euscaphis japonicus
SWEETHEART or EUSCAPHIS TREE

In the plant introduction business, hyperbole often overshadows reality. The gardening world is still debating the merits of this small tree that was advertised as heat- and drought-tolerant. In our garden, it flags at the first hint of drought and is not to be trusted without moist medium. Lustrous, dark green, compound pinnate leaves, composed of seven to eleven leaflets, each 2 to 4 in. long, are engaging and turn mahogany-purple in fall. Yellowish white flowers in 4- to 9- (to 12-) in.-diameter terminal panicles appear in May and June. The nifty fruit are rose to ruby-red and open to expose the shiny, steel-blue to black seeds. Quite spectacular at their best. Reddish brown stems are also beautiful, developing vertical gray-brown tissues that produce striated (snakeskin) patterns. Moist, organic laden soils and partial shade to full sun maximize performance. Possible use as an accent or novelty plant. Will *never* become an everyday tree! Grows 15 to 25 ft. high and wide. Zones 7 to 8. China, Korea, Japan.

Euscaphis japonicus foliage

Euscaphis japonicus, Sweetheart Tree

Euscaphis japonicus flowers

Euscaphis japonicus fruit and seeds

×*Fatshedera lizei*

Remarkable intergeneric hybrid between *Fatsia japonica* 'Moseri' and *Hedera helix* 'Hibernica' with scandent growth habit and evergreen leaves. Loose and snaky on its own. Makes a terrific espalier when trained on a wall, tree, or fence. Develops, like *Hedera helix*, rootlike hold-fasts that permit attachment to porous materials. Leathery, lustrous dark green, five-lobed, 4- to 10-in.-wide leaves are intermediate between the parents. The pale green-white flowers are held in a terminal panicle, 8 to 10 in. long, up to 4 in. wide, composed of 1-in.-diameter, 12- to 36-flowered hemispherical umbels. Flowers in October in the Dirr garden. Shade (some degree) and moist, well-drained soils suffice. Have grown it for 15 years with only cold (−3°F) killing it to the ground. Re-sprouted and now its vigorous self. Allow it to wind through multi-stemmed shrubs. Grows 3 to 5 ft. high; larger on a wall. Zones (7)8 to 10.

Cultivars and Varieties. 'Anna Mikkels' has irregular yellowish markings in center of leaf.

'Variegata' is splashed and bordered with white.

×*Fatshedera lizei*

×*Fatshedera lizei* foliage

×*Fatshedera lizei* flowers   ×*Fatshedera lizei* 'Variegata'

×*Fatshedera lizei* 'Anna Mikkels'

Fatsia japonica

JAPANESE FATSIA

Beautiful, seven- to nine- (to eleven-) lobed, 6- to 14-in.-diameter, lustrous dark green leaves provide bold texture to shady areas of the garden. In fact, even in England, the plant *requires* a shady environment to prevent leaf discoloration. Dense and rounded in habit. Flowers, white, appear in 1- to 1½-in.-diameter rounded umbels, in a 15- to 20-in.-high and -wide terminal panicle. Opening times vary from October to November, with full flower in early January in Savannah. Fruit are ⅓-in.-diameter, subglobose, blackish drupes. Transplant from containers into moist, acid soils high in organic matter.

Fatsia japonica foliage

Fatsia japonica, Japanese Fatsia

MORE ➤

Fatsia japonica **continued**

Provide adequate fertilizer, or leaves show nitrogen deficiency. Tolerant of air pollution and salt spray. One of the prized plants in our garden—nothing compares for textural accents. Grows 6 to 10 ft. high, 6 to 10 ft. wide. Zones (7)8 to 10. Japan.

Cultivars and Varieties. 'Variegata' has white margins and streaks and "shows" even better than the species in shade.

Fatsia japonica flowers

Fatsia japonica fruit

Fatsia japonica 'Variegata'

Feijoa sellowiana
PINEAPPLE GUAVA

This handsome gray-leaved evergreen shrub is a common element in Florida landscapes. Rounded and shrubby in outline but can be grown as a small tree. The broad, ovate, 1- to 3-in.-long leaves are reminiscent of juvenile *Eucalyptus* foliage, except whitish-felted below. Their upper surfaces are dark green. The flowers are like fuchsias, with four reflexed sepals, four petals red in center and whitish at margins, stamens numerous, ¾ to 1 in. long and rich crimson. Flowers in May and June. Fruit are 1- to 3-in.-long, egg-shaped berries, green, tinged red, turning yellow. Edible with taste likened to pineapple with overtones of spearmint. Full sun to partial shade in light loamy soil. Tolerates salt spray. Prune after flowering. Use for foliage effect as a screen, hedge, mass, or cut-back shrub. Grows 10 to 15 ft. high, 10 ft. wide. Zones (7)8 to 10(11). Southern Brazil and Uruguay.

Feijoa sellowiana, Pineapple Guava

Feijoa sellowiana foliage and foliage undersides

Feijoa sellowiana flower

Feijoa sellowiana young fruit

Ficus carica foliage

Ficus carica
COMMON FIG

Common in old homesteads throughout the South, often outlasting the house itself. Massive rounded shrub—bold leaves and coarse stems (winter) make it difficult to miss. The sandpapery, dark green leaves, three- to five-lobed, are 4 to 8 in. high and wide, even larger on vigorous shoots. Flowers are produced inside a concave structure that, when mature, enlarges and becomes fleshy. The tapering, top-shaped fruit, 2 to 4 in. long, 1 to 2½ in. wide, are green-purple-brown at maturity. Inexplicably, the fig in our garden, so beautiful in leaf, produces a fruit with the texture and taste of a dishrag. Tolerates about any soil and full sun. Plant it for foliage texture, fruit, and as a conversation piece. Good as a cut-back shrub for foliage. Grows 10 to 15 ft. high and wide. I have observed a 30-ft.-high and -wide rounded tree with a 14- to 16-in.-diameter trunk at Mompessan House, Salisbury, England. Could not believe it was a fig at first. Zones 7 to 10. Western Asia and Mediterranean regions.

MORE ➤

Ficus carica, Common Fig

Ficus carica continued

Ficus carica espaliered at Sissinghurst Garden, England

Ficus carica fruit

Ficus pumila
CLIMBING FIG

A rambunctious, true-clinging, evergreen vine that is famous for covering structures throughout the Southeast. The juvenile leaves, ¾ to 1¼ in. long, are appressed to the structure. Adult leaves, 2 to 4 in. long, are borne on woody stems that grow in all directions. Have observed the adult form pruned into a hedge in Savannah. Best growth occurs in shade and protected areas. Winter sun in Zone 7b has discolored leaves. Will grow in virtually any soil. Requires pruning to keep it neat. For a small-leaf vine, it is quite tenacious. Limited by structure: have seen it 3 ft. high on 3-ft. walls and 40 ft. up on columns. Zones 7b to 10. China, Taiwan, Japan.

Cultivars and Varieties. 'Variegata' has leaves with a creamy white margin.

Ficus pumila, Climbing Fig

Ficus pumila juvenile foliage

Ficus pumila 'Variegata'

Fontanesia fortunei
FORTUNE'S FONTANESIA

Rare and "Jurassic" shrub with nail-like durability. I remember seeing in my travels a planting near Clinton, Oklahoma, where the wind never stopped blowing. For some unearthly reason, the plant was taught in the woody plant course during my Ohio State days. Upright, multi-stemmed, graceful, almost unperturbable shrub. Leaves, opposite, willowlike, 1 to 4½ in. long, and lustrous dark green, hold late in fall without appreciable fall color. Foliage, from a distance, resembles a fine-textured bamboo and is a suitable alternative, especially since it does not "run." The greenish white flowers, in 1- to 2-in.-long panicles, do not inspire. Adaptable to varied soils and climatic conditions. Good massing and screening plant. Grows 10 to 15 ft. high. Zones 4 to 8. China.

Fontanesia fortunei foliage

MORE ➤

Fontanesia fortunei, Fortune's Fontanesia

Fontanesia fortunei **continued**

Cultivars and Varieties. 'Titan' is more upright in habit with prettier foliage; a 3-in.-high cutting grew 76 in. high, 65 in. wide in three growing seasons.

Fontanesia fortunei flowers

Fontanesia fortunei 'Titan'

Fuchsia magellanica
HARDY FUCHSIA

Although nowhere common in Zones 7 to 11, this small to medium-sized shrub produces an attractive arrangement of pendulous red flowers in summer. The habit is oval-rounded with slender branches clothed in lustrous dark green, ¾- to 2-in.-long, prominently toothed leaves. The beautiful flowers, solitary or paired and originating from the leaf axils in summer, average 2 in. long and range from deep crimson to occasionally white or pale pink. The red-purple, ¾-in.-long, oblong fruit are seldom produced on plants that I have observed. Best performance in moist, well-drained soils and cooler air temperatures. Almost weedlike in Ireland, England, and continental Europe, and one of the most asked about plants during our garden tours. Great border and container plant. Grows 2 to 10 ft. high and wide. Zones 7 to 9, 10 on the West Coast. Chile, Argentina.

Fuchsia magellanica, Hardy Fuchsia

Fuchsia magellanica flowers and foliage

Galphimia gracilis (*Thryallis glauca*)
SHOWER OF GOLD, SPRAY OF GOLD

I went (almost) crazy trying to identify this evergreen shrub, which was endowed with bright yellow flowers in October. A utilitarian, rounded shrub that is used in foundations, groupings, and mass plantings in central Florida and south. Leaves, opposite, gray-green, to 2 in. long, turn reddish purple in winter. The ½- to 1-in.-wide, yellow flowers open throughout the warm periods. Each flower is composed of five, free-clawed, bright yellow petals surrounding the ten, red, stalked stamens. Requires full sun and well-drained soil. Easily pruned and maintained. Flowers on new growth so removing old flowers encourages new shoot development. Grows 4 to 6 ft. high and wide. Zones 9 to 11. Central America.

Gardenia jasminoides (*G. augusta*)
GARDENIA, CAPE JASMINE

Fortuitous that this prose is penned just after sniffing a double-flowered gardenia in the garden. Powerful, heady aroma, equatable with a walk through the perfume section of a major department store. Wow! For the better half of May into June, sporadically thereafter, waxy, white flowers twinkle in the garden and cast their floral fragrance for meters. Shiny, dark green leaves, either opposite or in threes, grace the lustrous stems. The entire evergreen shrub, oval-rounded in outline, is elegant. Each flower, 2 to 3 (to 4) in. wide, with six (occasionally seven) wedge-shaped petals, lasts a brief time and ages to yellow. Fruit are 1- to 1½-in.-long, winged (ridged), fleshy berries that color a beautiful rich orange in November and persist into winter. Seeds are readily extracted and will germinate upon sowing. Have observed plants prospering in shade and sun. Tolerant of dry soils. White flies and scale can be bothersome. Bonnie and I grow four different cultivars and have never had any problems. Makes a good container plant, shrub border component, entrance plant. Grows 4 to 6 ft. high

MORE ➤

Gardenia jasminoides, Gardenia

Gardenia jasminoides foliage

Gardenia jasminoides flowers

Gardenia jasminoides fruit

Gardenia jasminoides 'Daruma'

Gardenia jasminoides **continued**

and wide. Zones 7b to 10. China, Taiwan, Japan.

Cultivars and Varieties. Numerous, embracing such double-flowered forms as 'Aimee Yoshida', 'August Beauty', 'Fortuniana', 'Michael', 'Mystery', 'Billie Holiday', and 'Chuck Hayes' (semidouble). Single forms include 'Daisy', 'Daruma', 'Grif's Se-lect', 'Kleim's Hardy', 'Shooting Star', and 'White Gem'.

'Radicans' is a compact rounded form, 2 to 3 ft. high, with 1- to 2-in.-diameter double white flowers. Quite common in commerce.

'Radicans Variegata' has restrained cream-margined leaves that occasionally revert to the species type.

Gardenia jasminoides 'Kleim's Hardy'

Gardenia jasminoides 'Shooting Star' (left), species (right)

Gardenia jasminoides 'Grif's Select'

Gardenia jasminoides 'Radicans'

Gardenia jasminoides 'Radicans Variegata'

Gaylussacia ursina, Bear Huckleberry

Gaylussacia ursina
BEAR HUCKLEBERRY

Huckleberries are not the easiest members of the Ericaceae to identify, and this 2½- to 5-ft.-high suckering shrub is the one I encounter most often during my hikes through north Georgia. Forms low thickets, suckering in all directions, of rather nondescript medium green leaves, 2 to 4 in. long, with tiny resinous dots on the lower leaf surface. In fall, leaves turn beautiful reddish purple, the effect lasting long into the season. The small rose flowers are mixed with the foliage and not greatly effective. The ⅓-in.-diameter shiny black drupe ripens in late summer. Grows in acid soils, often rocky, dry, and well-drained. Have observed only in the shade in the wild. Great naturalizing plant. The fall color is beautiful. Zones 6 to 7. Tennessee, North Carolina, and Georgia.

Gelsemium sempervirens
CAROLINA YELLOW JESSAMINE

The Head Gardener turns the light switch on in late March and April in the Southeast, for shrubs and trees are crawling with this glowing yellow-flowered vine, evergreen and twining, that appears to embrace every structure, yet never smothers a plant like kudzu or wisteria does. The shiny green leaves are 1 to 3½ in. long and may discolor (yellow) in winter sun. The 1½-in.-long, 1-in.-wide, funnel-formed, fragrant, yellow flowers often open from February into April across the South. Flowers are effective for a full month. Grows in any well-drained soil in sun to partial shade. Used on trellises, walls (with support), mailboxes, and as a groundcover. Beautiful early spring flowering vine. Grows 10 to 20 ft. on structures. Zones 6 to 9, probably to 10 and 11. Vir-

MORE ➤

Gaylussacia ursina fall color

Gelsemium sempervirens, Carolina Yellow Jessamine

Gaylussacia ursina foliage and flowers

Gelsemium sempervirens flowers

Gelsemium sempervirens **continued**

ginia to Florida westward to Texas and Arkansas, south to Central America.

   Gelsemium rankinii, Swamp Jessamine, differs from *G. sempervirens* by flowering in fall and spring and having no floral fragrance. Also grows in swamps in North Carolina to Florida to Louisiana. Zones 7 to 9.

Cultivars and Varieties. 'Pride of Augusta' produces double yellow flowers with the appearance of miniature rose buds.

   'Woodlander's Light Yellow' has cream-yellow flowers, larger than *Gelsemium sempervirens* but not as cold hardy. Zones 8 and higher.

Gelsemium rankinii flowers

Gelsemium sempervirens 'Pride of Augusta'

Gelsemium rankinii, Swamp Jessamine

Gelsemium sempervirens 'Woodlander's Light Yellow'

Gordonia lasianthus
LOBLOLLY-BAY

Native evergreen tree or shrub that grows in swamps but has a difficult time transitioning into garden culture. In central Florida, nursery plants grew contentedly in the sandy soils, supplemented only by drip irrigation. The habit is pyramidal-conical, somewhat open, with 4- to 6-in.-long, glossy dark green leaves. Flowers open in late May and continue sporadically into October. Each flower is 2½ in. across, five-petaled, with a central mass of yellow stamens. In cultivation, does best in well-drained soils. Fickle, and plants on the Georgia campus have inexplicably died. Probably no mass commercial appeal but a pretty tree, resembling *Franklinia alatamaha* in flower. Possibly 30 to 40 ft. high, under cultivation; generally never lives long enough. Zones 7 to 9. Virginia to Florida to Louisiana.

Cultivars and Varieties. 'Variegata' has irregular creamy white margins that turn rose-pink in cold weather. This is a weak grower and needs protection from sun and wind to keep it looking good.

Gordonia lasianthus foliage

Gordonia lasianthus bark

Gordonia lasianthus flower

Gordonia lasianthus 'Variegata'

Gordonia lasianthus, Loblolly-bay

Grevillea robusta
SILK OAK

Tried to grow this in Athens but the first fall freeze deep-sixed any hopes. A warm-climate tree, picking up steam in central Florida and south. Beautiful soft pyramidal habit with fernlike leaves, gray green above, silvery beneath, up to 12 in. long. Flowers, like many members of the Proteaceae, are showy by virtue of the stamens, in this case orange-yellow, in comblike, 4-in.-long racemes borne on short shoots in spring. Best in full sun and well-drained soil. Handsome specimen, shade, and street tree. Somewhat messy, with considerable leaf abscission in spring, sporadically thereafter. Grows 50 to 75 ft. high, about one-half as wide. Larger in its native haunts. Zones 9 to 11. Australia.

The related species *Grevillea rosmarinifolia*, a needle-like evergreen shrub to 5 ft. high, produces lovely red flowers in spring and summer. A yellow-flowered form, 'Sulfurea' is available. The species has been successfully grown near Commerce, Georgia (Zone 7b). Beautiful lustrous dark green foliage and refined texture. Zones 7b to 9. Australia.

Grevillea rosmarinifolia flowers

Grevillea rosmarinifolia

Hedera canariensis
ALGERIAN IVY

Another ivy, but not just another ivy. Large glossy dark green leaves with red petioles rise 8 to 10 in. above the ground to form a beautiful groundcover carpet. The leaves are 2 to 6 (to 8) in. long. Prefers partial shade and moist, organic, well-drained soil. Excellent salt tolerance. Have witnessed terrific injury (kill) to plantings on the coast of Georgia after exposure to 11°F. Best above 20°F. Excellent groundcover plant for warmer climates. Grows 10 to 20 ft. on a tree or structure. Zones 9 to 10. Canary Islands, Madeira, the Azores, Portugal, and northwest Africa.

Hedera canariensis, Algerian Ivy

Helianthemum nummularium, Sunrose

Helianthemum nummularium
SUNROSE

Smallish wee plants, with no charisma until they burst forth with white, yellow, orange, and red flowers, like starburst fireworks. Witnessing their beauty is the lure that entices the gardener to take the bait. I succumbed and have little to show for trying except the knowledge that heat and humidity wreak havoc. A small spreading evergreen, almost groundcover-like, is covered with 1-in.-wide, single or double flowers in late May and June. Flowers persist for a month. Leaves, ½ to 1 in. long, vary from dark green above, grayish below, to gray on both surfaces. Requires well-drained soil on the dry side, preferably in low to moderately fertile soils, slightly acid to neutral in full sun. A common rock garden or wall plant where drainage is excellent. Remove spent flowers to encourage new foliage. Grows 6 to 12 in. high, 2 to 3 ft. wide in rather uniform circles. Zones 7 to 8, 10 on the West Coast. Mediterannean region.

Helianthemum nummularium double flowers

Helianthemum nummularium single flowers

Hibiscus mutabilis
(*Hibiscus chinensis* var. *mutabilis*)
CONFEDERATE ROSE

This large, oafy, rounded shrub appears in late summer, almost like a mushroom after a rainstorm. What is truly remarkable is the die-back (herbaceous) nature of the species and its spirited growth in a single season, resulting in a large, coarse-stemmed, rounded shrub. Plants in Athens, Georgia, have reached 10 to 12 ft. high. The three- to seven-lobed, 4- to 10-in.-long, dark green leaves serve as the perfect foil for the 1½- to 3- (to 4-) in.-diameter, five-petaled, white, aging to pink, rose, and red, flowers. Flowers initiate on new growth in summer and continue until hard frosts. Fruit are hairy, subglobose, 1-in.-diameter capsules with rounded seeds. Ideally, remove capsules to keep plants in active growth. Prefers moist, well-drained, fertile soils in full sun to maximize growth. May require supplemental fertilizer during active growth to maintain dark green foliage color and flower production. Lovely for flower color in perennial and shrub borders. Could be used as a specimen plant but takes on the appearance of a large bundle of gray-brown sticks in winter. Grows 8 to 10 ft. high and wide. Zones 7 to 10(11). China.

Cultivars and Varieties. 'Plena' is a double form with cottonball-shaped flowers that transition through white, pink, rose, and red.

Hibiscus mutabilis 'Plena' flowers

Hibiscus mutabilis 'Plena'

Hibiscus rosa-sinensis
CHINESE HIBISCUS

Strictly a herbaceous perennial in Zone 9, becoming above-ground woody about central Florida into the Keys. Shrub or small tree, often used for container planting in the North or in conservatories. Remarkable flowers in a spectrum of colors and shapes (single to double). Leaves are waxy, rich green, 6 in. long and 4 in. wide. The flowers, 5 to 8 in. in diameter in white, yellow, pink, salmon, red, and combinations, cause shortness of breath. Over 120 cultivars are known. Full sun, any well-drained soil, and ample nutrition keep plants vigorous. Flowers on new growth of season, so remove spent flowers. Grows 8 to 15 ft. high. Zones 9 to 11. Tropical Asia.

Hibiscus rosa-sinensis, Chinese Hibiscus, as a container plant

Hypericum, ST. JOHNSWORT

A varied group of evergreen to deciduous shrubs, usually small in stature, with rich green leaves, almost needlelike in some species, and ⅓- to ½-in.-diameter, five-petaled, yellow flowers from May or June through September. Although largely unknown to cultivation, the following species are easy to cultivate and provide compactness, handsome foliage, and beautiful yellow flowers. Acid, well-drained, moist soil in full sun results in maximum performance. All are easy to grow from seed (sow on moist medium, do not cover) and root from softwood cuttings. At the Center for Applied Nursery Research, Dearing, Georgia, 12 species are being tested in replicated trials. The following are the best to date.

Hypericum brachyphyllum

Lustrous green, needlelike leaves, less than ½ in. long, 1/24 in. wide, occur in clusters along the two-winged stems. The flower buds are red and conical, opening to ½-in.-diameter yellow flowers. Grows 3 to 5 ft. high. in wet areas in Georgia to Florida and Louisiana. Zones 7 to 9.

Hypericum densiflorum

A rounded deciduous shrub with 1- to 2-in.-long, ⅛- to ⅓-in.-wide lustrous dark green leaves. Habit is oval-rounded with fine-textured, lax-arching shoots. The ½-in.-diameter yellow flowers occur in corymb-like panicles at the ends of the shoots from June through August. Variable habitats in the wild from mountain balds to swamps and bogs, New York to Georgia, west to Missouri, Louisiana, and Texas. Grows 1 to 3 (to 5) ft. high and wide. Zones 5 to 9.

Hibiscus rosa-sinensis flower

Hibiscus rosa-sinensis flower

Hypericum densiflorum

Hypericum fasiculatum, Sand-weed

Hypericum galioides, Bedstraw St. Johnswort

Hypericum fasiculatum
SAND-WEED

Lustrous dark green, needlelike, evergreen leaves, ½ in. long, about ¹⁄₁₂ in. wide, with many clustered at the nodes, producing a juniper-type texture. Habit is dense and compact to 3 ft. high and wide. The ½- to ⅔-in.-diameter yellow flowers open from May through September. Grows in moist soils (low pinelands, swamps), North Carolina to Florida, west to Mississippi. Zones 7 to 9.

Hypericum galioides
BEDSTRAW ST. JOHNSWORT

Similar to *Hypericum fasiculatum* with longer and wider, lustrous dark green evergreen leaves to 2 in. long. Forms a loose, lax cushion, 1 to 1½ ft. high, 3 ft. wide. Golden yellow flowers, ½ to ¾ in. in diameter, open in June and July. Grows in moist soils in the Coastal Plain from North Carolina to Louisiana. Zones 7 to 9.

Cultivars and Varieties. 'Brodie' is a uniform, broad-mounded selection with lustrous dark green leaves and ¾-in.-diameter flowers.

Hypericum galioides 'Brodie'

Hypericum galioides 'Brodie' foliage

Hypericum lissophoeus

A wonderful textural plant for borders, airy and feathery with asparagus-like leaves and exfoliating copper-brown bark. The habit is upright, 3 to 5 ft. high, loose and arching, and the gray-green, $\frac{1}{2}$- to 1-in.-long, needlelike evergreen leaves are elegant. The $\frac{1}{2}$-in.-diameter yellow flowers twinkle among the needles, producing just enough color to entice. Grows in wet depressions in north Florida. Zones 7b to 9.

Hypericum lissophoeus

Hypericum lloydii

Hypericum lloydii

Can be confused with *Hypericum reductum* but has longer, notched, evergreen leaves and sepals. Growth habit is decumbent and groundcover-ish. Needlelike leaves are more lustrous than *H. reductum*. The $\frac{1}{3}$-in.-diameter, yellow flowers open in August and continue until frost. Found in dry pine woods and rock outcrops, North Carolina to Alabama. Zones 7 to 9.

Hypericum reductum

An evergreen groundcover species, about 1 to $1\frac{1}{2}$ ft. high and spreading to form a carpet of dull green, needlelike leaves less than $\frac{1}{2}$ in. long. Flowers are $\frac{1}{3}$ in. in diameter, yellow, and open in August and beyond. Grows in drier soils (dunes, sand hills) from North Carolina to Florida and Alabama. Zones 7 to 9.

Hypericum reductum

Idesia polycarpa
IGIRI TREE

Quite an iconoclastic biological specimen that, although outlandish, has not attracted attention from gardeners. Becomes a rounded tree with coarse branches and 5- to 10-in.-long, deep green leaves. Bark is almost grayish white, and several multi-stemmed specimens in the University's Botanical Garden are about as close to white-bark birches as is possible in the South. Flowers (June) are dioecious, yellow-green, male in 5- to 6-in.-long panicles, female in up to 8-in.-long panicles. A fruiting tree is *spectacular* with dangling panicles of ¼- to ⅓-in.-diameter, bright red fruit. My fondest memories conjure fruiting trees, in a grove type planting, at the National Arboretum. Tolerates heat, drought, and *substandard* soils. Extremely fast growing as a young tree. Easily grown from freshly planted seed. Grows 40 to 60 ft. high and wide. Zones 6 to 9. Southern Japan, central and western China.

Idesia polycarpa, Igiri Tree, fruiting

Idesia polycarpa foliage

Idesia polycarpa fruit

Idesia polycarpa bark

Ilex, HOLLY

A garden-worthy group of plants of the first order of magnitude with beauty of foliage, fruit, and habit. Some 400 species, probably more, are recognized worldwide. They exist as wind-sculpted mountaintop to swampy shrubby denizens, 12 in. to 60 ft. high. Leaves are either evergreen or deciduous and, although usually depicted with spiny margins, can be lightly serrated to entire. Flowers open in late winter to spring, usually white, four-petaled or more, either quite fragrant or nondescript. Sexes are separate, with male flowers generally having four extended stamens; female flowers, with the green ovary in the center, recall a green basketball. Fruit are botanically drupes, not berries as often stated. Colors range from white to yellow, orange, red, purple, and black. The seedlike structures in the fleshy fruit pulp are called pyrenes. Various numbers are present per fruit depending on species. For ideal pollination and fruit set, it is best to have a male and female from the same species that flower at the same time. In truth, according to discussions with experts and personal observations, any male can pollinate any female if flowering overlaps. Holly boughs, particularly Ilex aquifolium, *make beautiful Christmas decorations. Prune holly in winter to rejuvenate entire plants. I witnessed 20-ft.-high 'Nellie R. Stevens' cut within 3 ft. of the ground with new shoots emerging from the large trunk the following spring. Sun- and moderately shade-tolerant. Any soil (preferably acid) except permanently wet; several species withstand wet feet. Minimal diseases and insects with root rot, spittlebugs, scale, leaf miner, and mites most prominent.*

The late Fred C. Galle's Hollies: The Genus Ilex *(Portland, OR: Timber Press, 1997) will forever stand as the classic reference on the large genus.*

Ilex ×altaclerensis fruit and foliage

Ilex ×altaclerensis
ALTACLERA HOLLY

A hybrid group of hollies with *Ilex aquifolium* and *I. perado* as parents. Medium-sized pyramidal trees with lustrous dark green, entire (almost) to spiny-margined leaves. Flowers white (early spring), and fruit bright red. Not the most cold- or heat-tolerant but adaptable in the Middle Atlantic States and on the West Coast. Over 50 cultivars are known. Good collection at Van Dusen Botanical Garden, Vancouver, British Columbia. Grows 20 to 40 ft. high, one-half as wide. Zones 6 to 8, 9 to 10 on the West Coast.

Cultivars and Varieties. 'Camelliifolia', with lustrous black-green leaves, to 5 in. long, 3 in. wide, and dark red fruit, is one of the most popular forms.

'James G. Esson', with beautiful, undulating, spiny, dark green leaves and lustrous red fruit, is smaller than 'Camelliifolia', and habit is more open.

Ilex ×altaclerensis, Altaclera Holly

Ilex aquifolium
ENGLISH HOLLY

The plant of hedgerows, shady woods, and roadsides throughout England. Long planted by the birds, and untended soil is often home to wayward seedlings. Has escaped from cultivation in the Pacific Northwest. Typically a dense pyramidal tree with spiny-margined, lustrous dark green leaves. Four-petaled, off-white, fragrant flowers in May give rise to $\frac{1}{4}$- to $\frac{7}{8}$-in.-diameter, rounded, red fruit. Grows in acid and higher pH soils, in sun or shade; displays great salt tolerance and is readily pruned. Some of the great hedges in English gardens are built of this biological material. Amazing number of cultivars, most best suited to the West Coast, although I have observed plants from Cape Cod to Pine Mountain, Georgia. Grows 30 to 50 ft. high with beautiful gray bark. Zones 6 to 7b, 10 on the West Coast. Europe, northern Africa, and western Asia.

Cultivars and Varieties. 'Argenteomarginata' with white-margined leaves and 'Aureomarginata' with gold-margined leaves are available.

'Balkans', 'Boulder Creek', Siberia™, and 'Zero' are more cold hardy forms with red fruit.

'Ferox', Hedgehog Holly, has small leaves with marginal and upper surface spines; several variegated selections of 'Ferox' are in cultivation.

Ilex aquifolium, English Holly

MORE ➤

Ilex aquifolium foliage

Ilex aquifolium fruit

Ilex aquifolium continued

Ilex aquifolium 'Argenteomarginata'

Ilex aquifolium 'Aureomarginata'

Ilex aquifolium 'Ferox'

Ilex cassine
DAHOON

A southeastern native evergreen species that grows in moist woods of the southern Coastal Plain into the Bahamas and Texas. Typically a small tree or large shrub, open and somewhat scraggly, with light green leaves, 2 to 4 (to 6) in. long, toothed (at apex) to entire. Leaves assume varied manifestations, with small ½- to 1-in.-long leaves constituting var. *myrtifolia* and a longer narrow leaf form representing var. *angustifolia*. The species and two varieties grow in Athens, and *none* inspire the average gardener. Most notably, the species hybridizes with *Ilex opaca* to form *I. ×attenuata*, from which 'East Palatka', 'Foster's #2', and 'Savannah' were selected. Fruit, ¼ in. in diameter, globose, commonly red, to yellow on

Ilex cassine, Dahoon

occasion, are borne on elongated pedicels (stalks). Fruit almost fluoresce and persist into winter in the South. Moist, well-drained, acidic soil suits it best. Terrifically susceptible to spittlebug damage. Prune to maintain a dense habit. Grows 20 to 30 ft. high, 8 to 15 ft. wide. Zones 7 to 9.

Cultivars and Varieties. 'Escatawba', 'Perdido', and 'Tensaw' are superior red-fruited selections from Tom Dodd III, Semmes, Alabama.

'Autumn Cascade' is a heavy red-fruited, semi-pendent selection of var. *myrtifolia*.

Ilex cassine fruit and foliage

Ilex cassine var. *myrtifolia* 'Autumn Cascade' fruit

Ilex cassine var. *myrtifolia* 'Autumn Cascade'

Ilex cassine var. *angustifolia* foliage

Ilex cornuta
CHINESE HOLLY

For the hot, dry areas of the country, this evergreen large shrub/small tree would rank in the top five safe choices. Typically a multi-stemmed shrub, occasionally a small tree, with five to seven (occasionally nine) sharp-spined, credit card–textured leaves. Indestructible—large plants pruned to within 6 to 12 in. of the soil line resprout and reform. Leaves, lustrous dark green, are 1½ to 4 in. long and maintain good coloration year-round. Flowers, four-petaled, dull white, fragrant, ¼ in. wide, are produced in prodigious quantities in the leaf axils. Bees hover about and consider these March flowers their first banquet of the season. If pollination is complete, fruit set is spectacular, with ¼- to ⅓-in.-diameter, bright red fruit ripening in September and October and persisting into winter. Full sun, moderate shade, heat, drought, and miserable soils, as long as they are well-drained, are adequate for successful culture. Can be pruned and maintained at any height. The cultivars discussed here are ideal for many landscape uses. Grows 8 to 10 (to 15) ft. high, often wider at maturity. Zones 7 to 9, 10 on the West Coast. China, Korea.

Cultivars and Varieties. 'Burfordii' is a spineless leaf form (except for the terminal spine) with large red fruit. Grows 20 ft. high and wide.

'Carissa' is a 3- to 4-ft.-high, 4- to 6-ft.-wide, compact form with an entire leaf margin. Female.

'Dwarf Burford' ('Burfordii Nana') is the smaller version of 'Burfordii', usually 5 to 6 (to 8) ft. high and wide but grows larger. Leaves are 1½ to 2 in. long, lustrous dark green and unevenly surfaced. A plant on the Georgia campus is over 15 ft. high. Female.

'Fine Line' ('Fineline') grows 12 ft. high, 5 ft. wide, with 1½- to 2½-in.-long, essentially spineless leaves and red fruit. Slower growing than 'Burfordii'.

'Needlepoint' is a Dirr favorite with narrow leaves, spineless leaf margins, and lustrous dark green color on a bulbous-conical framework. Grows 15 ft. high, 10 ft. wide, red fruit.

'Rotunda' is the porcupine of the group, 3 to 4 ft. high, 6 to 8 ft. across. Leaves are seven-spined and dangerous, making it a good "no cut-through," i.e., barrier planting. Female.

Ilex cornuta female flowers

Ilex cornuta, Chinese Holly

Ilex cornuta 'Burfordii'

Ilex cornuta 'Burfordii' bark

Ilex cornuta foliage

Ilex cornuta 'Burfordii' fruit

Ilex cornuta 'Carissa'

MORE ➤

Ilex cornuta continued

Ilex cornuta 'Dwarf Burford'

Ilex cornuta 'Dwarf Burford' fruit

Ilex cornuta 'Fine Line' fruit

Ilex cornuta 'Rotunda'

Ilex cornuta 'Rotunda' fruit and foliage

Ilex 'Emily Bruner'

A stately, dense, broad pyramid of leathery lustrous dark green leaves that is becoming more common in southern landscapes. This hybrid between *Ilex cornuta* 'Burfordii' and *I. latifolia* was brought to Don Shadow's (Shadow Nursery, Winchester, Tennessee) attention when he was a student at the University of Tennessee; he subsequently named and introduced it into cultivation. The 2- to 4- (to 5-) in.-long leaves have jagged, spiny margins, which several students described as rolling, white-capped seas. Leaves hold their color through the seasons, with slight discoloration in winter. Beautiful, ¼- to ⅓-in.-diameter, rounded, red fruit ripen in September and October and persist into winter. Intensity of red color diminishes with age. Sun or partial shade in well-drained soil. Suitable for use as a specimen plant and in groupings and screens. 'James Swan' is the male pollinator. Grows 20 to 25 ft. high, 10 to 15 ft. wide. Zones 7 to 9.

Ilex cornuta 'Fine Line'

Ilex cornuta 'Needlepoint'

Ilex 'Emily Bruner'

MORE ➤

Ilex 'Emily Bruner' continued

Ilex 'Emily Bruner' foliage and flowers

Ilex 'Emily Bruner' foliage and fruit

Ilex ×*koehneana*, Koehne Holly

Ilex ×*koehneana* 'Hohman'

Ilex ×*koehneana*

KOEHNE HOLLY

I frequently take visitors to the Horticulture Farm test area, where invariably I introduce them to *Ilex* ×*koehneana* growing next to *I. opaca*. Numerous comments concern the former: "How beautiful compared to *I. opaca*!" and "Why is it not in commerce?" No easy response, except with 400 or so holly species and thousands of cultivars worldwide, there is little wiggle room for another species or cultivar in the marketplace. Interestingly, in ten years, *I.* ×*koehneana* has outgrown the *I. opaca* by 50 percent and is much more dense, well shaped, and aesthetically pleasing: compact pyramid, densely branched, with bronze-purple new growth and lustrous dark green mature leaves. Leaves are 2 to 3½ (to 5) in. long with eight to twelve, ¹⁄₁₆-in.-long, spiny teeth on each margin. Brilliant red, ⅓-in.-diameter fruit ripen in early fall and persist. Any well-drained, acidic soil is suitable, full sun to partial shade. Displays high heat and drought resistance. Fast growing, about 1½ to 2 ft. per year in average soil. Grows 20 to 25 ft. high, 10 to 15 ft. wide. Zones 7 to 9. Hybrid between *I. aquifolium* and *I. latifolia*. Not as cold hardy as 'Nellie R. Stevens'.

Cultivars and Varieties. Many constituted through the years, with 'Hohman', 'San Jose', 'Wirt L. Winn' among the best. Two recent U.S. National Arboretum releases, 'Agena' (female) and 'Ajax' (male), are promising. Both grew 30 ft. high in 30 years.

Ilex ×*koehneana* 'Wirt L. Winn'

Ilex latifolia
LUSTERLEAF HOLLY

Serves as a *Magnolia grandiflora* substitute by virtue of the large, 4- to 6½- (to 8-) in.-long leaves; several large plants in Athens have been mistaken for Southern Magnolia. Matures into a broad pyramidal-oval shape with densely borne leaves, allowing for screening use. The thickish, lustrous dark green leaves are set with short, coarse, blackish gland-tipped teeth. The deep dull red, ⅓-in.-diameter, globose fruit ripen in fall and hold into February and March, eventually becoming a duller, washed-out red. Extremely durable plant, tolerating full sun, moderate shade, drought, and heat. Amenable to pruning, like all hollies, and can be effectively espaliered against a wall. Makes a noble specimen or accent, screening, or grouping plant. Typically 20 to 25 ft. high, one-half as wide. Have observed 40-ft.-high specimens in Greenville, South Carolina. Zones 7 to 9. Not as cold hardy as 'Nellie R. Stevens'. Japan, China.

Cultivars and Varieties. 'Mary Nell', named after the wife of the late J. C. McDaniel, a professor of horticulture at the University of Illinois, is a complex hybrid with *Ilex latifolia* as one part of the genetic puzzle. Has become more popular in southern nursery production because of glossy dark green leaves, red fruit, and pyramidal habit to around 20 ft. The only negative is the propensity to form multiple leaders, which requires considerable pruning during production.

Ilex ×koehneana 'Wirt L. Winn' fruit and foliage

Ilex ×koehneana 'San Jose'

Ilex latifolia, Lusterleaf Holly

Ilex latifolia foliage

MORE ➤

Ilex latifolia **continued**

Ilex 'Mary Nell' foliage

Ilex 'Mary Nell' fruit

Ilex 'Nellie R. Stevens' flowers

Ilex 'Nellie R. Stevens' fruit

Ilex 'Nellie R. Stevens'

The grand dame of landscape hollies in the Southeast: common, over-used, but functional to a pragmatic fault. Dense, broad-pyramidal outline, almost self-sustaining in maturity. The leaves, 2 to 3 (to 4) in. long, have two to three spines per margin. The long axis of the leaf is twisted, each leaf leathery lustrous dark green—the standard for other tree-type hollies. Flowers open in late March and April, and the ¼- to ⅓-in.-diameter, bright red fruit ripen in fall and are less persistent than those of 'Emily Bruner'. Sun- and shade-tolerant, adaptable to any soils except wet. Keep fertilized for best leaf color. Eminently prunable; great hedge or screen. From Washington, D.C., to Florida, the first choice. Hybrid between *Ilex cornuta* 'Burfordii' and *I. aquifolium*. In our garden, even in deep shade, the habit without pruning is sufficiently dense to effect a solid screen. Grows 15 to 25 ft. high, two-thirds as wide. Zones 6 to 9.

Ilex 'Nellie R. Stevens'

Ilex 'Red Hollies'

A new series embracing the names Cardinal™, Festive™, Little Red™, Oak Leaf™, and Robin™. The "red" refers to the color of the new growth, which is variable and not showstopping. All are females and produce ¼- to ⅓-in.-diameter, red fruit. All are small, pyramidal trees with lustrous dark green leaves. To date, Oak Leaf™ and Robin™ have grown the fastest; Little Red™ and Festive™ the slowest. Arose (supposedly) as open-pollinated seedlings of 'Mary Nell' in the 1980s. All are patented. Many southeastern nurserymen have grown the series, but their long-term commitment to continued production is in limbo. Certainly they offer new foliage textures but will be hard-pressed to supersede 'Nellie R. Stevens'. Grows 10 to 15 ft. high, one-half as wide, although size varies. Zones 7 to 9.

Ilex rotunda
LORD'S HOLLY

A rare species in cultivation but, based on my observation, one of the more heat-tolerant hollies. Reasonable specimens about 20 ft. high grow in the Coastal Plain of Georgia. The dark green leaves are entire and provide no clue as to holly affinity. The ¼-in.-diameter fruit are borne in umbels on ¼-in.-long stalks from the leaf axils. In full fruit, the effect resembles a fireworks display. I remember a large specimen at the University's Coastal Garden in Savannah that would change anyone into a believer. Difficult to propagate via cuttings and nowhere common in trade. Appears to have uses for breeding. A collector's plant for Zones 8b to 9(10). Japan and Korea.

Ilex vomitoria
YAUPON

The quintessential southern holly—native, used with impunity, prospering everywhere, multifunctional, and attractive. My airplane touches down at Houston's Intercontinental, and I peek out the window at fields of *Ilex vomitoria*. Bonnie and I visit Georgia's barrier islands, and I can barely contain myself before taking another photo of *I. vomitoria*. Variation is remarkable and has been exploited to select numerous cultivars. Typically a multi-stemmed, large, evergreen shrub, forming thickets. Bark, as on most hollies, is silver-gray to gray-brown. Finely serrated leaves, purplish tinged at emergence, eventually lustrous dark green, average ½ to 1½ in. long. The

MORE ➤

Ilex rotunda, Lord's Holly

Ilex 'Red Hollies' (Oak Leaf™)

Ilex rotunda fruit and foliage

Ilex vomitoria **continued**

four-petaled, greenish white, ¼-in.-diameter flowers open in mid- to late April. The translucent, ¼-in.-diameter fruit are produced in abundance and literally mask the branches. Fruit persist, often through winter, to the time of the next year's flowering cycle. Grows in wet and dry, acid to alkaline soils, in sun and shade, withstanding salt spray and interminable pruning. Many uses including topiaries, hedges, tree-forms, espaliers, loose screens, and groupings. Choice no-brainer selection for green meatballs, gobs-of-green, and innocuous spinach. Grows 10 to 20 ft. high and wide. The national champion in Texas is a surprising 45 ft. high, 40 ft. wide. Zones 7 to 10. Southeastern Virginia to central Florida, west to Texas, southeastern Arkansas, and Oklahoma.

Cultivars and Varieties. Bordeaux™ ('Condeaux') is a branch sport of 'Schillings' with more compact habit, smaller leaves, and wine-red winter leaf color.

'Katherine' is a large shrub form with beautiful golden yellow, long-persistent fruit.

'Nana' is a female dwarf form, 5 ft. high, wider at maturity, with larger leaves than 'Schillings'.

'Pendula' is a large (to 20 ft.) weeping form with red fruit; both male and female forms are offered. 'Folsum's Weeping' is included here.

'Schillings' ('Stokes Dwarf'), one of the best compact forms, is 3 to 4 ft. high and wide, male, with purplish new shoot extensions.

'Shadow's Female' (Hoskins Shadow™) has large lustrous dark green leaves and abundant bright red fruit.

'Will Fleming' is a fastigiate male form that is tight in youth but opens and splays to the point of no redemption with time.

Ilex vomitoria, Yaupon

Ilex vomitoria female flowers

Ilex vomitoria fruit

Ilex vomitoria 'Nana'

Ilex vomitoria 'Schillings'

MORE ➤

Ilex vomitoria 'Will Fleming'

Ilex vomitoria 'Katherine'

Ilex vomitoria continued

Ilex vomitoria 'Shadow's Female'

Ilex vomitoria 'Pendula'

Illicium anisatum
JAPANESE ANISE-TREE

Striking lustrous dark green leaves serve as the perfect contrast to the 1-in.-diameter, 20- to 30-petaled, white flowers that open in March. Habit is pyramidal-columnar, often with a central leader. The wavy-surfaced leaves range from 2 to 4 in. in length and are borne perpendicular to the stems. Requires shade and well-drained soil and is not as hardy as *Illicium floridanum* or *I. parviflorum*; in the Dirr garden, it does not flag in drought like these two species. Certainly a wonderful filler in the shady border. Always discernible because of the sheeny leaves. Grows 6 to 10 (to 15) ft. high, one-half as wide. Zones 7 to 9. China, Japan.

Cultivars and Varieties. 'Pink Stars' has pink-budded flowers that open pinkish white, new leaves reddish tinged fading to green. Introduced by J. C. Raulston Arboretum, Raleigh, North Carolina.

An exciting new form from Japan, with bronze-purple leaves and apricot-orange flowers, is now in production in the South.

Illicium anisatum, Japanese Anise-tree

Illicium anisatum foliage

Illicium anisatum flowers

Illicium anisatum 'Pink Stars'

Illicium floridanum foliage

Illicium floridanum
FLORIDA ANISE-TREE

Almost unknown in the Southeast until the devastating freezes of the early 1980s, when this species surfaced as a possible alternative to Redtip Photinia and evergreen privets. Variable in habit from a relatively dense to a large, open, loose shrub. Easily restrained by tip pruning. Leaves are 2 to 6 in. long, entire, wavy-surfaced, and dark green. Several students described the bruised leaf odor as resembling a gin and tonic. How would they know? Flowers, 1 to 2 in. in diameter, maroon-purple, composed of 20 to 30 strap-shaped petals, open in April for four to six weeks. Fragrance is *stinky*! The

1- to 1½-in.-diameter fruit are composed of 11 to 15 follicles in a star-like configuration. Grows in moist to wet soils. Shows drought stress. Requires shade in our Georgia garden to maintain dark green leaves. Wonderful in large groupings and masses. Grows 6 to 10 ft. high, wider at maturity. Zones 6 to 9. Florida, Georgia, Alabama, Mississippi, and Louisiana.

Cultivars and Varieties. 'Halley's Comet' offers abundant flowers in spring and sporadically into fall; the deep red flowers are larger than the typical species.

MORE ➤

Illicium floridanum, Florida Anise-tree

Illicium floridanum flower

Illicium floridanum fruit

Illicium floridanum 'Halley's Comet'

Illicium floridanum continued

'Semmes' produces white flowers on a compact, 6 ft. by 6 ft. shrub growing by our front door, where it looks like a rhododendron.

'Shady Lady' has wavy, gray-green leaves with gray-white margined variegation and pink flowers.

Additionally, there are compact forms ('Pebblebrook'), pink-flowered forms, and several variegated types.

Illicium henryi
HENRY ANISE-TREE

Among the anise-trees, this is the most aesthetic but least grown. Rhododendron-like leaves, rigidly held, on a rounded to pyramidal framework. The fragrant (when bruised) leaves, 4 to 5 (to 6) in. long, are lustrous dark green and maintain this color year-round. The rose-pink, ½- to 1-in.-diameter flowers open in April and May. Requires shade for best growth. More drought-tolerant than *Illicium floridanum*. In the Dirr garden, visitors frequently ask the identity of this species, which resides in an understory planting of eight other *Illicium* taxa. Superb textural element in the border, excellent screening ever-

Illicium floridanum 'Semmes'

Illicium floridanum 'Shady Lady'

Illicium henryi foliage

Illicium henryi, Henry Anise-tree

green under pines, the aristocrat of *Illicium* species. Grows 6 to 8 (to 15) ft. high, usually not quite as wide. Zones 7 to 9. China.

Illicium henryi flower

Illicium mexicanum flowers

Illicium mexicanum
MEXICAN ANISE-TREE

Try as I might, I am unable to bond with this species because of the sprawling growth and mediocre performance. The leaves are similar to *Illicium floridanum* except more lustrous, with an elongated apex. Flowers (reddish) open in March in Athens, each 1½ to 2 in. across. Does not appear as prosperous under cultivation as other species discussed but has hybridized with *I. floridanum*. Provide moist, well-drained soil in partial to moderate shade. Only for the collector. Grows 5 ft. high and wide (the biggest I have observed). Zones 7 to 10. Mexico.

Cultivars and Varieties. 'Woodland Ruby' is a hybrid between *Illicium mexicanum* and *I. floridanum* with greater vigor.

Illicium parviflorum
SMALL ANISE-TREE

The true everyday garden plant among the anise-trees, with sun and shade resiliency, ease of culture, and beautiful olive-green foliage that distinguishes it from its taxonomic colleagues. Small, ½-in.-diameter yellowish flowers are borne in the leaf axils from May through October. Fluffy, billowy masses of evergreen foliage drift through the understory, providing color, texture, and aromatic amenities. The 2- to 4-in.-long leaves are rich with safrole, the same oil that imparts fragrance to sassafras leaves. In the evening, the sweet odor is evident. A former graduate student, Andrea Southworth, determined that the insect resistance of *Illicium* species was related to the oil content of the leaves. Nurserymen do not spray *Illicium* for insects and

MORE ➤

Illicium mexicanum, Mexican Anise-tree

Illicium parviflorum foliage

Illicium parviflorum flower and flower bud

Illicium parviflorum **continued**

diseases in the production process. Prefers moist soil in sun or shade. Requires pruning to keep it in bounds. Grows 8 to 10 ft. high, wider at maturity. Zones 6 to 9. Found in wet areas in southern Georgia and Florida.

Cultivars and Varieties. Many years past, I named a shiny dark green, more rounded leaf form 'Forest Green'. Branches more fully and is decidedly darker green than the species.

Indigofera amblyantha

Seeds I collected at the Hillier Arboretum in late January produced flowering plants by June in Athens. The habit is rounded and fine-textured, not unlike *Indigofera heteranthera* but better behaved. The leaves, composed of seven to eleven, $\frac{1}{2}$- to 1-in.-long, gray-green to bright green leaflets bring a low-key color contrast to the dark green leaves of other *Indigofera* species. Flowers are unique, developing from each leaf axil and held upright in a slender, elongated, conical raceme, 2 to 5 in. long, that continues to lengthen as flowers open. Buds are deeper rose-pink, opening lighter, and effective from May into summer. Like the other indigoferas treated herein, this species flowers on new growth, so pruning promotes increased flower development. Save room for the indigoferas in the garden: they are trouble-free and aesthetically pleasing. Culture and use the same as *I. heteranthera*. Fits into herbaceous borders, for it functions as a cut-back shrub that when pruned in late winter will be glorious by summer. Grows 4 to 6 ft. high and wide. Zones 6 to 8. China.

Illicium parviflorum, Small Anise-tree

Illicium parviflorum 'Forest Green' leaf (top) vs. species type

Indigofera amblyantha flowers and foliage

Indigofera amblyantha

Indigofera decora, Chinese Indigo

Indigofera decora
CHINESE INDIGO

What a wonderful chance discovery about eight years past at an antebellum home across from the Georgia campus, where a low subshrub with pink wisteria-like flowers was growing in the shade of pecan trees. Another key-out quest was performed, with this species surfacing as the leading candidate. A suckering, spreading shrub with seven to thirteen, 1- to 2½-in.-long rich green leaflets per leaf. Flowers, each ¾ in. long, pink, in 4- to 8-in.-long, 20- to 40-flowered racemes, explode in May and continue sporadically into August and September on new growth. Have yet to observe fruit set. I hope to breed this species with the others for improved floral characteristics. Prefers moist, moderately fertile, acid soil in partial shade (best) to full sun. Some foliage lightening in full sun but no diminution in floral production. Displays excellent heat and drought tolerance. Use as a groundcover in shade, at the front of a border, and in bank plantings. One of Bonnie's favorite plants. Our fine colony prospers under the shade of a Southern Red Oak, *Quercus falcata*. Grows 12 to 18 in. high, spreads indefinitely. Zones 6 to 7(8). China, Japan.

Cultivars and Varieties. 'Alba', with white flowers, is in cultivation.

'Rosea' has deeper pink flowers with a hint of lavender.

Indigofera decora flowers

Indigofera heteranthera
(*I. gerardiana*)
HIMALAYAN INDIGO

A perpetual motion, i.e., flowering, machine, initiating in June and continuing through September on the new growth. I have tested the plant for ten years in the field plots at the University of Georgia, and its resilience in heat and drought is borderline miraculous. A rounded shrub, loose and refined, requiring some pruning to keep it tidy and presentable. The leaves are composed of 13 to 21 leaflets, each about ½ in. long and blue-green. The rose-purple, ½-in.-long flowers occur in a 3- to 5-in.-long raceme with 24 or more clustered along the axis of the raceme. Moderate moisture and fertility produce active growth, and as long as new growth emerges, new flowers are formed. Requires full sun, and moist, well-drained soils; pH adaptable. Excellent border plant. Functions as a "big" herbaceous perennial. Can be cut back in winter and will explode with new growth and flowers in summer. Grows 4 to 6 ft. high and wide. Zones 6 to 8. Himalayas.

Indigofera heteranthera flowers

Indigofera heteranthera, Himalayan Indigo

Ixora coccinea
IXORA, FLAME OF THE WOODS

Handsome broadleaf evergreen shrub with beautiful red to orange-red summer flowers. Densely branched and foliated with dark green, leathery, opposite to whorled leaves up to 4 in. long. Young leaves are bronze-colored. The tubular corolla is divided into four lobes at the end, each 1½ to 2 in. long, and borne in axillary corymbs during summer. Flowers are effective for a long period. The fruit, rounded, about ½ in. in diameter, purplish black, ripen in fall. Prefers moderate to high fertility, acid soils, and partial shade. Foliage becomes chlorotic in high pH soils. Use in groupings, foundations, hedges, and masses. Grows 4 to 6 ft. high and wide. Zones 9b to 11. Southeast Asia, India.

Jasminum floridum
SHOWY JASMINE

Unusual among the more than 200 *Jasminum* species in that the leaves are alternately arranged. The masses of slender, arching, angular, glabrous green stems merge into an irregular haystack. Appears a degree more "messy" than *Jasminum nudiflorum*. The smallish dark green leaves are semi-evergreen to evergreen, depending on the degree of cold. Yellow flowers appear on new growth from late April through June and flickeringly into fall. Makes a good massing plant. Prefers sun to partial shade in moist, well-drained soil. Grows 3 to 5 ft. high and wide. Zones 8 to 10. China.

Ixora coccinea, Flame of the Woods

Jasminum floridum foliage

Jasminum floridum, Showy Jasmine

Jasminum floridum flower

Jasminum humile
ITALIAN YELLOW JASMINE

Slightly different from the other jasmine species, more upright, in the 5- to 7-ft.-high range, with three to seven leaflets per alternate leaf. The dark green leaves are semievergreen to evergreen. The minimally fragrant yellow flowers open in June and do not overwhelm. Best sited in partial shade in well-drained soil. Has displayed good heat and drought tolerance in Athens. More of a novelty plant, nowhere common. Frequently brought to me for identification, as it does not fit the typical jasmine profile. Zones 7b to 9. Middle East, Burma, China.

Cultivars and Varieties. 'Revolutum' is larger, more cold hardy, and often with more leaflets.

Jasminum mesnyi
PRIMROSE JASMINE

The first time I spied the species, the primrose-yellow, semidouble flowers were sparkling in the March sun. Great billowy masses are forged when plants are sited in close proximity. Individually, the plant develops a mounded, broad-spreading habit with trailing branches. The lustrous dark green evergreen leaves are comprised of three leaflets, each 1 to 3 in. long. The 1½-in.-diameter, semidouble flower is composed of six to ten divisions. Wonderfully adaptable and tolerates sun and moderate shade. Terrific in bank plantings, mass groupings, or as a *tall* groundcover. Beautiful in flower and well suited to gardens in the Coastal Plain of the Southeast. Grows 5 to 6 (to 9) ft. high, wider at maturity. Zones 8 to 9. China.

Jasminum humile flowers and foliage

Jasminum humile 'Revolutum'

Jasminum humile, Italian Yellow Jasmine

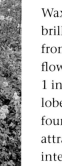

Jasminum nudiflorum
WINTER JASMINE

Waxy maroon-red buds explode to brilliant forsythia-yellow flowers from January through March. The flowers, each 1½ to 2 in. long, ¾ to 1 in. across, with five to six wavy lobes, appear on naked stems. The four-angled, olive-green stems are attractive and provide both winter interest and background for the flowers. Leaves are composed of three leaflets, lustrous deep green, each ½ to 1¼ in. long. For erodable slopes, banks, unmanageable areas, and groundcover use, this is the plant of choice. The branches root in contact with the soil, producing an interwoven fabric that is impenetrable. No special soil requirement; full sun to moderate shade permit ease of culture. Grows 3 to 4 ft. high, 4 to 7 ft. wide. Zones 6 to 10. China.

Cultivars and Varieties. 'Variegatum' is similar to the species but less vigorous, with whitish leaf margins and gray-green centers.

MORE ➤

Jasminum mesnyi, Primrose Jasmine

Jasminum mesnyi flowers and foliage

Jasminum nudiflorum flowers and buds

Jasminum nudiflorum 'Variegatum'

Jasminum nudiflorum, Winter Jasmine

Jasminum nudiflorum continued

Jasminum nudiflorum in flower

Jasminum nudiflorum in flower

Jasminum officinale 'Inverleith'

Jasminum officinale
COMMON WHITE JASMINE

A delightfully fragrant twining vine, deciduous to semi-evergreen, producing flowers throughout summer. The oppositely arranged leaves, rich green, are composed of five to nine leaflets, each ½ to 2½ in. long and ⅙ to 1 in. wide. The ¾- to 1-in.-long and -wide, four- to five-lobed white flowers open from June through October. Partial shade and moist, well-drained soil prove beneficial. Great plant for trellises, walls, fences—about any structure. One of the most cherished plants in English gardens. Grows 10 to 20 (to 30) ft. on a climbing structure. Zones 8 to 10. Caucasus, northern Iran, Afghanistan, Himalayas, China.

Cultivars and Varieties. Several cultivars are known. 'Affine' has pink-tinged flowers opening white.

'Aureovariegatum' ('Aureum') has yellow-blotched leaves.

'Inverleith' has red flower buds and backs of the outer petals that contrast with the pure white inner surface.

Jasminum officinale flowers and foliage

Jasminum officinale 'Aureovariegatum'

Jasminum officinale, Common White Jasmine

Jasminum parkeri
DWARF JASMINE

A wonderful, cute, diminutive evergreen shrub, mounded and spreading, that could serve as an effective groundcover. The alternate leaves, compound pinnate, composed of three to five, $\frac{1}{8}$- to $\frac{3}{8}$-in.-long, dark green leaflets, serve as a perfect contrast to the $\frac{1}{2}$- to $\frac{3}{4}$-in.-long, $\frac{1}{2}$-in.-wide, six-lobed, yellow flowers. Flowers appear in May and June and may be followed by greenish white, translucent, globose, $\frac{1}{6}$-in.-wide berries. Requires good drainage, wind protection. Useful rock garden or container plant, or as a filler at the front of a border. Grows 12 (to 24) in. high, 30 in. wide. Zones (8)9 to 10. Northwest India.

Jasminum parkeri flowers

Jasminum parkeri, Dwarf Jasmine

Juniperus salicicola
SOUTHERN RED CEDAR

In terms of taxonomic minutiae, possibly nothing more than the southern extension of *Juniperus virginiana*. However, extensive travels through central Florida and the Gulf Coast support horticultural differences. Typically a broad dense pyramid, finer in texture than its northern relative, with smaller bright green needles and cones. Trees in the Orlando area are 30 to 40 ft. high; the national champion in Alachua County, Florida, is 75 ft. high, 52 ft. wide. Grows on the sand dunes and coastal marsh edges in full sun. Use for screens, wind breaks, and hedges. Small, $\frac{1}{5}$-in.-diameter, blue-green cones provide feed for birds. Zones 7 to 9(10). Southeastern United States.

Cultivars and Varieties. 'Brodie' is an upright form, 20 to 25 ft. high, 4 to 6 ft. wide, with scalelike, grass-green foliage in summer becoming more sage-green in winter. One of the best upright screening evergreens for the South.

Juniperus salicicola, Southern Red Cedar

Juniperus salicicola 'Brodie'

Juniperus salicicola bark

Kadsura japonica

If only it were hardier (Zones 8 and higher), the commercial uses for this plant would exceed supply. Vigorous twining vine with delicate reddish young stems and 2- to 4-in.-long, dark green leaves that recall the common houseplant, *Hoya carnosa*. Cream-ivory, fragrant flowers emerge from the leaf axils and are followed by 1-in.-long, fleshy, scarlet berries. Place in partial to moderate shade in deep, moist soil high in organic matter. Not as wild as *Campsis radicans* and the *Wisteria* species. Grows 12 to 15 ft.; requires a structure for support. Zones (7b)8 to 9. Japan, China.

Cultivars and Varieties. 'Chirimen' has cream-white marbling and streaking throughout the leaf. Somewhat unstable and may revert to green.

'Fukurin' offers leaves edged to various degrees with cream and yellow; these same areas are rose-tinged in winter.

Kadsura japonica 'Fukurin'

Kadsura japonica 'Chirimen'

Koelreuteria bipinnata
BOUGAINVILLEA GOLDENRAINTREE,
CHINESE FLAMETREE

Medium-sized tree on the ascension in southern gardens because of the late summer yellow flowers and pink capsules. Habit is beanpole-like in youth, becoming vase-shaped to rounded with age. The bipinnately compound lustrous leaves produce a tropical aura. In our garden, two trees literally stop traffic in late August and early September when the immense panicles, 12 to 24 (to 30) in. long, 8 to 18 in. wide, are slathered with bright yellow flowers. Flowers occur at the end of the shoots, the entire tree an orb of floral sunshine. The papery, three-valved capsules, 1 to 2 in. long, pink to rose, color soon after flowering and hold for three to five weeks. Capsules collected at peak color can be dried and will hold their color. Withstands drought, full sun, and miserable soils.

MORE ➤

Koelreuteria bipinnata, Bougainvillea Goldenraintree

Koelreuteria bipinnata continued

Use as specimen or work into a border and underplant with shade-tolerant shrubs. Is weedlike and produces numerous seedlings; Bonnie and I hoe 1001 per garden year. Grows 20 to 30 (to 40) ft. high, about two-thirds as wide. Zones 6 to 8(9). China.

Koelreuteria elegans, Chinese Raintree, Flamegold, is closely allied to *K. bipinnata* but less cold hardy [Zones 9 to 10(11)], smaller and densely round-headed in habit. Flowers and fruit are similar in color. Generally 20 to 30 ft. high and wide. Taiwan, Fiji.

Koelreuteria bipinnata fall color

Koelreuteria bipinnata fruit

Koelreuteria elegans foliage

Lagerstroemia, CRAPEMYRTLE

Without question, the premier flowering tree/shrub for Zones 7 to 10, the Southeast, Southwest, and into California. Requires significant summer heat to ripen the wood. Remarkably, flowering specimens grow on Martha's Vineyard, Massachusetts. In Zone 7b (Athens), flowers develop on early cultivars in mid-June with July and August peak, and lingering flowers in September. Cultivars flower on new growth of the season and should always be pruned lightly in the dormant season, never stubbed back to large-diameter trunks and limbs. For all, full sun, good air movement, and well-drained, acid soil are ideal. Crapemyrtles are not "fussy" but may require fertilizer applications in late winter to keep the foliage rich green and spur good growth and flower development. The spectacular bark is often overlooked (flowers first), but the rich gray, cream, brown, rust, and sheathing combinations are equally beautiful. In our garden, a multi-stemmed row of 'Natchez' is remarkable for the beauty of the cinnamon-colored bark. Now 25 ft. high, the flowers are not even noticeable until petals fall. Food for landscape thought.

Fall color depends on climatic conditions with long, cool (no freezes) autumns ideal for the yellow, orange, and red displays. Some cultivars like 'Sioux' have excellent red fall color.

Koelreuteria elegans fruiting

Mildew, Cercospora *leaf spot, flea beetle, Japanese beetle (flowers and leaves), and Asian ambrosia beetle may cause problems. Ideally, plant the most disease-resistant cultivars and keep them actively growing. Easily propagated from softwood cuttings and seeds. Numerous seedling have been grown to flower in a single season with seed planted in January.*

True genetic dwarfs 2 to 3 ft. high (such as 'Chickasaw' and 'Pocomoke', bred by the late Dr. Donald Egolf, U.S. National Arboretum) to 50-ft. treelike Lagerstroemia fauriei *'Fantasy' reflect the great variation. Dr. Egolf introduced 27 cultivars over his remarkable career. Newer introductions are still emerging from his work. All are discussed in this treatment.*

Lagerstroemia 'Natchez'

Lagerstroemia 'Sioux' foliage

Lagerstroemia 'Sioux' fall color

Lagerstroemia 'Sioux'

Lagerstroemia 'Chickasaw'

Lagerstroemia 'Pocomoke'

Lagerstroemia fauriei

Introduced in the 1950s from Japan by the U.S. National Arboretum, it became a most important source of mildew resistance and rich cinnamon bark in Dr. Egolf's breeding program. Early seedlings were sent to cooperating institutions including North Carolina State University, where trees over 50 ft. high still exist. Habit is vase-shaped, similar to American Elm, with a cloud of medium green, almost peach leaf–like foliage that turns yellow in autumn. Cinnamon-brown, chestnut-brown to dark red-brown bark is the primary ornamental calling card. This wonderful trait has been transmitted to many of Dr. Egolf's hybrids. Flowers lack the pizzazz of *Lagerstroemia indica* and the hybrids. In Athens, moderately fragrant, white flowers in 2- to 4- (to 6-) in.-long, upright pyramidal panicles open in early June. Reflowering does nót occur, a trait that is inherent in *L. indica*. Fruit on the species are six-valved, dehiscent capsules with waferlike brown seeds. Transplant as container-grown plants. Growth is maximized in moist, well-drained soils and full sun. Useful as a specimen plant, perhaps as a street tree if properly pruned. Almost always low-branched and multi-stemmed, so single stems must be trained from youth. Grows 30 ft. high or more, one-half as wide. Zones (6)7 to 9. Japan.

Cultivars and Varieties. 'Fantasy' is a tight vase-shaped selection with beautiful cinnamon-brown bark, white flowers, and yellow fall color. Extremely fast growing, will grow 40 to 50 ft. high; mildew resistant.

'Kiowa' grew 30 ft. high, 25 ft. wide at the U.S. National Arboretum. White flowers and cinnamon-brown bark; mildew resistant. This was one of Dr. Egolf's favorite forms.

'Sarah's Favorite' is similar to 'Natchez' but more cold hardy and flowers over a longer period; mildew resistant. May be a hybrid like 'Natchez' but growth habit not as floppy. Grows 20 ft. high or more.

'Townhouse', from the J. C. Raulston Arboretum, has darker red-brown bark. Probably will grow 20 to 30 ft. high, almost as wide; mildew resistant.

Lagerstroemia fauriei

Lagerstroemia fauriei bark

Lagerstroemia fauriei 'Fantasy' bark

Lagerstroemia fauriei 'Fantasy'

Lagerstroemia fauriei 'Fantasy' flowers

Lagerstroemia fauriei 'Sarah's Favorite' flowers

MORE ➤

Lagerstroemia fauriei continued

Lagerstroemia fauriei 'Sarah's Favorite' fall color

Lagerstroemia fauriei 'Townhouse' bark

Lagerstroemia fauriei 'Townhouse' fall color

Lagerstroemia indica

The true "summer lilac" of southern gardens, with fluffy 6- to 12-in.-long, 3- to 6-in.-wide panicles of white, pink, lavender, melon-red, red, and purple, on plants 3 to 45 ft. high. To travel the South from June through August is to understand why this is the best flowering shrub/small tree for gardens large and small. Foliage, given little press, when free of mildew and leaf spot, is dark green, eventually reinventing itself in yellows, oranges, and reds. Early fall freezes render foliage hay brown and as dry. Bark is exfoliating, exposing smooth inner bark, with snakeskin-like molting in summer. Ancient trunks are sinewy, smooth, artistic, and sculptural. Colors are cream, light brown to brown, usually not as colorful as *Lagerstroemia fauriei*. Full sun, moist, well-drained soil are requisites. Once established, will withstand considerable drought. Choice plant for specimen use, groupings, containers, urban settings, large shrub/small street tree. Typically 15 to 25 ft. high; height range is extreme, have observed 40- to 45-ft. specimens in Savannah, Georgia. Zones (6)7 to 9. China, Korea.

Cultivars and Varieties. 'Byers Wonderful White' produces dense white flowers. Upright habit to 20 ft.

'Carolina Beauty' is the most common red-flowered form. Abundant yellow stamens; high susceptibility to mildew. Grows 20 ft. high.

Lagerstroemia indica bark

MORE ➤

Lagerstroemia indica branching habit

168

Lagerstroemia indica continued

'Catawba' (Egolf introduction) has lustrous dark green, leathery leaves, excellent orange-red fall color, dark purple flowers; good mildew resistance. Grows 10 to 15 ft. high.

'Cedar Red' is a smaller shrub form, 6 to 10 ft. high, with reddish purple new growth and red flowers with yellow stamens.

'Centennial' is a compact form with bright lavender flowers. Grew this for a time but flowers never measured up. Grows 3 to 5 ft. high.

'Cherokee' (Egolf introduction), a red-flowered form with high mildew

Lagerstroemia indica in flower

Lagerstroemia indica fall color

Lagerstroemia indica 'Byers Wonderful White'

Lagerstroemia indica 'Carolina Beauty'

Lagerstroemia indica 'Carolina Beauty'

Lagerstroemia indica 'Catawba'

Lagerstroemia indica 'Catawba'

susceptibility, never found commercial acceptance. Grows about 10 ft. high.

'Comanche' (Egolf introduction) is a loose, spreading form with coral-pink flowers. Grows 10 to 15 ft. high.

'Conestoga' (Egolf introduction) has lavender-pink flowers on long splaying shoots. Open habit, grows 10 to 15 ft. high..

'Dallas Red' is a "red" flowered selection that displayed excellent winter hardiness at the J. C. Raulston Arboretum. Grows 20 ft. high or more.

Dynamite™ ('Whit II') is just

Lagerstroemia indica 'Catawba' fall color

Lagerstroemia indica 'Conestoga'

MORE ➤

Lagerstroemia indica 'Dallas Red' fall color

Lagerstroemia indica Dynamite™

Lagerstroemia indica **continued**

that, with explosive red flowers smothering the foliage. I first witnessed it in early September in full flower and could not fully comprehend the intensity of the red. Vigorous upright habit to 20 ft. high; good mildew resistance. From Dr. Carl Whitcomb's breeding program, Stillwater, Oklahoma.

'Hardy Lavender' is an old-time selection with medium lavender flowers. An upright grower to 20 ft.

'Near East' produces soft pink flowers on enormous broad billowy panicles on a framework of 10 ft. or more; moderate mildew resistance.

'Ocmulgee' is a compact shrub with dark green leaves, red-maroon buds, red flowers. Grows 3 to 4 ft. high and wide; aphids and sooty mold are problematic.

'Peppermint Lace' produces deep pink, white-edged, picotee flowers. Grows 15 to 20 ft. high; mildew susceptible.

Pink Velour™, formerly Royal Velvet™ ('Whit III'), has crimson buds, opening pink; beautiful burgundy new growth turns purple-green to dark green. Grows 10 to 12 ft. high; mildew resistant.

'Potomac' (Egolf introduction) develops clear medium pink flowers. Upright growth habit, 10 to 15 ft. high, one-half as wide; mildew susceptible.

'Powhatan' (Egolf introduction) flowers are medium purple, on a 10- to 12-ft.-high and -wide shrub; mildew resistant.

Raspberry Sundae™ ('Whit I') has crimson buds that open cardinal-red to pink, similar to red raspberries. Upright growth habit to 15 ft. high; slight mildew.

'Regal Red' is more watermelon-red than red. Broad-spreading form,

Lagerstroemia indica 'Hardy Lavender'

Lagerstroemia indica 'Near East'

Lagerstroemia indica 'Ocmulgee'

Lagerstroemia indica 'Ocmulgee' flowers

Lagerstroemia indica 'Peppermint Lace'

Lagerstroemia indica Pink Velour™

Lagerstroemia indica 'Potomac'

Lagerstroemia indica 'Potomac' flowers

MORE ➤

Lagerstroemia indica **continued**

grows 15 ft. high; mildew resistance good.

'Seminole' is a favorite pink in the Dirr garden, rich, vibrant, and clear. The 10- to 15-ft.-high framework is smothered in July and August; mildew resistant.

'Velma's Royal Delight' was the most cold hardy form in the late Dr. John Pair's evaluations at Wichita, Kansas; small in stature, 5 ft. high, 4 ft. wide, it produces abundant magenta flowers in summer.

'Victor' is much like 'Ocmulgee' with dark red flowers on a 3- to 5-ft.-high and -wide shrub. Good mildew resistance; susceptible to aphids and sooty mold.

'Watermelon Red' is appropriately

Lagerstroemia indica 'Seminole'

Lagerstroemia indica 'Victor'

named, with flowers of this color on a 15-ft.-and-higher upright shrub; mildew susceptible.

'William Toovey' is similar to 'Watermelon Red' with pink-red flowers.

Lagerstroemia indica 'Watermelon Red'

Lagerstroemia limii

Rare species with thickish, large, blue-green leaves that suggest little affinity with the genus. Rather unkempt shrub that itself deserves minimal garden space, however, it has been used for breeding purposes by the U.S. National Arboretum. Flowers are lavender-purple in a compact inflorescence. Cultural requirements are similar to those discussed in the introduction. Possibly a collector's plant. Grows 10 to 15 ft. high. Zones 6 to 9. China.

Lagerstroemia Hybrids

These hybrids, all Egolf introductions, resulted from crosses of *Lagerstroemia indica* and *L. fauriei*, the latter parent providing mildew resistance and cinnamon-brown bark (on some selections). They are preferred for modern gardens because of mildew resistance. *Cercospora* leaf spot can be a problem.

Cultivars and Varieties. 'Acoma' is a white-flowered, broad spreading shrub, 10 to 12 ft. high and wide, with light gray-brown bark.

'Apalachee', with lavender flowers, glossy dark green leaves, upright habit to 15 ft. high, and cinnamon to chestnut-brown bark, is among the best for *Cercospora* resistance.

MORE ➤

Lagerstroemia 'Acoma'

Lagerstroemia Hybrids continued

Lagerstroemia 'Acoma' flowers

Lagerstroemia 'Apalachee' flowers

Lagerstroemia 'Apalachee' bark

Lagerstroemia 'Biloxi' bark

'Biloxi' is distinctly upright, 20 ft. high by 12 ft. wide, with pale pink flowers and dark brown bark.

'Caddo', relatively compact, 8 to 10 ft. high and wide, has bright pink flowers and light cinnamon-brown bark.

'Choctaw' offers bright pink panicles in loose structures, appearing on a vase-shaped, 20-ft.-high large shrub/small tree, with light to dark cinnamon-brown bark.

'Hopi', rich pink, profuse, and long-flowering, is a dense oval-rounded shrub, 10 ft. high, 8 ft. wide, with gray-brown bark.

'Lipan' is wide vase-shaped, 15 ft. high by 15 ft. wide at maturity; lavender-pink flowers, near white to beige bark.

'Miami' carries flaming dark pink flowers on a large upright shrub or small tree. Grows 20 ft. high or more, dark chestnut-brown bark.

'Muskogee', a 1981 introduction, is popular in the 21st century because of large shrub/small tree status (grows 20 ft. high or more), prolific lavender-pink flowers, and light gray-brown bark.

'Natchez' is the most common large-growing (20 ft.), white-flowered form, with rich cinnamon-brown bark. An allée in the Dirr garden (see

Lagerstroemia 'Biloxi' flowers

Lagerstroemia 'Choctaw'

Lagerstroemia 'Choctaw' bark

Lagerstroemia 'Choctaw' flowers

MORE ➤

Lagerstroemia **Hybrids continued**

Lagerstroemia 'Lipan' bark

Lagerstroemia 'Hopi'

Lagerstroemia 'Lipan'

Lagerstroemia 'Hopi' flowers

Lagerstroemia 'Miami'

Lagerstroemia 'Miami' bark

Lagerstroemia 'Muskogee'

MORE ➤

Lagerstroemia 'Muskogee' flowers

Lagerstroemia 'Muskogee' bark

Lagerstroemia 'Muskogee' fall color

Lagerstroemia **Hybrids continued**

photograph in "Reflections on Garden-making in Georgia") is beautiful throughout the seasons.

'Osage', with light pink flowers and chestnut-brown bark, has never attracted significant attention from gardeners. Grows 15 ft. high; shows considerable cold damage in Georgia (Athens) tests.

'Pecos' opens medium pink, grows 10 to 15 ft. high, and develops dark brown bark; like 'Osage', it is not common in commerce.

'Sioux', a Dirr favorite, is upright in habit, 12 to 15 ft. high, with rich pink flowers and lustrous dark green leaves that turn red in fall; gray-brown bark; photographs page 163.

'Tonto', the best "red" from Dr. Egolf's program, may contract slight mildew. Grew 10 ft. high, 8 ft. wide in five years in Georgia trials; gray-brown bark.

'Tuscarora' is a large upright tree type, 20 ft. or more in height, 10 ft. wide. Dark coral-pink flowers, light brown bark.

Lagerstroemia 'Osage' bark

Lagerstroemia 'Osage'

Lagerstroemia 'Pecos'

Lagerstroemia 'Tuscarora'

Lagerstroemia 'Tonto'

'Tuskegee' has deep coral-pink flowers, not too different from 'Tuscarora'. A wide-spreading shrub, over 20 ft. high and wide at maturity, with light brown bark.

'Wichita' offers light lavender flowers and russet-brown bark on a large upright shrub, over 20 ft. high at maturity. Difficult to propagate.

Lagerstroemia 'Tuskegee' bark

Lagerstroemia 'Tuscarora'

MORE ➤

Lagerstroemia 'Tuskegee' flowers

Lagerstroemia 'Wichita'

Lagerstroemia **Hybrids continued**

'Yuma', with abundant bi-colored lavender flowers and light gray bark, is remarkable in flower. Grows 12 to 15 ft. high, 12 to 15 ft. wide.

'Zuni' is as close to purple as possible in the hybrid group; the flowers are shaded with lavender, reducing intensity somewhat. Gray-brown bark; grows 10 to12 ft. high.

True genetic dwarfs. Dr. Egolf, over a period of approximately 20 years, crossed, crossed, crossed and developed a core of true compact types. Many are still being tested and may be released. The current introductions include 'Chickasaw' with mounded habit, 2 ft. high, 3 to 3½ ft. wide, rose-lavender flowers, small, glossy dark green leaves; and 'Pocomoke', slightly larger in size, 3 ft. high and wide, after ten years, better and bigger foliage than 'Chickasaw', flowers rose-lavender. See photographs on page 163.

Lagerstroemia 'Yuma'

Lagerstroemia 'Zuni'

Lagerstroemia 'Zuni' bark

Lantana camara
LANTANA

Among the top five flowering plants for summer color, South and North. In Zone 7 (0 to 10°F), several cultivars are die-back shrubs but regenerate new shoots from the base. In Zones 9 to 11, they become more perennial and woody and evergreen. In our garden, 'Miss Huff', orange-yellow flowers, has been perennial for over ten years and regrows to a 5- to 6-ft.-high and -wide shrub in a single season. Typically a rounded-arching shrub but, in many of the cultivars, often sprawling and groundcover-like. The medium to dark green leaves, 2 to 3 (to 5) in. long, are scabrous (sandpapery) above and aromatic when crushed. Flowers initiate on new growth from June through October in Athens. Each flower, four- to five-lobed, ¼ in. across, is held in a 1- to 2-in.-diameter inflorescence. The flowers, like the leaves, have a slight odor. Colors follow the rainbow, and the number of cultivars is beyond anyone's ability to remember. Favorite butterfly plant! Fruit are ⅓-in.-diameter, berrylike drupes that turn metallic blue-purple-black. Well-drained soil, slightly acid, moderate moisture and fertility, along with full sun, suit it best. Displays good salt tolerance. Hot weather accelerates flowering. Once in the garden, trouble-free and maintenance-free except for pruning to keep plants in check. Has become weedlike in the deeper South; I witnessed, north of Orlando, freeze-damaged orange grove acreage chockablock with lantana. Use in sunny borders, containers, and combined with annuals. Grows 1 to 5 ft. high, wider at maturity. Zones 9 to 11 for above-ground hardiness, otherwise treat as a subshrub. West Indies. Has naturalized in many warm temperate countries.

Cultivars and Varieties. 'Miss Huff' is a spectacular performer with orange-yellow flowers that has proven root hardy in Zone 7b. Grows 5 to 6 ft. high. Minimal to no fruit.

'New Gold' is a Georgia Gold Medal Winner, less cold hardy than 'Miss Huff' but a wonderful carpet of yellow-gold all summer long. Grows 1 to 1½ ft. high, 3 to 4 ft. wide. I have not observed fruit set on this cultivar.

MORE ➤

Lantana camara, Lantana

Lantana camara continued

Lantana camara trained as a standard

Lantana camara 'Miss Huff'

Lantana camara 'New Gold'

Lantana camara 'New Gold' (left) and 'Miss Huff'

Laurus nobilis
TRUE LAUREL

The bay leaves of the culinary arts are derived from this evergreen species. Its presence in gardens is rooted in antiquity. Densely pyramidal-oval to haystack-shaped with 2- to 4-in.-long, wavy margined, lustrous dark green leaves. The yellow-green flowers open in spring and do little to stir the aesthetic senses. Fruit are lustrous black, ½-in.-diameter berries. Best in semi-shade (grows acceptably in full sun) and moisture-retentive soils under cultivation. Serves as a great container plant. Useful for topiary and hedges; also a natural in the herb garden. Grows 8 to 12 ft. high in the South, larger on the West Coast. Zones 8b to 9, 10 on the West Coast. Mediterranean region.

Cultivars and Varieties. 'Aurea' sports yellow-gold new growth that loses much of the color in the heat of summer.

Laurus nobilis, True Laurel

Laurus nobilis foliage

Laurus nobilis flowers

Laurus nobilis 'Aurea'

Lavandula angustifolia
COMMON LAVENDER

Long established in herb gardens for oil of lavender (from flowers) and as a woody subshrub in Mediterranean climates. Beautiful, compact, broad-rounded habit with gray to blue-green evergreen leaves. Flowers rise above the foliage in elongated spires in shades of white, pink, blue, violet to lilac, and beyond. Flowers are profuse, and the best blue and purple cultivars are beautiful in their summer garb. Bonnie and I have grown lavenders our entire gardening life. In Illinois and Georgia, long-term presence is not guaranteed. Sun and well-drained, sandy soil, on the dry side, with neutral to alkaline reaction, are best. Use for foliage color, texture, and fragrance. Excellent in containers. Remove spent flowers to keep plant tidy. Grows 1 to 2 ft. high and wide, or wider. Zones (5)6 to 8(9). Southern Europe, northern Africa.

Cultivars and Varieties. Numerous cultivars, but the time-honored 'Hidcote', with rich purple-blue flowers on 10- to 15-in.-long stalks and compact habit, is still one of the best.

Lavandula angustifolia, Common Lavender

Leitneria floridana foliage

Lavandula angustifolia 'Hidcote'

Leitneria floridana male catkins

Leitneria floridana
FLORIDA CORKWOOD

One of the lightest woods in the world, with a specific gravity less than cork, ornamentally useful in wet soils and along stream banks for its tropical effect. Observed large, exotic plantings at the Arnold Arboretum and the Brooklyn Botanic Garden. Tends to sucker and, neither a tree nor a shrub but simply a rover, forms lush colonies. Flowers are dioecious (male and female on separate plants), with the male in fuzzy willowlike catkins in late winter. Best suited to moist and wet soils in sun to partial shade. A bamboo-like alternative without the rambunctiousness. Use for "naturalistic" effect in wet soil and stream bank areas. Grows 6 to 12 (to 20) ft. high, spreading to infinity. Zones 5 to 9. Southern Missouri to Texas and Florida.

Leitneria floridana female flowers

Leitneria floridana, Florida Corkwood

Leitneria floridana in winter

Leptospermum scoparium
BROOM TEATREE

Remarkable evergreen shrub or tree with sharp-pointed, needlelike foliage and beautiful white, pink, and red flowers in late spring and summer. Typically compact-rounded, densely branched shrub, although I have observed large, bordering on treelike specimens in southwest coastal England. The dark green, ½- to ¾-in.-long leaves develop bronzy purple hues in cold weather. Flowers, approximately ½ in. in diameter, are produced singly from the leaf axils. Single- (the norm) and double-flowered forms are available. Transplant from a container into moist, fertile, acid, well-drained soil in full sun to partial shade. In San Francisco, a great garden plant; in Athens, a container plant that needs overwintering in a cool greenhouse. Grows 6 to 10 (to 15) ft. high and wide. Zones (8)9 to 10. New Zealand, Australia, Tasmania.

Cultivars and Varieties. 'Ruby Glow', an old standard with deep red, fully double, ½-in.-diameter flowers, bronzy foliage, and red stems, is among the best. Grows 6 to 8 ft. high.

'Snow White' with double white flowers is compact-spreading, 2 to 4 ft. high.

Leptospermum scoparium, Broom Teatree

Leptospermum scoparium 'Ruby Glow'

Leptospermum scoparium foliage

Leptospermum scoparium flowers

Lespedeza bicolor
SHRUB BUSHCLOVER

Gangly shrub of loose-arching demeanor that, if pruned each winter, reinvents itself in fine style during late spring and summer with rosy purple flowers. The rich blue-green trifoliate leaves, each leaflet 1 to 2 (to 3) in. long, show no propensity toward fall coloration. The pea-shaped, ½-in.-long flowers are produced on 2- to 5-in.-long racemes on current season's growth from the leaf axils of the uppermost 2 ft. of the shoot. Full sun, well-drained soil, pH adaptable—actually hard to kill. Only for the shrub border or as a cut-back shrub in perennial borders. Grows 6 to 10 ft. high and wide. Zones 5 to 9. North China to Manchuria, Korea, and Japan.

Cultivars and Varieties. 'Li'l Buddy' is a compact form, 3 ft. high after four years, narrow leaflets, graceful arching habit, rose-purple flowers.

Leptospermum scoparium 'Ruby Glow' flowers

Lespedeza bicolor flowers

Lespedeza bicolor, Shrub Bushclover

Lespedeza bicolor foliage

Lespedeza thunbergii
THUNBERG LESPEDEZA

Technically not woody but a die-back (to ground) shrub that rejuvenates itself into a mound of delicate cascading branches. The leaflets are rich bluish green, in threes, each 1 to 2 in. long, ½ to 1 in. wide. Foliage color is a pleasing contrast to the bright and dark greens of neighboring shrubs. The flowers are amazing, with abundant displays showing in June and again in August and September in Athens. Rosy purple, pea-shaped flowers appear in 6-in.-long racemes from the upper portions of the shoot, the whole constituting a 2- to 2½-ft.-long panicle. Flowers are effective for two to four weeks. Easily grown and ideally transplanted from containers. The richer and moister the soil, the more rapid the growth. Tolerates drier soils also. Full sun to light shade. Excellent plant to combine with "soft" herbaceous perennials. Lends a light, airy touch to the garden. Tidy up by removing old stems to within 6 in. of the soil line.

Grows 3 to 6 ft. high and wide. Zones 5 to 8. China, Japan.

Cultivars and Varieties. 'Alba' is a white-flowered selection that has brighter green leaves and grows taller and more upright than the species.

'Gibraltar' produces deep rose-purple flowers and is a vigorous grower.

'Pink Cascade' is pink-flowered and not quite as rambunctious as the species, although in our garden it has reached a height of 4 to 5 ft.

Spring Grove® is a selection from Spring Grove Cemetery, Cincinnati, Ohio, with rich deep rose-purple flowers.

'Variegata' has white-streaked leaflets, rose-purple flowers.

Lespedeza thunbergii, Thunberg Lespedeza

Lespedeza thunbergii flowers

Lespedeza thunbergii 'Alba' flowers

Lespedeza thunbergii 'Variegata'

Lespedeza thunbergii 'Alba'

Lespedeza thunbergii 'Pink Cascade'

Leucophyllum frutescens

TEXAS SAGE

Enlightening how plants are promoted! This southwestern species was labeled as the next great "shrub" for East Coast gardens. Unfortunately, the plant did not read the hype and is simply not accustomed to the high humidity, heavy wet soils, and vagaries of temperatures. Beautiful when at peace, forming a rounded, dense, evergreen shrub, with ½- to 1-in.-long, silvery leaves. The entire shrub is similar to a gray-leaf *Artemisia*. Flowers, rose-purple, 1 in. wide, bell-shaped, appear in summer. Delicate and elegant when in flower. Use container-grown plants; place in perfectly drained, acid to higher pH soil in full sun. Avoid excessive fertility and root zone moisture. Have tried to grow the species in our garden, unfortunately with no success. Atlanta Botanical Garden has been successful with ideal siting of the plants. Beautiful in groupings and in shrub and perennial borders. The silver foliage is a real showstopper. Grows 5 to 8 ft. high, 4 to 6 ft. wide. Zones 8 to 9, 10 on the West Coast. Texas and Mexico.

Cultivars and Varieties. Many are hybrids of *Leucophyllum frutescens* and related species.

'Alba' has white flowers.

'Compactum' is smaller in stature, with orchid-pink flowers.

'Rain Cloud' has violet-blue flowers, grows 5 ft. high, 3 ft. wide in five years.

'Silver Cloud', dense, rounded form, 3 ft. high, 3 ft. wide, has silver-white leaves and violet-purple flowers.

'White Cloud' produces gray foliage and white flowers on a 6- to 12-in.-high by 4- to 6-ft.-wide shrub.

Leucophyllum frutescens, Texas Sage

Leucophyllum frutescens flowers and foliage

Leucophyllum frutescens 'Silver Cloud'

Leucothoe axillaris
COASTAL LEUCOTHOE

The church-mouse cousin of the more common *Leucothoe fontanesiana* but achieving increased attention because of more compact habit, better garden adaptability, and the infusion of new cultivars. A broadleaf evergreen shrub, densely branched, forming a broad mound. The emerging leaves are bronze-red, maturing to lustrous dark green, turning bronze-green to reddish purple in winter. The small, urn-shaped, white flowers are borne in 1- to 2½-in.-long racemes in April and May. Fruit are five-valved, brown capsules with no significant ornamental value. Site in moist, well-drained, acidic soils in partial to heavy shade. Detests winter sun, wind, and exposed locations. Great massing plant, combines seamlessly with its rhododendron brethren. Probably more resistant to the fungal leaf spot that devastates *L. fontanesiana*, however, still susceptible. Grows 2 to 4 ft. high, 1½ times as wide. Zones 5 to 9. Virginia to Florida and Mississippi in lowland areas.

Cultivars and Varieties. At least ten in literature, none common. Have also observed several bronze- and copper- to cream-splashed leaf forms in my travels; the Dodd form, Semmes, Alabama, is the best to date.

'Greensprite', with year-round green leaves, was released by Mt. Cuba Center, Greenville, Delaware. Grows 5 to 6 ft. high, 10 ft. wide.

'Redsprite' has refined, twiggy growth, new shoots reddish, and winter leaf color coppery bronze; leaves are flat and arranged in a herringbone pattern. Grows 4 ft. high, 5 to 6 ft. wide.

Leucothoe axillaris, Coastal Leucothoe

Leucothoe axillaris winter color

Leucothoe axillaris new foliage

Leucothoe axillaris flowers

Leucothoe populifolia
FLORIDA LEUCOTHOE

Unfortunately, the name was changed to *Agarista populifolia*, but most nurseries and pragmatists utilize *Leucothoe*. By either name, this evergreen shrub is the same. Graceful, arching, upright, and dense in structure, with bamboo-like clumping habit. The emerging leaves, tinged red to bronze-purple, turn glossy rich green and hold this color through winter. Flowers, about ⅓ in. long, appear in axillary clusters from each node in May and June, a month or so later than *Leucothoe fontanesiana* and *L. axillaris*. Flowers are fragrant and cream-colored. Great plant for shady, moist sites in the garden. May languish if sited in full sun and dry soils. Fast growing and requires pruning to keep it small. A 12-ft. plant in our garden was cut back to 1 to 1½ ft. high and completely rejuvenated. Excellent in groupings in shady settings, to screen and shape vistas. Stems are densely set, so pedestrian traffic is reduced. Typically grows 8 to 12 ft. high and wide. Have observed 15- to 18-ft.-high plants in South Carolina. Zones (6)7 to 9. South Carolina to Florida.

Leucothoe populifolia new foliage

Leucothoe populifolia foliage

Leucothoe populifolia, Florida Leucothoe

Leucothoe populifolia flowers

Leucothoe racemosa
SWEETBELLS LEUCOTHOE

What a beauty! Unfortunately, well known only by the native plant aficionados. Bonnie and I were hiking the Bartram Trail in Rabun County, Georgia, and spied a plant with elongated racemes and cylinder-shaped flowers. Had to key it out to be sure. A small, refined shrub that produces a suckering colony. The rich green, ½- to 2½-in.-long leaves turn shades of red in autumn. The red-budded flowers are visible the year prior to flowering and are quite handsome in mid-April (Athens). The ⅓-in.-long, white flowers open along the entire 4-in.-long raceme. Definitely a woodland plant for moist soils. Grows 4 to 6 ft. high. Zones 5 to 9. Massachusetts to Florida and Louisiana in moist to wet areas.

Leucothoe racemosa in bud

Leucothoe racemosa, Sweetbells Leucothoe

Leucothoe racemosa flowers

Leucothoe racemosa fall color

Leycesteria formosa

PHEASANT-EYE

The first meeting with the plant occurred in a garden in Kent, England, and I had no idea of the plant's identity. Now it is one never to be forgotten because of its unique features. The typical habit is an upright-spreading shrub that requires tidying up after winter's anguish because of dead branches. The new shoots are deep purplish red, the leaves maturing to deep green. Flowers open on new growth, cream, each ¾ in. across, and are borne in 3- to 4-in.-long pendulous racemes. Each flower is subtended by an ovate, claret-colored, 1- to 1¾-in.-long, persistent bract. The beadlike, berry fruit ripen from glossy sea-green to maroon then purple-black. Provide partial shade and moist, well-drained soils. Often, in Europe, integrated into shrub borders, occasionally herbaceous borders. Grows 3 to 5 ft. high, less in spread. Zones 7b to 9, 10 on the West Coast. Himalayas.

Leycesteria crocothyrsos, Golden Pheasant-eye, produces yellow flowers in whorls of six in arching terminal racemes to 7 in. long. Grows 3 ft. high. A hybrid between the two species is known. Zone 9. Himalayas.

Leycesteria formosa, Pheasant-eye

Leycesteria formosa foliage

Leycesteria formosa flowers

Leycesteria formosa fruit

Leycesteria crocothyrsos, Golden Pheasant-eye

Ligustrum japonicum
JAPANESE PRIVET

An absolute building block of southern and West Coast landscapes, with versatility and adaptability making it a decathelon species. A large, evergreen shrub, steely in framework, rounded in outline, that when limbed up (pruned) makes a nifty, small, artistic tree or large shrub. Bark is gray, smooth, covered with large bumpy lenticels. Leaves, 2 to 4 in. long, are leathery in texture, black-green, with a mirrorlike upper surface. The heavy-scented, cream-colored flowers occur in dense, 2- to 6-in.-long and -wide panicles at the end of the shoots in May and June. The ¼-in.-diameter, oval-rounded, dull grayish, flat-black drupes ripen in September and October, persist into winter, and are latently scavenged by the birds. Remarkably durable plant in all but permanently

MORE ➤

Ligustrum japonicum, Japanese Privet

Ligustrum japonicum foliage

Ligustrum japonicum flowers

Ligustrum japonicum fruit

Ligustrum japonicum continued

wet soils. Adaptable from full sun to heavy shade. Can be pruned into any shape and often is, to the limits of demented imaginations. One of the best hedging, screening, and massing plants. Grown by the millions in southern and West Coast nurseries. Grows 6 to 12 ft. high, 6 to 8 (to 12) ft. wide. Zones (6)7 to 10. Japan, Korea.

Cultivars and Varieties. Many selected through the garden ages. The following are available in commerce.

'Howard' ('Frazieri') has yellow new leaves that fade in heat to greenish; pretty strong color element, not for the faint of heart.

'Jack Frost', 'Silver Star', and 'Variegata' have leaves that are deep green in center with gray-green mottling, cream-silver edges. Compact, grows 6 to 8 ft. high, 4 to 6 ft. wide.

'Nobilis' is possibly the best large-leaved form; the leaves are waxy, glistening, dark green. Upright habit and grows faster than 'Recurvifolium'.

'Recurvifolium' has been a standard forever in southern gardens. Lustrous dark green leaves with undulating, recurved margins, are narrower than 'Nobilis'; habit is more compact and growth slower. Attractive form.

'Rotundifolium' ('Coriaceum') is a stiff, upright, confused-looking plant, akin to the person in shorts at a black-tie shindig. The rounded, 1- to 2½-in.-long leaves are curiously twisted and closely spaced along the stems. Has flowered and fruited. Grows 4 to 6 ft. high

Ligustrum japonicum 'Howard'

Ligustrum japonicum 'Jack Frost'

Ligustrum japonicum 'Nobilis' foliage

Ligustrum japonicum 'Nobilis' fruit

Ligustrum japonicum 'Rotundifolium' in flower

Ligustrum japonicum 'Recurvifolium'

Ligustrum japonicum 'Rotundifolium'

Ligustrum lucidum

WAXLEAF, GLOSSY, or CHINESE PRIVET

For most garden situations, not preferable to *Ligustrum japonicum* because of large size, lack of hardiness, and weedlike nature. A broadleaf evergreen tree, upright vase-shaped, with rounded canopy and smooth gray bark. Leaves are larger than *L. japonicum*, 3 to 6 in. long, thinner, and often with a reddish rim. The cream flowers in 5- to 8- (to 12-) in.-long and -wide panicles open about two to three weeks later than *L. japonicum*. The blue-black fruit are dusted with gray wax. Fruit persist through winter and, because of their weight, cause the branches to become semi-pendulous. Grows with ardor in almost any soil, becoming weedlike as birds move the seeds to and fro. Utilize as a large shrub/small tree. Grows 20 to 25 (to 50) ft. high. Zones 8 to 10. China, Korea, Japan.

MORE ➤

Ligustrum lucidum flowers

Ligustrum lucidum fruit

Ligustrum lucidum foliage

Ligustrum lucidum, Waxleaf Privet

Ligustrum lucidum **continued**

Cultivars and Varieties. 'Excelsum Superbum' is a strong-growing form with cream- yellow leaf margins.

'Tricolor' has mixed copper to purplish new leaves that settle down to irregular cream margins and green centers.

Ligustrum lucidum 'Excelsum Superbum'

Ligustrum lucidum 'Tricolor'

Ligustrum sinense foliage

Ligustrum sinense
CHINESE PRIVET

Take note—a terrible and devastating escapee that terrorizes flood plains, fence rows, and even open fields, reducing native vegetation to rubble. This species, as I view it, is a large, thickly branched, rounded shrub with dull dark green, 1- to 3-in.-long leaves. In northern climates (Zone 6) it is deciduous, becoming more evergreen in the lower South. Leaves emerge early, often by March in Athens, and have a competitive advantage, particularly in woodland situations, since the native broadleaf canopy is not full until late April or early May (Athens). Cream-white flowers in 2- to 3-in.-long axillary panicles open in May. The dull waxy black fruit are produced in abundance and persist through winter. Eventually the birds eat the fruit and spread the seeds. Tenaciously adaptable, growing in dry soils and flood plain conditions, in sun or shade. A few of the cultivars might be considered. As for the species, I urge abstinence. One of the most frequently pulled weeds in our garden. Grows 10 to 15 ft. high and wide. Zones (6)7 to 10. China.

Cultivars and Varieties. 'Green Cascade' has arching-weeping branches and green leaves.

'Variegatum' with cream- to white-margined leaves is common. Not as rampant as the species, typically 6 to 8 ft. high; however, I have observed 15-ft.-high plants. Will revert to green.

'Wimbei' ('Wimbish') has ¼-in.-long, dark green leaves and closely spaced nodes. Looks more like a boxwood. Grows 6 to 8 ft. high, with upright ascending branches.

Ligustrum sinense 'Wimbei'

Ligustrum sinense, Chinese Privet

Ligustrum sinense flowers

Ligustrum sinense fruit

Ligustrum sinense 'Variegatum'

Lindera, SPICEBUSH

Although little known in gardens south and north, a host of Lindera *species are available from specialty nurseries. Atlanta Botanical Garden; Woodlanders, Inc., Aiken, South Carolina; and Nurseries Caroliniana, North Augusta, South Carolina, have ferreted out the best.*

Lindera aggregata
JAPANESE EVERGREEN SPICEBUSH

A beautiful plant for shady borders. Sports 2-in.-long, 1-in.-wide, prominently three-veined, evergreen leaves on a 6- to 10-ft.-high, pyramidal shrub. Yellow flowers in spring. Zones 7 to 8. Japan.

Lindera aggregata, Japanese Evergreen Spicebush

Lindera angustifolia
ORIENTAL SPICEBUSH

This species has 3- to 4-in.-long, narrow-elliptical leaves, glossy green above, bluish green to silvery below that turn yellow-orange-red in fall and die off gray-brown, persisting into winter. Yellow flowers and black, rounded fruit. Full sun to moderate shade, any well-drained soil. Grows 6 to 8 ft. high; develops colonies. Zones 6 to 8. China.

Lindera angustifolia fall color

Lindera angustifolia flowers

Lindera angustifolia fruit

Lindera erythrocarpa

With dark green, 2½- to 5-in.-long leaves, this is a plant begging for scrutiny in autumn, when the leaves turn stunning yellow. Yellow flowers open in March and April, followed by red fruit. Tolerates dryness better than *Lindera benzoin*. A plant in the University's Botanical Garden was 18 ft. high, 20 ft. wide. Zones 6 to 8. China.

Lindera angustifolia, Oriental Spicebush, in fall

Lindera erythrocarpa in fall

Liquidambar formosana
FORMOSAN SWEETGUM

An excellent tree for southern and West Coast gardens, unique because of the three-lobed leaves and soft bristly fruit. A 90-year-old tree on the Georgia campus, now 50 ft. high and wide, produces soft butter-yellow fall color every November. In youth the habit is distinctly pyramidal, becoming rounded at maturity. The 2- to 5-in.-long, 3- to 6-in.-wide leaves, lustrous dark green in summer, turn yellow to red in fall. The 1-in.-diameter, rounded, soft bristly fruit are not as offensive as those of *Liquidambar styraciflua*. Tolerates drought and heat once established; I observed healthy trees in Tampa, Florida, and Mobile, Alabama. Selection work needs to be undertaken with the species for improved growth habit and fall color. Might prove an excellent tree for large areas, streets, and parks in warm climates. Grows 40 to 60 ft. high and wide. Zones 6 to 9. Taiwan, southern and central China.

Liquidambar acalycina sports rich reddish maroon new growth that matures dark green, turning burgundy in autumn. Similar to *L. formosana* and now offered by several nurseries. Displays excellent vigor and is cold hardy to −10°F. Zones 6 to 8. China.

MORE ➤

Liquidambar formosana fruit and foliage

Liquidambar formosana continued

Liquidambar formosana, Formosan Sweetgum, fall color

Liquidambar formosana foliage in fall   *Liquidambar acalycina* new foliage   *Liquidambar acalycina* flowers

Lithocarpus henryi

HENRY TANBARK OAK

I held great hope that this species and other *Lithocarpus* taxa would become major players in urban and suburban settings in the South. Alas, this has not come to pass because of the vast superiority of native *Quercus* species. This species is the most cold hardy and common, forming a rounded habit. The evergreen leaves, 4 to 8 (to 10) in. long, are leathery, lustrous, and entire along the margin. In cold weather the leaves become yellow-green. Bark is smooth and gray, similar to beech. The reproductive structure is an acorn, borne on an 8-in.-long spike at the end of the shoot. Usually sold in containers and easy to transplant. Adaptable; plants in Coastal Georgia are thriving in sandy soils. Probably will always be a collector's plant. Grows 25 to 30 ft. high and wide. Zones 6b to 9. Central China.

The related species *Lithocarpus densiflorus* has the most beautiful, toothed, dark green leaves, silvery on the underside, on a large shrub or small tree framework. The tree in our garden was killed by sapsucker feeding and subsequent canker. Grows 15 to 25 ft. high and wide. The national champion is 92 ft. high, 84 ft. wide. Zones 7 to 9. Southwestern Oregon, California.

Lithocarpus henryi, Henry Tanbark Oak

Lithocarpus henryi bark

Lithocarpus henryi foliage

Lithocarpus henryi fruit

Lonicera caprifolium
ITALIAN HONEYSUCKLE

A vining honeysuckle, not well known in the United States, but with fragrant, pretty, 1¾- to 2-in.-long, tubular, yellowish white, purple-tinged flowers in four- to ten-flowered whorls from the axils of the terminal three pairs of leaves. The 2- to 4-in.-long leaves are dark green above, glaucous blue-green below, the upper leaf bases fused into a disk shape, subtending the flowers. Fruit are orange-red, rounded, about ¼ in. in diameter. Best in a cooler climate or the West Coast. Grows 10 to 20 ft. high. Zones 5 to 7(8). Europe, western Asia.

Lonicera caprifolium, Italian Honeysuckle

Lonicera flava
YELLOW HONEYSUCKLE

A beautiful, twining, restrained species that is found only in collectors' gardens and even then infrequently. The upper leaves are fused at their bases and subtend the flowers. Leaves are rich green above, bluish green beneath. The orange-yellow flowers occur in whorls of one to three at the end of the shoot. Each flower is 1 to 1½ in. long, nonfragrant, with colors ranging from yellow to yellow-orange stained red in bud. The ¼-in.-diameter, orange-red fruit are seldom produced, at least on plants I observed. Requires shade and a cool, moist root run. Unusual vine for trellises, arbors, and fences. Grows 6 to 10 ft. Zones 5 to 8. North Carolina to Missouri, Arkansas to Oklahoma.

Lonicera flava flowers

Lonicera caprifolium flowers

Lonicera flava, Yellow Honeysuckle

Lonicera flava fruit

Lonicera nitida
BOXLEAF HONEYSUCKLE

Try as I might to successfully grow this evergreen species, results were abysmal. In Europe, the western United States, and occasionally the South, plants are successful. Typically, a dense, haystack-shaped mass of close-knit stems and dark green leaves. The leaves, about ½ in. long, are glossy dark green. Creamy yellow flowers, ¼ to ½ in. long, are produced in axillary, short-stalked pairs. Fruit are ¼-in.-diameter, translucent, amethyst-colored berries. Used extensively for hedges and masses in European gardens. Often confused with *Cotoneaster* species, but that genus has alternate leaves (those of *Lonicera* are opposite). Full sun to partial shade in any well-drained soil. Grows 6 to 8 ft. high and wide. Zones 7 to 9. China.

Cultivars and Varieties. Many, with 'Baggesen's Gold' probably the most common: golden leaves and mounded habit; leaf color fades, but not completely, with time; better color under cool conditions.

'Maigrun' has small, rounded, boxwood-like leaves and graceful, fountain-like habit.

MORE ➤

Lonicera nitida, Boxleaf Honeysuckle

Lonicera nitida continued

Lonicera nitida pruned as a hedge

Lonicera nitida 'Baggesen's Gold'

Lonicera periclymenum
WOODBINE

After following this vine throughout Europe (or was it the reciprocal?), I could not resist bringing the cultivars to Georgia for evaluation. A vigorous twining species with beautiful blue-green foliage, the new growth often tinged with bluish purple-red. Flowers are fragrant, 1½ to 2 in. long, and appear in peduncled spikes in three to five whorls at the end of the shoots. Typical flower color is yellowish white with a purplish pink tinge. Flowers open in May and June. Fruit are often abundant, red, ¼ in. in diameter, and showy. Adaptable to varied soils, full sun to partial shade. The cultivars are superior to the species for garden use. Grows 10 to 20 ft. Zones 4 to 8. Europe, north Africa, Asia Minor.

Cultivars and Varieties. 'Belgica' is a common selection with whitish to yellowish (inside the corolla) tinged purplish red flowers in great profusion.

'Graham Thomas' is soft cream-yellow, without traces of purple. Named after the great English plantsman.

'Serotina' (Late Dutch) has dark purple-red flowers (outside), yellowish inside. Flowers open over a longer period and are later than the species.

Lonicera periclymenum, Woodbine

Lonicera periclymenum fruit

Lonicera periclymenum 'Belgica'

Lonicera periclymenum 'Graham Thomas'

Lonicera periclymenum 'Serotina' flowers

Lonicera periclymenum 'Serotina'

Lonicera periclymenum
'Serotina' fruit

Lonicera pileata
PRIVET HONEYSUCKLE

Often confused with *Lonicera nitida* but with longer leaves shaped like those of *Ligustrum vulgare*, Common Privet. Also, consistently more cold hardy. Broad-spreading, evergreen shrub, with branches layered, building on each other, resulting in a rather elegant cotoneaster-like habit. Leaves, ½ to 1 in. long, are lustrous dark green and remain so through winter. Flowers and fruit are similar to *Lonicera nitida*. Well adapted to sun, partial shade, well-drained soil. Have utilized the species on the Georgia campus with minimal success. I thought this evergreen honeysuckle would prove the answer for broad swatches of green. Grows 2 to 3 ft. high, one and one-half to two times as wide. Zones 6 to 8. China.

Cultivars and Varieties. 'Moss Green' is a low-spreading, compact form with thickish dark green leaves; looks like a reduced-in-stature 'Otto Luyken' cherrylaurel.

Lonicera pileata, Privet Honeysuckle

Lonicera pileata 'Moss Green'

Lonicera pileata foliage

Lonicera pileata 'Moss Green' flowers

Loropetalum chinense

CHINESE LOROPETALUM,
CHINESE FRINGE-FLOWER

If prescriptions could be written for perfect garden plants, this species would come close to filling the order. Upright, dense, evergreen shrub or small tree, typically vase-shaped in large specimens. Foliage is densely borne in almost planar disposition along the stems. The ovate-roundish, 1- to 2½-in.-long leaves are dark green and rough above, gray pubescent below. Four-petaled, fleecy flowers occur in the axils of the leaves producing a mottle of cream and green. Flowers open in April (Athens) with an effective period of three to four weeks. Bark, on large specimens, is rich brown and exfoliating. Remarkably adaptable and drought-tolerant, full sun to moderate shade, best in acid soil. Responds to pruning; a loose screen in our garden is 4 ft. high through selective feather pruning. Superb screening evergreen; useful in groupings and masses; makes a good hedge; lovely touch in the shrub border. In my biased opinion, this shrub and the cultivars with red-purple leaves can be blended into any southern or West Coast garden. Grows 6 to 10 (to 15) ft. high, similar spread. Zones 7 to 9, 10 on the West Coast. China.

Cultivars and Varieties. Snow Dance™ is more compact in habit with smaller leaves; flowers are profuse. A worthy choice for smaller properties, easily pruned to maintain small stature. Grows 6 to 8 ft. high, wider at maturity.

'Snow Muffin' is close to commercialization by Head-Lee Nursery, Seneca, South Carolina. As I witnessed the plant, my salivary glands became active, almost like seeing a double cheeseburger with the trimmings. Large, leathery dark green leaves on a groundcover-like framework: the plant measured 15 in. high by 53 in. wide. Will make a great groundcover plant.

MORE ➤

Loropetalum chinense, Chinese Loropetalum

Loropetalum chinense foliage

Loropetalum chinense Snow Dance™

Loropetalum chinense continued

Loropetalum chinense

Loropetalum chinense flowers

Loropetalum chinense 'Snow Muffin'

Loropetalum chinense var. *rubrum*
REDLEAF CHINESE LOROPETALUM

A star on the rise, introduced from China about 1990, and currently among the most popular broadleaf evergreens in southern gardens. Initially two cultivars, 'Blush' with bronze-purple new growth and hot pink flowers, and 'Burgundy' with reddish purple new growth and hot pink flowers, were introduced. Reddish purple leaf color is most pronounced with high fertility and moisture. Color is almost equally good in sun and shade. With rabbit-like reproduction, these two cultivars became staples in southern nurseries. Currently more pink-flowered forms with reddish purple leaves, rather than green, are grown and sold. Bonnie and I have liberally sprinkled them about the garden. Easy to manage, unbelievably drought-tolerant, and pest-free. I consider it one of the top introductions of the past ten years. Grows 6 to 10 (to 15) ft. high and wide. Zones 7 to 9, 10 on the West Coast. China.

Cultivars and Varieties. Cultivars are the garden essence of this remarkable plant.

'Bicolor' produces deep bronze-maroon emerging leaves, turning dark olive-green, and white petals with pink striping. Large upright growth habit.

Fire Dance™, with reddish purple leaves and hot pink flowers, was introduced by Piroche Plants, British Columbia. Grows 8 to 10 ft. high and wide.

Plum Delight™ maintains excellent reddish purple foliage and hot pink flowers on a shrub of smaller stature; in the Dirr garden, not as vigorous as 'Bicolor', 'Blush', 'Burgundy', and 'Zhuzhou Fuchsia'.

'Ruby', along with 'Suzanne', is one of the small forms, about 4 to 6 ft. high and wide, leaves more rounded, deep reddish purple; pink flowers.

'Sizzlin' Pink' is a wide-spreading form, branches layered upon branches; reddish purple foliage and hot pink flowers. Grows 4 to 6 ft. high and wide.

'Suzanne' is a reddish purple branch sport of 'Variegata' with compact habit and more rounded leaves; flowers pink.

'Zhuzhou Fuchsia' is distinctly upright in habit, with narrower reddish purple to deep black-purple leaves and hot pink-red flowers. The most cold hardy red-purple leaf form, about 8 to 10 ft. high at maturity.

Worth noting that 'Blush', Razzleberri™, Piroche Form, and 'Daybreak's Flame' are the same; Plum Delight™, 'Hines Purpleleaf', 'Hines Burgundy', and Pizzazz™ are the same; and 'Pipa's Red' and 'Zhuzhou Fuchsia' are similar.

Loropetalum chinense var. *rubrum* 'Blush'

Loropetalum chinense var. *rubrum* Fire Dance™

Loropetalum chinense var. *rubrum* Plum Delight™

Loropetalum chinense var. *rubrum* 'Burgundy'

Loropetalum chinense var. *rubrum* 'Ruby' flowers

Loropetalum chinense var. *rubrum* 'Burgundy' flowers

Loropetalum chinense var. *rubrum* 'Bicolor'

Loropetalum chinense var. *rubrum* 'Sizzlin' Pink'

MORE ➤

Loropetalum chinense var. *rubrum* continued

Loropetalum chinense var. *rubrum* 'Ruby'

Loropetalum chinense var. *rubrum* 'Zhuzhou Fuchsia'

Loropetalum chinense var. *rubrum* 'Suzanne'

Loropetalum chinense var. *rubrum* 'Zhuzhou Fuchsia' flowers

Lyonia lucida
LYONIA

Could not wait to bring the species into the Dirr garden but less than stellar performance and abundant leaf spot resulted in early plant retirement. Occasionally, I experience healthy plants and, in their finest forms, they tempt me to try again. Suckering, spreading, broadleaf evergreen, branches arching and loose. Leaves, 1 to 3 in. long, leathery, and a lustrous dark green, are the principal reason for growing the plant. Pink to pinkish white to white flowers emerge from the leaf axils in May. Requires moisture, light shade, and no stress under cultivation. Suitable for wet areas; respectable colonies crossed my path in such situations. Grows 3 to 5 ft. high, wider at maturity. Zones 5 to 9. Virginia to Florida to Louisiana.

Lyonia lucida flowers

Lyonia lucida, Lyonia

Lyonia lucida foliage

Lyonia lucida buds of pink form

Magnolia ashei

(M. macrophylla subsp. ashei)
ASHE MAGNOLIA

A wonderful textural element in gardens because of the large bold-textured leaves, clubby stems, and 12-in.-diameter flowers in late May and June (Athens). More or less shrubby in habit, with dark green, 24- to 30-in.-long leaves, silvery on their lower surfaces. Fragrant flowers consist of six immense tepals often stained purple at the base. A three-year-old plant was 30 in. high in our garden when it first flowered. Almost a heavenly experience to witness such magnificent beauty. Requires moist, well-drained, acidic soils in partial to heavy shade. Much more heat- and drought-tolerant than hydrangeas. Utilize as a textural element in the shade garden. Grows 10 to 20 ft. high and wide. Zones 6 to 9. Florida to Texas along the Gulf Coast.

MORE ➤

Magnolia ashei stem in bud

Magnolia ashei, Ashe Magnolia

Magnolia ashei **continued**

Magnolia ashei foliage

Magnolia ashei flower

Magnolia ashei fruit

Magnolia campbellii
CAMPBELL MAGNOLIA

Without question, in flower, this species inflames the passion for plants unlike any other. Trees—with un-magnolia-like size and crowns that scrape the heavens with their cup-and-saucer flowers—infuse the soul. Allan Armitage and I, on our initial visit to the southwest of England, when first viewing the Sino-Himalayan magnolias, thought we had ascended to Heaven. Pretty heady plants! Flowers are fashioned from 12 to 15 tepals, the outer splaying to form a saucer, the inner a cup, in entirety 10 in. across. Flowers open in March and April on naked branches. Leaves are 6 in. long, dark green, and oval in outline. The bark is gray, relatively smooth, becoming platy-scaly with age. For the western United States only, in a belt from San Francisco to Vancouver Island, British Columbia. Specimen tree with no other use acceptable. Grows 50 to 60 ft. high. Zones 9 to 10 on the West Coast. Himalayas.

Cultivars and Varieties. Numerous selections for flower colors are known. The most beautiful is 'Lanarth' with cyclamen-purple buds that open to dark reddish purple.

Magnolia campbellii bark

Magnolia campbellii, Campbell Magnolia

Magnolia campbellii flower

Magnolia campbellii 'Lanarth' bud

Magnolia campbellii 'Lanarth' flowers

Magnolia grandiflora
SOUTHERN MAGNOLIA

The symbol of southern gardens, loved and cherished, accorded privilege and prestige, truly the broadleaf evergreen tree of noble lineage. Numerous selections in the past 20 years have provided a variety of habits, sizes, and leaf shapes that better serve the small landscape. Strong, dense pyramid, usually with central leader, occasionally almost rounded in outline. Leaves with the consistency of Plexiglas, waxy-surfaced and dark green above, green to fuzzy brown below. Bark, smooth, gray, somewhat beech-like, is attractive. The true religious experience comes from the nirvanishly fragrant flowers, 8 to 12 in. wide, composed of six to fifteen tepals (petals and sepals look the same), each thick, concave, broad-ovate. In Athens the floral parade begins in May, with cultivars like 'Little Gem' still flowering in October and November. Fruit, composed of follicles, develop in 3- to 5-in.-long, conelike aggregates. The individual seeds, orange-red, emerge from a single split and dangle from a white, threadlike stalk. Transplant small trees from containers, larger balled-and-burlapped material in August and later. Grows in sun, shade, wet and dry, acid soils. Once established, a drought- and heat-tolerant plant. Noble tree for grouping, street tree, hedge, and large screen use. Old leaves fall and accumulate; when tread upon, they sound like a loud bowl of Rice Krispies. Grows 60 to 80 ft. high, 30 to 50 ft. wide. Zones (6)7 to 9, 10 on the West Coast. North Carolina to Florida, Arkansas, and Texas.

Cultivars and Varieties. Over 150 named, 30 to 40 still extant, fewer available in commerce. Ray Bracken, Piedmont, South Carolina, started the introduction band-

Magnolia grandiflora, Southern Magnolia

Magnolia grandiflora foliage and foliage undersides

Magnolia grandiflora flower

Magnolia grandiflora fruit and seeds

wagon in the Southeast with 'Bracken's Brown Beauty', patented in 1985. I estimate a dozen *new* cultivars in the last 15 years.

Alta™ ('TMGH'), upright-columnar to narrow-pyramidal form, like 'Hasse', with dark green foliage, slightly brown below. Good root system, easy to transplant; terrific dense foliage and branches, will make a great screen.

'Bracken's Brown Beauty' is compact in youth, with foliage extremely lustrous dark green above, rusty brown below, 6 in. long with undulating surface. Possibly mature at 30 to 50 ft. high, 15 to 30 ft. wide. One of the more cold hardy forms. Zone 6.

'Claudia Wannamaker' is still one of the best, and it becomes better with age, not as flashy in youth. Grows 50 ft. or more with maturity; a large, old specimen in Atlanta Botanical Garden reflects stateliness over time.

'Edith Bogue', possibly the most cold hardy selection, is an ideal choice for Middle Atlantic States; West Coast nurserymen reported branches less susceptible to breakage in heavy wet snows. Opens with time in deeper South, 30 to 40 ft. high, 15 to 20 ft. wide.

MORE ➤

Magnolia grandiflora Alta™

Magnolia grandiflora 'Claudia Wannamaker'

Magnolia grandiflora 'Bracken's Brown Beauty'

Magnolia grandiflora **continued**

Greenback™ ('Mgtig') is unique: polished dark green convex leaves reflect the sun in all directions, leaf undersides have some brown pubescence, finally green. Original plant was 30 ft. high, 12 ft. wide.

'Hasse' is a tight pyramidal-columnar form with lustrous dark green leaves, rusty pubescence below. Parent tree is now 45 to 50 ft. high, 15 to 18 ft. wide; one of the best for screening. Somewhat difficult to propagate and transplant but worth the effort.

'Little Gem' is possibly the most popular selection because of precociousness to flower and smaller size. Small (to 4 in. long) lustrous dark green leaves are covered with bronze-brown pubescence below. The cream-white flowers, 3 to 4 (to 6) in. in diameter, initiate in May (Athens) and are still developing in October and November. Requires pruning to keep it dense. Grows 20 ft. high or more at maturity; excellent for screening and hedging.

'Saint Mary' ('Glen St. Mary'), introduced about 1905, has beautiful lustrous foliage, bronze pubescence below, and large and copious flowers on young plants. Pyramidal habit, grows probably 30 ft. or more.

'Victoria', another cold hardy form, has lustrous dark green leaves with brown undersides. More open-growing than the types presented here; used extensively in the Pacific Northwest.

Magnolia grandiflora 'Hasse'

Magnolia grandiflora 'Edith Bogue'

Magnolia grandiflora Greenback™

Magnolia grandiflora
'Little Gem' flowers

Magnolia grandiflora 'Little Gem'

Magnolia grandiflora 'Saint Mary'

Magnolia liliiflora
LILY MAGNOLIA

One of the parents of *Magnolia* ×*soulangeana*; the Little Girl Hybrids from the U.S. National Arboretum; 'Galaxy'; 'Spectrum'; and the Jury Hybrids. Never given credence in gardens, but one of the most beautiful shrub types because of the deep vinous purple flowers. Leaves are 4 to 7 in. long and resemble those of *M.* ×*soulangeana*. Unfortunately mildew is a problem, and foliage may appear tatty by summer's curtain call. The flowers, the deepest red-purple in bud of any species, remain upright when opening, finally relaxing and exposing lighter inner color. In Georgia, flowers open in late March and continue into April, before the leaves emerge. Reblooming is common, even into summer, a trait passed to *M.* ×*soulangeana*. Moist, acid, well-drained soil, full sun are ideal. Out of favor but attractive in flower, it often grows around old homesteads in the South. Grows 8 to 12 ft. high, similar spread. Zones 5 to 8. China.

Cultivars and Varieties. Several rich, deep reddish purple forms have been introduced with 'Nigra' the best: deep lustrous green foliage, compact habit, dark reddish purple flowers. During my 1999 sabbatical at Hillier Arboretum, England, this cultivar opened in April and was still flowering in July with a full complement of leaves.

The Little Girl Hybrids combine *Magnolia liliiflora* 'Nigra' and *M. stellata* 'Rosea' to produce shrubby, later-flowering cultivars that avoid the spring frosts. All flower on naked stems and continue flowering as the leaves develop. Foliage is often mildew-ridden in Boston and Athens. The Little Girls develop water sprouts, need

MORE ➤

Magnolia liliiflora flowers

Magnolia liliiflora continued

Magnolia liliiflora, Lily Magnolia

Magnolia liliiflora 'Nigra'

Magnolia liliiflora 'Nigra' foliage

Magnolia liliiflora 'Nigra' emerging flower

Magnolia liliiflora 'Nigra' flower

occasional pruning, and grow 10 to 20 ft. high and wide. 'Ann' (deep purple-red), 'Betty' (deep purple-red), 'Jane' (reddish purple), 'Judy' (deep red-purple), 'Pinkie' (pale red-purple fading to pink), 'Randy' (purple), 'Ricki' (deep purple), and 'Susan' (red-purple) constitute the Little Girls.

Magnolia 'Judy'

Magnolia 'Ann'

Magnolia 'Pinkie'

Magnolia 'Betty'

Magnolia 'Randy'

Magnolia 'Jane'

Magnolia 'Susan'

Mahonia bealei

LEATHERLEAF MAHONIA

Functional broadleaf evergreen with leathery, spiny leaflets useful for shady areas of the garden. Stiff, almost clumsy growth habit, with strong upright stems and leaves borne at right angles, results in a bumpy cloud of foliage at the top. Leaves are composed of nine to thirteen (occasionally fifteen), leathery, blue-green leaflets, each 1 to 4 in. long, 1 to 2 in. wide, with five to seven prominent spines. Leaves maintain consistent foliage color through the seasons. Lemon-yellow flowers, in 3- to 6-in.-high, 6- to 12-in.-wide terminal inflorescences, open in winter, remaining effective for four to six weeks. Flowers are wonderfully fragrant and attract all manners of bees for an early nectar harvest. Robin's-egg-blue fruit, each ⅓ to ½ in. long, ripen in late April and May. The color is beautiful, and birds quickly harvest the bounty. Tougher than rawhide and adaptable to any well-drained soil. Requires some shade for best appearance. Excellent in the woodland garden, in groupings and masses. Grows 6 to 10 ft. high. Zones 7 to 9. China.

The oft-confused *Mahonia japonica*, Japanese Mahonia, is similar. Leaflets are glossy green and are not strongly veined. Additionally, flowers are larger and brighter yellow. Grows 6 to 7 ft. high. Zones 6 to 8. Japan.

Mahonia bealei foliage

Mahonia bealei, Leatherleaf Mahonia

Mahonia bealei flowers

Mahonia bealei fruit

Mahonia japonica flowers

Mahonia bealei in flower

Mahonia fortunei, Chinese Mahonia

Mahonia fortunei
CHINESE MAHONIA

At first glance, difficult to associate with *Mahonia*, for the leaflets are narrow and soft to the touch. Also, the flowers appear in late summer to early fall. Almost fernlike in leaf texture, leaves are densely borne, producing a full-foliaged evergreen shrub. The dark green leaflets, 2 to 5 in. long, ½ to ¾ in. wide, lightly serrated, range from five to nine (occasionally thirteen) per leaf. The bright yellow flowers, in 2- to 3-in.-long, erect racemes, are melded into the foliage. Although fruit are described as purple-black, I have yet to discover them on cultivated plants. Adaptable like all *Mahonia* species; requires shade. Mildew occurs occasionally. Use in groupings and masses. Prospering in Savannah, killed to the ground in Athens. Grows 5 to 6 ft. high and wide. Zones (7)8 to 9. China.

Mahonia fortunei foliage and flowers

Mahonia japonica

Mahonia ×media

The more this evergreen shrub (*Mahonia japonica* × *M. lomariifolia*) crosses my path, the greater my appreciation for its floral attributes. A large, coarse evergreen with gray-brown checkered bark and foliage in the upper one-half. The dark green leaves are composed of 17 to 21 leaflets. The lemon to bright yellow flowers occur at the end of branches in 10- to 14-in.-long and -wide, racemose panicles. Flowers are variably fragrant and open over an extended period in winter. Fruit are robin's-egg blue, oval-round, and provide great bird food. Adaptable, but best in some shade. Great winter-flowering shrubs for the border. Combine beautifully with *Hamamelis ×intermedia* cultivars. Grows 8 to 15 ft. high. Zones (6)7 to 9.

Cultivars and Varieties. 'Buckland' (pale yellow), 'Charity' (yellow), 'Faith' (soft yellow), 'Hope' (bright yellow), 'Lionel Fortescue' (yellow), 'Underway' (yellow), and 'Winter Sun' (bright yellow, opening in December in Athens, lustrous dark green leaves) are the best known.

Mahonia ×media

Mahonia ×media 'Buckland'

Mahonia ×media 'Charity'

Mahonia ×*media* 'Underway'

Mahonia ×*media* 'Winter Sun'

Mahonia ×*media* 'Winter Sun' fruit

Malus
FLOWERING CRABAPPLE

Less than stellar small flowering trees in the southern states, with several cultivars, such as 'Adams', 'Callaway', 'Harvest Gold', 'Jewelberry', 'Liset', 'Prairifire', 'Red Jewel', and 'Sugar Tyme', the best performers over a ten-year period at the Milliken Arboretum, Spartanburg, South Carolina. The lone native southern crabapple, *Malus angustifolia*, is a rounded, 20- to 25-ft.-high and -wide tree, with dense, spinescent branches. Finely toothed, rich green leaves, 2 to 4 in. long, turn yellow in fall. Fragrant, pink, five-petaled, 1- to 1½-in.-diameter flowers appear in May among the leaves. The yellowish green, rounded, ¾-in.-diameter fruit ripen in late summer and fall. Serves as a great source of food for wildlife. Leaves are susceptible to rust. Not common but a worthy native tree for woodland edges, open fields, and remote areas. Not for the manicured landscape. Zones 7 to 9. Southeastern United States. See *Dirr's Hardy Trees and Shrubs* (Portland, OR: Timber Press, 1997) for greater breadth of *Malus* treatment.

MORE ➤

Malus 'Adams'

Malus 'Adams' fruit

Malus continued

Malus 'Harvest Gold'

Malus 'Harvest Gold' flowers

Malus 'Callaway'

Malus 'Callaway' fruit

Malus 'Prairifire'

Malus 'Red Jewel'

Malus 'Liset'

Malus angustifolia

Malus 'Red Jewel' fruit

Malvaviscus arboreus var. *drummondii*

TURK'S CAP, TURK'S TURBAN

A subshrub to herbaceous perennial, moving from South to North, with beautiful, twisted red flowers with prominent stamens, summer into fall. Develops a loose, shrubby outline, with 2- to 3-in.-wide, coarse-textured, yellow-green leaves on long petioles. The 1½- to 2-in.-long flowers are great hummingbird magnets and develop on new growth. The flower effect is not overwhelming like *Hibiscus*. Requires full sun, well-drained soils; pH adaptable and drought-tolerant. Fills a niche in the border or mixed annual planting. Grows 3 to 5 ft. high. Zones 8 to 9. Mexico to Brazil.

Mandevilla splendens (*Dipladenia splendens*)

PINK ALLAMANDA

Evergreen vine that finds a home on mailboxes, fences, walls, and trellises. Bonnie and I grew the plant in containers, and every autumn the fleshy roots and part of the top were removed to a cool greenhouse. The opposite, 3- to 8-in.-long, oval, deeply veined, lustrous dark green leaves are leathery and insect- and disease-resistant. The 2- to 4-in.-long and -wide, rich pink flowers open in summer and continue into fall. The five-lobed flower has a wide tubular base, flaring to flat-faced. Best in full sun and moderate fertility and moisture. Flowers develop on new shoots, so keep plants in active growth. Certainly one of the best summer-flower-

Malvaviscus arboreus var. *drummondii*, Turk's Cap

Mandevilla splendens, Pink Allamanda

Malvaviscus arboreus var. *drummondii* flowers

Mandevilla splendens 'Alice du Pont'

Mandevilla splendens 'Red Riding Hood'

ing vines, overwintering only in the Deep South. Grows 10 to 20 ft.; more restrained in containers and where climbing space is limited. Zones 10 to 11. Brazil.

Cultivars and Varieties. Not an easy species to chart taxonomically, for it was once included in *Dipladenia* and is still listed there.

'Alice du Pont', a large-flowered (to 4 in. wide) selection with deep pink buds, opening pink, is one of the most common selections.

'Red Riding Hood' has deeper rose-red flowers that are smaller than 'Alice du Pont'.

Melia azedarach, Chinaberry, in fruit

Melia azedarach
CHINABERRY

A scourge over much of the South, consuming fence rows and open spaces. On the flip side, a pretty round-headed tree with glossy dark green leaves, 1 to 2 ft. long, with 1½- to 2-in.-long toothed or lobed leaflets. Leaves die off yellow-green, not spectacular, but noticeable. In May, fragrant, lavender-lilac flowers, each ¾ in. across, appear in loose, 8- to 16-in.-long panicles. Leaves are present, so floral effect is dampened. Beautiful on close examination, the petals glistening bicolored lavender-lilac. Fruit, scary in their abundance, are ½-in.-diameter, rounded, yellow to yellow-brown drupes. Fruit persist through winter, providing ample forage for wildlife. Adaptable and weedy, prospers in heat and drought. A fruitless selection would prove a worthy small street tree. Grows 30 to 40 ft. high and wide. Zones 7 to 10. India, China.

Cultivars and Varieties. 'Jade Snowflake', with cream-speckled leaves and loose, lax, vase-shaped habit, and 'Umbraculiformis', Texas Umbrella-tree, multi-stemmed with umbrellalike crown, 20 to 25 ft. high, are occasionally available.

MORE ➤

Melia azedarach foliage

Melia azedarach flowers

Melia azedarach continued

Melia azedarach fruit

Melia azedarach 'Jade Snowflake' foliage

Melia azedarach 'Umbraculiformis', Texas Umbrella-tree

Melia azedarach 'Jade Snowflake'

Michelia figo foliage

Michelia figo flower

Michelia figo, Banana Shrub

Michelia doltsopa

Michelia figo
BANANA SHRUB

Appropriate name for this broadleaf evergreen shrub of upright-oval to rounded habit. The floral fragrance, reminiscent of banana oil, is a pleasing aroma in the spring garden. The newly emerging leaves are covered with silky brownish pubescence, at maturity glabrous, lustrous dark green, 1½ to 4 in. long. Foliage alone is reason to grow the plant. The 1- to 1½-in.-long and -wide, six- to nine-tepaled, yellowish green, tinged purple, cup-shaped flowers are borne on a ½-in.-long brown pubescent peduncle from April through June. The rich fragrance, particularly on still, warm days, trails one through the garden. Prefers rich, moist, well-drained acidic soils in some degree of shade, although plants succeed in sun. A plant in our garden is shrouded by several southern red oaks and *always* holds up in the heat and drought better than the next-door native azaleas, Japanese kerrias, and oakleaf hydrangeas. Excellent for shady areas of the garden. Withstands heavy pruning and still looks good. Grows 6 to 10 (to 15) ft. high. Zones 7 to 9, 10 on the West Coast. China.

In recent years, many *Michelia* species have become available in commerce. Most are Zones 8 to 9(10) adaptable and reserved for the collector. *Michelia doltsopa*, a large tree with multi-tepaled, fragrant white flowers; *M. maudiae* with fragrant white flowers; and the hybrid *M. ×foggii* (*M. doltsopa* × *M. figo*) are the most common.

Cultivars and Varieties. 'Port Wine' and 'Stubbs Purple', the flowers with more purple coloration, are probably one and the same selection of *Michelia figo*. MORE ➤

Michelia figo continued

Michelia doltsopa foliage

Michelia doltsopa flower

Michelia maudiae

Michelia ×foggii

Millettia reticulata
EVERGREEN RED WISTERIA

The Atlanta Botanical Garden has successfully grown this species for many years, but coming out of winter this twining vine often assumes the appearance of an alley cat after a brawl. When right, the leathery, lustrous dark green leaves, composed of seven to thirteen leaflets, each 1 to 2 in. long, provide a beautiful fence, trellis, and arbor cover. The dark purple-red, weakly fragrant flowers, in 6- to 10-in.-long inflorescences, develop from July and August into fall. The fruit are elongated, fat, bony pods, constricted between the seeds that mature in late fall. Fast growing in moist, acid, fertile, well-drained soil and full sun. Requires support. A true evergreen only in Zones 10 to 11. Grows 10 to 20 ft. Zones 7b to 11. China.

Millettia reticulata, Evergreen Red Wisteria

Mitchella repens
PARTRIDGEBERRY

Too often left behind in the dust of bigger, better, newer plants, this evergreen groundcover makes a wonderful woodland blanket. I remember teaching this in a wildflower course at the University of Illinois and then on a field trip showing the plant to students as we hiked Turkey Run State Park, Marshallville, Indiana. Sometimes the little things take center stage—such was the case with Partridgeberry. Almost pancake-like in habit, the dark green, whitish-veined leaves, ¼ to 1 in. long and wide, are oppositely arranged along the stems. The fragrant, ½-in.-long, pink to white flower with four-lobed corolla opens over a long period in spring and summer. The red, berrylike, ¼- to ⅓-in.-diameter fruit ripen in summer and fall and persist. Requires moist, woodsy, acid soil and shade. For that small segment of the woodland garden! To appreciate this small woodland citizen is a signal that all biological entities, great and small, are important. Grows 1 to 2 in. high, spreads indefinitely. Zones 4 to 9. Canada to Florida, Arkansas, and Texas.

Musa
BANANA

These large-leaved tropical plants have become the focal points of container and annual color gardening in much of the South. Even in Zone 7b, plants have overwintered, although die-back occurs. Develops soft, thickish stems, often clumping from offsets, with large 4- to 8-ft.-long, slightly arching to drooping leaves. Texture is bold, brash, and attention-grabbing. Yellow flowers with red to purple bracts develop in summer. Fruit set may occur in hottest parts of the South. Requires fertile, well-drained soils high in organic matter. Full sun to partial shade. Remove tattered leaves. In cooler areas of the South, cut off the top of the plant, dig roots (corms), and move to a protected (nonfreezing) site. Always exciting to drive through central

MORE ➤

Mitchella repens, Partridgeberry

Mitchella repens flowers

Mitchella repens fruit

Musa ornata, Rose Banana

234

Musa continued

Georgia (Zone 7b) and experience a lush banana in a garden setting. *Musa acuminata* 'Dwarf Cavendish', 6 to 8 ft. high; *M. coccinea*, Red Banana, 4 to 5 ft. high; *M. ornata*, Rose Banana, 8 to 10 ft. high; and *M. ×paradisiaca*, 15 to 20 ft. high, are the most common.

Musa ×paradisiaca

Myrica cerifera fruit

Myrica cerifera foliage

Myrica cerifera
SOUTHERN WAXMYRTLE

A walk along the beaches from southern New Jersey to the Florida Keys reveals this amazing evergreen species in myriad shapes and sizes. Prospers in pure sand, and frequent bicycle touring on the Outer Banks of North Carolina indicated that beach grass and this species are about the only vegetation holding the sand in place. A large spreading shrub, it reinvents itself from root suckers into impenetrable colonies. Beautiful grayish white bark develops on older branches and trunks. Olive-green foliage is dotted with small glands that, when broken, release the bayberry fragrance. On warm evenings, you can pick up the scent simply by passing by. Leaves are 1½ to 3 in. long, ⅓ to ¾ in. wide, and usually serrate toward the apex. The gray, globose fruit, ⅛ in. in diameter, are massed in clusters of two to six on the previous season's growth. Transplant from container into about any soil, dry to wet. Fixes atmospheric nitrogen, which assures survival in miserable soils. Full sun to moderate shade. Withstands the endless pruning required to keep it in check. Great seaside plant but also a large screening evergreen. Can be used for hedges. Grows 10 to 15 (to 20) ft. high and wide. Zones 7 to 11.

Myrica cerifera bark

Cultivars and Varieties. 'Don's Dwarf', with deep olive-green leaves and bluish gray fruit, grows 3 ft. high and wide. Many "dwarf" forms have been introduced and include 'Club Med', 'Georgia Gem', 'King's Dwarf', Luray', 'Lynn's Dwarf', and 'Tom's Dwarf'.

'Fairfax' is a densely foliaged and branched selection that grows 6 to 8 ft. high and wide. An improvement on the species because of restrained growth.

'Hiwassee' is more cold hardy and has withstood –4°F with minor foliage burn. A plant in my shop is vigorous and will become large like the species.

var. *pumila* is definitely lower growing than the species, perhaps 3 to 4 ft. high or less. The J. C. Raulston Arboretum has an excellent, compact, female form that is pictured herein.

Myrica cerifera 'Don's Dwarf'

MORE ➤

Myrica cerifera, Southern Waxmyrtle

Myrica cerifera continued

Myrica cerifera 'Georgia Gem'

Myrica cerifera var. *pumila*

Myrica cerifera 'Fairfax'

Myrica inodora fruit

Myrica inodora
ODORLESS BAYBERRY

Difficult to imagine a bayberry without foliar fragrance, but such is the situation with *Myrica inodora*. A handsome, rounded, evergreen shrub that becomes open with age. Leaves, dark green, 1½ to 3 in. long, are entire. Although glands are present on leaf, no fragrance is detectable. The ¼-in.-diameter, oblong-oval drupes, dark brown to black, are sometimes covered with white wax. Adaptable to wet soils and grows in swamps, bogs, and ponds in its native habitat. The species is beautiful in foliage but has never caught on in gardens. Excellent wetland mitigation species. Grows 15 to 20 ft. high and wide. Zones 8 to 9. Panhandle of Florida, Alabama, and Mississippi.

Myrtus communis
COMMON MYRTLE

The myrtle of antiquity, long a staple of garden-making throughout warm temperate regions. Handsome evergreen foliage and beautiful bark place it in the front ranks of broadleaf evergreens. In habit a dense, leafy shrub or small tree, upright in youth, more oval-rounded with age. Lustrous dark green leaves, 1 to 2 in. long, are oppositely arranged. In May and June, small pinkish buds open to ¾-in.-diameter, five-petaled, fragrant, white flowers. Flowers are effective over a long period. The ovoid, ½-in.-long, purplish black berry is masked by the foliage. Bark is beautiful, brown, smooth. Worthwhile to limb up lower branches to expose the bark. Full sun to partial shade; good drainage is essential.

MORE ➤

Myrica inodora, Odorless Bayberry

Myrtus communis bark

Myrtus communis flowers

Myrtus communis fruit

Myrtus communis continued

A superb hedge plant, quite common in European gardens. Lovely foliage accent in the border. Discovered a 5-ft.-high plant in an Athens garden that indicates more cold hardiness than I thought possible. Grows 10 to 12 ft. high and wide. Zones (8)9 to 10. Iran and Afghanistan.

Nandina domestica

NANDINA, HEAVENLY BAMBOO

A bread-and-butter broadleaf evergreen shrub with alley-cat toughness and durability. Mature plants remain extant in old home sites in the South long after the home has crumbled and disappeared. A member of the barberry family; the only easily discernible shared characteristic is the yellow cambium. Usually an upright, strongly caned shrub, with the foliage concentrated in the upper one-half of the plant; however, suckers and colonizes, thus forming densely foliated mounds. Tri-pinnately compound leaves, 1 to 2 (to 3) ft. long, are composed of ¾-

Myrtus communis, Common Myrtle

to 3-in.-long, rich metallic bluish green leaflets. Low temperatures induce reddish pigmentation that varies from a blush to deep reddish purple, depending on seedling or cultivar. Flowers appear in May and June as pink buds, in 8- to 15-in.-long terminal panicles, and open to six-petaled, ¼- to ⅓-in.-wide blooms, white with yellow anthers. The beautiful ⅓-in.-diameter globular red fruit ripen in September and October, persisting into and through winter. Their color and persistence lend great aesthetics to the winter garden. Adaptable to sun, shade, and varied soils, except permanently wet. Bulletproof to insects and diseases. Utilize for foundation plantings, masses, groupings, slope stabilizers, in shady borders and understory plantings. Plants will become leggy; rejuvenation pruning in late winter induces basal shoot development and subsequently fuller plants. Although beyond common, it is one of the most serviceable broad-leaf evergreens. Grows 6 to 8 ft. high, usually less in spread, but with time becomes more wide than high. Zones 6 to 9, 10 on the West Coast. China.

Cultivars and Varieties. Selections for foliage, fruit, and growth habit dominate the marketplace.

'Alba' has whitish to cream-yellow fruit and lighter green foliage. Grows 5 to 6 ft. high.

'Atropurpurea Nana' is a stiff meatball, light green in summer foliage, uniformly red with the advent of cold. Grows 2 ft. high, 2 to 3 ft. wide; no flowers.

'Firepower' ('Fire Power') is virus-free and with the noncontorted leaves of 'Atropurpurea Nana'. Similar to 'Wood's Dwarf'.

Gulf Stream™ is possibly the most popular cultivar in nursery production. Grows 3 to 3½ ft. high, slightly less

Nandina domestica, Heavenly Bamboo

Nandina domestica in winter

Nandina domestica flowers

MORE ➤

Nandina domestica continued

in spread, dense in habit and foliage. Winter coloration is variable, some years intense red, others red-green; inflorescences about 4 in. long with red fruit developing.

'Harbour Dwarf', with rich metallic blue-green foliage, reddish-tinged in winter, develops a spreading, suckering habit. Grows 2 to 3 ft. high, wider at maturity. Excellent for low masses, groupings; flowers and fruit develop.

Moon Bay™, a mounded grower, 1½ to 2½ ft. high and wide, has shinier, lighter green leaves that acquire red hues in winter. Good-looking selection but has not taken off like Gulf Stream™.

'Moyer's Red' is a large-growing form to 6 ft. or more, with typical species characteristics except winter foliage is glossy red. Reported to be slightly less cold hardy in the Atlanta area, compared to other cultivars. Both flowers and fruit are produced.

'San Gabriel' ('Kurijusi', 'Orihime') is truly unique, with individual leaflets modified into narrow fernlike segments that are reddish when young, then blue-green, and finally reddish purple in winter. Grows 1 to 2 ft. high. My observations indicate less cold hardiness than the species.

'Umpqua Warrior' is a 6- to 9-ft.-high form, not unlike the species, with large flowers and fruit. The J. C. Raulston Arboretum, Raleigh, North Carolina, holds the best collection of nandinas, including the Umpqua series, i.e., 'Chief' and 'Princess'; as I studied them, any good seedling is as notable.

'Wood's Dwarf', with rich green summer foliage and red winter leaf coloration, grows 2 to 2½ ft. high, not too different from 'Firepower'; developed by the late Ed Wood, when he was a student at Oregon State University.

Nandina domestica 'Firepower' winter color

Nandina domestica Gulf Stream™

Nandina domestica fruit

Nandina domestica 'Alba'

Nandina domestica 'Atropurpurea Nana'

Nandina domestica 'Harbour Dwarf'

Nandina domestica 'San Gabriel'

Nandina domestica 'Umpqua Warrior'

Nandina domestica Moon Bay™

Nandina domestica 'Wood's Dwarf'

Nandina domestica Moon Bay™ winter color

Nandina domestica 'Moyer's Red' winter color

Nandina domestica 'Wood's Dwarf' winter color

242

Nerium oleander
OLEANDER

Superb shrub or small tree for the
Deep South into the Florida Keys.
On a late March trip to Key West,
Bonnie and I marveled at the beautiful flowers in singles and doubles,
whites to reds. The flowers develop
on new growth and are most vibrant
in summer. A broadleaf evergreen,
upright-branched, oval-rounded
shrub, with 3- to 5- (to 8-) in.-long,
½- to ¾-in.-wide, leathery dark
green leaves. The 1- to 1½- (to 2-)
in.-diameter, five-petaled flowers are
phenomenal in their variations. Colors alone range from white, cream,
yellow, pink, lilac, salmon, apricot,
and flesh to copper, orange, red, carmine, and purple. Fruit are elongated, podlike structures, 5 to 7 in.
long, containing small, fringed
seeds. Tougher than a tick in terms
of adaptability. Withstands sun,
heat, wind, salt, drought, and pollution. Easily transplanted from containers. Cut back overgrown or cold-
damaged plants. Superb summer-
flowering plant for groupings, containers, and masses. All parts of the
plant are poisonous. Grows 6 to 12
ft. high and wide; 20-ft.-high plants
in Florida. Zones 8 to 11. Southern
Asia, Mediterranean region.

Cultivars and Varieties. Over 120
cultivars growing at Filippi Nursery,

Nerium oleander, Oleander

Nerium oleander in flower

Nerium oleander fruit

Nerium oleander foliage

Nerium oleander flower

Nyssa ogeche
OGEECHEE TUPELO, OGEECHEE-LIME

Mèze, France. Several compact forms, like Carnival™ (salmon-pink) and 'Petite Pink' (shell pink), as well as larger-growing, hardier forms (Zones 7b to 8a), like 'Hardy Pink', 'Hardy White', and 'Sugarland Red', are available in commerce.

Always on the watch for potential "new" urban and stress-tolerant trees. This swamp species, like many bottomland species, lends itself to more compacted soils. The late J. C. Raulston grew the species in the west side of the Arboretum in Raleigh, North Carolina, in soil so hard that roots barely penetrated. Yet the plant appeared remarkably robust. Habit in cultivation is rounded, branches coarse and covered with 4- to 6-in.-long, dark green leaves. On female trees, ovoid fruit, ¾ to 1½ in. long, change to red or remain green with a red blush. Fruit are extremely sour, which suggested the name Ogeechee-lime. Unusual tree for naturalizing; found in wet soils in the wild and excellent for wet soil areas. Requires

MORE ➤

Nerium oleander 'Petite Pink'

Nerium oleander 'Hardy Pink'

Nyssa ogeche bark

Nyssa ogeche, Ogeechee Tupelo

244

Nyssa ogeche continued

root pruning to facilitate easier transplanting. A few Georgia nurserymen produced the tree, but the market was not ready. Grows 30 to 40 ft. high and wide. Zones 6 to 9. South Carolina, Georgia, and Florida.

Nyssa ogeche foliage

Nyssa ogeche fruit

Orixa japonica foliage

Orixa japonica

Potential uses include quizzing guests relative to identity and checking their tolerances to one of the strongest odors in the leafy kingdom. A member of the citrus family (Rutaceae); the "curious" leaf odor recalls the oils of lemon, lime, orange, and feet. Back to horticulture—dense, mounded, spreading shrub, almost like floweringquince, *Chaenomeles*, in impenetrability. Lustrous bright green leaves, 2 to 5 in. long, become soft yellow in fall; greenish flowers in spring. The sel-

dom-produced fruit offer little ornament. Prefers partial shade in moist, well-drained, acid soil high in organic matter. Have observed plants in substandard soils yet still prosperous. Novelty shrub for the collector. Grows 6 to 8 ft. high, wider at maturity. Zones 6 to 7. Japan.

Cultivars and Varieties. 'Variegata', with irregular cream-white margined leaves, is striking when the shoots first emerge, settles down with maturity.

Orixa japonica

Orixa japonica flowers

Orixa japonica 'Variegata'

Osmanthus americanus
DEVILWOOD

Out of character for an *Osmanthus* species, as the leaves are spineless; the only
other *Osmanthus* species native to the
southeastern United States is *Osmanthus
megacarpus*, which is similar, except
smaller in habit and larger of fruit. At
times wispy and without great landscape
appeal; occasionally robustly foliated.
Bark is smooth gray on older trunks.
Leaves, 2 to 5 in. long, are lustrous dark
olive-green above, pale green beneath.
In March and April, the four-petaled, ¼-
in.-diameter, fragrant, cream-colored
flowers appear in axillary terminal panicles. Sexes are separate, and the ½-in.-
long, ovoid, dark blue-purple fruit develop on female plants. I have watched
fruit persist into the following spring,
then disappear in a day with the frenzied
feeding of feathered flocks. Wonderful
wet soil plant, growing naturally along
swamp margins, hammocks, and borders
of streams. Tolerates drier soils once
established. Bonnie and I grow several
plants; none will ever overwhelm, but
they do possess a latent beauty. Good
choice for naturalizing in moist soils.
Prune to maintain density. Used in a
grouping behind the first green at the
Augusta National Golf Course, home
of the Master's. Grows 15 to 25 ft. high,
variable spread. Zones 6 to 9(10). North
Carolina to Florida and Mississippi.

Osmanthus americanus, Devilwood

Osmanthus americanus habit and bark

Osmanthus americanus flowers

Osmanthus americanus fruit

Osmanthus americanus foliage

Osmanthus ×burkwoodii

A taxonomic enigma, at one time given the name ×*Osmarea burkwoodii*, but now contained within *Osmanthus*. A hybrid of *Osmanthus delavayi* and *O. decorus*, the species develops into a compact broadleaf evergreen shrub of haystack to rounded outline. Like most *Osmanthus* species, the 1- to 2-in.-long, serrated leaves are leathery, lustrous dark green. Flowers, fragrant, small, open in April and May. I have not observed fruit set. Another piece of ammunition in the *Osmanthus* arsenal that makes our gardens more beautiful. Easy to grow; several prospering plants in the Athens area indicate adaptability to southern heat and humidity. Place in moderate shade, well-drained soil. Useful as a filler in borders and the like. Grows 6 to 10 ft. high and wide. Zones 6 to 8, 9 and 10 on the West Coast.

Osmanthus ×burkwoodii flowers

Osmanthus ×burkwoodii foliage and flowers

Osmanthus delavayi foliage and flowers

Osmanthus ×burkwoodii

Osmanthus delavayi
DELAVAY TEAOLIVE

My many trips to English gardens provided the introduction to this species, and the first encounter at Lanhydrock, Bodmin, had me doubting myself. It was a chilly (actually bone-chilling) late March day when this unknown 15-ft.-high broadleaf evergreen shrub looked me in the eye, in full flower and fragrance, daring me to identify it. I simply could not put two and two together. The lustrous dark green leaves, ½ to 1 in. long, with strong teeth, are reminiscent of small holly leaves. The fragrant white flowers are produced in four- to eight-flowered cymes from each leaf axil, resulting in a swath of cream along the branches. Fruit are roundish, ½-in.-long, blue-black drupes. I have grown the plant in Athens, but it never lived up to Lanhydrock. Wonderful plant for foliage and late winter-spring flowers. Grows 6 to 10 ft. high and wide. Zones 7 to 8, 9 to 10 on the West Coast. China.

Osmanthus ×fortunei
FORTUNE'S TEAOLIVE

A hybrid of *Osmanthus heterophyllus* × *O. fragrans*, and among the most durable of plants for sun, shade, and dry soils in the Southeast. Introduced from Japan in 1856, the initial introduction was male. My monitoring of flowers indicates all in cultivation are males. Makes the most uniform, dense haystack of dark green. Occasionally limbed up to display the smooth gray bark. On the Georgia campus, two 20- to 25-ft.-high specimens attract the attention of

MORE ➤

Osmanthus delavayi, Delavay Teaolive

Osmanthus ×fortunei **continued**

the entire student body in mid- to late October, when the perfume of the flowers lays a sweet, smoglike blanket across the University. The small, four-petaled, white flowers appear in cymose clusters from the leaf axils and are effective for two to three weeks. The spiny juvenile leaves, thick leathery dark green, 2 to 4 in. long, have ten to twelve triangular teeth per margin. As the plant ages, serrations disappear; the large plants just mentioned have almost no serrated leaves. Mature plants also flower more intensely than the juvenile delinquents. Container-grown and easily transplanted. Shade and sun adaptable. Requires well-drained soil. A great screen or hedge plant. Grows 10 to 15 (to 20) ft. high, usually less in spread. Zones 7 to 9. Japan.

Cultivars and Varieties. 'Fruitlandii' has less stiff serrations and is more upright in habit, particularly in youth.

'San Jose', with more elongated leaves than the species, is more open in outline. Both grow in our garden, with 'Fruitlandii' possibly the best overall.

Osmanthus ×fortunei 'Fruitlandii'

Osmanthus ×fortunei 'San Jose'

Osmanthus ×fortunei, Fortune's Teaolive

Osmanthus ×fortunei foliage

Osmanthus ×fortunei flowers

Osmanthus fragrans new foliage

Osmanthus fragrans
FRAGRANT TEAOLIVE

For continuous floral fragrance, the Fragrant Teaolive has no peers. Starting in September, it provides sweet perfume, with flowers still emerging in April (Athens) and appearing sporadically in late spring and summer. Most passersby do not see the flowers but remark about the pleasing aroma. Upright, broad columnar, broadleaf evergreen shrub in youth becoming treelike at maturity. Leaves, 2 to 5 in. long, are finely toothed or entire and maintain the lustrous dark green color year-round. Bark, when exposed, is smooth, gray-brown, and attractive. The small, four-petaled, whitish flowers appear in small axillary clusters. Fruit are elongated, olivelike, purple-black drupes with a waxy coating and seldom develop on cultivated plants. Adaptable to varied soils, except permanently wet. Sun and shade adaptable. Like all *Osmanthus* species, no serious insects or diseases. Utilize in combinations with other broadleaf evergreens, mixed borders, screens, and even hedges. Great in shady situations and a wonderful container plant. Bonnie and I have "spotted" the species and cultivars throughout the garden for a continuum of floral fragrance. Cold is the prime enemy, and anything below 0°F will injure leaves. In fact, plants were killed, in some instances to the ground, at –3°F in the Athens area. Grows 10 to 15 ft. high, 20 to 30 ft. high in Zones 9 and 10. Zones 7 to 10. China, Japan.

Cultivars and Varieties. Many selected over the centuries, but differences, except for a few, are minor.

'Aurantiacus' (f. *aurantiacus*) produces pale to deep orange flowers in fall; typically does not repeat flower like the species. Leaves are more

MORE ➤

Osmanthus fragrans foliage and flowers

Osmanthus fragrans 'Aurantiacus'

Osmanthus fragrans, Fragrant Teaolive

***Osmanthus fragrans* continued**

leathery and darker green, less serrated, and habit is dense, pyramidal-conical. Gorgeous in flower and fragrance.

'Nanjing's Beauty' ('Fudingzhu') was recently introduced to America from China and produces more abundant, fragrant, cream-white flowers than the species.

Osmanthus heterophyllus, Holly Teaolive

Osmanthus fragrans 'Nanjing's Beauty'

Osmanthus heterophyllus adult foliage and flowers

Osmanthus heterophyllus juvenile foliage

Osmanthus heterophyllus 'Aureomarginatus'

Osmanthus heterophyllus 'Aureus'

Osmanthus heterophyllus
HOLLY TEAOLIVE

Appropriately named, for the spiny-margined leaves that, although smaller, otherwise resemble English Holly leaves. Many people misidentify this species as holly, but the leaves are always opposite on *Osmanthus*, alternate on *Ilex*. Dense upright-oval to rounded evergreen shrub that is virtually impenetrable. The 1- to 2½-in.-long, leathery lustrous dark green, spiny-margined leaves become, with age, entire. An ancient specimen is a thing of beauty and comes without the excruciatingly painful "sticky" leaves. White, four-petaled, ¼-in.-diameter, fragrant flowers open in mid- to late October into early November. The floral scent is heavenly and spices the entire garden. The fruit that occasionally develop, usually hidden among the leaves, are ⅜- to ½-in.-long, bluish purple-black drupes. Resilient and ironclad shrub that withstands sun, shade, heat, drought, pruning, and vandalism. Makes a superb hedge and barrier. Grows 8 to 10 ft. high; 20-ft. plants grow in Athens, Georgia, and Aiken, South Carolina. Zones 6 to 9. Japan.

Cultivars and Varieties. Certainly one of my favorite species for unusual cultivars; several offer greater breadth of landscape benefits, and many are great everyday garden plants.

'Aureomarginatus', with yellow-margined, green-centered leaves, forms a large haystack to 10 ft. or more.

'Aureus' has golden yellow leaves that fade to yellow-green and green. Leaves are strongly spiny in youth. Slower growing and smaller that the species.

'Goshiki' is a spectral rainbow with new growth tinged pink and bronze, flecked with gold, maturing gold, cream, and green—all rather pretty when finally settled down. Grows 6 ft. high and wide; good choice in shady areas of the garden to provide a touch of color.

'Gulftide', with extremely spiny young leaves, upright habit, white flowers, and fruit, is an excellent hedge or barrier plant. Leaves, with maturity, become entire. Grows 10 ft. high or more.

'Purpureus' derives its name from the appearance of the new shoots, which look as if they were dipped in purple-black tar. Leaves are extremely beautiful and eventually become dark green; spiny-margined when young, finally entire. One of the most cold hardy cultivars, forming a dense rounded outline to 10 ft. high.

'Rotundifolius' offers 1½- to 2-in.-

MORE ➤

Osmanthus heterophyllus 'Goshiki'

Osmanthus heterophyllus 'Gulftide'

Osmanthus heterophyllus 'Gulftide' flowers

Osmanthus heterophyllus 'Purpureus'

Osmanthus heterophyllus continued

long, 1- to 1¼-in.-wide, leathery dark green leaves without spines, fragrant white flowers, and bluish purple fruit. Habit is more compact, 4 to 5 (to 8) ft. high and wide. A superb foundation, grouping, and massing shrub.

'Sasaba', with extremely spiny leaves and upright habit, 8 to 10 ft. high, is more of a collector's item;

fragrant white flowers open in early November in the Dirr garden.

'Variegatus' is the most frequently available cultivar in commerce, with cream-white margined leaves that are not as spiny as the species; forms a pyramidal-oval to rounded outline, eventually reaching 8 to 10 ft. in height. About half a zone less hardy than the species.

Osmanthus serrulatus

One of the most beautiful teaolives for foliage, the 2- to 3½-in.-long, leathery, lustrous dark green leaves have 26 to 30, plastic, sawlike teeth per margin. As plants mature, the leaves become entire, and it is difficult to locate a single serrated leaf. Habit parallels a large, broad mound, truly impenetrable. Flowers, winter to spring, are white, fragrant, and produced in clusters of four to nine from the leaf axils. Fragrance is not as overpowering as that of *Osmanthus fragrans*. Fruit are oblong, blue-black drupes. Have grown the species in our Athens garden without the success of *O.* ×*fortunei*, *O. heterophyllus*, and *O. fragrans*. Appears to be in suspended animation. At the Hillier Arboretum, England, I witnessed a 15-ft.-high and -wide specimen. Remarkably beautiful where it can be grown. Grows 6 to 12 ft. high and wide. Zones 7 to 10. China.

Osmanthus heterophyllus 'Rotundifolius'

Osmanthus serrulatus foliage and flowers

Osmanthus heterophyllus 'Sasaba'

Osmanthus heterophyllus 'Variegatus'

Osmanthus serrulatus

Pachysandra procumbens
ALLEGHENY PACHYSANDRA

One of the most beautiful broadleaf evergreen groundcovers, forming a blanket of green that complements and enhances the shrubs and trees above. The habit is stoloniferous-spreading to form large mats of rich green (emerging) to dark blue-green leaves with grayish mottling at maturity. The 2- to 4-in.-long, almost rounded leaves are entire at the base with coarse teeth from the middle to the apex. Flowers occur at the base of the leaf stalk (stem) in 2- to 4-in.-long spikes in March and April. The pinkish white flowers are fragrant and often not visible, as they are buried in the crown of the plant. Requires moist, acid to higher pH, loose, friable soils, high in organic matter, and some degree of shade for best growth. Without equivocation, one of the most beautiful native groundcovers. In northern climates, snow tends to flatten the leaves, but with new growth in spring the sins of winter are absolved. Grows 6 to 10 in. high, spreading to infinity. Zones 5 to 9. Eastern Kentucky, West Virginia to Florida and Louisiana.

Cultivars and Varieties. 'Eco Treasure' is a more highly variegated selection; 'Forest Green' is listed as darker green, although I see little difference between it and the species type.

Pachysandra procumbens, Allegheny Pachysandra

Pachysandra procumbens 'Eco Treasure'

Pachysandra procumbens flowers

Palms

Approximately 2800 species of palms grow in the far-flung lands of the subtropical and tropical climates of the earth. A selected few are cold hardy to Zone (6)7 and in recent years have become fashionable elements in Atlanta landscapes, particularly Trachycarpus fortunei, *Chinese Windmill Palm. Over my gardening tenure in Georgia, six palm species have been grown, with only* Rhapidiophyllum hystrix, *Needle Palm, the clear-cut survivor. Fifty to 100 miles south of Athens-Atlanta, palms increase in landscape commonality.* Butia capitata, *Pindo Palm;* Trachycarpus fortunei; Sabal palmetto, *Cabbage Palm; and* Sabal minor, *Dwarf Palmetto, dot the countryside, looking somewhat out of place among the pines and deciduous trees.*

Palms are easily transplanted and often container-grown, making the process even easier. Palms have ropelike roots, like a corn plant, and large trees are often moved with a small root ball. I witnessed Sabal palmetto *lying on the ground in a garden center in Columbia, South Carolina, all parts exposed without protection. Plant in well-drained soil, provide adequate moisture and fertility. Palms require little care once established and from my observations withstand more abuse than most trees and shrubs. Palms are extremely wind-tolerant, and even Hurricane Hugo was unable to significantly dislodge* S. palmetto *from the South Carolina coast.*

Palms tolerate full sun and significant degrees of shade. The Needle Palm in the Dirr garden grows in the shade of a Southern Red Oak and has performed magnificently. The same species grows equally well in full sun. Palms like Caryota, Chamaedorea, Howea, Phoenix, Livistona, *and others function as indoor plants because of shade*

MORE ➤

Palms continued

tolerance. Mites and other sucking insects are occasional problems on indoor plants.

Palms elongate from the terminal meristem and increase in diameter via the primary thickening meristem. Take care not to injure the growing point in transplanting. I have observed large transplanted trees where the two or three leaves above the meristem are all that remain, and these are tied into a bundle for protection.

Cold is the major limiting factor to successful culture, and leaf edges, entire leaves, and often the growing point are injured by repeated low temperatures. Leaves may be killed outright, with growth renewed from the undamaged meristem. If cold damage occurs, wait until early summer for new growth before removing the plant. Typically, younger plants are more susceptible to severe cold damage than older, established plants.

Landscape uses are abundant: single specimen, groupings, containers, and foundation planting are the most common. Be adventurous, for palms offer foliage, texture, and form nowhere else available in the woody plant world. Ask yourself how many resort hotels utilize palms in lobbies and outdoor settings to evoke the aura of elegance, hospitality, and warmth.

Caryota mitis

Butia capitata
PINDO PALM

Beautiful small tree species with stout trunk and 3- to 6-ft.-long, pinnately compound, grayish to bluish green leaves. The leaves arch gracefully, creating a semi-pendent to weeping effect. The crown is relatively dense and full. Older, declining leaves should be removed by cutting the large woody petiole base as close to the trunk as possible. Fruit are orange-yellow drupes, about 1 in. wide, edible, and with a pineapple flavor. Species displays high salt tolerance and is often planted on the ocean side of houses and resort complexes. Used in parking lot islands, which attests to its high heat and drought tolerances. Grows 12 to 18 ft. high, about one-half this in spread. Zones 8 to 11. In the early 1980s, I was involved with assessing cold damage at a resort on the Georgia coast; low temperature was 11°F, and this species was largely uninjured. South America.

Butia capitata, Pindo Palm

Chamaerops humilis
MEDITERRANEAN or EUROPEAN FAN PALM

Handsome small clumping species that develops a rounded outline with 18- to 24-in.-wide leaves, each divided into narrow segments. Foliage color ranges from green to blue-green. Petiole is covered with sharp, spiny teeth that point toward the leaf blade. Provide well-drained soil in full sun to heavy shade. Slow-growing in more northern areas. Useful in a container, foundation plantings, and groupings. Grows 3 to 6 ft. high, often wider; potential in warmest areas to 15 to 20 ft. high. Zones (8)9 to 11. Listed as surviving 10 to 15°F; one reference noted 6°F. Mediterranean region.

Chamaerops humilis, Mediterranean Fan Palm

Livistona chinensis, Chinese Fan Palm

Livistona chinensis
CHINESE FAN PALM

Handsome species with large, coarse-textured, palmate leaves and smooth trunks resulting from the clean abscisson of the leaf bases. Often described as single-stemmed, but specimens I observed were full and dense, as wide as they were high. The emerald-green leaves are 3 to 6 ft. across, the segments cut one-third to one-half the diameter and the lobes arching at their extremities like a cupped hand facing the ground. The petiole is about as long as the blade, with brown, ¾- to 1-in.-long spines from the base to the middle. The trunk, about 1 ft. thick at maturity, is gray and marked with the scars of the fallen leaf bases. The plant in youth is trunkless and forms a large mound, eventually becoming tree-like. Grows best in well-drained, moist, fertile soil, in sun and partial shade. Protect in more northernly

MORE ➤

Livistona chinensis petiole

Livistona chinensis leaf

Livistona chinensis continued

areas. Handsome accent and container plant. Have observed it massed in an understory planting. Grows 10 to 15 (to 20 to 30) ft. high. Zones 9 to 11. Temperatures in the low to mid twenties will injure foliage. Southern Japan, Ryukyu Islands, Bonin Island, southern Taiwan.

Phoenix canariensis
CANARY ISLAND DATE PALM

A large specimen on St. Simons Island, Georgia, was killed outright by 11°F; however, the plant had grown in the location for around 30 years. A large, thickish, single-trunked palm with globular head of dark green, upright and arching fronds.

Each lustrous dark green, compound pinnate leaf is up to 15 ft. long. The thick, gray-brown trunk has diamond-shaped leaf bases, wider than high, on the mature trunk, with old petiole bases persisting below the crown. The yellow-red, oblong-ellip-

Phoenix canariensis trunk

Phoenix canariensis, Canary Island Date Palm

Phoenix roebelinii, Pygmy Date Palm

Rhapidiophyllum hystrix
NEEDLE PALM

soid fruit, ¾ in. in diameter, appear in large paniculate clusters during the warm months. Prefers full sun, fertile, well-drained soil. Used as an avenue, boulevard, street tree; specimen palm; and accent plant. Beautiful habit that elicits accolades from those who know little about palms. Grows 20 to 30 ft. high, 15 ft. wide; full-grown plants about 60 ft. high. Zones 9 to 11. Temperatures below 20°F injure foliage. Canary Islands.

The related species *Phoenix reclinata*, Senegal Date Palm, is used as a specimen palm at the Disney complexes in Orlando. A low-branched, clumping species, the branches recurving upward and wide-spreading. The dark green, pinnate leaves range from 10 to 20 ft. in length. Grows 15 to 25 ft. high, wider at maturity. Only for the warmest areas of Zone 9, into 10 and 11. Below 28 to 30°F, leaf damage will occur. Tropical Africa.

Phoenix roebelinii, Pygmy Date Palm, is a fine-textured, lustrous green, graceful arching, pinnate-leaved species that grows 4 to 6 ft. high, 5 ft. wide. A common container plant in northern gardens and conservatories. Bears slender, needlelike spines along the petiole base. Zones 10 to 11. Laos.

Without debate, the most cold hardy palm, with reports of its culture as far north as Cincinnati, Ohio. A rounded, dense-foliaged palm with the characteristic needlelike spines in the center of the clump from which the leaf bases arise. The palmate leaves, lustrous dark green, are divided almost to the base into seven to twenty stiff segments. Individual leaf blades are up to 3 ft. across on 2- to 3-ft.-long, slender, unarmed petioles. Trunk is thick and short, and does not elongate; it is covered with the leaf bases, spines, and brown matting. Found in a variety of soils in the wild, from river bluffs and limestone hammocks to seepage areas and moist to wet flood plains, often in shade. Tolerates drought and heavy soils under cultivation. Probably the best no-brainer for someone remotely interested in palms. Good evergreen shrub for containers, accent plant, shady border. Has been a winner in the Dirr garden. Grows 6 to 8 ft. high and wide. Zones 7 to 11. South Carolina, Georgia, Florida, Alabama, and Mississippi.

Rhapidiophyllum hystrix, Needle Palm

Phoenix reclinata, Senegal Date Palm

258

Rhapis excelsa
LADY PALM

Handsome small palm with dark green, fingerlike lobes and refined aesthetic habit. Forms clusters to clumps of canelike stems covered with brown fibers toward the top, becoming smoother with maturity. The overall effect is reminiscent of bamboo, particularly *Sasa palmata*. The palmate leaves are divided into five to ten segments, cut almost to the base, with the petiole unarmed. Leaves are 10 to 20 in. across. Requires moderate to heavy shade, deep, moist, organic, well-drained soils. Useful in foundations, containers, and shady borders, and as a textural accent. Grows 5 to 10 ft. high and wide. Zones 9 to 11, 8 with protection. Southern China.

Sabal palmetto
CABBAGE PALM

The most common tree palm in the Coastal Plain of the Southeast, utilized as a single specimen, in groupings, along streets, and in groves. Single-trunked, with the old leaf bases attached or cleanly abscising with a few below the crown. The crown is usually quite full, with the lower leaves gently arching. The leaves are costa palmate, somewhere between pinnate and palmate, to 6 ft. long and 3 ft. wide, divided one-third of the way to the base with many threadlike leaf pieces in the sinuses (indentations). Leaves vary from gray-green to green. Fruit are rounded, brown-black, ¼-in.-diameter drupes. I noticed fruiting specimens in Savannah, Georgia, that were dropping over the walks and streets. Adaptable species, tolerating urban conditions to the best garden soils. Extremely salt- and wind-tolerant and grows (happily) in coastal

Rhapis excelsa, Lady Palm

Sabal etonia

Sabal palmetto trunk

sands. Found wild in coastal forest, tidal flats, elevated areas in marshes. Wonderful hardy species for coastal South Carolina to Texas. Have observed as far north as Ocean City, Maryland, where it was struggling. Grows 30 to 40 (to 60) ft. high. Zones 8 to 11. Lower Coastal Plain of southeast Georgia and South Carolina into Florida.

I have tried a host of smaller shrubby species—*Sabal etonia, S. minor, S. mexicana (S. texana)*—with no success. The −3°F low temperature and back-to-back cold winters of 1984 and 1985 devastated marginal or borderline plants.

MORE ➤

Sabal minor, Dwarf Palmetto

Sabal palmetto, Cabbage Palm

Sabal palmetto continued

Sabal minor, Dwarf Palmetto, grows 6 to 10 ft. high with large, fan-shaped leaves, up to 3 ft. across, with 30 to 40 swordlike segments, 1 to 5 ft. long, pointing forward and arching; petioles up to 5 ft. long. Leaves are deeply cut to the base, producing 30 to 40 daggerlike segments varying from shiny dark green to blue-green in coloration. A distinct blue-foliaged form ('Glauca') is in cultivation. The stem usually is at or below ground level but with age may develop above ground. Forms suckering colonies in wet and poorly drained soils in the wild. Tolerates salt spray. Handsome foliage mass, textural accent, or foundation plant. Zones 8 to 11. North Carolina to Florida, Texas, and Arkansas.

Serenoa repens
SAW PALMETTO

Almost a frightening experience in the wild, where the spreading trunks, covered with leaf bases and brown fiber, look like large snakes. Habit is dense, suckering, colonizing, forming large-spreading, impenetrable thickets. I walked the shoreline of the north end of Jekyll Island, Georgia, where the trunks are exposed by the pounding sea; some are 9 to 12 in. thick—formidable antagonists to the ocean's eroding forces. The palmate leaves are 2 to 3 ft. wide, divided into 25 or 30 segments cut over halfway to the base. Each leaf segment is cleft and sharp to the touch. Additionally, the 3- to 4-ft.-long petioles have sharp saw-teeth on the basal portion. Leaf color is dark green, although bluish green to silver-green selections occur. Grows in shade and sandy soils in the wild; also found in wetter situations. I notice that coastal developments are preserving the species by limiting construction and building boardwalks over established plantings. Grows 6 to 10 ft. high, spreading indefinitely. Zones 8 to 11. South Carolina to Florida and Louisiana.

Sabal minor fruit

Serenoa repens, Saw Palmetto

Serenoa repens spreading trunks

Syagrus romanzoffianum leaflets

Syagrus romanzoffianum
(*Arecastrum romanzoffianum*)
QUEEN PALM

I learned this species as *Arecastrum* and then was subjected to the spelling-bee *Syagrus*. Nomenclature aside, the Queen Palm is an elegant, large, single-trunked species with feathery, dark green (both surfaces) leaves. Leaves range from 8 to 15 ft. in length, with the drooping leaflets up to 3 ft. long and the petiole entire. I first witnessed the species in H. P. Leu Gardens, Orlando, Florida, and this aristocratic species was forever imprinted as a standout among their large collection. The 1- to 2-ft.-diameter trunk is gray and smooth with irregular bulges over its length. Best sited in well-drained soils in full sun. Displays moderate salt tolerance. Use for streets, formal plantings, and as a specimen palm. Grows 40 ft. high or more. Zones 9 to 11. Expect some leaf damage at 25°F, but has recovered from temperatures in the mid teens. South America.

Syagrus romanzoffianum, Queen Palm

Trachycarpus fortunei
CHINESE WINDMILL PALM

'Tis difficult to reconcile that one is looking at a palm on the west coast of Scotland at the latitude of Newfoundland, but indeed at Inverewe Gardens, this most hardy tree species grew with great resolve. Usually a small tree in the 10- to 20-ft.-high range in Zones 7 and 8, a 30-ft.-high plant grew in a protected corner of a church in Athens, Georgia. The trunk, about 1 ft. in diameter, is usually smaller at the base, fattest toward the top, and densely covered with brown, stringy fibers and old leaf bases. Identification is easy for this palm, especially if it is growing in Zones 7 and upper 8, for there is nothing to confuse it with. The leaves are palmate, 2 to 3 ft. across, cut almost to the base with the segments arching near the tops. Color is dark green, grayish below, the petiole rough and bumpy but without teeth. The canopy is ovoid-globular, with the lowest leaves often tatty. Needs tidying to keep it smiling. Adaptable to any soil except wet, full sun to partial shade. Displays wind, drought, and salt tolerance. Grows slowly in colder climates, so can be craftily engaged in foundation plantings.

MORE ➤

Trachycarpus fortunei leaf

Trachycarpus fortunei continued

Good container plant or tropical look in annual and perennial plantings. Grows 10 to 20 (to 40) ft. high. Zones 8 to 11, 7 with protection. China.

Trachycarpus fortunei trunk

Washingtonia robusta
MEXICAN FAN or WASHINGTON PALM

Native to Mexico that is common in Florida, less so in California, where _Washingtonia filifera_ is the native and preferred species. Large growing with a narrow trunk, especially at the base, a rounded crown, and older leaves that persist, forming a dense skirt. The palmate leaves, divided halfway to the base, are bright green and 3 to 5 ft. across, with the tips slightly drooping. The 3- to 4-ft.-long petiole, reddish brown, is armed with prominent yellow-green spines. Prospers in dry, well-drained, sandy soils and full sun. The trunk is smooth toward the base, with leaf bases near the crown. Use as a specimen, in groupings, and for street plantings. Grows 40 to 80 ft. high. Zones 8 to 11. Temperatures of 20°F and below result in injury.

Washingtonia filifera, California or Desert Fan Palm, is similar but with a thicker trunk and the long-petioled, 3- to 6-ft.-long leaves form a more open crown. Grows 60 ft. high. Considered slightly more cold hardy than _W. robusta_. Hybrids occur between the two species.

Trachycarpus fortunei, Chinese Windmill Palm

Washingtonia robusta, Mexican Fan Palm

Washingtonia robusta at Longwood Gardens

Washingtonia robusta petioles

Parkinsonia aculeata
JERUSALEM THORN

Feathery, light, airy, small tree with bipinnately compound foliage composed of tiny, bright green leaflets. Habit is open-arching, broad-spreading, either single or multi-stemmed. The leaves range from 8 to 16 in. in length with ¼- to ½-in.-long, small, linear, rich green leaflets. The bark is green, becoming brown and fissured with age. Stems are armed with thorns at the nodes. The beautiful yellow flowers, with orange markings, ¾ to 1 in. wide, fragrant, open in spring and repeat in summer with new growth flushes. The fruit are gray-brown, 6-in.-long pods. On the Georgia Coastal Islands, the species performs magnificently in full sun and well-drained soil. Excellent drought and alkaline soil tolerance. Displays high degree of salt tolerance. Makes a small specimen tree; be careful in siting because of the thorns. Grows 15 to 20 ft. high and wide. Zones 8 to 11. Caribbean.

Parkinsonia aculeata, Jerusalem Thorn

Parkinsonia aculeata foliage and flowers

Parkinsonia aculeata flowers

Parrotiopsis jacquemontiana foliage and flowers

Parrotiopsis jacquemontiana

A unique member of the witchhazel family (Hamamelidaceae) with coarsely toothed leaves that resemble those of *Hamamelis*, witchhazel. Rare in cultivation and probably reserved for the collector of biological antiquities. An upright, oval to rounded shrub with stiff branches and dense foliage—kind of unmistakable when confronted. The roundish dark green leaves, 2 to 3½ in. long and wide, seldom develop appreciable fall color. The true flowers are borne in small clusters in April and May, subtended by four to six, petal-like, ½- to 1-in.-long, white bracts. Certainly the flowers do not overwhelm but are curiously interesting. Site in partial shade, although the plant will grow in full sun. Provide moist, acid, well-drained soil. Use for accent, for novelty, or to drive visitors loony. Grows 8 to 12 ft. high. Zones 5 to 7. Himalayas.

Parthenocissus henryana
SILVERVEIN CREEPER

For 22 years in Georgia, I observed this beautiful vine complete its seasonal cycles yet have *never* seen it offered in southern commerce. Like the close relatives *Parthenocissus quinquefolia* and *P. tricuspidata*, it is a true clinging vine, meaning small, cuplike holdfasts "glue" it to structures. The emerging leaves are bronze-purple, maturing to dark blue-green with silver veins above, purplish on the lower surface. In autumn, leaves become red to reddish purple. Best sited in some shade in moist, well-drained soil. Common in England and offers greater aesthetics than *P. quinquefolia* and *P. tricuspidata*. Grows 15 ft. or more. Zones (6)7 to 8. China.

MORE ➤

Parrotiopsis jacquemontiana

Parthenocissus henryana foliage

Parrotiopsis jacquemontiana foliage

Parthenocissus henryana, Silvervein Creeper

Parthenocissus henryana continued

Parthenocissus henryana fall color

Passiflora incarnata, Wild Passion Vine

Passiflora incarnata fruit

Passiflora caerulea, Blue Passion Flower

Passiflora incarnata
WILD PASSION VINE, MAYPOP

Native vine, almost invasive but with the most beautiful floral configuration of any flowering plant. The photograph does justice to the flower, which is best described as a complex of five petals, five sepals, a row (or two) of threadlike fringe above the petals, and five elevated anthers, each with a broad stigma that encircles three styles. Flowers, 2 to 3 in. wide, open from May through autumn, never in great numbers, the colors ranging from lavender to white. Leaves are three-lobed, dark green, 2 to 6 in. long and wide. Fruit are 1½- to 3-in.-diameter, ovoid berries, green ripening to yellow, containing numerous dark brown seeds. Grows on moist to dry sites in nature, full sun to semi-shade. Overwinters as a rootstock. Climbs by tendrils, similar to grapes. Not utilized enough in modern gardens. Good on trellises, arbors, fences. Attracts butterflies. Grows 10 to 20 ft. but easily restrained by pruning. Zones 6 to 9. Pennsylvania to Illinois, Missouri, Oklahoma, south to Florida and Texas.

About 500 species worldwide, but only a few are in commerce. *Passiflora caerulea*, Blue Passion Flower, is semi-evergreen to evergreen in Zones 9b to 11. Leaves are five-lobed, compared to the three-lobed leaves of *P. incarnata*. Flower colors vary from white to pale pink and blue. Fruit are orange. Brazil, Argentina.

Passiflora coccinea, Red Passion Flower, is semi-evergreen to evergreen with brilliant scarlet flowers. Zones 10 and 11. Southern Venezuela, Peru, Bolivia, Brazil.

Persea borbonia
REDBAY

A broadleaf evergreen native shrub or tree that grows in standing water yet also withstands drier conditions. On the Outer Banks of North Carolina, plants were growing in water; on Georgia's Jekyll Island, a 40-ft.-high tree was prospering in sandy soil. Leaves are lustrous medium green, 2 to 6 in. long, becoming yellow-green in exposed (to wind or sun) locations. The ovoid-rounded, dark blue to black, ½-in.-long drupes ripen in October. Useful for naturalizing in difficult sites. Leaves are often infested with a gall and appear swollen, water-soaked, and ugly. Grows 20 to 30 ft. high, two-thirds to equal this in spread. Zones (7)8 to 9. Southern Delaware to Florida, westward to southeastern Texas.

Persea borbonia foliage

Persea borbonia fruit

Philadelphus inodorus
MOCKORANGE

Native southeastern member of the *Philadelphus* clan that to most gardeners is represented only by *Philadelphus coronarius*. I first identified the plant 22 years past, growing in the shade garden area of the University's Botanical Garden. I kept smelling the flowers with no resultant odor detected, and the name *P. inodorus* was brought into nasal focus. Habit is upright-oval, multistemmed, with opposite, 2- to 4-in.-long, dark green, three-veined, serrate to entire leaves engulfing the upper one-third to one-half of the plant. The four-petaled, white flowers are 1 to 1½ in. in diameter and are borne in terminal axillary cymes of three. Flowers are present from May into June and are followed by small, brown capsules. Tough plant that requires only sun, and moderately moist, well-drained soil for maximum effect; however, plants in half shade flower respectably. Good border plant, as a filler along woodland edges, and for a screen in partial shade. Grows 6 to 10 ft. high, 6 to 8 ft. wide. Zones (5)6 to 9. Pennsylvania to Tennessee, south to Florida and Mississippi.

Philadelphus pubescens, Hairy Mockorange, has leaves pubescent on their undersides and flowers borne in racemes, otherwise similar to *P. inodorus*. Zones 6 to 9. Illinois, south to Tennessee and Arkansas.

MORE ➤

Persea borbonia, Redbay

Philadelphus inodorus flowers and foliage

Philadelphus pubescens, Hairy Mockorange

Philadelphus pubescens underside of leaf

Philadelphus inodorus continued

Philadelphus inodorus, Mockorange

Phillyrea angustifolia

Closely related to *Osmanthus* and often confused with that genus. The habit is dense and rounded with smallish, narrow, lustrous dark green, 1- to 1½-in.-long leaves. Small, white, fragrant flowers open in spring, followed by blackish fruit. Like *Osmanthus* species, grows in sun to moderate shade in any well-drained soil. Useful for screens, hedges, and fillers. Grows 10 ft. high and wide. Zones 7 to 9. China, Japan.

Phillyrea angustifolia foliage

Phillyrea angustifolia flowers

Phillyrea angustifolia

Photinia ×fraseri
FRASER or REDTIP PHOTINIA

Both a blessing and a curse, for at one time it was the most widely grown and sold hedging/screening plant in the Southeast. The beautiful ruby-red new growth has enticed gardeners worldwide to utilize the plant. In the southeastern United States, millions were planted. The allure and economic power of an aesthetic hedging plant are phenomenal. Unfortunately, a devastating fungal disease (caused by *Entomosporium maculatum*) has wreaked havoc. In its finest form, an upright, oval, broadleaf evergreen shrub becoming treelike if left to itself. Often pruned into a block of red and green for screening purposes, it makes a pretty small tree when trained to a single stem. In fact, some southern cities have used the species for street tree plantings. The young leaves emerge ruby-red, mature to dark green, and subsequent growth is also reddish turning to green. White, malodorous flowers occur in 5- to 6-in.-wide, terminal corymbs in April. Red fruit mature in late summer. At its finest, one of the most adaptable plants growing in hot, dry, miserable soils in sun to moderate shade but thriving where moisture and sunlight are available. Also quite salt-tolerant. At one time, the premier hedging and

MORE ➤

Photinia ×fraseri new foliage

Photinia ×fraseri foliage

Photinia ×fraseri flowers

Photinia ×fraseri **continued**

screening plant. To appreciate the numbers produced, one Georgia nursery's wholesale sales were $3 million in redtips out of $20 million total sales. Grows 10 to 15 ft. high. Zones 7 to 9, 10 on the West Coast. Originated as a chance seedling at the Fraser Nurseries, Birmingham, Alabama, around 1940.

Cultivars and Varieties. 'Red Robin', with darker ruby-red foliage and more rounded, spreading habit, is popular in Europe.

'Robusta' is larger growing, more treelike, with coppery red leaves; a 25-ft.-high specimen grows in the Hillier Arboretum.

Photinia ×fraseri 'Red Robin'

Photinia glabra 'Rubens'

Photinia glabra 'Rubens' new foliage

Photinia glabra 'Variegata'

Photinia glabra
JAPANESE PHOTINIA

Quite a handsome broadleaf evergreen shrub with red new growth that settles to a life of green. One of the parents of *Photinia ×fraseri* and, unfortunately, the carrier of the genes for susceptibility to leaf spot. Several plants on the Georgia campus have formed dense oval-rounded outlines. The leaves are 1½ to 3½ in. long, emerge rich bronzy red, finally glossy dark green, and are without hairs, hence, *P. glabra*. Flowers and fruit are similar to *P. ×fraseri*, except smaller. The limiting factor is leaf spot, so where annual rainfall is high, resist the temptation to plant. Grows 10 to 12 ft. high and wide. Zones (7)8 to 10. Plants were killed to the ground at −3°F. Japan, China.

Cultivars and Varieties. The species and cultivars prosper in European climates and the West Coast; 'Rubens', a bright, bronze-red leaf form, and 'Variegata', pink and bronze-red new leaves, maturing white and green, are reasonably common.

Photinia serrulata new foliage

Photinia serrulata
CHINESE or ORIENTAL PHOTINIA

Although uncommon, it is the most disease-resistant species and, in its own aesthetic matrix, a respectable broadleaf evergreen shrub or tree. Habit is upright in youth, gradually evolving into an oval-rounded form. Makes a respectable small tree and, if trained single-stemmed, could be utilized along streets. The new leaves are apple-green to bronze-tinted, maturing lustrous dark green. Immense clusters of stinky, white flowers appear in late March and early April. With the advent of autumn, the ¼-in.-diameter fruit turn their characteristic red. Fruit persist into winter and are foraged by the birds. Stray seedlings pop up in fence rows and woodland habitats, the leaves strongly cut and incised like holly. As leaves mature, the serrations become less dramatic and uniform; actually difficult to believe the young leaves come from the same species. Prospers in any soil except wet, in full sun to moderate shade.

MORE ➤

Photinia serrulata, Chinese Photinia

Photinia serrulata **continued**

Could prove useful for screens, hedges, and as a small tree. Does not have the calling-card red new growth of *Photinia ×fraseri* and *P. glabra* but is the preferred choice because of high disease resistance. Grows 20 to 25 (to 30) ft. high, about two-thirds that in spread. Witnessed a 50-ft. specimen in England. Zones 6 to 9, 10 on the West Coast. China.

Cultivars and Varieties. 'Green Giant' is an oval-rounded form, 30 to 45 ft. high, 20 to 30 ft. wide, with apple-green new growth, lustrous dark green at maturity; selected by the author from the Univeristy of Georgia campus.

Photinia serrulata flowers

Photinia serrulata fruit

Photinia serrulata 'Green Giant'

Pieris formosana var. *forrestii*
HIMALAYAN PIERIS

One of the most beautiful of all the *Pieris* species, with the electric-red new growth literally stopping people in their tracks. During our English garden tours, this plant receives as much attention as any. The new growth transitions from red to cream then to green, and any subsequent new growth is similar in coloration. The habit is quite dense, eventually rounded in outline. The 2- to 4-in.-long leaves are larger than other *Pieris* species. Flowers in large, to 6-in.-long, terminal clusters appear in late winter to spring. The urn-shaped, $1/3$-in.-long, fragrant flowers are effective for four to six weeks. Provide cool, moist environment akin to San Francisco and the Pacific Northwest. Unbelievably colorful in a border. A great conversation piece. Grows 10 ft. high and wide. Zones 8 to 10 on the West Coast. Western China, Burma.

Cultivars and Varieties. Two relatively common selections in Europe include 'Wakehurst', with brilliant red leaves, and 'Forest Flame', with similar foliage coloration.

Pieris formosana var. *forrestii* 'Wakehurst'

Pieris formosana var. *forrestii*, Himalayan Pieris

Pieris formosana var. *forrestii* 'Wakehurst' flowers

Pieris formosana var. *forrestii* 'Wakehurst' new foliage

274

Pieris phillyreifolia
VINE-WICKY

This humble broadleaf evergreen vine/shrub is found in swampy habitats in the Southeast, often growing on Baldcypress, *Taxodium distichum*. Typically a vine in the previous habitat, it develops into a small shrub when brought into garden culture. Beautiful leathery lustrous dark green leaves, ¾ to 2½ in. long, are revolute (turned under) around the margins. Milk-white, ⅓-in.-long, urn-shaped flowers appear in three- to nine-flowered racemes in late winter to early spring. Beautiful plant for the collector. Would appear to have potential for breeding root-rot resistance and heat tolerance into *Pieris japonica*. Grows 1 to 2 ft. high as a shrub. Zones 7 to 9. South Carolina, Georgia, Florida, and Alabama.

Pinckneya pubens
(*P. bracteata*)
PINCKNEYA, FEVERBARK

One of the early (1979–82) plants in the Dirr garden because of its beautiful flowers (bracts). Cold in the early 1980s (–3°F) killed it to the ground, yet 120 or so miles south near Macon, Georgia, it grows naturally in abundance. Large shrub to small tree, often loose and open. Needs to be integrated with other plants to look its best in a garden setting. Large leaves, up to 8 in. long, oppositely arranged and semi-dog-eared, emerge bronze-green, becoming medium to dark green. True flowers are yellowish green, mottled brown and purple, ½ to 1 in. long, with five reflexed corolla lobes resulting in a distinct trumpet-shaped flower. The large bracts, white to

Pieris phillyreifolia, Vine-wicky

Pinckneya pubens foliage, bracts, and flowers

Pinckneya pubens, Feverbark

pink, subtend the flowers and provide the pizzazz. Flowers, which open in June in Athens, are effective for several weeks and beyond. Fruit are ¾-in.-diameter, two-valved capsules that contain numerous flattish seeds. Seeds germinate immediately upon sowing. Provide moisture and soils rich with organic matter. Have observed plants in sun and partial shade. The plant in the Dirr garden was on the north side of the house. Unique and quite beautiful signature plant. Not common but worth pursuing. Grows 10 to 20 ft. high, less in spread. Zones (7b)8 to 9. Found in low wet woods in South Carolina to Florida.

Pinus clausa
SAND PINE

A pine that is grown only in the Deep South, where I observed it functioning as a windbreak. A soft, pyramidal tree, short-statured compared to many pines. Bark is relatively smooth in youth, becoming reddish brown and scaly. Needles are rich green, in twos, sometimes threes, often twisted or bent, 1½ to 3 in. long. Cones are ovoid-oblong, 2 to 3 in. long, brown, with hard, inflexible scales, and a prickle on each scale back. Open and closed cones may be on the same tree. Strictly for use in deep, sandy soils, where it is found in the wild. Picturesque growth habit. Has been domesticated for Christmas tree use. Grows 30 to 40 ft. high, 20 ft. wide, although the national champions are all over 90 ft. high. Zones 8 and 9. Florida, southwestern Alabama.

Pinus echinata
SHORTLEAF PINE

Among the most beautiful southern pines in old age. Artistically assembled, with a long slender bole (trunk), a narrow pyramidal crown with sinuous, contorted branches, and scalelike bark that is arranged in jigsaw puzzle pieces. I tell my students the easiest way to distinguish this from *Pinus taeda*, Loblolly Pine, is by the puzzle-piece bark and sinuous branches compared to the ridged and furrowed bark and straight branches of *P. taeda*. Needles occur in fascicles (bundles) of two, occasionally three, dark bluish green, 2 to 4½ in. long. Cones are dark brown-black, 1½ to 2½ in. long, and 1 to 1½ in. wide. Extremely tolerant of harsh sites, it grows naturally on dry, upland soils. Useful in groupings and groves. Towering mature specimens on the Georgia campus inspire and humble. Grows 80 to 100 ft. high. Zones 6 to 9. New Jersey, south to Georgia, Texas, Oklahoma.

MORE ➤

Pinus echinata, Shortleaf Pine

Pinus echinata sinuous branches

Pinus echinata continued

Pinus echinata bark

Pinus elliottii bark

Pinus elliottii cones

Pinus elliottii

SLASH PINE

Another important southern timber species with a more coastal distribution. I frequently mistake this species for *Pinus taeda*. A tall tree, trunk slender, with an ovoid crown. The 4- to 9- (to 12-) in.-long, glossy dark green needles appear in fascicles of two, occasionally three. The cones are ovoid, 3½ to 6 in. long, lustrous chestnut-brown, and armed with a short prickle at the end of each scale. With age, the red-brown to purple-brown bark is fractured into large, irregular blocks with scaly, flaking plates, similar to that of *P. echinata*. Excellent species for use in the Coastal Plain of the Southeast. Grows in wet soils, inter-dune hollows, and near coastal sands. Like *P. taeda* and *P. echinata*, excellent in groupings and groves. Grows 80 to 100 ft. high. Zones 8 to 10. South Carolina to Florida, west to southeastern Mississippi and Louisiana.

Pinus elliottii, Slash Pine

Pinus glabra
SPRUCE PINE

Unique two-needled pine that I envisioned as the next great Christmas tree and screening pine for the Southeast: a beautiful oval-rounded crown, dark green summer needles, and varied soil tolerances suggested landscape greatness. It was tested in Athens and grown by a local nursery, but it became obvious that the winter yellowing of needles precluded wholesale acceptance. Open-grown trees tend to hold their branches to the ground. The spirally twisted needles are 2 to 4 in. long. Cones, 1¾ to 3¾ in. long, brown, the scales with minute prickles, often persist two to four years. Bark is dark gray, closely ridged and furrowed, producing small, thin, reddish brown plates suggestive of *Picea* bark. Beautiful pine for naturalizing in the Deep South. Grows 40 to 60 ft. high. Zones 8 to 9(10). South Carolina to northern Florida to Louisiana.

Pinus glabra, Spruce Pine

Pinus glabra in youth

Pinus glabra bark

Pinus glabra needles

Pinus palustris, Longleaf Pine

Pinus palustris
LONGLEAF PINE

Ecologically, an important pine which survives through fires that burn off the competing grasses and weedy vegetation. Great acreages have been lost because of development and lack of natural fires. In youth the grass stage is apparent, a single stem with long needles producing a drooping mane. Eventually, side branches develop producing a Saguaro cactus look-alike. With age, a narrow crown of loosely arching needles develops. The brown bark becomes platy-scaly with age. The dark green needles, in fascicles of three, are 6 to 12 (to 18) in. long. The brown, ovoid-oblong cones, 6 to 8 (to 10) in. long, up to 5 in. wide, open promptly and abscise over winter. Extremely adaptable and common in the sandy or clay-sand ridges of Georgia. Useful in coastal landscapes, as it adds texture and unique architecture to large-scale plantings. Grows 60 to 70 ft. high. Zones 7 to 10. Southeastern Virginia to Florida, east to Texas.

Pinus palustris developing side branches

Pinus palustris cone

Pinus palustris bark

Pinus taeda
LOBLOLLY PINE

The forester's primary timber species in the Southeast and the landscaper's most reliable, fast growing, screening species. I have grown to admire its tenacity and persistence in colonizing highway cuts, banks, ditches, open grassy fields, abandoned agricultural land, and marsh edges along the coast. Pyramidal in youth, more open, with a slender trunk and wide-spreading, straight branches. Open-grown, large trees are enchanting. The needles, 6 to 10 in. long, in fascicles of three, occasionally two, are dark green. The ovoid-cylindrical, buff to rust-brown cones, 3 to 6 in. long, have sharp, recurved prickles on the backs of the scales. Several trees in our garden appear to "spit" cones on a daily basis. I have filled large garbage cans in a single cleanup. Easy to transplant from containers or when balled and burlapped. Settles in quickly, yielding 10 to 20 ft. of linear (height) growth in five to ten years. The best screening, massing, situational pine for the Southeast. It will establish where broadleaf trees cannot establish a toehold. Grows 60 to 90 ft. high. Zones 6 to 9. Southern New Jersey to Florida, west to eastern Texas and Oklahoma.

Pinus taeda, Loblolly Pine

Pinus taeda bark

Pinus taeda cones

Pistacia chinensis
CHINESE PISTACHE

An unheralded and largely unknown small to medium-sized tree that provides Sugar Maple–like fall color in the middle to Deep South. Oval-rounded to broad-rounded in outline, coarsely and irregularly branched in youth, becoming more uniform and dense with maturity. Bark becomes scaly, gray to gray-black, and as the scales flake off they expose salmon to orange inner bark. Compound pinnate leaves with ten to twelve leaflets, each 2 to 4 in. long and lustrous dark green, turn brilliant orange and orange-red in fall. I have walked seedling populations in autumn displaying every color from yellow-green to fluorescent red in their plumage.

Male and female flowers are greenish to purplish and open before the leaves in April. The robin's-egg-blue, ¼-in.-diameter, rounded drupaceous fruit ripen in October. Prospers in a wide range of soils and pH levels; once established, amazingly drought-tolerant. Full sun for best growth and fall foliage. High insect and disease tolerance. Great lawn, street, and park tree for South and West. When a selection for a male clone with excellent fall color that propagates easily is eventually made, the species will become the next, only better, Bradford Pear. Grows 30 to 35 ft. high, 25 to 35 ft. wide. Zones 6 to 9, 10 on the West Coast. China, Taiwan, Philippines.

Pistacia chinensis male flowers

Pistacia chinensis fruit

Pistacia chinensis, Chinese Pistache

Pistacia chinensis fall color

Pittosporum tenuifolium
TAWHIWHI, KOHUHO

A truly unique broadleaf evergreen of tight pyramidal-conical habit, possibly reserved only for the Mediterranean climate around San Francisco and other parts of the West Coast. Singularly beautiful in foliage, each 2- to 3-in.-long leaf has rolled (undulating) edges and lustrous dark green coloration. Numerous leaf selections have been introduced, including silver, yellow, purple, green maturing to purple, cream-edged, yellow-edged, and other permutations. Flowers (purple) and fruit are somewhat inconspicuous. Tolerant of sun and shade. Best in well-drained soil. Useful for a color accent in mixed plantings, screens, groupings, and even hedges. Grows 10 to 20 (to 30) ft. high. Zones 8 to 10 on the West Coast. New Zealand.

Pittosporum tenuifolium, Tawhiwhi, foliage and flowers

Pistacia chinensis in fall

Pistacia chinensis bark

Pittosporum tobira, Japanese Pittosporum

Pittosporum tobira 'Wheeler's Dwarf'

Pittosporum tobira
JAPANESE PITTOSPORUM

One of the most essential broadleaf evergreen shrubs for southern and West Coast landscapes, growing in sand, seaside conditions, full sun or shade, heat and drought. Wonderful, robust, dense, compact shrub, usually broad-mounded at maturity. Have observed the species pruned to small tree status and, indeed, picturesque plants 20 to 25 ft. high are known. Tough-as-rawhide leaves, recurved at the margins, measure 1½ to 4 in. long, up to 1½ in. wide. The lustrous dark green foliage color persists year-round in sun and shade. Flowers appear in April and May, when not removed by the pruning shears, and are borne in 2- to 3-in.-diameter, terminal umbels. Each ½- to 1-in.-diameter, five-petaled flower opens white, finally yellow, and provides orange-blossom fragrance. The fruit are pear-shaped, three-valved, ½-in.-diameter capsules. Easy to grow, withstands heavy pruning and salt spray. Used in foundation plantings; terrific under trees, in hedges, screens, buffers, and barrier plantings; effective in containers and raised planters. Grows 10 to 12 ft. high, one and one-half to two times this in width. Zones (7)8 to 10. Japan, Korea, China.

Cultivars and Varieties. 'Variegata' is one of the more genteel cream-edged forms, with the center of the leaf gray-green. Reasonably vigorous to 6 ft. and higher, same sweet floral fragrance as the species. A common house and conservatory plant in the North.

'Wheeler's Dwarf' is the best compact form of the species, 3 to 4 ft. high, slightly wider, forming a dense mound of lustrous green leaves.

Pittosporum tobira 'Variegata'

Pittosporum tobira pruned as a small tree

Plumbago auriculata
(*P. capensis*)
PLUMBAGO

Strictly a conservatory plant or summer annual in Zone 7 and north, but a fine evergreen vine to scandent shrub in Zone 8b and south. Forever it has been a remembrance of my visits to Longwood Gardens, where in the conservatory it grew across the aisle from the tropical Chinese Hibiscus, *Hibiscus rosa-sinensis*. Longwood visitors photograph the beautiful pale blue flowers while shunning the bright yellow, orange, and red flowers of the hibiscus. In Orlando, Florida, at Leu Gardens, this grew in the parking lot island planting next to *Callistemon* species. In habit, shoots fall over each other, producing a shrublike mass. Can also be trained on a trellis or similar structure. The light green leaves, ¾ to 3 in. long, are arranged alternately and clustered along the stem, providing a pleasing backdrop to the flowers. The azure-blue flowers, 1 to 1½ in. across, five-lobed, trumpet-shaped, occur on short racemes over much of the year. Heaviest flowering is from May through November, although flowers appear throughout the year. Well-drained, moderately fertile soils, and full sun are ideal. Flowers on new growth, so maintain active shoot production via pruning. Used as a groundcover and in bank and mass plantings; excellent spilling over the edges of

MORE ➤

Plumbago auriculata flowers

Plumbago auriculata, Plumbago

284

Plumbago auriculata continued

large containers. Grows 2 to 3 ft. high, 5 ft. wide; to 10 ft. on a climbing structure. Zones 9 to 11. South Africa.

Cultivars and Varieties. 'Alba' (var. *alba*) produces white flowers but is otherwise similar to the species.

Podocarpus macrophyllus 'Maki' seeds and receptacles

Podocarpus macrophyllus 'Maki' (var. *maki*)
SHRUBBY CHINESE PODOCARPUS

The true species has largely yielded landscape space to 'Maki' (var. *maki*), often called the Shrubby Chinese Podocarpus. The leaves of the species are 3 to 4 in. long; those of 'Maki' are ½ to 2¾ in. long and narrower. In youth an irregular columnar pyramid of feathery branches and needles, easily sculpted into any shape. In fact, in Florida and California, this is often used for topiary. The lustrous waxy dark green needles have two glaucous (gray) bands below. Bark is similar to yew, *Taxus*, reddish brown and loosely affixed in strips. Fruit (actually naked seeds), red to red-purple, ½ in. long, are attached to a fleshy receptacle, generally the same color. The species is dioecious, and the seeds are produced only on female plants. Adaptable to most soils, full sun to heavy shade. Abhors wet soils and cold; anything below 5 to 10°F produces injury or death. One of the best hedge and topiary plants. Grows 20 to 35 ft. high. Zones 8 to 10. Japan, southern China.

I have tested other *Podocarpus* species in Georgia with limited resultant enthusiasm. *Podocarpus alpinus*, Tasmanian Podocarp, and *P. nivalis*, Alpine Totara, are two of the hardiest. In well-drained soil, i.e., raised beds, such as provided by the Atlanta Botanical Garden, they persevered. In Georgia red clay and exposed conditions, the two species languished.

Podocarpus macrophyllus 'Maki' needles and seeds

Podocarpus macrophyllus bark

Podocarpus macrophyllus 'Maki', Shrubby Chinese Podocarpus

Podocarpus nivalis, Alpine Totara

Podocarpus macrophyllus

Podocarpus alpinus, Tasmanian Podocarp

Podocarpus salignus, Willowleaf Podocarp

MORE ➤

286

Podocarpus macrophyllus 'Maki' continued

Podocarpus salignus, Willowleaf Podocarp, develops a graceful pyramidal-rounded habit with 3- to 5-in.-long, lustrous dark green, "willowy" leaves. A beautiful evergreen but cold hardy only in Zones 8 to 10. Grows 20 to 30 ft. high. Southern Chile.

Cultivars and Varieties. Several spreading-bushy types: 'Brodie' is 3 ft. high, 6 ft. wide.

'Nana' is rounded and compact.

'Spreading' has a groundcover-like habit.

Podocarpus salignus foliage

Podocarpus nagi foliage

Podocarpus nagi
(*Nageia nagi*)
BROADLEAF PODOCARPUS

If appearance is everything, then this distant relative of the *Podocarpus* group needs shaping up. In fact, recent taxonomic treatment provided a new nomenclatural identity, *Nageia nagi*. The typical habit is softly pyramidal with lustrous dark green leaves, 1 to 3 in. long, ½ to 1¼ in. wide, with numerous veins running lengthwise. Could be mistaken for a *Eucalyptus* species or some member of the Liliaceae. Naked seeds are ½ in. wide, purple-red with a waxy plumlike bloom. Adaptable but cold sensitive. Utilize as a specimen or accent plant. Grows 30 to 40 ft. high, usually smaller. Zones 9 to 10. Southern Japan, Taiwan, and southern China.

Podocarpus nagi, Broadleaf Podocarpus

Poliothyrsis sinensis

For future generations to decide its garden merits, compelling facts are herein aggregated. My first exposure occurred in 1991 at the Arnold Arboretum, where in late July the white, aging to yellow, flowers were developing in 6- to 8-in.-long, loose, terminal panicles. The foliage, a rather nondescript medium green, turns yellow-burgundy in autumn. Emerging leaves are yellowish before maturing. Each leaf is 3 to 6 in. long with dentate margins and three prominent veins. Habit is shrublike, vase-shaped, with arching branches. Prefers full sun, moist, well-drained soil. Once established, tolerates drought. Could be utilized as a large shrub or fashioned into a small tree. Possibly lacks the aesthetic "oomph" necessary for the smaller contemporary landscape. Grows 15 to 20 ft. high and wide. Zones 6 to 8. Central China.

Poliothyrsis sinensis

Poliothyrsis sinensis flowers and foliage

Poliothyrsis sinensis new foliage

Prunus americana
AMERICAN RED PLUM

My old jogging treks introduced me to this species in both the tree form and colonizing habit. A handsome, small, oval-rounded tree or suckering thicket, not unlike sumac. The shiny dark green leaves, 2 to 4 in. long, sharply and doubly serrate, turn yellow to red in autumn. The pure white flowers, plum-fragrant, two to five together, open in March. Interestingly, the variation in flowering times is extensive, with one colony in full flower, another in tight bud. The yellow to red, 1-in.-long, yellow-fleshed fruit ripen in June and July. Tougher than cement and grows in comparable soils along roadsides, ditches, banks, and fence lines. Excellent wildlife plant, also useful for naturalizing. Appears to take care of itself with no grooming necessary. Grows 15 to 25 ft. high, 10 to 15 ft. wide. Zones 4 to 8. Massachusetts to Manitoba, south to Georgia, New Mexico, and Utah.

Prunus angustifolia, Chickasaw Plum, is similar and prevalent in comparable habitats. More colonizing, not as treelike. Flowers, ½ in. in diameter, white, plumlike fragrance, are evident by early March in Athens.

Prunus americana flowers

Prunus americana, American Red Plum

Prunus americana fall color

Prunus campanulata
BELL-FLOWERED or
TAIWAN CHERRY

The best flowering cherry for the Deep South, requiring minimal chilling hours to send its carmine-rose buds bursting forth. In the Dirr garden, it typically flowers in late February and early March, complementing the witchhazels. In fact, the two make a pretty bouquet. Small, graceful, rounded in outline with spreading branches, it is among the most admired plants in our garden. Typical cherry leaves: glands on the petiole, margins set with fine, slightly incurved teeth, lustrous dark green, occasionally yellow-bronze-red in autumn. The carmine-rose flowers, 1½ in. long, ¾ in. wide, five-petaled, open along the naked branches. If untainted by freezing temperatures, flowers may be expected to provide three weeks or more of color. When the petals fall, the calyx tube, a deep ruby-rose color, is exposed and extends the overall effect. The fruit are red, ½ in. long, ⅜ in. wide, appearing almost rounded. Adaptable to sand and clay soil, preferably acid and well-drained. Full sun to partial shade (pine) in coastal areas. Wonderful small garden tree. Should be in every gardener's top ten where it can be grown successfully. Grows 20 to 30

MORE ➤

Prunus angustifolia, Chickasaw Plum

Prunus angustifolia fruit

Prunus campanulata flowers

Prunus campanulata foliage

Prunus campanulata continued

ft. high and wide. Zones 7 to 9, 10 on the West Coast. Taiwan, southern China, Ryukyu Islands of Japan.

Cultivars and Varieties. 'Okame', a hybrid between *Prunus campanulata* and *P. incisa*, is discussed in *Dirr's Hardy Trees and Shrubs* (Portland, OR: Timber Press, 1997). Zones 5 to 8.

'Dream Catcher', an open-pollinated seedling of 'Okame', produces bright pink flowers one week after 'Okame'; dark green leaves turn orange-red in fall. A recent introduction from the U.S. National Arboretum, it grows 25 ft. high, 20 ft. wide in 12 years.

Prunus campanulata, Bell-flowered Cherry

Prunus caroliniana, Carolina Cherrylaurel

Prunus caroliniana pruned as a hedge

Prunus caroliniana

CAROLINA CHERRYLAUREL

A weed in the Coastal Plain of the Southeast, prevalent in fence rows and planted with regularity by the birds. Large evergreen shrub or small pyramidal-oval tree, although becomes more rounded and open with age. I questioned the identity of a 40-ft.-high tree in Orlando, Florida, never having observed one that large. The national champion, 47 ft. high and 55 ft. wide, resides in Lakeland, Florida. Bark is relatively smooth in youth, more irregular with time, dark gray to almost black. The scent of almond extract, inherent in the leaves and stems, is released when they are bruised; in fact, the odor equates with maraschino cherries. The 2- to 3- (to 4-) in.-long, lustrous dark green leaves are serrated in youth, entire on older plants. The sickeningly sweet, white flowers, each ¼ to ⅓ in. across, appear on 1½- to 3-in.-long racemes from the leaf axils in March and April. Flower effect is not potent but reliably effective for a long period. The top-shaped drupes, ⅜ to ½ in. in diameter, lustrous black, ripen in October and to some degree are present the next flowering cycle. Birds resist eating them until other, more palatable fruit are taken, but eat they do, and distribute with reckless abandon. Adaptable to well-drained sandy and clay soils in sun to partial shade. Utilize for screens and hedges and to soften harsh vertical lines. On the Georgia campus, hedges have been maintained for more than 21 years and are no less effective or aesthetic. Grows 20 to 30 (to 40) ft. high, 15 to 25 ft. wide. Zones 7 to 10. Coastal Virginia to northern Florida, west to Louisiana.

Cultivars and Varieties. Bright 'N Tight™ is a compact, tightly branched form, almost flame-shaped in outline, with lustrous dark green leaves. Grows 10 to 20 ft. high; makes a good hedge, screen, and barrier.

Prunus caroliniana fruit

Prunus caroliniana flowers and fruit

Prunus caroliniana Bright 'N Tight™

Prunus caroliniana foliage

Prunus laurocerasus
COMMON CHERRYLAUREL, ENGLISH LAUREL

A serviceable broadleaf evergreen shrub with cosmopolitan adaptability from Atlanta to Boston to the Pacific Coast. 'Tis a favorite of the landscape architecture clan and appears on their plans with the regularity of eraser marks. The numerous cultivars fill many landscape niches and have superseded the species, which is rarely planted. The species develops into a large evergreen shrub, oval-rounded to broad-spreading, of solid, dense constitution. Dark green, almost black-green, lustrous leaves, 2 to 6 (to 10) in. long, rank with yew for somber expression. To be sure, no broadleaf evergreen matches it leaf-to-leaf for effectiveness. Flowers, much like those of *Prunus caroliniana*, occur in 2- to 5-in.-long racemes from the leaf axils in April and May. The fragrance is a haunting, never-to-be-forgotten, plum aroma. Fruit are conical-rounded, purple to black, $\frac{1}{3}$- to $\frac{1}{2}$-in.-long drupes; seldom set on plants in the Southeast, more so in the West and Europe. Adaptable to sun and shade, requires well-drained soil. Shot hole—a disease complex that produces buckshot-like holes in leaves which enlarge, rendering the plant "mad dog" ugly—can be troublesome. Used for screens, groupings, hedges, foundations, and massing. Grows 10 to 18 ft. high and wide, or wider. Zones 6 to 8. Southeastern Europe into Asia.

Cultivars and Varieties. Many, over 40 described with four to five key players in North American horticulture.

Prunus laurocerasus foliage

Prunus laurocerasus, Common Cherrylaurel

'Magnoliifolia', with immense 10- to 12-in.-long, 3- to 4½-in.-wide, lustrous black-green leaves, grows 20 to 25 ft. high, one and one-half times as wide at maturity. At a distance, could be mistaken for *Magnolia grandiflora*.

'Majestic Jade' is a seedling selection from 'Otto Luyken' that grows 6 to 10 ft. high, 3 to 4 ft. wide, upright-oval in habit, with lustrous dark green leaves. It is more resistant to shot hole than 'Otto Luyken'.

'Marbled White', 'Marbled Dragon', and 'Castlewellan' are probably the same. Leaves splotched and streaked cream and green; unstable, reverting to green. Grows upright vase-shaped, 6 to 10 ft. high.

'Otto Luyken', the crown prince of cultivars, is small, 3 to 4 ft. high, 6 to 8 ft. wide, with 2- to 4-in.-long, lustrous black-green leaves. Upper leaves are borne at a 45° angle to stem; abundant flowers on mature plant.

'Schipkaensis' grows 4 to 5 (to 10) ft. high and wide, forming a dense mound of 2- to 4½-in.-long, lustrous dark green leaves, each leaf with a few serrations toward the apex. Several different forms masquerade

MORE ➤

Prunus laurocerasus flowers

Prunus laurocerasus 'Magnoliifolia' foliage

Prunus laurocerasus 'Magnoliifolia'

Prunus laurocerasus continued

under this name, with 'West Coast Schipkaensis' distinctly different—more upright with prominently serrated leaves.

'Zabeliana' has that dog-eared, gracefully arching, willowlike leaf appearance; leaves are not toothed, lustrous dark green, narrower than either 'Otto Luyken' or 'Schipkaensis'. Grows 5 ft. high and considerably greater in spread.

Prunus laurocerasus 'Otto Luyken' flowers

Prunus laurocerasus 'Otto Luyken' foliage

Prunus laurocerasus 'Otto Luyken'

Prunus laurocerasus 'Marbled White'

Prunus laurocerasus 'Majestic Jade'

Prunus laurocerasus 'Schipkaensis' fruit

Prunus laurocerasus 'Schipkaensis'

MORE ➤

Prunus laurocerasus continued

Prunus laurocerasus 'Zabeliana'

Prunus laurocerasus 'Zabeliana' foliage

Prunus mume 'Pendula'

Prunus mume

JAPANESE APRICOT

A favorite tree of the late great J. C. Raulston, North Carolina State University, who advocated its use in southern gardens with preacher-like zeal. Unique because it flowers in January and February, when gardening lies dormant in reality and in mind. But the explosion of fragrant white, pink, and red flowers on dormant stems turns the tide in this species' favor. A small tree, upright vase-shaped, finally with a rounded head, stems glistening green, it blends into any garden niche. A rooted cutting planted eight years ago in our garden is now 15 ft. high and wide. Foliage is nondescript medium green in summer, yellow-green at best in fall. The five-petaled flowers, 1 to 1¼ in. in diameter, occur singly or in pairs on long stems of the previous season and on short spurs on larger branches. The delicate fragrance is an added bonus, along with the extended, four- to eight-week floral period. A well-drained, reasonably fertile, acid soil in full sun is ideal. Many uses, with single specimen, groupings, and border use among the best. Handsome specimens from Washington, D.C., to Charleston, South Carolina, have crossed my path. Grows 15 to 20 ft. high and wide. Zones 6 to 9, 10 in California. Japan, China.

Cultivars and Varieties. Over 250 named selections with unique growth habits and flower characteristics.

'Dawn' has large, ruffled, double pink flowers and is later flowering.

MORE ➤

Prunus mume, Japanese Apricot

Prunus mume foliage

Prunus mume flowers

Prunus mume 'Peggy Clarke'

Prunus mume continued

'Matsurabara Red' produces double, dark red flowers on an upright tree to 20 ft. high.

'Peggy Clarke' bears double, deep rose flowers with extremely long stamens and a red calyx.

'Pendula' has single or semidouble, pale pink flowers and a weeping habit.

'Rosemary Clarke' has large, double, fragrant white flowers with red calyces.

'W. B. Clarke' offers double pink flowers on a weeping framework.

Punica granatum foliage and flower buds

Punica granatum flowers and flower buds

Punica granatum fruit

Punica granatum
POMEGRANATE

Beautiful shrub that receives minimal press in southern garden literature yet produces beautiful five- to seven-petaled, orange flowers in June, lustrous foliage, and edible, reddish fruit. In Zone 7, plants are injured by low temperatures, and tender spring foliage may be killed by a late freeze. These liabilities aside, the species develops into a large upright-oval to spreading rounded shrub composed of numerous slender branches. The "bundle-of-sticks" appearance in winter scares some gardeners. The 1- to 3-in.-long, oval-lanceolate, lustrous dark green leaves change to soft yellow-green in fall. The 2-in.-long, 2-in.-wide flowers—petals like crepe paper, calyx cup rindy like an orange—open in late May and June (Athens), with an occasional flower present into late summer. The 2- to 3½- (to 5-) in.-diameter fruit, with thick leathery rind and edible fleshy-coated seeds, ripen in September and October. Site in full sun, well-drained soil; pH adaptable, tolerates sand and clay. Handsome shrub in flower and worthy of inclusion in the border. Tolerates partial shade and still flowers with moderate gusto. Spring frost damage has killed three different cultivars to the ground in our garden. Grows 12 to 15 ft. high and wide. Zones (7)8 to 10. Eastern Mediterranean to the Himalayas.

Cultivars and Varieties. 'Legrellei' produces double salmon-pink flowers on a large shrub.

var. *nana* ('Nana') grows 3 to 4 (to 6) ft. high and wide, with red-orange single flowers and 2-in.-diameter, orange-red fruit. Beautiful in mass; a planting on the Georgia campus persisted for 18 years. Described as more cold hardy than the species, and my observations indicate that this is true.

Punica granatum var. nana

Punica granatum, Pomegranate

Punica granatum var. *nana* flowers

Punica granatum var. *nana* fruit

Punica granatum 'Legrellei'

Pyracantha koidzumii

FORMOSA FIRETHORN

This species picks up the landscape slack in the South, about where *Pyracantha coccinea* ends. A large, upright, wild, splaying, "thuggy," broadleaf evergreen shrub with sharp spines that consumes large chunks of real estate. Lustrous dark green, spatulate-shaped, 1- to 3-in.-long leaves, essentially without marginal teeth, permit separation from the toothed margins of *P. coccinea* in the North. The white flowers smother the foliage in April and May, each five-petaled, ¼ in. in diameter, and with hawthorn-like odor. Fruit are spectacular, persistent into winter, and, along with *Nandina*, provide maximum effect for extended periods. The ¼-in.-diameter, red pome colors in September and October. Full sun, hot, dry locations in well-drained soil suit it best. Transplant from a container and do not move once located. Best use is espaliered on south and west walls and fences. Reasonable barrier plant but a maintenance nightmare. Pyracanthas in general have descended from favor due to rampaging growth, spiny branches, and insect and disease problems. Grows 8 to 12 (to 20) ft. high and wide. Zones 8 to 10. Taiwan.

Cultivars and Varieties. 'Low-Dense' grows in a mounded form to 6 ft.

high and produces orange-red fruit. Less cold hardy than the species.

'Santa Cruz' is a more prostrate form, almost groundcover-like, 2½ to 3 ft. high, 5 to 6 ft. wide, with beautiful dark green leaves and red fruit. Highly resistant to fruit scab.

Pyracantha koidzumii fruit

Pyracantha koidzumii, Formosa Firethorn

Quercus acuta
JAPANESE EVERGREEN OAK

Often confused with and sold as *Quercus myrsinifolia* or *Q. glauca* because of similar evergreen leaf and growth habit; however, the leaves of *Q. acuta* are entire—those of the other two are serrated. Not as cold hardy in Athens, but a 20-ft.-high and -wide, low-branched, rounded tree grows in Aiken, South Carolina, about 140 miles southeast. The 2½- to 5½-in.-long leaves are leathery, lustrous dark green through the seasons. Bark is smooth and gray. Acorns are similar to those of *Q. myrsinifolia*, with the cap covering about one-third of the ¾-in.-long nut. Excellent for use in small spaces. Should be tested for container and street tree potential in the lower Southeast. Will grow in sandy soils with an acid reaction in full sun to moderate shade. Zones 8 to 9. Japan.

Quercus acuta, Japanese Evergreen Oak

Pyracantha koidzumii 'Santa Cruz'

Quercus acuta bark

Quercus acuta foliage

Quercus falcata
SOUTHERN RED OAK

The large oak growing in the most infertile, worn-out soil is, in most instances, *Quercus falcata*. Truly, a biologically tough *hombre*, bearing up and even thriving where other oaks would sputter. At maturity, rounded to broad-rounded, as a juvenile delinquent, pyramidal and without distinction. Massive, large, muscular branches lend credence to its tough-guy persona. Leaves appear in numerous manifestations, from three- to seven-lobed and 5 to 12 in. long, lustrous dark green above, grayish green below. Leaves may turn russet-red in autumn, but color is never spectacular. The leaf base is usually rounded, a distinction separating the species from other southern oaks. Acorns, ½ in. long, with the cap sitting on top of the striated (alternating brown and black stripes) nut, are borne in abundance. Difficult to transplant in large sizes and has not gained commercial acceptance. Grows anywhere except swamps. Full sun to partial shade. Worthy tree for difficult (impossible) sites. Drought and heat tolerances are legendary. Grows 70 to 80 ft. high and wide. National champion is 104 ft. high, 135 ft. wide. Zones (6)7 to 9. New Jersey to Florida, west to Missouri and Texas.

Cultivars and Varieties. var. *pagodifolia*, Cherrybark Oak, is found in bottomland habitats from Virginia to Florida, west to southern Illinois and Arkansas. The leaves are more uniformly five- to eleven-lobed, sinuses not as deeply cut, and the bark is blackish and scaly. Trees I have grown maintain a central leader and more uniform habit. I believe this variety has landscape and street tree possibilities. Zones 6 to 9.

Quercus falcata, Southern Red Oak

Quercus falcata branches and bark

Quercus falcata foliage and foliage undersides

Quercus falcata acorns

Quercus georgiana
GEORGIA OAK

An honor to have a tree named after the great state of Georgia, and this smallish round-headed species appears to have landscape and street tree potential. A few southern growers have produced quality field-grown trees. The ultimate test will be the degree of acceptance by the landscape profession. Small, dapper, broad-rounded in outline with 1½- to 4½-in.-long, three- to seven-lobed leaves, sinuses shallow, upper surface lustrous dark green, lower pale green with tufts of hairs in the vein axils. Fall color is red, reddish purple to burgundy in November. The ½-in.-long, dark brown nuts are covered about one-quarter by the cap. Grows on granite outcrops and thin soils. High degree of drought and heat tolerance. Easy to transplant. Choice small tree for planters, lawns, and streets. Grows 15 to 30 ft. high and wide. Zones 6 to 8. South Carolina, Georgia, and Alabama.

MORE ➤

Quercus falcata var. pagodifolia fall color

Quercus georgiana fall color

Quercus falcata var. pagodifolia, Cherrybark Oak

Quercus georgiana, Georgia Oak

Quercus georgiana in fall

Quercus glauca
BLUE JAPANESE OAK

Probably the most commonly cultivated evergreen oak, with the exception of *Quercus virginiana*. Upright-oval habit with such a tight, dense canopy that the species can be utilized for large screen plantings. In Atlanta, I witnessed plants skirted to the ground with branches that served as handsome buffers. The 2½- to 5½-in.-long leaves are strongly toothed in their upper one-half, lustrous dark green, gray-green beneath. Upon emergence, leaves range from rich green, bronze, to purple-green. Acorn is similar to that of *Q. myrsinifolia*. Prospers in clay-based and sandy soils in full sun to partial shade. Handsome small specimen tree, useful as large screen; looks, as do the other evergreen oaks, more like a holly. Grows 20 to 30 ft. high, spread one-half to three-quarters the height. Witnessed a 30-ft.-high, 40-ft.-wide specimen with low-slung, wide-spreading branches. Zones (7)8 to 9. Japan and China.

Quercus glauca foliage

Quercus glauca acorns

Quercus hemisphaerica
LAUREL OAK

Although terribly confused and misidentified in commerce, this semi-evergreen species is a respectable tree for planting in infertile, sandy to clay-based upland soils. Plants on the Georgia campus have weathered the years and emerged as stately specimens. Distinctly pyramidal in youth, becoming more rounded with age. In fact, the national champion is 96 ft. high and 95 ft. wide, which reflects "roundability." Leaves may have a few teeth; they are almost entire on old trees. Each is about 1 to 4 in. long, ½ to 1½ in. wide, lustrous dark green above, lighter green below. New leaves emerge bright yellow-green before settling down. Acorn is striated, ½ in. long, enclosed ¼ to ⅓ in. by the saucer-shaped cap. Relatively easy to transplant. Tolerates substandard soils from sand to clay; pH adaptable. Utilize for residential, park, urban, and street tree. Leaves hold into February and March in Zone 7. Densely branched in youth and makes a good early appearance. Grows 40 to 60 ft. high, 30 to 60 ft. wide. Zones 6 to 9. Southeastern United States.

Quercus laurifolia, Swamp Laurel Oak, is frequently confused with *Q. hemisphaerica* but is distinguished by diamond-shaped leaves and earlier leaf drop (late December and January). Grows in wetter habitats in the wild.

MORE ➤

Quercus glauca, Blue Japanese Oak

Quercus glauca new foliage

Quercus laurifolia, Swamp Laurel Oak

Quercus hemisphaerica continued

Quercus hemisphaerica, Laurel Oak

Quercus hemisphaerica acorns

Quercus hemisphaerica foliage

Quercus lyrata foliage

Quercus lyrata acorns

Quercus lyrata
OVERCUP OAK

A hidden gem; overlooked and, by some, scorned because of the large acorns. Now receiving acceptance by southern nurserymen because of uniform growth habit, fast growth, handsome foliage, and ease of transplanting. A Georgia nurseryman told me it was the most uniform oak he ever grew. Pyramidal-oval in youth, rounded at maturity. Branches are upturned, translating to effective and safe use along streets and trafficked areas. The 6- to 8-in.-long, lustrous dark green leaves, with three to five lobe pairs, become yellow-brown in autumn. Acorns are chunky, ¾ to 1 in. high and wide, covered for the bulk of their length by the acorn cap. Readily transplanted; tolerates wet, dry, and moist well-drained sites; pH adaptable. A great tree for urban use. Have observed large (75 ft.) specimens in Cincinnati, Ohio. Grows 45 to 50 ft. high and wide. Zones 5 to 9. New Jersey to Florida, west to Missouri and Texas.

Quercus lyrata, Overcup Oak

Quercus lyrata bark

Quercus lyrata in winter

308

Quercus michauxii
SWAMP CHESTNUT OAK

Acorns as big as golf balls, and I forage like a famished squirrel to collect every nut possible for propagation. Yes, true, as I groveled under an 80- to 100-ft.-high behemoth at Brookgreen Garden, Murrells Inlet, South Carolina, on a late November day. The leaves, similar to *Quercus prinus*, perhaps thicker textured and more pubescent, were bronze-red. A mammoth tree, rounded in outline with 4- to 8-in.-long, dark green leaves. Bark, even on young trees, is gray-brown and quite scaly. The species is taxonomically similar to *Q. prinus*, with the former growing in wetter soils. At Weeks Bay Wildlife Refuge near Mobile, Alabama, the tree is common in the swampy habitat. Acorns are similar to *Q. prinus*. Small trees on the Georgia campus were transplanted without difficulty and have grown exceedingly fast. I believe this is, like *Q. lyrata*, *Q. nuttallii*, and *Q. prinus*, a noble tree for southern landscapes. Grows 80 to 100 ft. high and wide. National champion is 200 ft. high, 148 ft. wide. Zones 5 to 9. New Jersey, Delaware to Florida, west to Indiana, Missouri, and Texas.

Quercus michauxii, Swamp Chestnut Oak

Quercus michauxii foliage, foliage undersides, and acorns

Quercus michauxii fall color

Quercus michauxii bark

Quercus myrsinifolia
CHINESE EVERGREEN OAK

Rare and unusual evergreen oak that grows in Savannah, Georgia, and Washington, D.C., with equal facility. Oval to rounded outline, small branches and leaves, result in refined texture, somewhat atypical for an oak. Newly emerging foliage is exquisite purple-bronze. Leaves mature lustrous medium green, gray-green below, with finely serrated margins from the basal third to the apex of the leaf. The smooth gray bark is comparable to that of the beech. Nifty, ½- to 1-in.-long, brownish black, oval-oblong acorns are one-third to one-half covered by a cap with three to six concentric rings. Transplanting can be difficult unless trees are root-pruned. Tolerates extremes of soil (except wet). Sapsuckers, a type of woodpecker, drill rings of holes in concentric circles that may serve as avenues for fungal invasion. I lost two trees via these "critters." When well grown, a beautiful lawn, park, and street tree. Grows 20 to 30 (to 40 to 50) ft. high, slightly less in spread. Zones 7 to 9. Japan, China, Laos.

Quercus myrsinifolia, Chinese Evergreen Oak

Quercus myrsinifolia new foliage

Quercus myrsinifolia acorns

Quercus myrsinifolia foliage

Quercus myrsinifolia bark

Quercus nigra
WATER OAK

Ubiquitous tree in the Southeast! Native but relentless in its pursuit of open ground, where it takes hold and acts like an obnoxious, exotic weed. With that said, it is remarkable in its ability to reach monumental sizes in miserable soils. Large, almost overwhelming in stature, it can quickly become the dominant tree if left to its reseeding capabilities. A tree survey of the Georgia campus taken in 2000 reflected its dominance over the 25 other oak species. Leaves are dull, dark bluish green to lustrous dark green, paler beneath. Shape is three-lobed at apex to entire, with each leaf 1½ to 4 in. long, ½ to 2 in. wide. Acorns rain in October and November, literally mulching the ground. Each is ½ in. long and wide, striated brown and black, enclosed one-quarter to one-third by the cap. Ironclad in tough soil from wet to stone dry, moderate shade to full sun; pH adaptable. Weaker wooded than other oaks but still more stable than the widely planted, weak-wooded *Acer saccharinum*, Silver Maple. Seldom available in nursery commerce. Pretty much the domain of "Squirrel Nursery Company." Grows 50 to 80 ft. high and wide. National champion is 128 ft. high, 79 ft. wide. Zones 6 to 9. Southern New Jersey, south to Florida, west to eastern Texas, and northward in the Mississippi valley to southeastern Missouri and eastern Oklahoma.

Quercus nigra, Water Oak

Quercus nigra foliage

Quercus nigra acorns

Quercus nigra in fall

Quercus nuttallii

NUTTALL OAK

One of those rare discoveries that excites the pragmatist and researcher because of aesthetics and cultural adaptability. A bottomland species that is closely allied to *Quercus coccinea*, *Q. palustris*, and *Q. shumardii*, the real differences reside in its development of a full canopy at an early age, its rapidity to caliper, its greater range of pH adaptability, its wet soil tolerance, and the ease with which it may be dug in early summer. I have walked nurseries and observed this growing next to *Q. shumardii*: uniformity of crown, density of foliage, and consumer appeal are heavily weighted toward *Q. nuttallii*. In short, it is a nurseryman's oak. Pyramidal in youth, more rounded with age. Leaves, five- to nine-lobed, 4 to 9 in. long, 2 to 5 in. wide, lustrous dark green, turn red in fall, followed by complete leaf drop. New growth is rich red to reddish purple. Acorns are ¾ to 1¼ in. long, ovoid-oblong, and one-third to one-half covered by the cap. Easy to transplant and grow. A grower's tree as well as a gardener's tree. Use as a specimen and street tree, for parks, campuses, and golf courses. I asked a friend how to separate this from *Q. shumardii* with reliability; his answer—if there is standing water around the tree in the wild, then it is *Q. nuttallii*. Grows 40 to 60 ft. high. National champion is 110 ft. high, 85 ft. wide. Zones 5 to 9. Western Alabama to east Texas and Oklahoma, north to southeastern Missouri and southern Illinois.

Quercus nuttallii, Nuttall Oak

Quercus nuttallii foliage

Quercus nuttallii fall color

Quercus phillyraeoides, Urbame Oak

Quercus phillyraeoides
URBAME OAK

Oaks, with about 400 species, assume myriad growth habits and leaf types. This evergreen may be at the furthest end of the variation curve with its upright-oval, large shrub or small tree habit. The new growth emerges bronze-red, settling to shiny dark green and pale green beneath. Each leaf is 1 to 2½ in. long, almost as wide. I have yet to observe acorns on cultivated plants. Has prospered at the J. C. Raulston Arboretum, Raleigh, North Carolina. Best in the collector's garden. Grows 15 to 25 ft. high. Zones 7 to 8. China, Japan.

Cultivars and Varieties. 'Emerald Sentinel', distinguished for its upright growth habit, is a selection from the J. C. Raulston Arboretum.

Quercus phillyraeoides foliage

Quercus phillyraeoides 'Emerald Sentinel' foliage

Quercus phillyraeoides 'Emerald Sentinel'

Quercus prinus
CHESTNUT OAK

An unheralded oak species but worthy of landscape respect; and, for little more than a walk in the woods, the hiker will be treated to one of nature's most important cafeterias. The species provides sweet acorns for the gray squirrel, black bear, white-tailed deer, and other wildlife. My son Matt, a Civil War history buff, and I toured battlefields from Kings Mountain, South Carolina (Revolutionary), to Gettysburg, Pennsylvania, and the species was a constant. As we ascended the dry ridge of Big Roundtop, the blocky bark signaled the presence of the species, some trees clearly descending from that part of American history. It is certainly a tree for the ages. Oval-rounded, eventually vase-shaped, with large spreading branches. The 4- to 6- (to 12-) in. long, 1½- to 4-in.-wide leaves, with ten to fourteen pairs of roundish teeth, are dark green, changing to orange-yellow and yellow-red-brown in fall. Plump, rich brown acorns, 1 to 1¼ in. high, ¾ in. wide, are one-third to one-half enclosed by the cap. Moderately easy to transplant, with an affinity for rocky, dry, upland sites in the wild. An excellent large area tree and even grows in parking lot islands in South Carolina. Truly a beautiful species that should be a greater part of southern and northern tree planting initiatives. Grows 60 to 70 ft. high, about as wide. Zones 4 to 8. Southern Maine and Ontario to South Carolina and Alabama.

Quercus prinus, Chestnut Oak

Quercus prinus bark

Quercus prinus fall color

Quercus prinus acorns

314

Quercus shumardii fall color

Quercus shumardii acorns

Quercus shumardii
SHUMARD OAK

Long a staple in the southeastern and southwestern landscapes but natively growing into Michigan and southwestern Ontario. The first large (80 ft.) tree I experienced was at the Missouri Botanical Garden, on an October day; the 30-year-old memory of its yellowish bronze fall color has followed me throughout my career. On the Georgia campus, the species has been planted in spades with great success. Pyramidal when young, rounded with maturity. Seven- to nine-lobed, lustrous dark green, 4- to 8-in.-long, 3- to 4-in.-wide leaves turn yellow-bronze to reddish in autumn; I have yet to experience outstanding pure red fall color. Acorns are ¾ to 1½ in. long, striated with brown-black lines, covered only at the base by the cap. Relatively easy to transplant; pH adaptable, tolerant of dry and moist soils. Rated superior in 13-year shade tree evaluations at Auburn University. Tremendously drought-tolerant shade, street, or large area tree. Grows 40 to 60 ft. high and wide. Co-national champions are 144 ft. high, 112 ft. wide, and 112 ft. high, 111 ft. wide. Zones 5 to 9. Kansas to southern Michigan to North Carolina, Florida to Texas.

Quercus shumardii, Shumard Oak

Quercus stellata
POST OAK

A mid-June day on Martha's Vine-yard, studying the native vegeta-tion—and what jumps in the way but a beautiful, 40- to 50-ft.-high and -wide Post Oak. In my beloved Georgia, I have jogged by the species on numerous occasions. While visit-ing Oklahoma, I saw a lone wind-modulated specimen standing in a grassy field. Pretty adaptable tree! Pyramidal initially, becoming round-topped with spreading branches. The 4- to 8-in.-long leaves, tough as rawhide, reflective dark green above, grayish to brownish below, develop, on occasion, a golden brown fall patina. The egg-shaped, ¾- to 1-in.-long acorns are one-third to one-half covered by the top-shaped cap. Considered difficult to transplant. Grows on dry, gravelly or sandy soils and rocky ridges but is extremely adaptable. Grows 60 to 70 ft. high and wide. Zones 5 to 9. Southern Massachusetts to Florida, west to Iowa and Texas.

Quercus stellata, Post Oak

Quercus stellata foliage

Quercus stellata acorn

Quercus stellata fall color

Quercus virginiana
LIVE OAK

This crown jewel of evergreen oaks consumes large swaths of real estate from coastal Virginia to Texas. In cities from Savannah, Georgia, to Houston, Texas, and in between, it is the dominant landscape tree for streets, parks, and residential areas. Truly excessive in size but without equal for majesty. Rounded in youth, wide-spreading with time, the low-slung branches stretch great distances from the trunk. Bark is blackish and cross-checked into well-defined blocks. The 1- to 3- (to 5-) in.-long, leathery leaves are convex-surfaced, lustrous dark green, with recurved margins. The gray-green, pubescent lower surface allows separation from *Quercus hemisphaerica* (which see). The acorns, ¾ to 1 in. long, dark brown to black, enclosed one-third by the cap, are held on a ½- to 3-in.-long stalk. Finicky during transplanting; most tree growers root-prune field-grown trees to ensure successful establishment. A number of southern nurserymen grow the trees in containers. Adaptable to about any soil type in full sun to partial shade. A climax species in the coastal Southeast. Tolerant of salt, drought, and wind. A magnificent tree for large area use. Grows 40 to 80 ft. high, 60 to 100 ft. wide. Zones (7)8 to 10. Virginia to Florida, west to Oklahoma and Texas into Mexico.

Cultivars and Varieties. Highrise™ ('QVTIA'), a fastigiate to upright-oval form, is the first Live Oak produced on a large scale via cutting propagation; will prove effective as a street tree and in sites where lateral space is limited. Estimated ultimate size: about twice as high as wide.

Quercus virginiana, Live Oak

Quercus virginiana branching habit

Quercus virginiana

Quercus virginiana bark

Quercus virginiana foliage and acorns

Rhamnus carolinianus, Carolina Buckthorn

Rhamnus carolinianus
CAROLINA BUCKTHORN

This was one of the first of the unknown plants I agonized over for hours upon arriving in Athens. Looked like a buckthorn, but I had never discovered one so rich and vibrant with red fruit, ripening to black, and the darkest of green leaves. Often planted by the birds, it appears in the oddest places, usually as a large shrub or small tree. The 2- to 6-in.-long leaves have eight to ten, deeply impressed vein pairs, resulting in a corrugated appearance. Flowers, inconspicuous yellowish green, open in spring, followed by the 1/3-in.-diameter globose, red to black fruit. Prefers shady, moist soils but is quite adaptable. Worthy naturalizing species, particularly in the understory. Simply not well known but rivals a good deciduous holly in rich red fruit. Grows 10 to 15 ft. high and wide. Zones 5 to 9. New York to Florida, west to Nebraska and Texas.

Rhamnus carolinianus mature fruit and fall color

Rhamnus carolinianus new fruit and foliage

Rhaphiolepis umbellata
INDIAN HAWTHORN

An essential element of warm-climate landscapes from the sea coast to Atlanta, Birmingham, Little Rock, and the Southwest. I am amazed at the numbers used for mass effect in residential and commercial settings. Mounded in habit and thickly set with heavy foliage, plants meld together into dark green to blue-green fabrics. Leaves are extremely variable in shape, 1 to 3 in. long, almost as wide, toothed to entire. In winter, plants often assume a purplish tinge. New growth emerges gray-green and extremely pubescent in March and April. White to pink flowers in 2- to 3-in.-high and -wide inflorescences open in late April and May. The fruit, ⅜- to ½-in.-diameter, purple-black to bluish black, one- to two-seeded berries, ripen in fall and persist attractively through winter. Easily cultivated in sun and shade but suffers from fungal leaf spot and deer browsing; in fact, it is occasionally referred to as "deer candy." When grown to optimum, a worthy plant for numerous landscape niches. Grows 4 to 6 ft. high and wide; cultivars smaller (2 to 3 ft. high) and larger (to 15 ft. high) are known. Zones 7b to 10. Japan, Korea.

The related hybrid species *Rhaphiolepis ×delacouri*, with pretty pink flowers, grows 4 to 5 ft. high and wide.

Cultivars and Varieties. Retired Georgia researcher Will Corley tested numerous cultivars for leaf spot resistance and found little. Two newer introductions, 'Eleanor Taber' (pink) and 'Olivia' (white), have proven more resistant and are good growers. 'Olivia' performed the best in my Georgia tests.

Rhaphiolepis umbellata, Indian Hawthorn

Rhaphiolepis umbellata foliage

Rhaphiolepis umbellata flowers

Rhaphiolepis umbellata fruit

Rhaphiolepis ×delacouri flowers

MORE ➤

Rhaphiolepis umbellata continued

Rhaphiolepis ×*delacouri*

Rhaphiolepis umbellata 'Eleanor Taber'

Rhaphiolepis umbellata 'Olivia'

Rhododendron, RHODODENDRON, AZALEA

Among the most common evergreen and deciduous woody flowering shrubs in the Southeast with myriad shapes, sizes, flower colors, and flowering times. The gardener is too often confronted with the standard 20 evergreen azaleas like 'Hino-Red', 'Delaware Valley White', 'Fashion', and 'Coral Bells'. Amateur breeders have expanded the horizons of this great genus, and enterprising nurserymen have tied their wagons to the newer introductions. They are discussed herein in groups, along with some of the cultivars. A good example of a major new group of southern azaleas is the Encore™ group that flowers in late summer to fall and again in spring. Truly re-markable at their best but absolute cold hardiness, even in Zone 7, is suspect.

My experiences with evergreen and deciduous azaleas point toward excellent drainage, even moisture, mulch, shade, and monitoring for lace bugs! Millions are sold annu-ally, and millions die annually. In flower the azaleas are "wow" plants; the rest of the year they beg for attention. Pro-ceed with the knowledge that azaleas have a place in warm-climate landscapes, but many other plants offer beauty of flower, fruit, and foliage and long-term performance.

For best cultural success, plant high, especially in heavy, poorly drained soils, and provide partial shade, even mois-ture, and mulch. Drought and lace bug are the most serious maladies. Most flower on old wood, so pruning is best accom-plished after flowering.

Rhododendron alabamense flowers

Rhododendron alabamense
ALABAMA AZALEA

A favorite in the Dirr garden. Enticingly sweet flowers, white often with a yellow blotch, open in mid-April. Foliage and flowers develop at the same time, so the floral show is somewhat diminished. Flowers are borne in six- to ten-flowered clusters. Usually a refined, rounded shrub with dark green leaves. Utilize under pines, mixed with broadleaf evergreens, and in groupings. Every visitor to the Dirr garden is enthralled with this species. Grows 5 to 6 (to 8) ft. high and wide. Zones (6)7 to 8. Found in dry open woodlands and rocky hill sites in north central Alabama and isolated areas of west central Georgia.

Rhododendron austrinum
FLORIDA AZALEA

Another native azalea with sweet fragrance and a vivid color range from pale yellow, yellow to orange. Flowers open before the leaves and are often still effective as the leaves emerge. Many seedlings grow in our garden, and all are different in flower color. An upright shrub, loose, arching, almost rounded at maturity. Dark green leaves may develop yellow to bronze-orange fall coloration. Flowers open in mid-April, anywhere from eight to fifteen per cluster. The effect is tremendous, especially in mass. A planting on the Georgia campus of eight to ten large plants generates abundant questions when in flower. Same uses as *Rhododendron alabamense* and even easier to grow. Grows 8 to 10 ft. high and wide. Zones (6)7 to 9. Northern and eastern Florida to southwest Georgia, southern Alabama, and southeastern Mississippi.

Rhododendron austrinum, Florida Azalea

Rhododendron alabamense, Alabama Azalea

Rhododendron austrinum flowers

Rhododendron canescens, Piedmont Azalea

Rhododendron canescens
PIEDMONT AZALEA

In many respects, a white to pink counterpart of *Rhododendron austrinum* and, in fact, hybridizes freely with that species to produce a range of intermediates. One of the taller growing species, often 10 to 15 ft. high, particularly in shady habitats; more "compact" when open-grown. Plants in full sun set liberal quantities of flower buds. The dark green leaves develop reddish hues when environmental conditions in the fall are perfect. Fragrant, white, pink to rose flowers in nine- to fourteen-flowered clusters open in late March and early April on naked stems. Their delicate color and texture blend with any landscape situation. As understory plants, they are at home. Grows 6 to 10 (to 15) ft. high and wide. Zones 5 to 9. North Carolina, Tennessee to north Florida, Georgia, Alabama, and Texas. The most common and widely distributed native azalea.

Cultivars and Varieties. 'White Canescens' ('Alba') has pretty, pure white flowers.

'Brooke' bears fragrant, pink flowers.

'Varnadoes Phlox Pink' has fragrant, vivid pink flowers in April; this is a favorite in the Dirr garden.

Rhododendron canescens flowers

Rhododendron canescens 'White Canescens'

Rhododendron canescens 'Varnadoes Phlox Pink'

Rhododendron chapmanii
(*R. minus* var. *chapmanii*)
CHAPMAN RHODODENDRON

Unique because of its northwest Florida nativity, it would appear the perfect species to increase heat tolerance in rhododendrons. By itself, unremarkable but intriguing, with 1- to 2-in.-long, dark green leaves, often with rolled, curled, undulating margins. The habit is loose, open, and spreading, and selections would have to be made to bring it to commerce. The rose-pink-lavender flowers open in late spring, although in north Florida, I observed plants in flower during October. Worthy candidate for the adventuresome warm-season garden. A collector's plant. Grows 6 to 10 ft. high and wide. Zones (6)7 to 9.

Rhododendron chapmanii, Chapman Rhododendron

Rhododendron flammeum
(*R. speciosum*)
OCONEE AZALEA

One of the more easily identified native azaleas because the flowers are slightly later than *Rhododendron canescens* and have no fragrance. A rounded shrub, relatively dense and full, with dark green leaves. Unbelievable range of flower colors from yellow to pink, salmon, orange-red, and red. Another excellent native azalea that lives in harmony with other garden shrubs. Grows 6 to 8 ft. high and wide. Zones 6 to 7(8). Georgia to South Carolina.

Rhododendron flammeum, Oconee Azalea

Rhododendron flammeum flowers

Rhododendron prunifolium

PLUMLEAF AZALEA

At the distant end of the flowering spectrum lies this most beautiful orange-red to red flowered native azalea. In July and August, nonfragrant flowers snap to attention yet are so far embedded in the foliage that their powerful colors are somewhat masked. Terrific plant for attracting hummingbirds; in August, I watch the remarkable creatures work their magic on the flowers. A large shrub, 10 to 15 ft. high; the few plants in the Dirr garden are 6 ft. high after six years. Has been used for hybridizing to extend flowering season. Worthwhile garden plant for woodland edges, borders, and irregular groupings. Zones 5 to 8. Southwestern Georgia and eastern Alabama.

Rhododendron prunifolium, Plumleaf Azalea

Rhododendron prunifolium buds

Rhododendron prunifolium flowers

Rhododendron 'Colonel Mosby'

Confederate Azaleas

A new group of heat-tolerant azaleas meshing the floral characteristics of the Exbury Hybrids and *Rhododendron austrinum*, Florida Azalea. This work was carried by Alabama plantsmen Bob Schwalt, Tom Dodd Jr., and Tom Dodd III. The selections have terrific flowers, before and with the leaves. The dark green leaves, to date, are mildew-free. Flowers are knockouts, appearing in 3- to 4- (to 5-) in.-diameter trusses in April. Great potential for the warm southern gardens where Exbury and Knap Hill types turn to rot, ruin, and mildew. Grows 6 to 10 ft. high. Zones 6 to 9.

'Admiral Semmes' has fragrant yellow flowers.

'Colonel Mosby' is a personal favorite, with beautiful foliage and fragrant, deep rose flowers that fade to pink, each with a yellow blotch.

'Stonewall Jackson' is a southern 'Gibraltar', with fragrant, large, solid, rich orange flowers. A vigorous grower and happy garden camper.

Encore™ Azaleas

A novel concept indeed: extend the flowering season from spring, with a summer gap, to resume in late summer to fall. Such is the case with this well-crafted and marketed group of azaleas, the introductions of which carry the prefix "autumn" to distinguish them from spring azaleas. All are spreading to rounded, evergreen shrubs, 1 to 2 (to 3) ft. high, 3 ft. wide and more. Early introductions are pink, rose to purple, single and double. Bonnie loves the colors and the fact that flowers open in fall and spring. Not as blowsy as the Kurume Hybrids and Southern Indicas. Cold hardiness is suspect, since *Rhododendron oldhamii* is one parent. Probably best in Zones 7 to 9.

The best performers in the Dirr garden are Autumn Amethyst™ (rosy purple), Autumn Coral™ (salmon-pink), Autumn Embers™ (orange-red), Autumn Rouge™ (pink-red), Autumn Royalty™ (rich purple), and Autumn Ruby™ (salmon-red).

Rhododendron 'Admiral Semmes'

Rhododendron Autumn Amethyst™

Rhododendron Autumn Coral™

Rhododendron 'Stonewall Jackson'

Rhododendron Autumn Rouge™

Rhododendron Autumn Royalty™

Girard Hybrids

The skilled plantsmanship of Ohio's Girard Nursery, through the generations, resulted in these improved evergreen azaleas. I first grew them over 25 years ago in our Illinois garden. 'Hot Shot', 'Pleasant White', and 'Renee Michelle' proved stellar performers. Most have excellent, lustrous foliage, large flowers, and −5 to −15°F flower bud hardiness. Size ranges from about 3 to 6 ft. in height. The southern nursery industry is replacing many of the smaller-flowered Kurume Hybrids with the Girards. I counted over 35 cultivars released by Girard Nursery. Based on observations and performance in the Dirr garden, I recommend 'Hot Shot' (deep orange-red to scarlet flowers), 'Pleasant White' (large white flowers), 'Renee Michelle' (clear pink flowers), 'Rose' (rose flowers, glossy deep green leaves, deep red in winter), and 'Scarlet' (strong red). Zones (5)6 to 8.

Kurume Hybrids

Although often associated with northern gardens, particularly the coastal Northeast into the Middle Atlantic States, this hybrid Japanese group is more commonly grown and utilized in the Southeast. At their best, 4- to 6-ft.-high and -wide, broadleaf evergreen shrubs with smallish, 1-in.-long leaves and 1- to 2-in.-diameter flowers. In this author's opinion, they could be replaced by the Girard and Robin Hill Hybrids in Zones 7 and 8. Callaway Garden's famous azalea bowl was largely planted with Kurume Hybrids. Petal blight and susceptibility to lace bug necessitate abundant maintenance. Zones 6 to 8(9).

'Coral Bells', with coral-pink, ½-in.-diameter, hose-in-hose (double) flowers, on a 3- to 4-ft.-high and -wide shrub, remains one of the most popular.

'Hershey's Red' has 2-in.-diameter, bright red flowers.

'Hinodegiri' produces vivid red, 1½-in.-diameter flowers and dark green summer foliage that turns wine-red in fall.

'Mother's Day' has large, red flowers on a wide-spreading plant.

Rhododendron 'Renee Michelle'

Rhododendron 'Mother's Day'

Rhododendron 'Coral Bells'

Rhododendron 'Hinodegiri'

Robin Hill Hybrids

A group of delicate-hued, large-flowered, evergreen azaleas with the lateness and large flowers of the Satsuki Hybrids. Flowers are large, 2½ to 4 in. across. Habit is spreading, and, for selected cultivars, size in ten years ranges from 15 in. high, 34 in. wide, to 25 in. high, 28 in. wide. Starting to make inroads in southern gardens. Zones 7 to 8(9).

'Hilda Niblett' produces large pink and white flowers on a compact mounded plant.

'Nancy of Robin Hill' is a beautiful light pink, hose-in-hose (double), low-growing form.

Rutherfordiana Hybrids

Beautiful, ruffled flowers, evergreen foliage, and compact habit, 2 to 4 ft. high and wide, make these azaleas common in the Coastal Plain of the Southeast. The forms most often encountered in cultivation are 'Pink Ruffles', with pink-violet, semidouble, 2-in.-diameter flowers, and 'Red Ruffles', with large, 3-in.-diameter, deep red, ruffled flowers. Zones 8 to 9.

Satsuki Hybrids

Called "fifth-month azaleas" because they flower in May. About the latest of the commonly grown evergreen azaleas in southern gardens. Spreading branches clothed with evergreen leaves, less than 1 in. long, serve as the perfect framework for the 2- to 4-in.-diameter flowers, which open in mid- to late May into June in Athens. Require shade for best performance. Excellent massing plants under pines and broadleaf trees. Numerous cultivars boggle the aesthetic senses. Grows 1 to 2 (to 3) ft. high, wider at maturity. Zones 7 to 9, 10 on the West Coast. Japan.

'Gumpo Pink' (pink) and 'Gumpo White' (white) are extremely popular.

Southern Indica

Amazing evergreen azaleas, large-flowered with a rich color range and ability to tolerate full sun (once established) to Live Oak shade. A staple on Jekyll Island, Georgia, and at several resort hotels the dominant understory shrub. Habit is broad-mounded, with 1- to 3-in.-long,

MORE ➤

Rhododendron 'Hilda Niblett'

Rhododendron 'Gumpo Pink'

Rhododendron 'G. G. Gerbing'

Rhododendron 'Red Ruffles'

Rhododendron 'Formosa'

Rhododendron 'George L. Taber'

Southern Indica continued

dark green leaves. Flowers appear in late March and April in clusters, each flower 2½ to 3 in. across, sometimes greater. Colors range from white to deepest purple. From my observations, one of the most adaptable evergreen azaleas. Grows 5 to 10 ft. high and wide. Zones (7)8 to 10.

Time-tested and time-honored, with greater cold hardiness, the most common cultivars are 'Formosa' (magenta with deep blotch), 'G. G. Gerbing' (pure white), and 'George L. Taber' (bright orchid-pink).

Rhus michauxii
MICHAUX'S SUMAC

Rare but worthy species that is definitively more restrained than *Rhus copallina*, *R. glabra*, and *R. typhina*, all featured in *Dirr's Hardy Trees and Shrubs* (Portland, OR: Timber Press, 1997). The habit is low-growing, suckering, the end result large colonies. Leaves are composed of nine to fifteen leaflets, each 2 to 4 in. long, dark green, and coarsely toothed. Fall color is beautiful and long persisting, yellow-orange to deep reddish purple. The yellow-green flowers occur in 6- to 8-in.-long panicles in June and July, followed on female plants by pubescent, compressed red drupes. Like all *Rhus* species, extremely adaptable; plants I witnessed were prospering in low-fertility, rocky soils. A collector's plant as well as a good plant for naturalizing. Grows 2 to 3 ft. high, spreading indefinitely. Zones 5 to 7. North Carolina to Georgia.

Rhus michauxii, Michaux's Sumac

Rhus michauxii fall color

Rosa banksiae 'Lutea' flowers

Rosa banksiae 'Lutea'
LADY BANKS' ROSE

A mainstay in southern landscapes and often used for entryways, espaliers, and along fences. Almost a scandent, evergreen shrub, exhibiting vinelike tendencies if trained to a structure. Left alone, it forms an arching, rounded shrub. The evergreen leaves consist of three to five (occasionally seven), 1- to 2½-in.-long, lustrous dark green leaflets. Stems are shiny grass-green and without prickles. In late March and April, the double, soft primrose-yellow, delicately fragrant flowers appear. A profusion of yellow engulfs the shoots and makes for a spectacular and lovely effect. At one time, I considered this form disease-free but have observed considerable mildew. To date, black spot has not been a problem. One of the easiest roses to culture, with numerous garden uses. At Powys Castle, Wales, a 30-ft. specimen climbs the castle wall. Grows 15 to 20 ft. high. Zones 7 to 8(9). China.

Cultivars and Varieties. 'Normalis' ('Alba') might be considered the species type with 1-in.-wide, slightly fragrant, single, white flowers.

Rosa banksiae 'Lutea'

Rosa banksiae 'Lutea'

Rosa banksiae 'Lutea' mature prickleless canes

Rosa laevigata
CHEROKEE ROSE

For some unusual reason, this species was chosen as the state flower of Georgia. An unruly, evergreen to semi-evergreen, scandent shrub forming wide-spreading, impenetrable tangles of sharply prickled stems. Great place for rabbits and vermin to establish residency. The three to five leaflets, thick-textured, lustrous dark green, are 1½ to 4 in. long. The thickish canes are armed with red-brown prickles that cut to the quick. Be careful! Five-petaled, fragrant, solitary, pure white, 3- to 4-in.-diameter flowers open in April and May. The pear-shaped fruit, densely set with bristles, mature reddish brown to red, each 1½ to 1¾ in. long, ¾ in. wide. Tougher than a nail. Have observed excellent flowering in sun and moderate shade. Difficult to keep in bounds and has no place in the small landscape. Grows 8 to 10 ft. high, 15 to 18 ft. wide; canes as long as 30 ft. occur. Zones 7 to 9. China, Taiwan, Burma.

Cultivars and Varieties. 'Anemone' is a pink-flowered form that has hybrid blood. A member of the Dirr garden until it outgrew the boundaries of hospitality.

Rosa laevigata, Cherokee Rose

Rosa laevigata cane and prickles

Rosa laevigata flowers

Rosa laevigata fruit

Rosa laevigata 'Anemone'

Rosmarinus officinalis foliage

Rosmarinus officinalis flowers

Rosmarinus officinalis
ROSEMARY

"Woody shrub?", you ask. Actually one of the best evergreen woody plants if sited in sun and well-drained soil. A plant in our garden is over 15 years old and still prospering. Each time I visit Sissinghurst Garden, England, I marvel at the large rosemary plants by the tower. Rounded, spreading, they form billowy, cloudlike masses. The evergreen leaves range from ¾ to 2 in. in length and are gray-green to dark green, depending on the cultivar. Close inspection reveals a green upper surface, gray to white-tomentose lower. The bruised leaves emit a potent, unmistakable aromatic odor. The pale to dark blue, ½-in.-long flowers are borne in the leaf axils from fall to spring. In our garden, flowers are most pronounced in December, January, and February. Easily cultured, requiring well-drained soils. Best in full sun, but partial shade is acceptable. Hand-some foliage color and texture contrast with other shrubs. Easily pruned and maintained, even for hedging use. Simply brushing the hand across the foliage is sufficient to release the sweet pungence. Grows 2 to 4 ft. high and wide. Zones (6)7 to 8(9). Southern Europe, Asia Minor.

Cultivars and Varieties. Numerous and confused; the following have crossed my path.

'Benenden Blue' ('Collingwood Ingram') has a semi-erect habit, dark green narrow leaves, and vivid, almost gentian-blue flowers.

'Lockwood de Forest' is similar to 'Prostratus' with lighter green foliage and blue flowers. Grows 2 ft. high, 4 to 8 ft. wide.

'Roseus' produces pinkish flowers.

'Severn Sea' has fine blue flowers on a free-flowering, arching-spreading shrub.

MORE ➤

Rosmarinus officinalis, Rosemary

Rosmarinus officinalis continued

Rosmarinus officinalis pruned as a hedge

Rosmarinus officinalis 'Lockwood de Forest'

Rubus, BRAMBLE

The story goes that Liberty Hyde Bailey, the father of American horticulture and one of the world's great taxonomists, gave up trying to organize the genus Rubus in frustration. I applaud the efforts of the fruit industry to produce easy-to-grow and more palatable blackberries, dewberries, raspberries, boysenberries, tayberries, and loganberries; and on the aesthetic side of the equation, several forms with colorful foliage and stems are offered. Be forewarned: most carry a prickly chip on their stems and are aggressive to the degree of being combative. All require well-drained soil and full sun for best foliage and stem coloration. Rubus idaeus 'Aureus' produces bright yellow foliage. Rubus thibetanus 'Silver Fern' has silver-gray, attractively dissected leaves and waxy, silver-white stems. Rubus biflorus *and its variety* quinqueflorus, R. cockburnianus, R. coreanus, R. koehneanus, R. lasiostylus *and its variety* hubeiensis—*all have silvery white stems. Zones 6 to 9. All are Asiatic in origin.*

MORE ➤

Rubus idaeus 'Aureus'

Rubus thibetanus

Rubus thibetanus 'Silver Fern'

Rubus cockburnianus stems

Rubus biflorus

Rubus cockburnianus foliage

Rubus continued

Rubus lasiostylus var. *hubeiensis*

Rubus lasiostylus var. *hubeiensis* stems

Rubus pentalobus
(*R. calycinoides*)

I never envisioned this species making inroads into the commercial groundcover sector, but its use has increased on the West Coast and some parts of the South. A broad-leaf evergreen groundcover with bristly, brown, pubescent stems and three- to five-lobed, wrinkled, leathery, lustrous dark green leaves. Flowers are white, the fruit red, but I have yet to see them on cultivated plants. Requires well-drained soil in partial shade, although colonies in full sun have prospered. I question long-term performance in heavy, wet soils. Have observed die-back in a planting on the Georgia campus. Excellent groundcover with beautiful foliage. Grows 3 to 9 in. high, spreading indefinitely. Zones 7 to 9. Taiwan.

Cultivars and Varieties. 'Emerald Carpet' is a more compact clone with smaller leaves that turn burgundy in autumn.

A yellow-leaved form has been discovered and will be introduced in the near future.

Rubus pentalobus foliage

Rubus pentalobus

Ruscus aculeatus
BUTCHER'S BROOM

Neat, tidy, smallish broadleaf ever-green shrub that prospers in the heat and drought of the Southeast. One of the great nook-and-cranny plants, for it survives in the most shade-laden, forsaken spots in the garden. Develops into a neat mound of erect, rigid stems, suckering and coloniz-ing as it matures. Dull gray-white flowers appear in the middle of the cladophyll (modified stem); on fe-male plants, these are followed by 1⁄3- to 1⁄2-in.-diameter, rounded, glossy bright red fruit, ripening in September and October, and persist-ing through winter. Requires shade and dryish, well-drained soil. "Foli-age" is quite prickly, so handle with care. Makes a good border or mass planting. Foliage is often dried and dyed for Christmas decorations. Holds up forever. Grows 1 1⁄2 to 3 ft. high, wider at maturity. Zones 7 to 9. Europe, northern Africa, Middle East.

Cultivars and Varieties. Several bi-sexual forms are in commerce. My

MORE ➤

Ruscus aculeatus foliage

Ruscus aculeatus flower

Ruscus aculeatus fruit

Ruscus aculeatus, Butcher's Broom

Ruscus aculeatus **continued**

first introduction to the hermaphrodite- (perfect-) flowered form was at Kew Gardens in 1993, where the gardener was dividing the plant and offered me a piece; in the backpack it traveled, jabbing me senseless but making it to the Dirr garden. Beautiful—fruit like small red cherries cover the branches without the need for pollination.

'Wheeler's Variety' grows 2 ft. high and wide; produces brilliant scarlet berries without the presence of a male.

Ruscus aculeatus hermaphrodite-flowered form

Santolina chamaecyparissus foliage

Santolina chamaecyparissus flowers

Santolina chamaecyparissus
LAVENDER COTTON

From Cape Cod to Georgia, this small, evergreen member of the daisy family performs with remarkable resilience. A tight, dense, silver-gray mound in its best incarnation; however, with heat and humidity, it tends to open up and splay. The evergreen leaves are ½ to 1½ in. long, ⅛ in. wide, whitish tomentose, with strong aromatic odor. I love the flowers, which look like yellow lollipops: no petals, just fertile flowers in a ball-like head, arising 4 to 6 in. above the foliage from June through August. Flowers are set on new growth of the season; after flowering, remove spent inflorescences and tidy the plant. Prefers relatively dry, low fertility soils in full sun. Will grow in sand. Displays salt tolerance. Use for foliage contrast and in borders, low edges, and herb garden–type hedges. Does not last "forever," and some replacements are necessary. Grows 1 to 2 ft. high, 2 to 4 ft. wide. Zones 6 to 9. In our Illinois garden I grew this and *Santolina virens* (which see), and *S. chamaecyparissus* was more cold hardy. Southern Europe.

Santolina virens (*S. rosmarinifolia*), Green Santolina, is a dead ringer for *S. chamaecyparissus* except for the deep green, glabrous foliage and more compact growth habit.

Cultivars and Varieties. 'Lemon Queen', a selection of *Santolina chamaecyparissus*, produces pale lemon flowers on a compact mound of gray foliage. Grows 2 ft. high and wide.

Santolina chamaecyparissus, Lavender Cotton

Santolina virens flowers

Sapindus drummondii
WESTERN SOAPBERRY

Quite exciting to discover this species in the wild in western Oklahoma, where it was growing in dry soils. In Athens, Georgia, a lone specimen, 30 to 35 ft. high, 40 ft. wide, thrives in the heat, humidity, and drought, yet nowhere in cultivation is the tree common. Broad-oval to rounded crown of stiff branches with a scaly patchwork of gray-brown, orange-brown to reddish brown bark. The pinnate leaves, 10 to 15 in. long, are composed of eight to eighteen leaflets, each 1½ to 3 in. long, to 1 in. wide, lustrous medium green. The leaves turn beautiful yellow-orange in autumn. The yellowish white flowers, each ⅕ in. across, are produced in 6- to 10-in.-long, loose, pyramidal, terminal panicles in May and June. The ½-in.-diameter, round, yellow-orange drupe ripens in October and remains on the tree through winter and into spring; in the later stages, it may turn black. Adaptable species that should be utilized for urban sites. Only drawbacks are the fruit, which can be untidy. Grows 40 to 50 ft. high and wide. National champion is 62 ft. high, 67 ft. wide. Zones 6 to 9. Southern Missouri, Kansas, New Mexico, and Arizona to Louisiana, Texas, and northern Mexico.

MORE ➤

Santolina virens, Green Santolina

Sapindus drummondii flowers

Sapindus drummondii fruit

Sapindus drummondii fall color

Sapindus drummondii continued

Sapindus drummondii, Western Soapberry

Sapium sebiferum flowers

Sapium sebiferum seeds

Sapium japonicum

Sapium sebiferum
CHINESE TALLOW TREE

Entertaining and educational how one person's weed is another's garden treasure. This species is such a double-edged sword, with rampageous, self-seeding, noxious weed status in the Coastal South and respectable small tree status in Zone 7. Habit is pyramidal to rounded with a thin, airy canopy. The poplarlike leaves are bright to medium green, 1½ to 3 in. long and wide, turning yellow to reddish purple in fall. The inner leaves color first, with the outer following along; the effect is never overwhelming in Zone 7. Flowers, greenish yellow, appear in the same structure, the male at the apex, females at base. The eventual fruit are three-valved capsules containing white, wax-coated seeds. I have seen it in south Georgia, Alabama, and northern Florida, where it has wreaked havoc upon the native vegetation. Grows 30 to 40 ft. high and wide. Zones (7)8 to 10. China.

Sapium japonicum has longer, darker blue-green leaves that turn handsome reddish purple in fall. Each leaf is 3 to 5 in. long, 2 to 4 in. wide, and broad-ovate rather than deltoid like *S. sebiferum*. Trees I observed were small, 20 to 30 ft. high. Zones 8 to 9. China, Korea, Japan.

Sapium sebiferum, Chinese Tallow Tree

Sapium sebiferum fruit

Sapium sebiferum fall color

Sarcandra glabra

A visit to the health food store finds *Sarcandra* berries, an important plant in Chinese medicine. Although minimally cold hardy in our garden, it picks up steam 100 miles southeast near Augusta. A rounded-mounded, broadleaf evergreen with 4- to 6-in.-long, 1½- to 2-in.-wide, sharply and coarsely serrated leaves that maintain their lustrous dark green color year-round. Flowers are yellowish and inconspicuous; however, the ¼-in.-diameter, rounded, showy, orange-scarlet drupes ripen in September and October and persist into the following year. Prefers moist, acid, woodsy soil in partial to heavy shade. In the wild it grows as an understory plant, often near streams. Grows 1 to 3 ft. high and wide. Zones 8 to 9. Japan, Korea, Taiwan, China, India, and Malaysia.

Sarcococca confusa

The name says it all: the taxonomy is confused; however, the unique leaf shape permits separation from all cultivated taxa. Long a staple in the Dirr garden, it often shows up in older southern gardens. In youth somewhat loose, with age more dense and rounded, with dark olive-green, splaying stems and lustrous black-green leaves. Each leaf is 1 to 2½ in. long with an undulating (wavy) surface and margin. From the leaf axils, in February and March, small, white, fragrant, apetalous flowers emerge and maintain their effectiveness for four or more weeks.

The fruit, red changing to black, mature in fall and persist into spring. On numerous occasions I have grown seedling populations (clean pulp from seed and sow) and have observed essentially no variation in leaf or habit. A great plant for shade (requires such) in moist, woodsy soils; however, once established it tolerates drought. Superb in mass and as a single plant mixed with other broadleaf evergreens. No insects or diseases plague it, making it a great choice for environmentally conscious gardeners. Grows 3 to 5 ft. high and wide. Zones 6b to 8. China.

Sarcococca confusa

Sarcandra glabra

Sarcococca confusa foliage

Sarcococca confusa fruit

Sarcococca confusa flowers

Sarcococca orientalis

A relatively new species to modern cultivation, but one that, I believe, will become a staple of the southern landscape. Tough and durable like *Sarcococca confusa*, yet more rounded, compact, and actually "better looking" in youth. Leaves are closely spaced along the stems, each 1½ to 3 in. long, lustrous dark green and flat-surfaced, without the wavy margins of *S. confusa*. Flowers, fragrant, enticingly so, have opened as early as late December in the Dirr garden and still perfume the atmosphere in April. Two to five buds on a short, crooked stalk open white, the males with pink-blushed anthers and sepals. The shining black fruit are similar to those of *S. confusa* but do not initiate red before turning black. Tremendous plant in our garden, surviving under a Southern Red Oak, *Quercus falcata*, while *Hydrangea quercifolia* 'Snowflake' gasps for moisture. Requires shade and forms large masses if planted 2 ft. apart. My belief is the garden boat was missed in the Southeast by not utilizing *Sarcococca* species to greater advantage. This species, introduced from China by the great British plant explorer Roy Lancaster, is among the five most beautiful broadleaf evergreen plants ever to grace our garden. Grows 2 to 3 ft. high, slightly wider. Zones 6b to 8(9). China.

Sarcococca ruscifolia
FRAGRANT SARCOCOCCA

Often confused with and sold as *Sarcococca confusa* but, in my opinion, not as garden worthy or beautiful. The habit is more irregular than those of other *Sarcococca* species, with branches developing willy-nilly from the crown. Habit is eventually rounded, with the arching branches touching the ground. Leaves at their best are lustrous dark green, flat in disposition, with an elongated apex. The milk-white, fragrant flowers open in the axils of the terminal leaves in January and February. Fruit are rounded, ¼ in. in diameter, and persist into winter. Culture and uses similar to other species. Not as cold hardy as *S. confusa* and *S. orientalis*; leaf browning occurred at 7°F in our garden. Variety *chinensis* is similar, with longer, narrower leaves, but what I see in cultivation is similar to *S. ruscifolia*. Grows 3 ft. high and wide. Zones (7b)8 to 9. China.

Cultivars and Varieties. Roy Lancaster introduced 'Dragon's Gate', a var. *chinensis* selection, that appears more compact, with smaller, narrower leaves. Based on early evaluations in Georgia, it has significant landscape merit.

MORE ➤

Sarcococca orientalis

Sarcococca ruscifolia, Fragrant Sarcococca

Sarcococca orientalis flowers and foliage

Sarcococca ruscifolia fruit

Sarcococca ruscifolia continued

Sarcococca ruscifolia var. *chinensis*

Sarcococca ruscifolia var. *chinensis* foliage

Sarcococca ruscifolia var. *chinensis* 'Dragon's Gate'

Sarcococca saligna flowers

Sarcococca saligna

The largest-leaved species, looking minimally like a member of the genus *Sarcococca*. The habit is rhizomatous-spreading, dense, but with gracefully arching branches. The evergreen leaves are 3 to 5 in. long, less than ¾ in. wide, and reminiscent of willow leaves in shape. The flowers, green with yellow stamens, nonfragrant, open in March and look nothing like other *Sarcococca* species. Fruit are dark purple to black. In our Zone 7b garden, the plant dies to the ground every winter. Useful grouping and groundcover plant, where adaptable. Grows 2 to 4 ft. high, wider at maturity. Zones 8 to 9. Himalayas.

Sarcococca saligna

Sarcococca saligna foliage

Sequoia sempervirens
CALIFORNIA or COASTAL REDWOOD

The quiet giant of the West Coast from southern Oregon to California, easily reaching 300 ft. high along the fog-shrouded coast. In the East, the species will grow 30 to 60 ft. high, and a 40-ft.-high specimen grows in Atlanta, Georgia. Imposing conifer, densely branched and gracefully pyramidal in youth, with age losing the lower branches yet maintaining a relatively narrow pyramidal crown. I walked among the redwoods at Muir Woods and wondered how anyone could ever cut one. They are sacred, noble trees. The needles, ¼ to 1 in. long, are dark blue-green above, with two, top-of-the-exclamation-point, whitish bands below. The rich red-brown bark, fibrous on the surface, develops deep ridges and furrows. Cones are ¾ to 1¼ in. long, ½ to ¾ in. wide, somewhat egg-shaped and dark brown. Plant container-grown trees in deep, moist, organic, acid soils; shelter from wind and extreme winter sun. I noticed 'Cantab' (see "Cultivars and Varieties") at Hillier Arboretum was growing in significant shade and was still full to the base. Use for specimen and novelty. Grows 40 to 60 ft. high on East Coast; over 300 ft. high in native habitat. Zones 7 to 9.

Cultivars and Varieties. 'Adpressa' ('Prostrata') has shorter needles and compact habit: grows 4 ft. high and wide in ten years. Apparently more cold hardy than the species; survived –9°F at the J. C. Raulston Arboretum, Raleigh, North Carolina, while the species died. Will revert and produce upright shoots that, if not pruned, result in a tree.

'Cantab' is a reversion shoot of 'Adpressa', with tight pyramidal-conical habit and shorter dark green needles. Grows 30 to 40 ft. high.

Sequoia sempervirens, California Redwood

Sequoia sempervirens bark

Sequoia sempervirens foliage

Sequoia sempervirens cone

MORE ➤

Sequoia sempervirens continued

Sequoia sempervirens 'Adpressa'

Sequoia sempervirens 'Adpressa' foliage

Sequoia sempervirens 'Cantab'

Sequoiadendron giganteum bark

Sequoiadendron giganteum
BIG TREE

Related to and often confused with *Sequoia sempervirens*. The needles are awl-shaped, triangular in cross section, slightly appressed, and pointing forward to the apex. The Europeans planted the species in parks and botanical and private gardens. The 100-ft.-high, garden variety *Sequoiadendron giganteum* is as common in Europe as the meatball broadleaf evergreen shrubs that serve as foundation plants in the South. Beautiful, dense, broad-pyramidal in youth, maintaining a similar outline in old age yet devoid of lower branches. The spongy bark, somewhat corklike in texture, is rich reddish brown, ridged and furrowed. Needles, ⅛ to ½ in. long, broad at the base tapering to a sharp point, are bluish green through the seasons. Cones are larger than those of *Sequoia*, similar in shape, 1½ to 3 in. long, 1 to 2 in. wide, and reddish brown. In the eastern United States, this species is better adapted than *Sequoia sempervirens*,

MORE ➤

Sequoiadendron giganteum, Big Tree

Sequoiadendron giganteum in youth

Sequoiadendron giganteum foliage

Sequoiadendron giganteum cones

Sequoiadendron giganteum continued

although moving further south to Zone 7, *Sequoia* picks up steam. Soil requirements are similar to *Sequoia*. I knew of a 100-ft.-high specimen at Tyler Arboretum, Lima, Pennsylvania. Strictly a specimen plant. Grows 60 ft. high in eastern and southern United States. National champion is 275 ft. high, 107 ft. wide. Zones 6 to 8. California in the Sierra Nevada Mountains at elevations of 4500 to 8000 ft.

Cultivars and Varieties. 'Hazel Smith' is a strong-growing, upright tree with bluish needles and greater hardiness. Has not performed well in Zone 7b.

'Pendulum' has an erratic leading stem that zigs, zags, dips, dives, arches, and bends to form living sculpture; the secondary branches hang mop- (mane-) like. If staked, grows 30 ft. or so, more often simply gliding above ground level.

Sequoiadendron giganteum 'Pendulum'

Serissa foetida
YELLOW-RIM

A much-loved bonsai plant that transitions to a semi-evergreen to deciduous shrub in Zones 7 to 9. A large grouping on the Georgia campus, now 3 to 4 ft. high, grows in the shade and root competition of Live Oak, *Quercus virginiana*, and flowers with abandon. A rounded shrub, densely branched, but fine-textured and airy in character. The deep green, 1- to 1½-in.-long leaves have a marginal yellow rim. The four- to six-lobed, ⅓-in.-diameter flowers twinkle like Christmas lights for four weeks or more in May and June. Never overwhelming in flower but with enough allure to entice even the sedentary gardener. Site in partial shade; full sun is acceptable, with adequate moisture. Nifty in small hedges, groupings, masses, containers and for bonsai. No insects and diseases. Grows 3 to 4 ft. high and wide. Zones (6)7 to 9. Southeastern Asia.

Cultivars and Varieties. 'Rosea' includes the single and double pink-flowered forms.

'Variegata' is used herein in a universal sense to umbrella the more prominently cream- and white-margined forms; in general these are less hardy than the species.

Serissa foetida flowers

Serissa foetida 'Variegata' foliage

Serissa foetida, Yellow-rim

Serissa foetida 'Rosea'

Serissa foetida 'Variegata'

Sesbania punicea
(*Daubentonia punicea*)
RATTLE BOX

Superb orange-red, yellow-spotted flowers, in wisteria-like racemes, droop from the branches in summer and fall. This South American native has become rather widespread in Zones 9 and 10 and self-seeds freely. Forms an irregular shrub habit with spreading canopy and pinnately compound leaves, composed of 12 to 14 leaflets, each ½ to 1 in. long and rich green. Flowers as described are formidable, and the long flowering season invites use in the garden. Requires sun and well-drained soil, although on St. Simons Island, Georgia, it grows along ditch banks. Grows 4 to 6 ft. high and wide. Zones 9 to 10. Southern Brazil, Uruguay, northeast Argentina.

Sesbania punicea, Rattle Box

Sinocalycanthus chinensis, Chinese Sweetshrub

Sinocalycanthus chinensis
CHINESE SWEETSHRUB

This robust shrub, oval to rounded in outline, is remarkable for the glossy dark green leaves, 6 to 10 in. long and up to 6 in. wide. Leaves turn soft yellow in autumn. The flowers, bulbous in bud, open cream-white. Each flower is 2½ to 3 in. in diameter, nonfragrant, opening sporadically in May. Based on performance in the Dirr garden, moist, well-drained soils rich with organic matter and partial shade are ideal. Drought induces premature defoliation. Grows 6 to 10 ft. high and wide. Zones (6)7 to 8. Eastern China.

Cultivars and Varieties. The J. C. Raulston Arboretum hybridized this species with *Calycanthus floridus* (*C. floridus* × *Sinocalycanthus chinensis*); the offspring were intermediate in leaf size, with large red-maroon flowers. The hybrid will probably be a better garden plant, but it is a large, floppy grower. Its correct name is ×*Sinocalycalycanthus raulstonii* 'Hartlage Wine'.

Sinocalycanthus chinensis fall color

×Sinocalycalycanthus raulstonii

×Sinocalycalycanthus raulstonii 'Hartlage Wine'

Sinocalycanthus chinensis foliage and flower

Sinojackia rehderiana
JACKTREE

A mysterious and clandestine member of the silverbell family (Styracaceae) that has gained some momentum in southern gardens. Its virtues are many, particularly the spectacular, lustrous dark green foliage that remains green into October in Zone 7. Habit is several degrees irregular and, without staking, becomes arching and unkempt. Also, displays a shrublike propensity if left alone. Each 1- to 3- (to 4-) in.-long leaf is leathery, lustrous dark green with fine, marginal teeth. I have yet to experience any significant fall color. The five- to seven-petaled, white flowers, 1 in. wide, appear in three- to five-flowered cymes at the ends of lateral shoots in April and May. Flowers are suspended like spiders on webs. The woody drupe is ¾ in. long, ½ in. wide, with a broad conical apex. Pleasantly surprised by the species' heat and drought, as well as full sun to heavy shade, tolerances. I have yet to observe insect and disease problems. Growers had a difficult time marketing this species, and it will take a second and third effort to launch the career. Small specimen tree or large shrub for about any location. Grows 15 to 20 ft. high and wide. Zones 6 to 8. China.

Sinojackia rehderiana, Jacktree

Sinojackia rehderiana flowers   *Sinojackia rehderiana* fruit

Sinojackia rehderiana foliage

Smilax
GREEN-BRIER

An immense genus with 200 species of deciduous or evergreen, woody or herbaceous climbers, the stems often lethally prickly. The real beauty resides in the evergreen foliage and blue-black to red fruit. My arms ran red from the attacks of *Smilax rotundifolia* during early efforts to clean the one and three-quarter acres now lovingly termed the Dirr garden. The only species cultivated to any degree in the South is *S. smallii*, Bamboo or Jackson Vine; this essentially thornless, evergreen form offers the most beautiful, waxy, lustrous dark green foliage, which is utilized for Christmas decorations. *Smilax walteri*, Coral Green-brier, produces red fruit and grows in wet soil areas. Utilize sparingly for foliage effect and naturalized plantings. Zones 7 to 9. Southeastern United States.

Smilax rotundifolia foliage

Smilax smallii foliage

Sophora secundiflora
TEXAS MOUNTAIN LAUREL, MESCAL BEAN

When I first saw it, during a visit to San Antonio, Texas, I thought this was one of the most beautiful flowering plants I had ever laid eyes upon. Attempts to grow the plant in Athens, Georgia, met with disaster. Often, plants native to areas with dry climates and soils perform inadequately in humid climates. Evergreen large shrub or small tree, upright-spreading and low-branched. The leaves, compound pinnate, 4 to 6 in. long, are composed of seven to nine, rich green, oblong or obovate, notched leaflets, each to 2 in. long.

The great aesthetics are embodied in the fragrant, violet-blue, 1-in.-long flowers, borne in a wisteria-like raceme in late winter to spring. Fruit are 6- to 9-in.-long, silver-gray, woody pods with ½-in.-wide, red seeds. Transplant from containers into well-drained, drier soils; best suited for the Southwest. Tolerates alkaline soils. Use as an accent plant and small street tree, and in courtyards, containers, and groupings. Grows (15 to) 20 to 30 ft. high. Zones 8 to 10. Texas, New Mexico, northern Mexico.

Sophora secundiflora foliage

Sophora secundiflora flowers

Smilax smallii, Bamboo Vine

Staphylea trifolia
AMERICAN BLADDERNUT

I stumbled upon this species, growing contentedly in an alluvial plain above the Oconee River, during a hike through a local woodland. A small side shoot was extricated and moved to the Dirr garden; ten years later, root pieces are still throwing up suckers. Not an unworthy plant, upright-spreading, either a small tree or eventually a large, rounded shrub. The genetic propensity to sucker soon renders the small tree a large shrub. Bark is striated, greenish gray with vertical white fissures, reminiscent of the Striped Maple, *Acer pensylvanicum*, one of the snakebarks. The trifoliate leaves, each leaflet 2 to 4 in. long and dark green, turn green-yellow in autumn. The greenish white, bell-shaped, $\frac{1}{3}$-in.-long flowers are borne in $1\frac{1}{2}$- to 2-in.-long, nodding panicles in April and May. Not overwhelming but noticeable and daintily pretty. The inflated capsule, 1 to $1\frac{1}{2}$ in. long, is three-lobed, green to brown, with yellowish brown seeds. Prefers moist soil and shade, although I observed plants in full sun. Good naturalizing species that suckers and colonizes. Grows 10 to 15 ft. high, wider at maturity. Zones 4 to 8. Quebec to Ontario and Minnesota south to Georgia and Missouri.

MORE ➤

Staphylea trifolia bark

Staphylea trifolia flowers

Sophora secundiflora, Texas Mountain Laurel

Staphylea trifolia, American Bladdernut

Staphylea trifolia continued

Staphylea trifolia fruit

Staphylea trifolia fall color

Stewartia malacodendron
SILKY STEWARTIA

Every gardener's dream plant but, unfortunately, difficult to culture. Four times, I tried and failed. The great Hillier Arboretum, England, has a perfect, 18-ft.-high specimen that flowers in June. A bushy shrub or small tree, low-branched and densely foliaged with 2- to 4-in.-long, dark green leaves. Bark is gray-brown, lightly ridged and furrowed. The five-petaled, 2½- to 3½- (to 4-) in.-diameter, white, purple-fila-mented, blue-anthered flowers appear singly from the leaf axils in June and July. The base of each petal may be streaked or stained with vinous purple coloration. To my way of thinking, few flowers are more beautiful. Flowers open over a long time frame, and I have stood in place for minutes simply appreci-ating their beauty. Fruit are woody, egg-shaped, ½-in.-diameter, five-valved, dehiscent, beaked capsules containing wingless, lustrous brown seeds. Plant high for maximum drainage, mulch for even moisture, and site in partial shade. A real gar-dener's plant, like the finest piece of art or sculpture. Those who grow this species with success have climbed the ladder of garden achievement. I am still on the bot-tom rung. Have observed a wonder-ful plant at the Polly Hill Arboretum, Martha's Vineyard, Massachusetts. Grows 10 to 15 (to 18) ft. high, not quite as wide. Zones (6)7 to 9. Vir-ginia and Arkansas to Florida, Louisiana, and Texas.

Stewartia malacodendron, Silky Stewartia

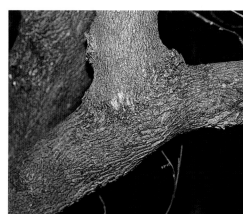

Stewartia malacodendron bark

Stewartia malacodendron buds

Stewartia malacodendron flowers

Stewartia ovata, Mountain Stewartia, bark

Stewartia ovata var. *grandiflora*

Stewartia ovata
MOUNTAIN STEWARTIA

This, along with *Stewartia malacodendron*, represents the southeastern contribution to the genus. Mountain Stewartia typically grows as an understory shrub on slopes above streams, often in moist soils. Spreading, bushy habit, vase-shaped in outline, although most garden plants are rounded and without great character. Bark, unlike its Asiatic relatives, is gray-brown and slightly ridged and furrowed. The dark green summer leaves offer a promise of orange to scarlet fall color that seldom materializes. Exquisite, glistening white, five- to six-petaled flowers with yellow-white stamens, each 2½ to 3 (to 4) in. in diameter, open in June and July. Flowers are not simply beautiful but romantic. Fruit, as for all *Stewartia* species, are five-valved, dehiscent capsules, containing flattish, brown seeds. Culture is ripe with landmines, and I continue to agonize over my inability to successfully grow this and *S. malacodendron*. Provide moist, acid, woodsy, well-drained soil under high shade in the South. Combine with ericaceous plants, which have similar garden habitat requirements. To successfully flower the species is a great feeling. I patiently wait for the day when I will experience that feeling to come. Grows 6 to 15 ft. high and wide. Zones 5 to 8. North Carolina to Tennessee and Florida.

Cultivars and Varieties. var. *grandiflora* has larger flowers, to 4 in. in diameter, and blue-purple stamens; the validity of this taxonomic unit is truly doubtful, since the purple-stamened types occur in wild populations of the true species.

Styrax grandifolius
BIGLEAF SNOWBELL

Abundant number of *Styrax* species, hovering around 100, with most better suited to garden culture in cooler climates. The two southeastern species, *Styrax americanus* and *S. grandifolius*, are worthy garden choices if correctly sited. The former is discussed in *Dirr's Hardy Trees and Shrubs* (Portland, OR: Timber Press, 1997). *Styrax grandifolius* is a large shrub or small tree with 2½- to 7-in.-long, 1½- to 3¾-in.-wide, dark green, denticulate to almost entire leaves. Leaves resemble those of *S. obassia*. In May and June, the fragrant, white, ¾- to 1-in.-wide flowers open in seven- to twelve- (occasionally twenty-) flowered, 4- to 8-in.-long, nodding racemes. In nature, it occurs as an understory tree where I observed it mixed with mountain laurel. Typically found along the banks of streams, although it grows in drier woods. Has been difficult to root from cuttings and is seldom available in commerce. Certainly a most beautiful native woody plant for woodland edges and naturalizing. Not as easy to culture as *S. obassia*. Grows 8 to 12 (to 15) ft. high. Zones 7 to 9. Virginia to Georgia.

MORE ➤

Styrax grandifolius foliage and flowers

Styrax grandifolius, Bigleaf Snowbell

Sycopsis sinensis
CHINESE FIGHAZEL

The common name must be rethought if the plant is to have any chance in commerce. My crazy affinity for the species runs tangential to my great love for the witch-hazel family (Hamamelidaceae). Loose, oval-rounded, shrubby forms exist as well as rather narrow, small, tree forms with smooth, gray bark. The evergreen leaves, 2 to 4 in. long, are essentially entire, lustrous dark green, and hold their color year-round. In winter, typically February and March, the small, yellowish flowers with red anthers and dark reddish brown tomentose bracts appear. Never overwhelming but, like *Parrotia persica*, with color sufficient to perk up the winter garden. Tolerates sun and shade (best) in acid, well-drained soils. Has possibilities for screening and hedge use. Observed thriving specimens in Washington, D.C., and Savannah, Georgia. Grows 10 to 15 ft. high and wide. Zones 7 to 9. Central China.

×*Sycoparrotia semidecidua*, an intergeneric hybrid between *Sycopsis* and *Parrotia*, is a botanical curiosity and potentially worthy small street tree. In 15 years in our garden, it has never exhibited heat or drought stress, and a large robust plant in Aiken, South Carolina, corroborates these tolerances. Leaves look like those of *Parrotia*, flowers like *Sycopsis*. Foliage is semi-evergreen senescing to yellow-green to yellow. Grows 10 to 15 (to 20) ft. high. Zones 7 to 9. Originated around 1950 in Basel, Switzerland.

Sycopsis sinensis flowers and foliage

Sycopsis sinensis, Chinese Fighazel

×*Sycoparrotia semidecidua* foliage

×*Sycoparrotia semidecidua* flowers

Symplocos tinctoria, Horse-sugar

Symplocos tinctoria
HORSE-SUGAR

Related to the more garden-worthy *Symplocos paniculata* but not itself without several attributes that might endear it to southern gardeners. The biggest problem is nondescriptness in habit and foliage, for few people can ever identify the plant. In the woodsy understory from the Piedmont to the Coastal Plain of the Southeast, it is either a loose, upright, broadleaf evergreen shrub of no distinction or a suckering, colonizing shrub that one could grow to love. The 3- to 6-in.-long leaves, thickish, lustrous dark green, are entire or obscurely serrate toward the apex. Leaves range from semi-evergreen to deciduous, depending on low temperatures. I love the fragrant cream-yellow flowers, which occur in dense, axillary clusters from the previous season's growth in April and May. Fruit are orange to brown, ⅓- to ½-in.-long, ellipsoidal drupes. Tolerates a wide range of soils, from drier woods to bottomlands and swamps. Strictly a naturalizing plant. Called Horse-sugar because the leaves are sweet. Grows 15 to 25 ft. high. Zones 7 to 9. Delaware to Florida to Louisiana.

Symplocos tinctoria flowers

Taxus chinensis foliage

Symplocos tinctoria foliage

Taxus chinensis
CHINESE YEW

The genus is one of the most essential components of cold temperate gardens but runs out of adaptability about Zone 7b. The late J. C. Raulston championed the Chinese Yew because it performed so magnificently in the Arboretum at Raleigh, North Carolina, where it is still growing in full sun next to the lath area. The habit on this plant is pyramidal-conical, almost like *Taxus cuspidata* 'Capitata' but with slightly longer needles and much faster growth. Since J. C.'s initial introduction, I observed other forms of the species that are more shrubby and wide-spreading. The dark green needles, 1 to 1½ in. long, have two bands on their lower surface. Needles hold good color through winter. Seemingly, the plant has potential in Zones 7 and 8 for screens, hedges, and foundation plantings but has not yet been embraced by commerce. Easy to root from cuttings; takes pruning; tolerant of heat and drought, sun and shade. Susceptible to deer browsing. Grows 5 to 10 ft. high, spread variable. Zones (6)7 to 8. Morton Arboretum mentioned growing the plant in Lisle, Illinois. China.

The related species *Taxus floridana*, Florida Yew, grows naturally in a narrow area along the Apalachicola River in northwestern Florida. Typically shrubby in cultivation, plants are treelike in the wild; the national champion is 20 ft. high, 26 ft. wide. Some discoloration of needles in exposed situations in winter. I thought it might serve as a breeding partner for introducing heat tolerance into the genus. Zones (6)7 to 9.

Taxus chinensis, Chinese Yew

Taxus floridana, Florida Yew

Tecomaria capensis
(*Tecoma capensis*)
CAPE HONEYSUCKLE

Much like *Campsis radicans* in appearance but more refined and less aggressive. My original introduction to the species occurred in a garden in Orlando, where I agonized over the identity of this bright orange-red flowered vine. The compound pinnate leaves are composed of five to nine, lustrous dark green, ½- to 1½-in.-long, sharply serrate leaflets. The 2- to 3-in.-long, tubular flowers, orange to orange-red, develop in terminal racemes from fall into winter, with sporadic flowering at other times. Requires no special care, other than well-drained soil and full sun. Like *C. radicans*, displays reasonable salt tolerance. Provide fence, trellis, post, or other suitable structure. Have observed it pruned into a free-standing shrub. Useful for covering banks, slopes, hard-to-maintain areas. Grows 10 to 15 ft. or more. Zones 9 to 11. South Africa.

Cultivars and Varieties. 'Apricot' has orange-yellow flowers.

Tecomaria capensis 'Apricot'

Ternstroemia gymnanthera new foliage

Ternstroemia gymnanthera fruit

Tecomaria capensis, Cape Honeysuckle

Ternstroemia gymnanthera

JAPANESE TERNSTROEMIA

Fast assuming the garden responsibilities of Redtip Photinia, *Photinia ×fraseri*, because of the colorful new growth, wide soil adaptability, and sun and shade tolerances. The young foliage varies from apple-green to bronze, red, reddish purple, and almost blackish purple. With maturity leaves turn lustrous dark green and in winter often assume rich reddish bronze coloration. Leaves are obovate, entire, somewhat spatulate in shape, 2½ to 4 in. long with a blunt apex, usually with an indentation. The five-petaled, white, ½-in.-diameter flowers are borne on reflexed stalks from the previous season's growth in May and June. Their effect is masked by the current season's foliage. Fruit are cute, 1-in.-long, ½-in.-diameter, egg-shaped, green to red, speckled berries that ripen in September. Primarily seed-grown; easily transplanted and grown in all but heavy, wet soils. Responds to pruning and can be kept in check. Excellent foundation, hedge, screen, or massing plant. One of the best alternatives to Redtip Photinia for everyday use. No serious insects or diseases. Grows 8 to 10 ft. high, 5 to 6 ft. wide. Have observed 20-ft.-high specimens in South Carolina. Zones 7 to 9(10). Japan, Korea, Taiwan, China, India, Borneo.

Cultivars and Varieties. Many nurseries interested in selections for foliage color and growth habit. To date Flowerwood Nursery, Loxley, Alabama, and Greenleaf Nursery, Park Hill, Oklahoma, are the prime movers.

'Burnished Gold' has yellow-gold-bronze foliage that diminishes with the heat of summer.

'Variegata' has a cream-white to yellow-white margin that turns rose-pink in winter; one of the more colorful variegated plants for shade and does not revert.

Ternstroemia gymnanthera, Japanese Ternstroemia

Ternstroemia gymnanthera 'Burnished Gold'

Ternstroemia gymnanthera 'Variegata'

Teucrium chamaedrys
WALL GERMANDER

A broadleaf evergreen subshrub that is utilized for hedges and masses in southern landscapes. The smallish, rounded-mounded habit, ¼- to 1-in.-long, dark green leaves, and rose-purple, summer flowers have endeared it to gardeners worldwide. Often used in formal gardens, it is time-honored for knot and herb gardens. Prefers well-drained, sandy soil, slightly on the dry side, in full sun. Prune to reinvigorate the plant and maintain dense branching. Grows 12 to 15 in. high and wide. Zones 6 to 8(9). Europe, northern Africa, western Asia.

Teucrium chamaedrys, Wall Germander

Teucrium chamaedrys foliage and flowers

Torreya taxifolia
STINKING CEDAR,
FLORIDA TORREYA

The first inclination is to identify this species as yew, *Taxus*, but a clasp of the foliage indicates something else. The stiff and prickly pointed needles literally penetrate the skin, compared to the soft, flexible needles of yew. A handsome needle evergreen, usually loosely pyramidal in outline. A dense, broad-pyramidal specimen in Monticello, Florida, is, at 30 to 35 ft. high, the largest I have observed. The gray-brown bark, ridged and furrowed, forms a woven pattern. Each 1- to 1¾-in.-long needle is flat, lustrous dark green with gray-green bands below. When bruised, a stinky odor is evident, hence, one of the common names. The olivelike, naked seed, dark green with purplish stripes, 1 to 1¼ in. long, ½ to ¾ in. wide, develops on female plants. Listed federally as an endangered species; the Atlanta Botanical Garden and Arnold Arboretum have contributed greatly to propagation and preservation. Not for the everyday garden, but for the gardener to know, appreciate, and preserve at all its worth. Most plants I observed range from 10 to 20 ft. in height. Zones 6 to 9. Found on wooded slopes and bluffs east of the Apalachicola River and northward into Georgia.

Torreya taxifolia male flowers

Trachelospermum asiaticum
JAPANESE STAR or ASIATIC JASMINE

I first experienced this species over 25 years ago, used as a groundcover on the Louisiana State University campus at Baton Rouge, and thought it one of the most beautiful plants. Calmer, cooler, even-tempered, and more "together" than *Trachelospermum jasminoides*, it provides the uniform lustrous dark green effect that remains the domain of "true" groundcovers. The evergreen leaves are ¾ to 2 in. long, elliptic to ovate, and glossy dark green. I have yet to experience flowers on the species in a groundcover planting but have observed the yellowish white, ¾-in.-diameter, fragrant flowers on climbing specimens. Occasionally, *T. jasminoides* is mixed with *T. asiaticum* in groundcover plantings; the former grows taller and flowers. In recent years, *T. asiaticum* is utilized

MORE ➤

Trachelospermum asiaticum, Japanese Star Jasmine

Torreya taxifolia, Stinking Cedar

Torreya taxifolia foliage

Trachelospermum asiaticum **continued**

more frequently in Zone 7b. Tolerates full sun and shade. Drought-tolerant compared to *Vinca* species. Full-sun plantings are often damaged by late winter to early spring freezes, which render the foliage brown. I suspect the plant dehardens and the leaves become sensitive to low temperatures. By June, foliage has regenerated. Excellent groundcover and in Zones 8 and 9 has few peers. Grows 6 to 12 in. high, spreading and rooting laterally. Grows 15 to 20 ft. high on a structure. Zones 7 to 9. Japan, Korea.

Cultivars and Varieties. Extremely dark green, smaller leaf forms like 'Elegant' and 'Nortex' are in cultivation. Variegated leaf forms, usually cream-splotched or -margined, are available.

Trachelospermum jasminoides, Confederate Jasmine

Trachelospermum asiaticum foliage

Trachelospermum asiaticum variegated leaf form

Trachelospermum asiaticum flowers

Trachelospermum jasminoides new foliage

Trachelospermum jasminoides
CONFEDERATE or STAR JASMINE

Multi-talented, broadleaf evergreen groundcover or vine, with sweetly scented flowers in spring to summer and terrific cultural adaptability. Used as a groundcover on the Georgia campus to cover slopes, it has outcompeted English ivy and blanketed the entire area. As a groundcover, the stems twine around each other, producing a carrot-top effect. It grows no more than 18 in. high but does not provide the carpetlike effect of *Vinca* and *Pachysandra*. A climbing structure like a trellis, coarse tree trunk, or wire is required if it is to be utilized as a vine. I had lunch in Augusta, Georgia, where a woven fence surrounding the eating area was covered with this species. Never did a cheeseburger taste (and smell) so delectable. The 1½- to 3½-in.-long leaves emerge bronze-purple and mature lustrous dark green. Flowers, shaped like boat propellers, five-petaled, cream to yellow, and fragrant, appear in April and May and sporadically thereafter. Easy to culture, requiring only good drainage. Best in some shade, but plants in full sun grow well. Winter sun and wind may cause some degree of discoloration. Uses as mentioned above—but it is worth the space to reiterate the garden excellence of this twining vine. Grows 10 to 12 (to 20) ft. high as a vine. Zones (7)8 to 10. Japan, China.

Cultivars and Varieties. 'Madison' is a more cold hardy selection with heavy pubescence on the underside of the leaf.

'Variegatum' is bordered and blotched with cream, the interior of the leaf is gray-green; in winter, creamy areas turn pinkish red to carmine.

More than one variegated form in cultivation—at Hannay's of Bath, Bath, England, a rare plant nursery, I obtained var. *wilsonii* 'Variegatum', which is hardier and more prominently cream-variegated than 'Variegatum'.

Trachelospermum jasminoides 'Madison'

Trachelospermum jasminoides 'Variegatum'

Trachelospermum jasminoides flowers

Trochodendron aralioides, Wheel Tree

Trochodendron aralioides
WHEEL TREE

Rare broadleaf evergreen tree, relegated to the sanctuaries of arboreta and botanical gardens. At Hillier Arboretum, there are so many that, in cleaning and thinning an area, I was afforded the privilege of cutting down a 20-ft.-high tree. My hands trembled, the blade quivered, the Wheel Tree groaned. Never again will I be coerced into such a heinous act. Develops a pyramidal outline with tiered branches. Foliage is lustrous dark green, each leaf 3 to 6 in. long, with prominent crenate serrations toward the apex. Flowers are bright green, ¾ in. in diameter, with a spokelike arrangement of 40 to 70 stamens. Locate in moist, acid, woodsy, well-drained soil in shade. Protect from wind. Strictly a conversation piece, but the unique habit and foliage combine favorably with other evergreens. Grows 10 to 20 ft. high, one-half this in spread. Zones 6 to 7. Japan, Korea, and Taiwan, where it grows in mountain forests.

Trochodendron aralioides flowers

Trochodendron aralioides foliage

Ulmus alata bark

Ulmus alata foliage and winged stem

Ulmus alata
WINGED ELM

Afforded not even casual glances by the woody cognoscenti because of commonality, perceived miserable habit, and mildew-laden leaves. Hold the negatives! I too was disrespectful, having seen many trees overrun with mildew that turned the entire tree ghostly gray in late summer and fall. However, selected trees appear resistant. The habit can be scruffy, but large, 70-ft. trees, like *Ulmus americana*, American Elm, in outline, are reasonably common. Leaves are smaller versions of American Elm leaves, 1 to 2½ in. long, dark green, turning yellow in autumn. Flowers, greenish red, appear

Ulmus alata, Winged Elm

MORE ➤

Ulmus alata in fall

Ulmus alata continued

in February and are followed by oval, ⅓-in.-long, hairy samaras. Tends to seed everywhere and becomes weedlike. Grows in the most miserable soils. With selection for desirable traits, it has the potential for street tree use in urban settings. Grows 50 to 60 ft. high, two-thirds this in spread. Zones 6 to 9. Virginia to Florida, west to Illinois, Oklahoma, and Texas.

Cultivars and Varieties. 'Lace Parasol' is an introduction from the J. C. Raulston Arboretum with stiffly weeping habit and strongly two-winged stems that resemble a weeping *Euonymus alatus*. Leaves contract mildew in summer and fall. A beautiful accent plant, particularly in the winter garden. The original plant is now 15 ft. high, 20 ft. wide, kind of like a giant multi-legged spider.

Ulmus crassifolia
CEDAR ELM

Like *Ulmus alata*, left behind in the commercial world but used with some regularity in the Southwest. I remember seeing numerous specimens in San Antonio, Texas. A large tree, oval-rounded, with dense branches and 1- to 2-in.-long, dark green leaves, stiff and rough to the touch, like sandpaper. Flowers and fruit are unremarkable. Withstands drought and heavy, infertile soils; pH adaptable. A reasonable street and lawn tree for drier areas of the South. Not superior to *Ulmus parvifolia*. Grows 50 to 70 ft. high, 40 to 60 ft. wide. Zones 7 to 9. Mississippi to Arkansas and Texas.

Ulmus alata 'Lace Parasol'

Ulmus crassifolia, Cedar Elm, foliage

Ulmus alata 'Lace Parasol' branches

Ulmus parvifolia
LACEBARK ELM

Although this species is discussed in detail in *Dirr's Hardy Trees and Shrubs* (Portland, OR: Timber Press, 1997), it is necessary to reiterate its remarkable adaptability to full sun, heat, drought, and miserable soils. It is also easy to transplant and can be successfully summer-dug. 'Drake' was not mentioned in the first book but is the most widely grown and planted cultivar in the Deep South and the West. Habit is broad-rounded, with lustrous dark green leaves, arching, semi-pendent branches, and early exfoliating gray, brown, orange bark. 'Drake' grows 20 to 30 ft. high and wide. Zones 7 to10. China.

Ulmus parvifolia 'Drake' bark

Ulmus parvifolia 'Drake'

Ungnadia speciosa
MEXICAN BUCKEYE

A member of the family Sapindaceae that for all the taxonomic world looks like a buckeye, *Aesculus*, of the family Hippocastanaceae. Shrubby, often multi-stemmed, it develops a rounded outline. Leaves are compound pinnate with three to thirteen leaflets. Leaves are lustrous dark green turning golden yellow in fall. Showstopping beauty is provided by the rich rosy pink, redbud-like flowers that, in Georgia, open on naked stems in March and April and continue as the leaves develop. Each fragrant flower is up to 1 in. wide and composed of four to five petals with prominent stamens. The capsular, brown fruit, with three cells, resemble buckeye and dehisce to release the black, ½-in.-diameter, rounded seeds. Durable species that grows in sandy, limestone soils in the wild but has performed well in the heavier soils of Georgia. Useful as a specimen plant and in borders and groupings. Grows 10 to 15 ft. high and wide. Zones 8 to 10. Texas, New Mexico, and northern Mexico.

MORE ➤

Ungnadia speciosa foliage (leaflet)

Ungnadia speciosa continued

Ungnadia speciosa, Mexican Buckeye

Ungnadia speciosa flowers

Ungnadia speciosa fruit

Ungnadia speciosa mature fruit and fall color

Vaccinium arboreum
FARKLEBERRY

Absolutely beautiful, native, large shrub/small tree that offers the garden an aesthetic attribute in every season. Native on our property—I love to watch it sing and dance. Spring brings small, white flowers in profusion; summer the leathery, glossiest foliage imaginable; fall provides rich red to crimson leaves and shiny black fruit; and winter the exposed bark in grays, rich browns, oranges, and reddish browns. Sound worthy? It knows how to dress for the seasons, but even better is its street (cultural) toughness. Found as an understory plant, often in drier woods, with hickories, oaks, tupelos, and beeches. With all the hype, the truth must be told: it is difficult to find in commerce. Virtually impossible to root from shoot cuttings, so seed propagation is necessary. Root cuttings would probably work. Great understory filler. A stunning native that has resisted commercialization. Grows 15 to 20 ft. high. Zones 7 to 9. Virginia to North Carolina to Florida, southern Illinois and Texas.

Vaccinium arboreum bark

Vaccinium arboreum, Farkleberry

Vaccinium arboreum flowers

Vaccinium arboreum fruit

Vaccinium arboreum fall color

Vaccinium ashei
RABBITEYE BLUEBERRY

Many botanists consider this species little more than the southern extension of *Vaccinium corymbosum*. Taxonomically, perhaps—horticulturally, no! The Rabbiteye Blueberry, like its northern relative, has been hybridized, and numerous fruit-producing cultivars have been introduced. The large, upright-spreading habit with coarse, gray-brown stems makes it a poor fit for smaller landscapes. The 1- to 2½-in.-long, blue-green leaves turn shades of red in autumn. Fall color can be spectacular and is often long persistent, up to four weeks. The ¼-in.-long, urn-shaped, white flowers appear on naked stems in March and April. The fruit mature in late June and July (Athens) and are the most beautiful powder blue to purplish blue. Each cultivar has its own rich blue patina. Fruit are rounded, ⅜ to ½ in. across, sweet and scrumptious. Provide moist, acid soil and full sun, and let them be. Wise to plant two different cultivars to ensure cross-pollination and heavy fruit set. Excellent for use along the side of the vegetable garden. Also blends well in the shrub border. Grows 8 to 10 (to 12) ft. high. Zones 7 to 9. Southeastern United States.

Cultivars and Varieties. 'Climax', 'Tifblue', and 'Woodard' are among the best of the approximately 20 cultivars for home-garden fruit production.

Vaccinium ashei, Rabbiteye Blueberry

Vaccinium ashei flowers

Vaccinium ashei fruit

Vaccinium ashei fall color

Vaccinium crassifolium

CREEPING BLUEBERRY

Unusual evergreen groundcover blueberry with lustrous dark green, finely serrate, ⅓- to ¾-in.-long, ⅛- to ⅜-in.-wide, oval leaves. Rose-red, ¼-in.-diameter flowers occur in short lateral and terminal racemes in May. Requires sandy, acid, well-drained soil in partial shade. Creeping Blueberry was part of the breeding program at North Carolina State University; several cultivars were selected but have had a difficult time in commerce because of susceptibility to *Phytophthora* root rot and stem anthracnose. Beautiful in the right situation, simply not an adaptable groundcover. Grows 6 in. high (as I witnessed the plant), although heights of 2 ft. are mentioned in the literature; continuously spreading and rooting. Zones 7 to 8. North Carolina to Georgia.

Cultivars and Varieties. 'Bloodstone' is a subsp. *sempervirens* form with reddish new growth that matures to lustrous dark green. Grows 6 to 8 in. high and makes a rather pretty groundcover.

'Wells Delight' offers lustrous dark green elliptic leaves.

Vaccinium elliottii

What a beauty, especially in November, when the leaves become rich red to purplish red. Exists as an understory shrub, finely branched, gently upright-spreading, and finally arching. Stems are green in summer, becoming red in autumn. The mirror-surfaced, rich green leaves, ½ to 1¼ in. long, finely serrate, turn rich red and reddish

MORE ➤

Vaccinium elliottii fall color

Vaccinium elliottii in fall

Vaccinium elliottii continued

purple and persist into December (Athens). White flowers occur in two- to six-flowered fascicles from buds of the previous season's wood. The ⅓-in.-diameter, black fruit ripen in summer. Prospers in well-drained, acid, moist soils. Appears to tolerate considerable drought. Terrific naturalizing shrub for the shade. Grows 6 to 12 ft. high and wide. Zones 6 to 9. Southeastern Virginia to north Florida, westward to east Texas and Arkansas.

Vaccinium stamineum
DEERBERRY

Variable shrub with green to glaucous blue-green foliage, often wispy and arching habit, but capable of growing to 15 ft. high. The ¾- to 3-in.-long leaves are either entire or slightly toothed. The small, white flowers resemble miniature bells with the pistil-stamen complex about twice as long as the corollas. Flowers hang from the leaf axils and combine quite harmoniously with the foliage in April and May. Fruit are ⅓ in. in diameter, whitish to purple, globose to pear-shaped berries. Found in shade and sandy soils in the wild. I have walked through large, wild seedling populations with no two plants exactly alike. Excellent native shrub for naturalizing. Grows 2 to 10 ft. high (my observations). Zones 5 to 9. Massachusetts to Minnesota, south to Florida and Louisiana.

Vaccinium elliottii flowers

Vaccinium stamineum, Deerberry

Vaccinium stamineum flowers

Viburnum awabuki foliage and flower buds

Viburnum awabuki

Forever called *Viburnum japonicum*, *V. macrophyllum*, and *V. odoratissimum* in the South but in recent years provided its correct name, largely through the efforts of the late J. C. Raulston. The more I travel through the South, the more often this species surfaces, and an immense old specimen to the left of the number 10 hole at the Augusta National Golf Course reflects its true beauty. Almost pyramidal at maturity, the foliage is so thickly set that the outline resembles a solid green structure. The leaves are beyond leathery, lustrous and dark green, 3 to 7 in. long, ½ to 2 in. wide. Leaves hold their color through the seasons. A plant in the Dirr garden, sited by the front door, has been pruned to 8 ft. to keep it in check. For more than 12 years, it has been assaulted yet returns quickly to its former glory. White flowers appear in June, in rounded cymose-panicles. Fruit are red, but for great numbers a cross-pollinator is necessary. Ubiquitously adaptable, growing in any soil except wet. Tolerates sun and shade with equal facility. Large specimen broadleaf evergreen for screens, borders, and heavy shade plantings. Grows 10 to 15 (to 20) ft. high. Zones (7)8 to 9. Japan.

Cultivars and Varieties. 'Chindo' was introduced by J. C. Raulston for its large, pendulous, red fruit clusters.

Viburnum awabuki

Viburnum awabuki fruit

Viburnum awabuki fall and winter color

Viburnum ×bodnantense

Simply could not omit these early-flowering (December through March), fragrant viburnums from this work. Hybrids between *Viburnum farreri* (see *Dirr's Hardy Trees and Shrubs* [Portland, OR: Timber Press, 1997]) and *V. grandiflorum*, they are suited to culture in Zone 7 if properly sited in shade and provided moisture in hot, dry weather. The habit is ragged to rugged, upright-spreading with a rounded top. The leaves, 2 to 4 in. long, are heavily pleated with impressed veins, rich green with red petioles. Fall foliage color seldom develops. Flowers occur in small, 1- to 2-in.-wide panicles in winter. Colors, depending on cultivar, are deep pink ('Charles Lamont'), rich pink ('Dawn'), and shell-pink buds to white ('Deben'). The fragrance is sweet with a slight edge. I observed fruit only once, ovoid, ⅓ in. long, red, finally black in fall. Adaptable species; provide protection from winter wind and sun. Flowers are often browned (burned) by extreme cold. The smallest amount of warmth induces sporadic flowering. *Never* spectacular but always worth waiting for. Grows 8 to 10 (to 15) ft. high and wide. Zones 6 to 7.

Viburnum ×bodnantense foliage

Viburnum ×bodnantense flowers

Viburnum ×bodnantense 'Charles Lamont'

Viburnum ×bodnantense 'Dawn'

Viburnum ×bodnantense fruit

Viburnum ×bodnantense 'Dawn' in flower

Viburnum ×bodnantense 'Deben'

Viburnum bracteatum foliage

Viburnum bracteatum, Bracted Viburnum

Viburnum bracteatum in fall

Viburnum bracteatum
BRACTED VIBURNUM

A rare but singularly beautiful species that is often confused with *Viburnum dentatum* but offers more leathery, lustrous dark green, heat-resistant leaves and is self-fruitful, based on the heavy fruit that occurs on 'Emerald Luster'. Habit is oval-rounded with even-diameter, arrow-shaft stems that eventually arch to form a rounded outline. As I pen this description, I peer out the window at a 12-ft.-high behemoth growing in the shade of Southern Red Oak, *Quercus falcata*. Leaves are coarsely dentate, with scalloped margins, 2 to 4 in. long and almost as wide, lustrous dark green turning bronze-yellow in fall. In May, the cream-white flowers appear at the end of every shoot in 5-in.-diameter, flat-topped cymes. Flowers are showy for a white-flowered viburnum. The beautiful rich blue-purple-black fruit ripen in late summer and are taken by the birds. Tougher-than-nails species that receives little press. Adaptable to anything but wet soil, in sun to moderate shade; flowering is maximized in sun. Excellent for the border, in shade and groupings, and for screening. Stems are so thickly set that the plant

MORE ➤

Viburnum bracteatum fruit

Viburnum bracteatum continued

serves as an effective screen even in winter. Grows 10 ft. high and wide, easily kept smaller by pruning. Zones 6 to 8. Southeastern United States.

Cultivars and Varieties. 'Emerald Luster', an introduction from my program, embodies all the traits just mentioned in a single genetic unit.

Viburnum bracteatum 'Emerald Luster'

Viburnum bracteatum fall color

Viburnum bracteatum 'Emerald Luster' flowers

Viburnum cassinoides, Witherod Viburnum, Cadillac Mountain, Maine

Viburnum cassinoides new foliage

Viburnum cassinoides flowers

Viburnum cassinoides fruit

Viburnum cassinoides fall color

Viburnum cassinoides var. *angustifolium* fall color

Viburnum cassinoides
WITHEROD VIBURNUM

A longtime favorite that has followed me from Georgia to Maine and back home again. Lovely, rounded shrub with spreading, arching branches and 1½- to 3½-in.-long, dull, dark green leaves, morphing into dull red and purple in autumn. The new shoots are bronze to chocolate-tinted. The white flowers with yellow stamens are borne in 2- to 5-in.-diameter, flat-topped cymes in May and June. The fruit are beautiful, transmogrifying themselves from green to pink-rose to blue to purple-black, often all colors in the same cluster. Fruit ripen in September and October. Adaptable species that grows in granite cracks and crevices on Cadillac Mountain, Maine, and along Panther Creek in north Georgia. More compact and heavy-fruiting in full sun but tolerates considerable shade. Beautiful in mass, in borders, and as a filler in shade. Grows 6 to 10 (to 15) ft. high and wide. Zones 3 to 8. Canada to Georgia.

Cultivars and Varieties. var. *angustifolium* has smaller, narrower leaves and a more open habit.

Viburnum cassinoides in fall

Viburnum davidii

DAVID VIBURNUM

A favored evergreen viburnum among the cognoscenti but temperamental in the Southeast. Better suited to the Mediterranean climate around San Francisco and into British Columbia. In Europe, it is as common as privet and thrives with neglect. The habit is distinctly rounded to mounded, dense, and bulletproof. Possible to bounce a quarter off the tightly affixed foliage. The conspicuous, three-nerved leaves, leathery, lustrous dark green, are 2 to 6 in. long. The pink-budded flowers open dull white in dense, 2- to 3-in.-wide, convex cymes in April and May. Plant two or more specimens to ensure cross-pollination. The ¼-in.-long, oval fruit are lustrous metallic blue and persist into winter. Requires moist, well-drained soil and shade protection in the South. Beautiful when properly grown. Used in groupings and masses and for textural accent. Grows 3 to 5 ft. high and wide. Zones (7)8 to 9. China.

Viburnum cinnamonifolium is a large version of *V. davidii*, reaching 6 to 10 (to 15) ft. high. Atlanta Botanical Garden houses a respectable 6- to 8-ft. specimen. Hardier than *V. davidii* and better adapted to the Southeast.

Cultivars and Varieties. 'Jermyn's Globe' is a hybrid between *Viburnum davidii* and *V. calvum* that originated at Hillier Arboretum. Leaves are smaller and not as lustrous as *V. davidii*. Grows 10 to 12 ft. high and wide. Taxonomically categorized as a cultivar of *V. ×globosum*.

Viburnum davidii, David Viburnum

Viburnum davidii foliage

Viburnum davidii flowers

Viburnum davidii fruit

Viburnum cinnamonifolium foliage and flowers

Viburnum cinnamonifolium

Viburnum japonicum

JAPANESE VIBURNUM

If a gardening friend tells you they have this species, provide the quizzical "are you sure?" look. Misidentified by pro and amateur, the true species is evergreen, white-flowered, and red-fruited, with broad-ovate leaves. Habit is rounded and relatively dense; leaves, each 2 to 5 in. long, about as wide, are leathery, lustrous dark green, with a few remote teeth toward the apex. The fragrant, white, ⅜-in.-wide flowers are produced in 2- to 4-in.-diameter cymes in May. Beautiful red fruit, ⅓ in. long, oval-rounded, ripen in fall and persist into winter. Requires some shade protection, moist, acid, well-drained soil. Rare species, possibly for the collector. Dr. Egolf used it to breed 'Chippewa' (*Viburnum japonicum* × *V. dilatatum*) and 'Huron' (*V. lobophyllum* × *V. japonicum*), two 8- to 10-ft.-high and -wide cultivars with leathery dark green foliage and red fruit. *Viburnum japonicum* grows 6 to 8 ft. high and wide. Zones 7 to 9. Japan.

MORE ➤

Viburnum japonicum foliage

Viburnum japonicum fruit

Viburnum ×globosum 'Jermyn's Globe' foliage and flowers

Viburnum japonicum flowers

Viburnum ×globosum 'Jermyn's Globe' winter color

Viburnum japonicum continued

Viburnum 'Chippewa' fall color

Viburnum macrocephalum forma *keteleeri* fruit

Viburnum japonicum, Japanese Viburnum

Viburnum macrocephalum, Chinese Snowball Viburnum

Viburnum macrocephalum

CHINESE SNOWBALL VIBURNUM

Visitors to the Dirr garden are intrigued and mystified by the large, white, poofy flowers that cover this plant in April and May. When I tell them it's a viburnum, the usual retort reverberates, "I thought it was a hydrangea!" Large, robust, dominating, vase-shaped shrub with a rounded top. The 2- to 4-in.-long leaves are dark green, hold late, and develop little fall color. The flower buds are naked (no covering scales), similar to small cauliflower heads, and send forth apple-green florets that mature glistening white. The entire process is stretched over six to eight weeks. Inflorescences range from 5 to 8 in. in diameter. Fruit are not formed because the inflorescence is sterile. Site in full sun (partial shade acceptable), in moist, acid, well-drained soil. Have never witnessed any pest problems. A strong flowering element in the shrub border. Our lone plant is stationed in front of a large *Cedrus deodara* and captures the spotlight when in flower. Often overgrows its boundaries; I cut it to within 2 to 3 ft. of the ground after flowering. The new growth does not flower the next year, but terrific rebloom occurs thereafter. Also possesses the curious and welcome initiative of flowering in autumn. Grows 12 to 15 (to 20) ft. high, about as wide. Zones 6 to 9. China.

Cultivars and Varieties. Forma *keteleeri*, the reproductive member of the species, produces sterile, showy florets on the outside, fertile on the interior, in 4- to 5-in.-diameter, flat-topped cymes. The brilliant red fruit that follow are spectacular.

Viburnum macrocephalum forma *keteleeri*

Viburnum macrocephalum foliage

Viburnum macrocephalum flowers

Viburnum macrocephalum forma *keteleeri* flowers

Viburnum nudum
SMOOTH WITHEROD

Considered by some authorities a subspecies of *Viburnum cassinoides* but logically a distinct entity based on leaf and habitat characteristics. Large shrub, similar to *V. cassinoides* in outline but with extremely lustrous dark green leaves that turn red to reddish purple in fall. The lustrous, sheeny, waxy cuticle accentuates the fall colors. Each leaf is 2 to 5 in. long, oval in outline, and usually entire, compared to those of *V. cassinoides*, which have serrated margins. The musky-scented, creamy white flowers, in 3- to 5-in.-diameter, flat-topped cymes, open in May and June. Fruit, much like those of *V. cassinoides*, start green on their way to pink, rose, bluish, and purplish black. In the wild, it is found in wet soil areas, and near Mobile, Alabama, I witnessed the species at home in the swamps of Weeks Bay Wildlife Refuge. Many southern nurserymen produce splendid container-grown plants. Beautiful for foliage effect. Grows 6 to 10 ft. high and wide. Zones 5 to 9. Connecticut, Long Island to Florida, west to Kentucky and Louisiana.

Cultivars and Varieties. 'Count Pulaski' is a multi-stemmed, loosely structured form with flowers and fruit in 6- to 10-in.-diameter clusters.

'Pink Beauty' has beautiful lustrous dark green leaves and pink fruit.

'Winterthur' is seemingly more compact than the two selections just mentioned, with lustrous dark green foliage, reddish purple fall color, and typical flowers and fruit.

Viburnum nudum, Smooth Witherod

Viburnum nudum foliage and flowers

Viburnum nudum flower buds

Viburnum nudum fruit

Viburnum nudum fall color

Viburnum nudum 'Winterthur'

Viburnum obovatum
SMALL VIBURNUM

Although considered a "small" viburnum, this is only from the standpoint of the ¾- to 2-in.-long, spatulate leaves, lustrous dark green, tardily deciduous, and early leafing. A plant in the University's Botanical Garden started petite and is now 10 to 12 ft. high and wide—a rounded, dense matrix of stems. The white flowers, in 1¾- to 2¼-in.-diameter cymes, open with the emerging leaves in April. Flowers do not shout, so engage them at

MORE ➤

Viburnum obovatum flowers

Viburnum obovatum fall color

Viburnum obovatum foliage

Viburnum obovatum, Small Viburnum

Viburnum obovatum continued

close quarters. The red, ellipsoidal, ⅓-in.-long fruit mature to black. Adapted to wet areas in nature but tolerant of dry soils once established. Found along stream banks and low woods. A worthy massing shrub, it is used in commercial landscapes in Tampa, Florida. More evergreen in the Deep South, progressing to deciduous in Zones 6 and 7. Grows 10 to 12 ft. high and wide. National champion is 23 ft. high and wide. Zones 6 to 9. South Carolina to Florida and Alabama.

Cultivars and Varieties. At least three dwarf forms have been introduced, with 'Reifler's Dwarf' and the Superior Tree Form the best I have observed. Both grow less than 5 ft. high and maintain more compact habit and dense foliage.

Viburnum odoratissimum

The species that is most often misidentified as *Viburnum awabuki* and *V. japonicum*. Unique because of dull, flat green leaves and stinky odor of bruised leaves, which recalls that of green peppers. Also the least cold hardy species, adapted only to Zones 8 and higher. A large, broadleaf evergreen shrub or small tree, oval-rounded in habit. The 2- to 4-in.-long, elliptic-oval leaves are dull olive-green. The white flowers are followed by red fruit. Extremely durable species for the Coastal Plain of the Southeast; large plants grow in Florida and Louisiana. Full sun and moderate shade adaptability. Good hedge plant. Grows 10 to 20 (to 30) ft. high. Zones 8 to 10. India, Burma, China to Japan and Philippines.

Cultivars and Varieties. 'Red Tip', with reddish green young foliage, is occasionally offered in commerce.

Viburnum odoratissimum foliage

Viburnum odoratissimum

Viburnum odoratissimum as a hedge

Viburnum rafinesquianum
DOWNY ARROWWOOD,
RAFINESQUE VIBURNUM

What started as a small, rather forlorn shrub in the University's Botanical Garden has matured into a broad-rounded meshwork of fine-textured stems and deeply veined, smallish leaves. Leaves are medium to dark green, 2 to 3 in. long, narrow-ovate with strong serrations; autumn entices a stubborn pale yellow from them, just enough to notice. The dull white flowers appear after the leaves in 2-in.-diameter clusters and are followed by blue-black fruit. In the wild, grows in drier basic or neutral soils but is quite adaptable under cultivation. Full sun to partial shade prove ideal. A good wildlife plant, naturalizing shrub, grouping, or massing. An enterprising nurseryman grew hundreds in the hopes of creating a market and still has hundreds. Grows 6 to 10 ft. high and wide. Zones 5 to 8. Quebec to Manitoba, south to Georgia, Kentucky, and Missouri.

Viburnum rafinesquianum flowers

Viburnum rafinesquianum, Downy Arrowwood

Viburnum suspensum
SANDANKWA VIBURNUM

Another broadleaf evergreen shrub, thickly set with branches and leaves—a perfect combination for hedge and screening uses. From the coast of Georgia to Key West, Florida, it increases in frequency. Leaves, 2 to 5 in. long, leathery, lustrous dark green, remain so through the seasons. In April, the white, faintly tinged pink, fragrant flowers open. Typically, they remain an enigma, because the plants are pruned for hedges and so flowers are removed. The globose fruit start red, maturing black. Appears well adapted to full sun, moderate shade, heat, drought, and sandy soils. Grows 6 to 12 ft. high and wide. Zones (8)9 to 11. Ryukyu Islands of Japan.

Viburnum suspensum, Sandankwa Viburnum

Viburnum suspensum foliage

Viburnum suspensum pruned as a hedge

Viburnum tinus
LAURUSTINUS

Never have I observed so many variations on a *Viburnum* species as occur within the genetic plasticity of *Viburnum tinus*. At Hillier Arboretum, from my arrival in mid-February to my return on July 27, 1999, one cultivar or another still produced the odd flower. Peak period is late winter (England), January and February (Athens). Habit is upright-rounded, evergreen, dense, thickly branched, and wall-like. The leaves are beautiful, lustrous dark, almost black-green, 1½ to 4 in. long, maintaining this beauty through the seasons. The pink-budded flowers open white in 2- to 4-in.-diameter cymes. Flower effect seems forever because cool temperatures prolong the effectiveness. Ever so slightly fragrant, but especially pleasant to be around when thoughts of the new gardening season are strong. The metallic blue fruit mature blue-black to black and persist into the next flowering cycle. This is a stalwart plant in Europe, less so in the South and West. Great shade plant, also tolerant of full sun.

Grows in gravel and clay; pH adaptable and salt-tolerant. Great plant for the winter garden. Serviceable, functional, and aesthetic in one mass of green. Hedge, barrier, screen, grouping, and shrub border use. Grows 6 to 12 ft. high, slightly less in spread. Zones (8)9 to 10. In Athens, killed to the ground at −3°F; in Washington, Georgia, 40 miles southeast, two 10-ft.-high shrubs thrive on an old estate. Southern Europe, northern Africa.

Cultivars and Varieties. Many, with 'Spring Bouquet', 'Eve Price', and 'Compactum' pink-budded and smaller in stature than the species.

'Bewley's Variegated' and 'Variegata' have cream-margined leaves and are less vigorous than the species.

'Clyne Castle', 'Gwenllian', and 'French's White' are larger types with good foliage.

MORE ➤

Viburnum tinus, Laurustinus

Viburnum tinus continued

Viburnum tinus foliage

Viburnum tinus flowers

Viburnum tinus 'Eve Price'

Viburnum tinus 'Compactum'

Viburnum tinus fruit

Viburnum tinus 'Bewley's Variegated'

Viburnum tinus 'Gwenllian' fruit

Viburnum tinus 'Gwenllian'

Viburnum tinus 'Variegata'

Viburnum utile
SERVICE VIBURNUM

The great breeding partner that resulted in the *Viburnum ×burkwoodii* complex and superior cultivars like 'Conoy', 'Eskimo', and 'Chesapeake'. Multiplicity of ornamental traits—leaf, flower, fruit—are transmitted to its offspring. The species is a broad-leaf evergreen shrub, somewhat loose and open in habit, with 1- to 3-in.-long, lustrous black-green leaves, wavy-margined and -surfaced. The underside is covered with thickish gray-white pubescence. The slightly fragrant flowers appear in 2- to 3-in.-diameter, rounded cymes in April. Buds are pink and open to white, five-petaled flowers. Fruit is a flattened, ovoid, ¼-in.-long, red to black drupe. Durable and resilient, it displays drought and heat tolerance as well as shade and sun adaptability. A small plant in our garden exhibited no drought stress in the disastrously hot, dry summers of 1998, 1999, and 2000. In some measure, a collector's and breeder's plant but quite beautiful in flower and foliage. Excellent shrub border plant. Grows 4 to 6 ft. high and wide. Zones 6 to 8. China.

Viburnum utile, Service Viburnum

Viburnum ×burkwoodii 'Conoy'

Viburnum utile flowers

Viburnum utile foliage

Viburnum ×burkwoodii 'Conoy' foliage

Vinca major, Large Periwinkle

Vinca major
LARGE PERIWINKLE

The standard window box or container plant, located in the front and allowed to trail over the edges. Such creativity! It is also a respectable broadleaf evergreen groundcover that becomes rampageous. Entire areas, bordered by walks, were eaten by the species at the University's Botanical Garden. Initially, I planted the variegated form in the heavily shaded area of the Dirr garden and ten years later was still trying to eradicate it. With that said, the plant forms a rolling sea of lustrous dark green, with 1½-in.-diameter, five-petaled, lilac-blue flowers in March and April. Flowers are lovely but never overwhelming. Soils should be evenly moist, well-drained, and acid. Shade is preferred. Displays drought intolerance by flagging like a limp lasagne noodle. Less drought-tolerant than *Vinca minor*. For rapid cover in shade, a reasonable choice. Nooks and crannies on the east and north sides of houses and structures are good locations. Frisky when left to the wide-open, shady places. Grows 12 to 18 in. high, rooting as it spreads, forming large colonies. Zones 6 to 9. France, Italy, former Yugoslavia.

Cultivars and Varieties. A number of variegated leaf types are known, with 'Variegata' the most common; its leaves are broadly margined with cream. 'Aureomaculata' has a central blotch of yellow-green that is not as visually potent as 'Variegata'.

Vinca major flower

Vinca major 'Variegata' flower

Vinca major 'Variegata'

Vinca minor, Common Periwinkle

Vinca minor owning the woods

Vinca minor
COMMON PERIWINKLE

Along with *Liriope* species, *Pachysandra terminalis*, *Hedera helix*, and *Euonymus fortunei* 'Coloratus', one of the big five of American groundcovers. A low, ground-hugging, broadleaf evergreen, with ½- to 1½-in.-long, medium to dark green leaves, it forms a perfect carpet. Flowers are 1 in. in diameter, lilac-blue, opening in March and April. Prefers moist, well-drained soil in shade. More drought-tolerant than *Vinca major*. Blight, canker, and die-back are attributable to several fungi. I have observed significant infection in wet soils and with prevalent rainfall. Also, the species is invasive, and entire woodlands have been digested. At its best, a worthy groundcover in a garden situation. The clump you dig up and throw in the woods may some day own the woods. Grows 3 to 6 in. high, rooting at the nodes and spreading indefinitely. Zones 4 to 8. Europe, western Asia.

Cultivars and Varieties. Many, several worth exploring for foliage and flower colors.

'Alba' represents the white-flowered types, which are not as vigorous as the typical species.

'Atropurpurea' bears deep plum-purple flowers and has always been one of my favorites.

'Bowles White', 'Emily', and 'Gertrude Jekyll' are white-flowered clones.

'Bowles Variety' ('La Grave') produces large, 1½-in.-diameter, lavender-blue flowers on a clump-forming plant.

Variegated forms. Variegated leaf forms with blue or white flowers are common. 'Albovariegata' (white flowers, yellow-edged leaves); 'Argenteovariegata' (blue flowers, white-margined leaves); 'Illumination' (blue flowers, yellow-centered leaf); 'Ralph Shugert' (blue flowers, cream-white to white margins, dark green centers); and 'Sterling Silver' (pale violet-blue flower, cream-margined leaf) are available.

Double-flowered forms. Several, including 'Azurea Flore Pleno' (sky blue), 'Florepleno' (purple-blue), and 'Rosea Plena' (violet-pink), are known.

Vinca minor foliage

Vinca minor flowers

Vinca minor 'Illumination'

MORE ➤

Vinca minor **continued**

Vinca minor 'Alba'

Vinca minor 'Atropurpurea'

Vinca minor 'Bowles Variety'

Vinca minor 'Azurea Flore Pleno'

Vitex rotundifolia

Unusual species that looks nothing like a vitex. The habit is sprawling-spreading, and a single five-year-old plant in our test plots is now 12 ft. wide and about 2 ft. high. The leaves are beautiful bluish green, about 2 in. long, 1½ in. wide, suborbicular in outline. The bluish purple flowers appear in short inflorescences from the leaf axils in May and thereafter on new growth of the season. Noted for its salt tolerance and ability to prosper in dry, sandy soils. Excellent for stabilizing oceanfront real estate. Also prospers in heavy soils. Requires full sun for best development. Utilize in rough areas of the garden or commercial landscape. Remember, it is deciduous and has an overstated disheveled look in winter. Grows 1 to 2 ft. high, infinitely spreading. Zones 7 to 10. Asia to Australia.

Vitex rotundifolia

Vitex rotundifolia foliage

Vitis rotundifolia
MUSCADINE

Mentioned ever so briefly in *Dirr's Hardy Trees and Shrubs* (Portland, OR: Timber Press, 1997) but deserving of more eloquent verbiage, since it is native throughout the Southeast and has been domesticated for garden and commercial fruit production. A phenomenally vigorous and long-lived vine that grows in the understory, almost groundcover-like and can climb a tree like no creature on earth. Leaves are 2½ to 5 in. high and wide, glossy dark green, and coarsely serrate. In fall, leaves turn soft mellow yellow. The ⅓- to 1-in.-diameter, rounded fruit are greenish to purplish with a thick skin. Fruit are utilized for jellies, jams, and wine. Alternatively, pop in your mouth, extract the skin, savor the sweet juice in the interior, and remove the rest. Unbelievably adaptable, but best fruit set occurs in the sun. Use trellises and arbors in garden settings. Requires considerable pruning to keep it in harmony with the structure and the rest of the garden. Grows 100 ft. high. Zones 5 to 9. Delaware to northern Florida, west to Missouri, Kansas, Texas, and Mexico.

Vitis rotundifolia, Muscadine, in fall

Vitis rotundifolia foliage

Vitis rotundifolia fruit

Wedelia trilobata
WEDELIA

I first spied this beautiful plant on the Louisiana State University campus at Baton Rouge, Louisiana, where it functioned as a utilitarian groundcover. A wide-spreading, trailing habit, rooting where stems touch moist soil, allows it to cover large expanses of real estate. I tried it in our Georgia garden; it covered an entire bed in a single season, but the following winter killed it to the root tips. Grows into neighboring shrubs, creating an untidy composition. The lustrous dark green, evergreen (Zone 10) leaves are opposite, to 4 in. long, one-half as wide, often three-lobed. They serve as a background for the yellow, daisy-like, ½- to ¾-in.-diameter flowers that develop on 4- to 6-in.-long stalks over much of the growing season. Best grown in full sun to partial shade. Well-drained soils are important. Becomes unkempt with time and should be cut or mowed to rejuvenate. Amazingly fast coverage for banks, slopes, difficult to mow locations. Grows 12 to 15 in. high, spreading forever. Zones 9 to 11. Tropical America.

Wedelia trilobata, Wedelia

Wisteria frutescens
AMERICAN WISTERIA

Years past, the species was meshed into our garden and never really impressed. Recently, I experienced a plant in flower (late April, Athens) and was smitten. The great attributes over the Asiatic species like *Wisteria floribunda* and *W. sinensis* are lateness to leaf out and flower, thus avoiding spring frosts, and less rambunctious growth habit. Still a vigorous, twining vine that requires support to look its best. Leaves consist of nine to fifteen, bright green leaflets, each 1½ to 2½ in. long, that turn yellowish in fall. The fragrant flowers, pale lilac-purple, ¾ in. long, are compressed into 4- to 6-in.-long, dense, villous racemes. Flowering is most pronounced in May (in Athens) but sporadically occurs on new growth into the summer. The flowers are not as impressive (or as large) as the Asiatic relatives but are more delicately beautiful and restrained. Fruit are 2- to 4-in.-long, glabrous pods with rounded, lima bean–like seeds. Best in moist soil in sun to partial shade. The plant in our garden was in dry soil and simply never performed. In the wild, it occurs naturally along moist shores of streams, ponds, and lakes, on the borders of wet woodlands and swamps, and in moist to wet thickets. This tells the gardener something about best siting in the garden. Grows 20 to 30 ft. high. Zones 5 to 9. Virginia to Florida and Texas.

Wisteria macrostachys, Kentucky Wisteria, is similar and by taxonomists described as a variety of *W. frutescens*. Appears more cold hardy, flowering in June in the Chicago area, with the typical lilac-purple flowers. 'Clara Mack' produces white flowers, later and in longer racemes than the species. Grows 15 to 25 ft. high. Zones (4)5 to 8(9). Missouri to Tennessee and Texas.

Cultivars and Varieties. 'Amethyst Falls', a selection of *Wisteria frutescens*, is appropriately named for the most beautiful, fragrant, lavender-blue flowers.

'Nivea' is a white-flowered form.

Wisteria frutescens, American Wisteria

Wisteria frutescens flowers

Wisteria frutescens 'Amethyst Falls'

Zamia pumila
(Z. floridana)
COONTIE

Delicate, elegant, broadleaf evergreen, spreading "shrub" that is utilized throughout Florida in foundation and mass plantings. The deep green, lustrous, leathery leaflets are held on 3- to 5-ft.-long, compound pinnate leaves. Each leaflet is less than ½ in. wide and either planar along the rachis or twisted and curved. The species is dioecious; female plants develop conelike structures with orange to scarlet seeds that mature in fall to winter. Adaptable species that grows in any well-drained soil. Prefers partial shade, but I have observed plants in full sun in north Florida. Brought plants to Athens for testing, and they were burned beyond recognition by a single winter. Irresistibly beautiful, with many landscape uses. Grows 1 to 3 ft. high, wider at maturity. Zones 8 to 11. Florida, West Indies, Cuba.

Zamia furfuracea, Cardboard Palm, has 2- to 6-in.-long, 1- to 3-in.-wide leaflets with cardboard-like texture. Not as cold hardy as *Z. pumila* but unique because of the foliage. Zones 9 to 11. Mexico, on sand dunes.

Zamia pumila, Coontie

Zamia furfuracea, Cardboard Palm

Zamia pumila foliage

Zamia furfuracea foliage

Zanthoxylum americanum flowers

Zanthoxylum americanum
PRICKLY-ASH, TOOTHACHE TREE

Seldom utilized for the contrived landscapes but a worthy native for naturalizing and wildlife food. Almost always a colonizing shrub, rather unruly in outline, prominently armed with 1/3- to 1/2-in.-long prickles. The compound pinnate leaves, composed of five to thirteen, 1½- to 2½-in.-long, lustrous dark green leaflets, are insect- and disease-resistant. Yellowish green flowers open on naked stems in April and May. Fruit, on female plants, are 1/5-in.-long, red capsules that ripen in July and August and contain small, lustrous black seeds. Adaptable, tough, durable species for sun or partial shade. Could be utilized as a barrier plant in infertile soils. Might prove a respectable massing plant for cuts or fills along highways. The bark was chewed to alleviate toothaches. Grows 15 to 25 ft. high and wide; usually smaller, to 10 ft. high. Zones 3 to 7. Quebec to North Dakota, south to Georgia and Louisiana.

The related species *Zanthoxylum clava-herculis*, Hercules-club, Pepperwood, is a shrub or tree with glossy dark green leaves, white to yellow-green flowers, and thornlike prickles on a platform base. Stems are coarse and chubby. Grows on sand dunes along the coast and is quite salt-tolerant. Important source of butterfly-caterpillar food. Grows 25 to 30 ft. high. Zones 7 to 10. Virginia, along coast to Texas and Oklahoma.

Zanthoxylum americanum, Prickly-ash

Zanthoxylum clava-herculis, Hercules-club

Zanthoxylum americanum fruit

Zanthoxylum clava-herculis stem and prickles

Zelkova sinica
CHINESE ZELKOVA

Forever second fiddle to *Zelkova serrata* but a handsome genetic unit with uniform habit and unique bark. Rare in all but arboreta with notable trees in the Arnold Arboretum, Jamaica Plain, Massachusetts; Morton Arboretum, Lisle, Illinois; and the former USDA Bamboo Station, Savannah, Georgia. Vase-shaped habit, narrower than the average *Z. serrata*, 1- to 2½-in.-long, scabrous, dark green leaves, and multi-colored gray, orange, brown, exfoliating bark offer seasonal aesthetics. Leaves turn yellow-orange in fall but with no degree of certainty. A tough species, from Chicago to Boston to Savannah. Clay, sand, and drought present no problem to successful culture. Selection for desirable traits is necessary before it can become an everyday street and urban tree. Grows 20 to 40 ft. high. Zones (5)6 to 9. Eastern China.

Zelkova sinica, Chinese Zelkova

Zelkova sinica in winter

Zelkova sinica bark

Zelkova sinica foliage

Ziziphus jujuba
CHINESE DATE

Beautiful, lustrous, mirror-reflective, dark green foliage seems sufficient reason to utilize the species. However, habit—upright-spreading to rounded—is often rumpled. The 1- to 2½-in.-long, strongly three-veined leaves are uniquely crenate-serrulate along the margin. The ¼-in.-diameter, grape-soda fragrant, yellowish flowers occur two to three together from the leaf axils of the current season's growth. Flower effect is masked, for the leaves develop simultaneously. Fruit are prized in China as a commercial staple. The egg-shaped, ½- to 1-in.-long fruit are brownish on the outside with a dried apple–like consistency on the inside. Several trees at the University's Horticulture Farm yielded tons of fruit. I sample a fruit each visit and still have not found a window of time when the taste is palatable. I know, I know—to each their own. Concrete-like tenacity in heat. If paired stem spines and fruit could be removed, it might make a good street tree. Grows 15 to 20 (to 25) ft. high. Zones 6 to 9. Southeastern Europe to southern and eastern Asia.

Ziziphus jujuba, Chinese Date

Ziziphus jujuba bark

Ziziphus jujuba foliage and flowers

Ziziphus jujuba fruit

Selecting Plants for Specific Characteristics or Purposes

Many readers require ready access to information on specific plants for specific purposes. In compiling the following lists of the plants best suited to certain purposes or offering specific commonly desired characteristics, I limited the entries to those plants that are most appropriate. Certainly a tad of personal bias is evident, but in the main, I erred on the side of objectivity. Use these lists as ready references to possible solutions for planting design problems. Perhaps salt tolerance is a criterion for landscaping a beach house; *Fuchsia magellanica, Myrica cerifera,* and *Serenoa repens* appear on the list of salt-tolerant shrubs. Look them up in the main body of the book, read the text, peruse the photographs, and decide which plants will create the desired effects.

Plant Lists

Flower Color

The following trees bear flowers of notable color. The primary flower color(s) is indicated for each plant. Variations of flower color will exist in certain cultivars or varieties of a plant, and flowers can often be ornamented with stripes or blotches of a different color.

WHITE

Aesculus californica
Aesculus indica
Alangium platanifolium
Aleurites fordii
Arbutus ×andrachnoides
Arbutus menziesii
Arbutus unedo
Bauhinia variegata
Butia capitata
Camellia japonica
Castanea pumila
Chilopsis linearis
Cinnamomum camphora
Clethra arborea
Clethra barbinervis
Crataegus aestivalis
Crataegus opaca
Crataegus rufula
Diospyros kaki
Ehretia dicksonii
Elliottia racemosa
Emmenopterys henryi
Eriobotrya japonica
Eucryphia glutinosa
Euscaphis japonicus
Gordonia lasianthus
Ilex ×altaclerensis
Ilex aquifolium
Ilex cassine
Ilex cornuta
Ilex 'Emily Bruner'
Ilex ×koehneana
Ilex latifolia

Ilex 'Nellie R. Stevens'
Ilex 'Red Hollies'
Ilex rotunda
Ilex vomitoria
Lagerstroemia fauriei
Lagerstroemia hybrids
Lagerstroemia indica
Ligustrum lucidum
Lithocarpus densiflorus
Lithocarpus henryi
Magnolia ashei
Magnolia grandiflora
Malus 'Callaway'
Malus 'Harvest Gold'
Malus 'Jewelberry'
Malus 'Red Jewel'
Malus 'Sugar Tyme'
Michelia doltsopa
Michelia ×foggii
Michelia maudiae
Myrtus communis
Osmanthus americanus
Osmanthus fragrans
Phoenix canariensis
Phoenix reclinata
Photinia serrulata
Pinckneya pubens
Poliothyrsis sinensis
Prunus americana
Prunus caroliniana
Prunus mume
Sabal palmetto
Sinojackia rehderiana
Stewartia malacodendron

Styrax grandifolius
Syagrus romanzoffianum
Vaccinium arboreum
Washingtonia filifera
Washingtonia robusta

YELLOW

Acacia dealbata
Acer barbatum
Acer leucoderme
Aesculus sylvatica
Alangium platanifolium
Alnus serrulata
Broussonetia papyrifera
Cornus capitata
Euscaphis japonicus
Grevillea robusta
Idesia polycarpa
Koelreuteria bipinnata
Koelreuteria elegans
Laurus nobilis
Parkinsonia aculeata
Persea borbonia
Sapindus drummondii
Sapium japonicum
Sapium sebiferum
×Sycoparrotia semidecidua
Sycopsis sinensis
Trachycarpus fortunei
Trochodendron aralioides
Ziziphus jujuba

PINK/ROSE

Aesculus californica

Aesculus indica
Aleurites fordii
Arbutus unedo
Camellia japonica
Chilopsis linearis
Lagerstroemia hybrids
Lagerstroemia indica
Magnolia campbellii
Malus angustifolia
Pinckneya pubens (bracts)
Prunus campanulata
Prunus mume

RED

Callistemon citrinus
Callistemon viminalis
Camellia japonica
Erythrina crista-gallii
Lagerstroemia hybrids
Lagerstroemia indica
Malus 'Adams'
Malus 'Liset'
Malus 'Prairifire'
Prunus mume

PURPLE

Bauhinia variegata
Chilopsis linearis
×Chitalpa tashkentensis
Lagerstroemia hybrids
Lagerstroemia indica
Melia azedarach
Pittosporum tenuifolium
Sophora secundiflora

Fragrant Flowers

The following trees bear flowers with notable fragrance.

Acacia dealbata
Aesculus californica
Aesculus indica
Alangium platanifolium
Chilopsis linearis
Clethra arborea
Clethra barbinervis
Diospyros kaki
Ehretia dicksonii
Elliottia racemosa
Eriobotrya japonica

Eucryphia glutinosa
Gordonia lasianthus
Ilex ×altaclerensis
Ilex aquifolium
Ilex cassine
Ilex cornuta
Ilex 'Emily Bruner'
Ilex ×koehneana
Ilex latifolia
Ilex 'Nellie R. Stevens'
Ilex 'Red Hollies'

Ilex rotunda
Ilex vomitoria
Lagerstroemia fauriei
Lagerstroemia hybrids
Lagerstroemia indica
Ligustrum lucidum
Magnolia ashei
Magnolia campbellii
Magnolia grandiflora
Malus 'Adams'
Malus angustifolia

Malus 'Callaway'
Malus 'Harvest Gold'
Malus 'Jewelberry'
Malus 'Liset'
Malus 'Prairifire'
Malus 'Red Jewel'
Malus 'Sugar Tyme'
Melia azedarach
Michelia doltsopa
Michelia ×foggii
Michelia maudiae

Myrtus communis
Osmanthus americanus
Osmanthus fragrans
Parkinsonia aculeata
Prunus americana
Prunus caroliniana
Prunus mume
Sinojackia rehderiana
Sophora secundiflora
Styrax grandifolius
Ziziphus jujuba

Fruit

The following trees offer ornamental or sizeable fruit. The primary fruit color(s) is indicated for each plant, although variations will occur within a species, and many fruit change color as they mature.

TREE	COLOR/COMMENTS	TREE	COLOR/COMMENTS
Aesculus californica	brown	Ilex cassine	red
Aesculus indica	brown	Ilex cornuta	red
Aesculus sylvatica	brown	Ilex 'Emily Bruner'	red
Aleurites fordii	green, poisonous	Ilex ×koehneana	red
Alnus serrulata	brown	Ilex latifolia	red
Arbutus ×andrachnoides	red	Ilex 'Nellie R. Stevens'	red
Arbutus menziesii	orange-red	Ilex 'Red Hollies'	red
Arbutus unedo	red	Ilex rotunda	red
Broussonetia papyrifera	orange-red	Ilex vomitoria	red
Butia capitata	yellow	Juniperus salicicola	silver-blue cones, good bird munchies
Camellia oleifera	green to brown, oil extracted from seeds	Koelreuteria bipinnata	rose
Castanea pumila	brown, edible, prickly covering	Koelreuteria elegans	rose
Cinnamomum camphora	black, messy	Laurus nobilis	black
Cornus capitata	red, beautiful	Ligustrum japonicum	black
Crataegus aestivalis	red, edible, used in mayhaw jelly	Ligustrum lucidum	blue-black
Crataegus opaca	red, edible, used in mayhaw jelly	Liquidambar acalycina	brown
Crataegus rufula	red, edible, used in mayhaw jelly	Liquidambar formosana	brown
Diospyros kaki	orange, edible	Lithocarpus densiflorus	brown
Eriobotrya japonica	yellow-orange, edible	Lithocarpus henryi	brown
Euscaphis japonicus	pink-rose, black seeds	Magnolia ashei	rose-red
Idesia polycarpa	red, spectacular on female trees	Magnolia campbellii	rose-red
Ilex ×altaclerensis	red	Magnolia grandiflora	rose-red
Ilex aquifolium	red	Magnolia liliiflora	rose-red

TREE	COLOR/COMMENTS	TREE	COLOR/COMMENTS
Malus 'Adams'	red	*Quercus falcata*	brown
Malus angustifolia	green	*Quercus georgiana*	brown
Malus 'Callaway'	red, edible	*Quercus glauca*	brown
Malus 'Harvest Gold'	yellow	*Quercus hemisphaerica*	brown
Malus 'Jewelberry'	red	*Quercus laurifolia*	brown
Malus 'Liset'	red	*Quercus lyrata*	brown
Malus 'Prairifire'	red	*Quercus michauxii*	brown
Malus 'Red Jewel'	red	*Quercus myrsinifolia*	brown
Malus 'Sugar Tyme'	red	*Quercus nigra*	brown
Melia azedarach	yellow	*Quercus nuttallii*	brown
Myrtus communis	black	*Quercus phillyraeoides*	brown
Nyssa ogeche	red, used like limes to flavor drinks	*Quercus prinus*	brown
Osmanthus americanus	blue-purple	*Quercus shumardii*	brown
Osmanthus fragrans	blue-black-purple	*Quercus stellata*	brown
Persea borbonia	blue-black	*Quercus virginiana*	brown-black
Phoenix canariensis	yellow tinged red	*Rhamnus carolinianus*	red to black
Phoenix reclinata	pale yellow to red	*Sabal palmetto*	black
Phoenix roebelinii	black	*Sapindus drummondii*	yellow-orange
Photinia serrulata	red	*Sapium sebiferum*	white seeds
Pistacia chinensis	blue	*Sinojackia rehderiana*	brown
Prunus americana	yellow-red, edible	*Styrax grandifolius*	brown
Prunus caroliniana	black	*Vaccinium arboreum*	black
Prunus mume	yellow	*Ziziphus jujuba*	brown, edible
Quercus acuta	brown		

TREES: DESIGN CHARACTERISTICS
Fall Color

The following trees exhibit attractive fall foliage color. Many will display the full range of fall colors, from pale yellows to deep reds and purples, often on the same tree or even on the same leaf. For the purposes of this list, fall color has been broken down into broad categories; "red," for example, can signify anything from pinks to deep maroon tints.

YELLOW
Acer barbatum
Acer leucoderme
Aesculus californica
Aesculus indica
Aesculus sylvatica
Alangium platanifolium
Castanea pumila
Diospyros kaki
Idesia polycarpa
Koelreuteria bipinnata
Koelreuteria elegans
Lagerstroemia fauriei
Lagerstroemia hybrids
Lagerstroemia indica
Lindera erythrocarpa
Malus angustifolia
Nyssa ogeche
Pistacia chinensis
Poliothyrsis sinensis
Prunus americana
Prunus mume
Quercus lyrata
Quercus nuttallii
Quercus prinus
Quercus shumardii
Quercus stellata
Rhamnus carolinianus
Sapindus drummondii
Sapium sebiferum
×*Sycoparrotia semide-cidua*
Ulmus alata
Ulmus crassifolia
Ulmus parvifolia
Zelkova sinica
Ziziphus jujuba

ORANGE
Quercus nuttallii
Quercus shumardii
Sapindus drummondii
Sapium sebiferum

RED
Acer barbatum
Acer leucoderme
Clethra barbinervis
Diospyros kaki
Elliottia racemosa
Euscaphis japonicus
Lagerstroemia hybrids
Lagerstroemia indica
Pistacia chinensis
Prunus americana
Prunus campanulata
Quercus falcata
Quercus falcata var. pagodifolia
Quercus georgiana
Quercus michauxii
Quercus nuttallii
Quercus prinus
Quercus shumardii
Sapium japonicum
Sapium sebiferum
Vaccinium arboreum

BRONZE
Castanea pumila
Clethra barbinervis
Elliottia racemosa
Prunus campanulata
Quercus michauxii
Quercus prinus
Zelkova sinica

YELLOW-GREEN
Broussonetia papyrifera
×*Chitalpa tashkentensis*
Melia azedarach

Bark

The following trees have bark with interesting texture or color.

Aesculus californica
Aesculus indica
Alnus serrulata
Arbutus ×andrachnoides
Arbutus menziesii
Broussonetia papyrifera
Butia capitata
Cinnamomum camphora
Clethra barbinervis
Crataegus aestivalis
Crataegus opaca
Crataegus rufula
Cunninghamia lanceolata
Cupressus glabra
Cupressus macrocarpa
Cupressus sempervirens
Dicksonia antarctica
Diospyros kaki
Ehretia dicksonii

Eucalyptus gunnii
Eucalyptus niphophila
Eucalyptus urnigera
Eucryphia glutinosa
Euscaphis japonicus
Idesia polycarpa
Juniperus salicicola
Lagerstroemia fauriei
Lagerstroemia hybrids
Lagerstroemia indica
Ligustrum japonicum
Ligustrum lucidum
Magnolia campbellii
Magnolia grandiflora
Malus 'Adams'
Malus angustifolia
Malus 'Callaway'
Malus 'Harvest Gold'
Malus 'Jewelberry'

Malus 'Liset'
Malus 'Prairifire'
Malus 'Red Jewel'
Malus 'Sugar Tyme'
Myrtus communis
Osmanthus americanus
Phoenix canariensis
Phoenix reclinata
Photinia serrulata
Pinus echinata
Pinus elliottii
Pinus glabra
Pinus palustris
Pinus taeda
Pistacia chinensis
Prunus campanulata
Prunus caroliniana
Quercus acuta
Quercus glauca

Quercus myrsinifolia
Quercus virginiana
Sabal palmetto
Sapindus drummondii
Sequoia sempervirens
Sequoiadendron giganteum
Sophora secundiflora
Styrax grandifolius
Syagrus romanzoffianum
Torreya taxifolia
Trachycarpus fortunei
Trochodendron aralioides
Ulmus parvifolia
Vaccinium arboreum
Washingtonia filifera
Washingtonia robusta
Zanthoxylum clava-herculis
Zelkova sinica

Weeping Habit

The following trees display a weeping habit or offer gracefully arching branches.

Acacia dealbata
Ilex vomitoria 'Pendula'
Prunus mume 'Pendula'

Prunus mume 'W. B. Clarke'
×Sycoparrotia semidecidua
Ulmus alata 'Lace Parasol'

Columnar or Fastigiate Habit

The following trees are columnar or fastigiate in habit.

Ilex vomitoria 'Will Fleming'
Juniperus salicicola 'Brodie'
Lagerstroemia 'Apalachee'
Lagerstroemia 'Sioux'
Magnolia grandiflora Alta™
Magnolia grandiflora 'Hasse'

Prunus caroliniana Bright 'N Tight™
Quercus phillyraeoides 'Emerald Sentinel'
Quercus virginiana Highrise™

Principal Species of Commerce

The following trees have the greatest number of cultivars
or the greatest volume of sales in the landscape trade.

Arbutus menziesii	Eucryphia glutinosa	Ligustrum lucidum	Phoenix reclinata	Quercus nuttallii
Butia capitata	Ilex ×altaclerensis	Liquidambar formosana	Photinia serrulata	Quercus prinus
Callistemon viminalis	Ilex aquifolium	Magnolia grandiflora	Pinus echinata	Quercus shumardii
Camellia japonica	Ilex cornuta	Malus 'Adams'	Pinus elliottii	Quercus virginiana
Cinnamomum camphora	Ilex 'Emily Bruner'	Malus angustifolia	Pinus palustris	Sabal palmetto
Cunninghamia lanceo-	Ilex ×koehneana	Malus 'Callaway'	Pinus taeda	Sapindus drummondii
lata	Ilex latifolia	Malus 'Harvest Gold'	Pistacia chinensis	Sophora secundiflora
Cupressus glabra	Ilex 'Nellie R. Stevens'	Malus 'Jewelberry'	Prunus campanulata	Syagrus romanzoffianum
Cupressus macrocarpa	Ilex 'Red Hollies'	Malus 'Liset'	Prunus caroliniana	Trachycarpus fortunei
Cupressus sempervirens	Ilex vomitoria	Malus 'Prairifire'	Prunus mume	Ulmus crassifolia
Eriobotrya japonica	Koelreuteria bipinnata	Malus 'Red Jewel'	Quercus hemisphaerica	Ulmus parvifolia
Eucalyptus gunnii	Koelreuteria elegans	Malus 'Sugar Tyme'	Quercus lyrata	Washingtonia filifera
Eucalyptus niphophila	Lagerstroemia hybrids	Parkinsonia aculeata	Quercus michauxii	Washingtonia robusta
Eucalyptus urnigera	Lagerstroemia indica	Phoenix canariensis	Quercus myrsinifolia	

Underutilized Species

The following trees are underutilized but deserve greater
consideration for landscape use.

Acer barbatum	Emmenopterys henryi	Michelia doltsopa	Quercus falcata	Sinojackia rehderiana
Acer leucoderme	Euscaphis japonicus	Nyssa ogeche	Quercus falcata var.	Stewartia malacodendron
Aesculus indica	Idesia polycarpa	Osmanthus americanus	pagodifolia	Styrax grandifolius
Aesculus sylvatica	Lagerstroemia fauriei	Pinckneya pubens	Quercus georgiana	Trochodendron aralioides
Alangium platanifolium	Liquidambar acalycina	Poliothyrsis sinensis	Quercus glauca	Vaccinium arboreum
Chilopsis linearis	Magnolia ashei	Quercus acuta	Quercus phillyraeoides	Zelkova sinica
Clethra barbinervis	Magnolia campbellii	Quercus coccinea	Rhamnus carolinianus	Ziziphus jujuba
Diospyros kaki				

A Guide to Tree Sizes

SMALL (15 TO 30 FT.)	Arbutus ×andrachnoides	Chilopsis linearis	Dicksonia antarctica	Ilex cassine
Acer barbatum	Arbutus unedo	×Chitalpa tashkentensis	Diospyros kaki	Ilex cornuta
Acer leucoderme	Bauhinia blakeana	Clethra arborea	Ehretia dicksonii	Ilex 'Emily Bruner'
Aesculus californica	Bauhinia variegata	Clethra barbinervis	Elliottia racemosa	Ilex ×koehneana
Aesculus sylvatica	Butia capitata	Cornus capitata	Eriobotrya japonica	Ilex latifolia
Alangium platanifolium	Callistemon viminalis	Crataegus aestivalis	Erythrina crista-gallii	Ilex 'Nellie R. Stevens'
Aleurites fordii	Camellia japonica	Crataegus opaca	Euscaphis japonicus	Ilex 'Red Hollies'
Alnus serrulata	Castanea pumila	Crataegus rufula	Gordonia lasianthus	Ilex rotunda

Ilex vomitoria
Juniperus salicicola
Koelreuteria bipinnata
Koelreuteria elegans
Lagerstroemia hybrids
Lagerstroemia indica
Laurus nobilis
Ligustrum lucidum
Lithocarpus densiflorus
Lithocarpus henryi
Magnolia ashei
Malus 'Adams'
Malus angustifolia
Malus 'Callaway'
Malus 'Harvest Gold'
Malus 'Jewelberry'
Malus 'Liset'
Malus 'Prairifire'
Malus 'Red Jewel'
Malus 'Sugar Tyme'
Myrtus communis
Osmanthus americanus
Osmanthus fragrans
Parkinsonia aculeata

Persea borbonia
Phoenix canariensis
Phoenix reclinata
Photinia serrulata
Pinckneya pubens
Pittosporum tenuifolium
Poliothyrsis sinensis
Prunus americana
Prunus campanulata
Prunus caroliniana
Prunus mume
Quercus acuta
Quercus georgiana
Quercus glauca
Quercus myrsinifolia
Quercus phillyraeoides
Rhamnus carolinianus
Sapium japonicum
Sinojackia rehderiana
Sophora secundiflora
Stewartia malacodendron
Styrax grandifolius
×Sycoparrotia semide-
    cidua

Sycopsis sinensis
Torreya taxifolia
Trachycarpus fortunei
Trochodendron aralioides
Vaccinium arboreum
Zanthoxylum clava-
    herculis
Ziziphus jujuba

MEDIUM (30 TO 50 FT.)
Arbutus menziesii
Broussonetia papyrifera
Cunninghamia lanceo-
    lata
Cupressus glabra
Cupressus macrocarpa
Cupressus sempervirens
Emmenopterys henryi
Idesia polycarpa
Ilex ×altaclerensis
Ilex aquifolium
Lagerstroemia fauriei
Liquidambar acalycina
Liquidambar formosana

Melia azedarach
Michelia doltsopa
Nyssa ogeche
Pinus clausa
Pinus glabra
Pistacia chinensis
Quercus hemisphaerica
Quercus laurifolia
Sabal palmetto
Sapindus drummondii
Sapium sebiferum
Ulmus parvifolia
Washingtonia robusta
Zelkova sinica

LARGE (50 FT. OR GREATER)
Aesculus indica
Araucaria araucana
Cinnamomum camphora
Eucalyptus gunnii
Eucalyptus niphophila
Eucalyptus urnigera
Grevillea robusta
Magnolia campbellii

Magnolia grandiflora
Pinus echinata
Pinus elliottii
Pinus palustris
Pinus taeda
Quercus falcata
Quercus falcata var.
    pagodifolia
Quercus lyrata
Quercus michauxii
Quercus nigra
Quercus nuttallii
Quercus prinus
Quercus shumardii
Quercus stellata
Quercus virginiana
Sequoia sempervirens
Sequoiadendron gigan-
    teum
Syagrus romanzoffianum
Ulmus alata
Ulmus crassifolia
Washingtonia filifera

TREES: CULTURAL CHARACTERISTICS
Tolerance to Compacted Soils, Drought, and Heat

The following trees offer tolerance to compacted, infertile soils
and other environmental stresses, such as heat and drought.

Acer barbatum
Acer leucoderme
Aesculus californica
Aleurites fordii
Bauhinia blakeana
Bauhinia variegata
Broussonetia papyrifera
Butia capitata
Callistemon citrinus
Callistemon viminalis
Chilopsis linearis
×Chitalpa tashkentensis
Cinnamomum cam-
    phora
Crataegus aestivalis
Crataegus opaca
Crataegus rufula
Cupressus glabra

Cupressus macrocarpa
Cupressus sempervirens
Diospyros kaki
Erythrina crista-galli
Eucalyptus gunnii
Eucalyptus niphophila
Eucalyptus urnigera
Grevillea robusta
Ilex cornuta
Ilex 'Emily Bruner'
Ilex ×koehneana
Ilex latifolia
Ilex 'Nellie R. Stevens'
Ilex rotunda
Ilex vomitoria
Juniperus salicicola
Koelreuteria bipinnata
Koelreuteria elegans

Lagerstroemia fauriei
Lagerstroemia hybrids
Lagerstroemia indica
Ligustrum lucidum
Liquidambar formosana
Magnolia grandiflora
Malus angustifolia
Melia azedarach
Osmanthus fragrans
Parkinsonia aculeata
Persea borbonia
Phoenix canariensis
Phoenix reclinata
Photinia serrulata
Pistacia chinensis
Prunus campanulata
Prunus caroliniana

Quercus acuta
Quercus falcata
Quercus falcata var. pa-
    godifolia
Quercus georgiana
Quercus glauca
Quercus hemisphaerica
Quercus laurifolia
Quercus lyrata
Quercus michauxii
Quercus myrsinifolia
Quercus nigra
Quercus prinus
Quercus shumardii
Quercus stellata
Quercus virginiana
Sabal palmetto

Sapindus drummondii
Sapium japonicum
Sapium sebiferum
Sinojackia rehderiana
Sophora secundiflora
Syagrus romanzoffi-
    anum
Trachycarpus fortunei
Ulmus alata
Ulmus crassifolia
Ulmus parvifolia
Washingtonia filifera
Washingtonia robusta
Zanthoxylum clava-
    herculis
Zelkova sinica
Ziziphus jujuba

409

Street and Urban Planting

The following species and cultivars offer the genetic plasticity to produce offspring that are better able to adapt to a variety of environmental stresses. From these trees, tomorrow's cultivars will be bred and selected.

Acer barbatum	*Lagerstroemia* hybrids	*Pistacia chinensis*
Cinnamomum camphora	*Lagerstroemia indica*	*Prunus campanulata*
Diospyros kaki	*Liquidambar acalycina*	*Quercus* spp.
Ilex spp.	*Liquidambar formosana*	*Sapindus drummondii*
Lagerstroemia fauriei	*Magnolia grandiflora*	*Zelkova sinica*

Tolerance to Moist to Wet Soils

The following trees are tolerant of moist to wet soil conditions.

Alnus serrulata	*Magnolia grandiflora*	*Quercus laurifolia*
Crataegus aestivalis	*Nyssa ogeche*	*Quercus michauxii*
Crataegus opaca	*Osmanthus americanus*	*Quercus nigra*
Crataegus rufula	*Persea borbonia*	*Quercus nuttallii*
Gordonia lasianthus	*Pinckneya pubens*	*Quercus virginiana*
Ilex cassine	*Pinus taeda*	*Sabal palmetto*
Ilex vomitoria	*Quercus falcata* var. *pagodifolia*	

Salt Tolerance

Trees listed show various degrees of tolerance to aerial- and/or soil-deposited salts.

Broussonetia papyrifera	*Ilex cornuta*	*Ligustrum japonicum*	*Phoenix reclinata*	*Syagrus romanzoffianum*
Butia capitata	*Ilex* 'Emily Bruner'	*Ligustrum lucidum*	*Pistacia chinensis*	*Trachycarpus fortunei*
Callistemon spp.	*Ilex* ×*koehneana*	*Magnolia grandiflora*	*Prunus caroliniana*	*Ulmus alata*
Chilopsis linearis	*Ilex latifolia*	*Melia azedarach*	*Quercus virginiana*	*Ulmus crassifolia*
Cinnamomum camphora	*Ilex* 'Nellie R. Stevens'	*Myrtus communis*	*Sabal palmetto*	*Ulmus parvifolia*
Diospyros kaki	*Ilex* 'Red Hollies'	*Parkinsonia aculeata*	*Sapindus drummondii*	*Washingtonia filifera*
Ilex ×*altaclerensis*	*Ilex rotunda*	*Persea borbonia*	*Sapium sebiferum*	*Washingtonia robusta*
Ilex aquifolium	*Ilex vomitoria*	*Phoenix canariensis*	*Sophora secundiflora*	*Zelkova sinica*
Ilex cassine	*Koelreuteria elegans*			

TREES: CULTURAL CHARACTERISTICS
Shade Tolerance

The following trees have moderate to good shade tolerance.

Acer barbatum
Acer leucoderme
Aesculus sylvatica
Alangium platanifolium
Castanea pumila
Clethra arborea
Clethra barbinervis
Cornus capitata

Ilex ×altaclerensis
Ilex aquifolium
Ilex cassine
Ilex cornuta
Ilex 'Emily Bruner'
Ilex ×koehneana
Ilex latifolia
Ilex 'Nellie R. Stevens'

Ilex 'Red Hollies'
Ilex rotunda
Laurus nobilis
Ligustrum japonicum
Ligustrum lucidum
Magnolia ashei
Magnolia grandiflora
Michelia doltsopa

Michelia ×foggii
Michelia maudiae
Myrtus communis
Osmanthus americanus
Osmanthus fragrans
Photinia serrulata
Prunus caroliniana
Rhamnus carolinianus

Sinojackia rehderiana
Stewartia malacodendron
Styrax grandifolius
×Sycoparrotia semide-
cidua
Sycopsis sinensis
Trochodendron aralioides
Vaccinium arboreum

SHRUBS: DESIGN CHARACTERISTICS
Flower Color

The primary flower color(s) is indicated for each species of flowering shrub. Variations of flower color will exist in certain cultivars or varieties of a plant, and flowers can often be ornamented with stripes or blotches of a different color.

WHITE
Abelia chinensis
Abelia ×grandiflora
Abutilon pictum
Adina rubella
Arbutus unedo
Ardisia crenata
Brugmansia ×candida
Brunfelsia pauciflora
Buddleia loricata
Camellia japonica
Camellia oleifera
Camellia reticulata
Camellia sasanqua
Camellia sinensis
Carissa macrocarpa
Chilopsis linearis
Choisya ternata
Cistus laurifolius
Clethra arborea
Clethra barbinervis
Cleyera japonica
Cliftonia monophylla
Cotoneaster lacteus
Cyrilla arida

Cyrilla racemiflora
Edgeworthia chrysantha
Edgeworthia papyrifera
Elaeagnus ×ebbingei
Elaeagnus macrophylla
Elaeagnus pungens
Elliottia racemosa
Eriobotrya japonica
Escallonia rubra
Euonymus japonicus
Eurya japonica
×Fatshedera lizei
Fatsia japonica
Fontanesia fortunei
Gardenia jasminoides
Gordonia lasianthus
Helianthemum nummularium
Hibiscus mutabilis
Hibiscus rosa-sinensis
Ilex cornuta
Ilex vomitoria
Illicium anisatum
Lagerstroemia hybrids
Lagerstroemia indica
Lantana camara

Leptospermum scoparium
Leucophyllum frutescens
Leucothoe axillaris
Leucothoe populifolia
Leucothoe racemosa
Ligustrum japonicum
Ligustrum lucidum
Ligustrum sinense
Loropetalum chinense
Lyonia lucida
Magnolia ashei
Michelia figo
Michelia ×foggii
Michelia maudiae
Myrtus communis
Nandina domestica
Nerium oleander
Osmanthus americanus
Osmanthus ×burkwoodii
Osmanthus delavayi
Osmanthus ×fortunei
Osmanthus fragrans
Osmanthus heterophyllus
Osmanthus serrulatus
Parrotiopsis jacquemontiana

Philadelphus inodorus
Philadelphus pubescens
Phillyrea angustifolia
Photinia ×fraseri
Photinia glabra
Photinia serrulata
Pieris formosana var. forrestii
Pieris phillyreifolia
Pinckneya pubens
Pittosporum tobira
Poliothyrsis sinensis
Prunus americana
Prunus angustifolia
Prunus caroliniana
Prunus laurocerasus
Pyracantha koidzumii
Rhaphiolepis umbellata
Rhododendron alabamense
Rhododendron Girard Hybrids
Rhododendron Kurume Hybrids
Rhododendron Robin Hill
  Hybrids
Rhododendron Satsuki Hybrids
Rhododendron Southern Indica
Rosa laevigata

411

Shrubs: Design Characteristics

Flower Color, White, continued

Rubus biflorus
Rubus idaeus 'Aureus'
Rubus koehneanus
Sarcococca confusa
Sarcococca orientalis
Sarcococca ruscifolia
Serissa foetida
Sinocalycanthus chinensis
Sinojackia rehderiana
Staphylea trifolia
Stewartia malacodendron
Stewartia ovata
Styrax grandifolius
Symplocos tinctoria
Ternstroemia gymnanthera
Vaccinium arboreum
Vaccinium ashei
Vaccinium stamineum
Viburnum awabuki
Viburnum bracteatum
Viburnum cassinoides
Viburnum cassinoides var.
    angustifolium
Viburnum cinnamonifolium
Viburnum davidii
Viburnum japonicum
Viburnum macrocephalum
Viburnum macrocephalum f.
    keteleeri
Viburnum nudum
Viburnum obovatum
Viburnum odoratissimum
Viburnum rafinesquianum
Viburnum suspensum
Viburnum tinus
Viburnum utile
Zanthoxylum clava-herculis

YELLOW

Abutilon pictum
Aesculus sylvatica
Agave americana
Alnus serrulata
Brugmansia ×candida
Callistemon salignus
Callistemon sieberi
Cassia bicapsularis
Cassia marilandica
Croton alabamensis

Edgeworthia chrysantha
Edgeworthia papyrifera
Euonymus americanus
Galphimia gracilis
Helianthemum nummularium
Hibiscus rosa-sinensis
Hypericum brachyphyllum
Hypericum densiflorum
Hypericum fasiculatum
Hypericum galioides
Hypericum lissophoeus
Hypericum lloydii
Hypericum reductum
Illicium parviflorum
Ixora coccinea
Jasminum floridum
Jasminum humile
Jasminum mesnyi
Jasminum nudiflorum
Jasminum parkeri
Lantana camara
Leycesteria crocothyrsos
Lindera aggregata
Lindera angustifolia
Lindera erythrocarpa
Lonicera nitida
Lonicera pileata
Mahonia bealei
Mahonia fortunei
Mahonia japonica
Mahonia ×media
Michelia figo
Myrica cerifera
Nerium oleander
Rhododendron austrinum
Rhododendron Confederate
    Azaleas
Rhus michauxii
Rosa banksiae 'Lutea'
Santolina chamaecyparissus
Santolina virens
×Sycoparrotia semidecidua
Sycopsis sinensis
Symplocos tinctoria

YELLOW-GREEN

Daphniphyllum macropodum
Laurus nobilis
Persea borbonia

Rhamnus carolinianus
Sarcococca saligna
Trochodendron aralioides
Zanthoxylum americanum

PINK/ROSE

Abelia ×grandiflora
Abutilon pictum
Arbutus unedo
Ardisia crenata
Brugmansia ×candida
Camellia japonica
Camellia reticulata
Camellia sasanqua
Ceanothus ×pallidus
Chilopsis linearis
Daphne odora
Escallonia rubra
Gaylussacia ursina
Helianthemum nummularium
Hibiscus mutabilis
Hibiscus rosa-sinensis
Illicium henryi
Indigofera amblyantha
Indigofera decora
Indigofera heteranthera
Lagerstroemia hybrids
Lagerstroemia indica
Lantana camara
Leptospermum scoparium
Loropetalum chinense var.
    rubrum
Lyonia lucida
Magnolia liliiflora
Nerium oleander
Pinckneya pubens
Rhaphiolepis ×delacouri
Rhaphiolepis umbellata
Rhododendron canescens
Rhododendron Confederate
    Azaleas
Rhododendron Encore™ Azaleas
Rhododendron Girard Hybrids
Rhododendron Kurume Hybrids
Rhododendron Robin Hill
    Hybrids
Rhododendron Rutherfordiana
    Hybrids
Rhododendron Satsuki Hybrids

Rhododendron Southern Indica
Rubus coreanus
Ungnadia speciosa
Vaccinium ashei
Vaccinium crassifolium
Vaccinium elliottii
Viburnum ×bodnantense

ORANGE/RED

Abutilon megapotamicum
Abutilon pictum
Callistemon citrinus
Callistemon linearis
Callistemon rigidus
Callistemon speciosus
Callistemon viminalis
Camellia japonica
Camellia reticulata
Camellia sasanqua
Desfontainia spinosa
Erythrina ×bidwellii
Erythrina herbacea
Escallonia rubra
Feijoa sellowiana
Fuchsia magellanica
Grevillea rosmarinifolia
Helianthemum nummularium
Hibiscus rosa-sinensis
Illicium floridanum
Illicium mexicanum
Ixora coccinea
Lagerstroemia hybrids
Lagerstroemia indica
Lantana camara
Leptospermum scoparium
Loropetalum chinense var.
    rubrum
Malvaviscus arboreus var.
    drummondii
Musa acuminata (bracts)
Musa coccinea (bracts)
Musa ornata (bracts)
Musa ×paradisiaca
Nerium oleander
Punica granatum
Rhododendron Confederate
    Azaleas
Rhododendron Encore™ Azaleas
Rhododendron flammeum

Rhododendron Girard Hybrids
Rhododendron Kurume Hybrids
Rhododendron prunifolium
Rhododendron Rutherfordiana
  Hybrids
Rhododendron Satsuki Hybrids
Rhododendron Southern Indica
Sesbania punicea
×Sinocalycalycanthus raulstonii
Tecomaria capensis

BLUE/PURPLE
Aucuba japonica
Brunfelsia pauciflora

Buddleia lindleyana
Buddleia salvifolia
Ceanothus ×delilianus
Chilopsis linearis
×Chitalpa tashkentensis
Cistus ×purpureus
Distylium racemosum
Duranta erecta
Hibiscus rosa-sinensis
Lagerstroemia hybrids
Lagerstroemia indica
Lantana camara
Lavandula angustifolia

Lespedeza bicolor
Lespedeza thunbergii
Leucophyllum frutescens
Leycesteria formosa
Musa acuminata (bracts)
Musa coccinea (bracts)
Musa ornata (bracts)
Musa ×paradisiaca
Pittosporum tenuifolium
Plumbago auriculata
Rhododendron chapmanii
Rhododendron Encore™ Azaleas
Rhododendron Girard Hybrids

Rhododendron Kurume Hybrids
Rhododendron Southern Indica
Rosmarinus officinalis
Rubus cockburnianus
Rubus lasiostylus
Rubus thibetanus 'Silver Fern'
×Sinocalycalycanthus raulstonii
Sophora secundiflora
Teucrium chamaedrys
Vitex rotundifolia

BLACK
Eurya emarginata

SHRUBS: DESIGN CHARACTERISTICS

Fragrant Flowers

The following shrubs have fragrant flowers.

SHRUB	FRAGRANCE STRENGTH/COMMENTS	SHRUB	FRAGRANCE STRENGTH/COMMENTS
Abelia chinensis	light to medium	Eriobotrya japonica	light
Abelia ×grandiflora	light to medium	Euonymus japonicus	vinegary
Adina rubella	light	Gardenia jasminoides	heavy
Aesculus californica	light	Gordonia lasianthus	light
Aesculus indica	light	Ilex cornuta	heavy
Alangium platanifolium	light	Illicium anisatum	light
Buddleia loricata	light	Illicium floridanum	malodorous
Buddleia salvifolia	light	Illicium mexicanum	malodorous
Camellia sinensis	light	Jasminum humile	light
Carissa macrocarpa	medium	Lagerstroemia hybrids	light
Castanea pumila	heavy, malodorous	Lagerstroemia indica	light
Ceanothus ×delilianus	light	Lantana camara	light
Ceanothus ×pallidus	light	Leucothoe axillaris	light, somewhat malodorous
Chilopsis linearis	light	Leucothoe populifolia	medium
Choisya ternata	heavy	Leucothoe racemosa	light
Clethra arborea	light	Ligustrum japonicum	heavy
Clethra barbinervis	medium	Ligustrum lucidum	heavy
Cliftonia monophylla	light	Ligustrum sinense	heavy
Cotoneaster lacteus	malodorous	Loropetalum chinense	light
Cyrilla arida	light	Loropetalum chinense	
Cyrilla racemiflora	light	var. rubrum	light
Daphne odora	heavy, sensuous	Lyonia lucida	medium
Edgeworthia chrysantha	medium	Magnolia ashei	heavy, sweet
Edgeworthia papyrifera	medium	Magnolia liliiflora	heavy
Ehretia dicksonii	light	Magnolia Little Girl Hybrids	heavy
Elaeagnus ×ebbingei	heavy	Mahonia bealei	heavy
Elaeagnus macrophylla	heavy	Mahonia fortunei	barely detectable
Elaeagnus pungens	heavy	Mahonia japonica	heavy
Elliottia racemosa	light	Mahonia ×media	medium

413

SHRUB	FRAGRANCE STRENGTH/COMMENTS	SHRUB	FRAGRANCE STRENGTH/COMMENTS
Michelia figo	heavy	*Rhododendron alabamense*	heavy
Michelia ×foggii	medium	*Rhododendron austrinum*	heavy
Michelia maudiae	light	*Rhododendron canescens*	heavy
Mitchella repens	heavy	*Rhododendron* Confederate Azaleas	heavy
Myrtus communis	medium	*Rosa banksiae* 'Lutea'	medium
Osmanthus americanus	heavy	*Rosa laevigata*	medium
Osmanthus ×burkwoodii	medium	*Sarcococca confusa*	heavy
Osmanthus delavayi	medium	*Sarcococca orientalis*	heavy
Osmanthus ×fortunei	heavy	*Sarcococca ruscifolia*	heavy
Osmanthus fragrans	heavy	*Sophora secundiflora*	heavy
Osmanthus heterophyllus	heavy	*Styrax grandifolius*	medium
Osmanthus serrulatus	medium	*Symplocos tinctoria*	medium
Parkinsonia aculeata	medium	*Ternstroemia gymnanthera*	light
Phillyrea angustifolia	medium	*Vaccinium ashei*	light
Photinia ×fraseri	heavy, malodorous	*Viburnum ×bodnantense*	heavy
Photinia glabra	heavy, malodorous	*Viburnum bracteatum*	malodorous
Photinia serrulata	heavy, malodorous	*Viburnum cassinoides*	musky
Pieris formosana var. *forrestii*	light	*Viburnum cassinoides* var. *angustifolium*	musky
Pieris phillyreifolia	light		
Pittosporum tobira	heavy	*Viburnum japonicum*	medium
Prunus americana	medium, sickeningly sweet	*Viburnum nudum*	musky
Prunus angustifolia	medium, sickeningly sweet	*Viburnum rafinesquianum*	malodorous
Prunus laurocerasus	medium, sickeningly sweet	*Viburnum suspensum*	light
Prunus mume	light	*Viburnum tinus*	light
Pyracantha koidzumii	heavy, malodorous	*Viburnum utile*	light
Rhaphiolepis ×delacouri	light		
Rhaphiolepis umbellata	light		

SHRUBS: DESIGN CHARACTERISTICS
Flowering Sequence

The following list serves as a guide to the flowering habits of shrubs. Many shrubs flower over extended periods, providing color for several months at a time, and they are listed here for each of the months that they are in bloom. These dates are for Zones 5 and 6 and are only approximate. In any given year spring may come two weeks earlier or later than the norm, and bloom times will change accordingly; therefore, this list should be used only as a guide.

JANUARY
Callistemon spp.
Camellia japonica
Camellia oleifera
Camellia reticulata
Daphne odora
Eriobotrya japonica
Eurya emarginata
Eurya japonica
Fatsia japonica
Jasminum nudiflorum
Osmanthus fragrans
Rosmarinus officinalis
Viburnum ×bodnantense
Viburnum tinus

FEBRUARY
Alnus serrulata
Callistemon spp.
Camellia japonica
Camellia reticulata
Daphne odora
Eurya emarginata
Eurya japonica
Jasminum nudiflorum
Mahonia bealei
Mahonia japonica
Mahonia ×media
Osmanthus fragrans
Rosmarinus officinalis
Sarcococca spp.
×Sycoparrotia semidecidua
Sycopsis sinensis
Viburnum ×bodnantense
Viburnum tinus

MARCH
Alnus serrulata
Aucuba japonica
Callistemon spp.

Camellia japonica
Camellia reticulata
Cliftonia monophylla
Croton alabamensis
Daphne odora
Edgeworthia chrysantha
Edgeworthia papyrifera
Eurya emarginata
Eurya japonica
Ilex cornuta
Illicium anisatum
Illicium mexicanum
Jasminum mesnyi
Jasminum nudiflorum
Lindera erythrocarpa
Magnolia liliiflora
Magnolia Little Girl Hybrids
Mahonia bealei
Mahonia japonica
Mahonia ×*media*
Myrica cerifera
Myrica inodora
Osmanthus americanus
Osmanthus delavayi
Osmanthus fragrans
Osmanthus serrulatus
Photinia serrulata
Pieris formosana var. *forrestii*
Pieris phillyreifolia
Prunus americana
Prunus angustifolia
Rhododendron canescens
Rhododendron Southern Indica
Rosa banksiae 'Lutea'
Rosmarinus officinalis
Sarcococca spp.
Sophora secundiflora
×*Sycoparrotia semidecidua*
Sycopsis sinensis
Ungnadia speciosa
Vaccinium ashei
Viburnum ×*bodnantense*
Viburnum tinus

APRIL
Aesculus sylvatica
Aucuba japonica
Brunfelsia pauciflora
Buddleia salvifolia
Callistemon spp.
Camellia japonica

Camellia reticulata
Carissa macrocarpa
Cliftonia monophylla
Croton alabamensis
Edgeworthia chrysantha
Edgeworthia papyrifera
Ilex vomitoria
Illicium floridanum
Illicium henryi
Jasminum floridum
Leucothoe axillaris
Leucothoe racemosa
Lindera aggregata
Lindera angustifolia
Lindera erythrocarpa
Loropetalum chinense
Loropetalum chinense var.
    rubrum
Magnolia liliiflora
Magnolia Little Girl Hybrids
Michelia figo
Michelia ×*foggii*
Michelia maudiae
Orixa japonica
Osmanthus americanus
Osmanthus ×*burkwoodii*
Osmanthus delavayi
Osmanthus fragrans
Osmanthus serrulatus
Parkinsonia aculeata
Parrotiopsis jacquemontiana
Phillyrea angustifolia
Photinia ×*fraseri*
Photinia glabra
Photinia serrulata
Pieris formosana var. *forrestii*
Pieris phillyreifolia
Pittosporum tenuifolium
Pittosporum tobira
Prunus americana
Prunus angustifolia
Prunus caroliniana
Prunus laurocerasus
Pyracantha koidzumii
Rhaphiolepis ×*delacouri*
Rhaphiolepis umbellata
Rhododendron alabamense
Rhododendron austrinum
Rhododendron canescens
Rhododendron Confederate
    Azaleas

Rhododendron Encore™ Azaleas
Rhododendron Girard Hybrids
Rhododendron Kurume Hybrids
Rhododendron Rutherfordiana
    Hybrids
Rhododendron Southern Indica
Rosa banksiae 'Lutea'
Rosa laevigata
Rubus spp.
Sarcococca spp.
Sinojackia rehderiana
Sophora secundiflora
Staphylea trifolia
Symplocos tinctoria
Trochodendron aralioides
Ungnadia speciosa
Vaccinium arboreum
Vaccinium ashei
Vaccinium elliottii
Vaccinium stamineum
Viburnum cinnamonifolium
Viburnum davidii
Viburnum macrocephalum
Viburnum obovatum
Viburnum suspensum
Viburnum utile
Zanthoxylum americanum
Zanthoxylum clava-herculis

MAY
Abelia ×*grandiflora*
Aesculus sylvatica
Brunfelsia pauciflora
Buddleia lindleyana
Buddleia salvifolia
Callistemon spp.
Carissa macrocarpa
Ceanothus ×*delilianus*
Ceanothus ×*pallidus*
Choisya ternata
Cotoneaster lacteus
Distylium racemosum
Euonymus americanus
Feijoa sellowiana
Fontanesia fortunei
Gardenia jasminoides
Gaylussacia ursina
Gordonia lasianthus
Grevillea rosmarinifolia
Helianthemum nummularium
Hypericum brachyphyllum

Hypericum fasiculatum
Hypericum lissophoeus
Illicium henryi
Illicium parviflorum
Indigofera decora
Jasminum floridum
Jasminum parkeri
Leucothoe axillaris
Leucothoe populifolia
Leycesteria crocothyrsos
Leycesteria formosa
Ligustrum japonicum
Ligustrum sinense
Lonicera nitida
Lonicera pileata
Lyonia lucida
Magnolia ashei
Magnolia liliiflora
Magnolia Little Girl Hybrids
Michelia figo
Myrtus communis
Nandina domestica
Orixa japonica
Osmanthus ×*burkwoodii*
Osmanthus fragrans
Parkinsonia aculeata
Parrotiopsis jacquemontiana
Persea borbonia
Philadelphus inodorus
Philadelphus pubescens
Phillyrea angustifolia
Photinia glabra
Pittosporum tobira
Plumbago auriculata
Prunus laurocerasus
Punica granatum
Pyracantha koidzumii
Rhaphiolepis ×*delacouri*
Rhaphiolepis umbellata
Rhododendron Encore™ Azaleas
Rhododendron flammeum
Rhododendron Girard Hybrids
Rhododendron Kurume Hybrids
Rhododendron Robin Hill
    Hybrids
Rhododendron Rutherfordiana
    Hybrids
Rhododendron Satsuki Hybrids
Rosa laevigata
Rubus spp.
Serissa foetida

×*Sinocalycalycanthus raulstonii*
Sinocalycanthus chinensis
Sinojackia rehderiana
Staphylea trifolia
Styrax grandifolius
Symplocos tinctoria
Ternstroemia gymnanthera
Trochodendron aralioides
Vaccinium arboreum
Vaccinium crassifolium
Vaccinium stamineum
Viburnum bracteatum
Viburnum cassinoides
Viburnum cinnamonifolium
Viburnum davidii
Viburnum japonicum
Viburnum macrocephalum
Viburnum nudum
Viburnum odoratissimum
Viburnum rafinesquianum
Vitex rotundifolia
Zanthoxylum americanum
Zanthoxylum clava-herculis

JUNE
Abelia chinensis
Abelia ×*grandiflora*
Adina rubella
Brunfelsia pauciflora
Buddleia lindleyana
Buddleia loricata
Callistemon spp.
Carissa macrocarpa
Ceanothus ×*delilianus*
Ceanothus ×*pallidus*
Chilopsis linearis
Choisya ternata
Cistus laurifolius
Cistus ×*purpureus*
Cleyera japonica
Cyrilla arida
Cyrilla racemiflora
Desfontainia spinosa
Duranta erecta
Elliottia racemosa
Erythrina ×*bidwellii*
Erythrina herbacea
Escallonia rubra
Euonymus americanus

Euonymus japonicus
Feijoa sellowiana
Fontanesia fortunei
Galphimia gracilis
Gardenia jasminoides
Gordonia lasianthus
Grevillea rosmarinifolia
Helianthemum nummularium
Hibiscus rosa-sinensis
Hypericum brachyphyllum
Hypericum densiflorum
Hypericum fasiculatum
Hypericum galioides
Hypericum lissophoeus
Illicium parviflorum
Indigofera amblyantha
Indigofera decora
Indigofera heteranthera
Jasminum floridum
Jasminum humile
Jasminum parkeri
Lagerstroemia hybrids
Lagerstroemia indica
Lantana camara
Lavandula angustifolia
Leptospermum scoparium
Lespedeza bicolor
Lespedeza thunbergii
Leucothoe populifolia
Leycesteria crocothyrsos
Leycesteria formosa
Ligustrum japonicum
Ligustrum lucidum
Lonicera nitida
Lonicera pileata
Magnolia ashei
Magnolia liliiflora
Michelia figo
Myrtus communis
Nandina domestica
Nerium oleander
Parkinsonia aculeata
Philadelphus inodorus
Philadelphus pubescens
Pinckneya pubens
Plumbago auriculata
Punica granatum
Rhododendron Robin Hill
    Hybrids

Rhododendron Satsuki Hybrids
Rhus michauxii
Santolina chamaecyparissus
Santolina virens
Serissa foetida
Sesbania punicea
Stewartia malacodendron
Stewartia ovata
Styrax grandifolius
Ternstroemia gymnanthera
Teucrium chamaedrys
Viburnum awabuki
Viburnum cassinoides
Viburnum nudum
Viburnum odoratissimum
Vitex rotundifolia

JULY
Abelia chinensis
Abelia ×*grandiflora*
Abutilon pictum
Adina rubella
Brugmansia ×*candida*
Brunfelsia pauciflora
Buddleia lindleyana
Callistemon spp.
Carissa macrocarpa
Cassia marilandica
Ceanothus ×*delilianus*
Ceanothus ×*pallidus*
Chilopsis linearis
×*Chitalpa tashkentensis*
Cistus laurifolius
Cistus ×*purpureus*
Clethra arborea
Clethra barbinervis
Desfontainia spinosa
Duranta erecta
Elliottia racemosa
Erythrina ×*bidwellii*
Erythrina herbacea
Fuchsia magellanica
Galphimia gracilis
Gordonia lasianthus
Grevillea rosmarinifolia
Hibiscus mutabilis
Hibiscus rosa-sinensis
Hypericum brachyphyllum
Hypericum densiflorum

Hypericum fasiculatum
Hypericum galioides
Hypericum lissophoeus
Illicium parviflorum
Indigofera amblyantha
Indigofera decora
Indigofera heteranthera
Ixora coccinea
Lagerstroemia hybrids
Lagerstroemia indica
Lantana camara
Lavandula angustifolia
Leptospermum scoparium
Lespedeza bicolor
Leucophyllum frutescens
Malvaviscus arboreus var.
    drummondii
Musa spp.
Nerium oleander
Parkinsonia aculeata
Plumbago auriculata
Poliothyrsis sinensis
Punica granatum
Rhododendron prunifolium
Rhus michauxii
Santolina chamaecyparissus
Santolina virens
Sesbania punicea
Stewartia malacodendron
Stewartia ovata
Teucrium chamaedrys
Vitex rotundifolia

AUGUST
Abelia chinensis
Abelia ×*grandiflora*
Abutilon pictum
Adina rubella
Brugmansia ×*candida*
Brunfelsia pauciflora
Buddleia lindleyana
Callistemon spp.
Carissa macrocarpa
Cassia marilandica
Chilopsis linearis
×*Chitalpa tashkentensis*
Clethra arborea
Clethra barbinervis
Desfontainia spinosa

416

Duranta erecta
Erythrina ×bidwellii
Erythrina herbacea
Fuchsia magellanica
Galphimia gracilis
Gordonia lasianthus
Grevillea rosmarinifolia
Hibiscus mutabilis
Hibiscus rosa-sinensis
Hypericum brachyphyllum
Hypericum densiflorum
Hypericum fasiculatum
Hypericum galioides
Hypericum lissophoeus
Hypericum lloydii
Hypericum reductum
Illicium parviflorum
Indigofera amblyantha
Indigofera decora
Indigofera heteranthera
Ixora coccinea
Lagerstroemia hybrids
Lagerstroemia indica
Lantana camara
Lavandula angustifolia
Leptospermum scoparium
Lespedeza thunbergii
Leucophyllum frutescens
Mahonia fortunei
Malvaviscus arboreus var.
    drummondii
Musa spp.
Nerium oleander
Parkinsonia aculeata
Plumbago auriculata
Poliothyrsis sinensis
Rhododendron prunifolium
Santolina chamaecyparissus
Santolina virens
Sesbania punicea
Vitex rotundifolia

SEPTEMBER
Abelia chinensis
Abelia ×grandiflora
Abutilon pictum
Adina rubella
Brugmansia ×candida
Brunfelsia pauciflora
Buddleia lindleyana
Callistemon spp.
Camellia sasanqua
Camellia sinensis
Carissa macrocarpa
Cassia marilandica
Chilopsis linearis
×Chitalpa tashkentensis
Clethra arborea
Desfontainia spinosa
Elaeagnus ×ebbingei
Elaeagnus macrophylla
Elaeagnus pungens
Eriobotrya japonica
Fuchsia magellanica
Galphimia gracilis
Gordonia lasianthus
Grevillea rosmarinifolia
Hibiscus mutabilis
Hibiscus rosa-sinensis
Hypericum brachyphyllum
Hypericum fasiculatum
Hypericum galioides
Hypericum lissophoeus
Hypericum lloydii
Hypericum reductum
Illicium parviflorum
Indigofera amblyantha
Indigofera decora
Indigofera heteranthera
Ixora coccinea

Lantana camara
Leptospermum scoparium
Lespedeza thunbergii
Leucophyllum frutescens
Mahonia fortunei
Malvaviscus arboreus var.
    drummondii
Musa spp.
Nerium oleander
Osmanthus fragrans
Plumbago auriculata
Rhododendron Encore™
    Azaleas
Sesbania punicea
Tecomaria capensis
Vitex rotundifolia

OCTOBER
Adina rubella
Arbutus unedo
Callistemon spp.
Camellia oleifera
Camellia sasanqua
Camellia sinensis
Cassia bicapsularis
Clethra arborea
Desfontainia spinosa
Elaeagnus ×ebbingei
Elaeagnus macrophylla
Elaeagnus pungens
Eriobotrya japonica
×Fatshedera lizei
Fatsia japonica
Gordonia lasianthus
Hibiscus mutabilis
Hypericum lloydii
Hypericum reductum
Illicium parviflorum

Lantana camara
Osmanthus ×fortunei
Osmanthus fragrans
Osmanthus heterophyllus
Plumbago auriculata
Rhododendron Encore™
    Azaleas
Sesbania punicea
Tecomaria capensis

NOVEMBER
Arbutus unedo
Callistemon spp.
Camellia japonica
Camellia oleifera
Camellia sasanqua
Camellia sinensis
Elaeagnus ×ebbingei
Elaeagnus macrophylla
Elaeagnus pungens
Eriobotrya japonica
Fatsia japonica
Osmanthus fragrans
Osmanthus heterophyllus
Plumbago auriculata
Tecomaria capensis

DECEMBER
Arbutus unedo
Callistemon spp.
Camellia japonica
Camellia oleifera
Camellia sasanqua
Eriobotrya japonica
Fatsia japonica
Osmanthus fragrans
Rosmarinus officinalis
Tecomaria capensis

Fruit

The following shrubs have colorful ornamental fruit.
The primary fruit color(s) is indicated for each plant,
although variations will occur within a species, and
many fruit change color as they mature.

SHRUB	COLOR/COMMENTS	SHRUB	COLOR/COMMENTS
Arbutus unedo	yellow-red	*Magnolia ashei*	red
Ardisia crenata	red	*Mahonia bealei*	robin's-egg blue
Ardisia japonica	red	*Mahonia fortunei*	purple-black
Aucuba japonica	red	*Mahonia japonica*	robin's-egg blue
Baccharis halimifolia	white	*Mahonia ×media*	robin's-egg blue
Carissa macrocarpa	red	*Mitchella repens*	red
Cleyera japonica	black	*Myrica cerifera*	gray
Cotoneaster lacteus	red	*Myrica inodora*	brown-black, sometimes covered with white wax
Cycas revoluta	orange-brown seeds		
Danae racemosa	orange-red	*Myrtus communis*	black
Daphniphyllum macropodum	blue-black	*Nandina domestica*	red
Duranta erecta	yellow	*Osmanthus americanus*	blue-purple
Elaeagnus ×ebbingei	red	*Osmanthus delavayi*	blue-black
Elaeagnus macrophylla	red	*Osmanthus fragrans*	purple-black
Elaeagnus pungens	red	*Osmanthus heterophyllus*	blue-purple-black
Eriobotrya japonica	yellow-orange	*Osmanthus serrulatus*	blue-black
Euonymus americanus	red	*Persea borbonia*	blue-black
Euonymus japonicus	pink-orange	*Phillyrea angustifolia*	black
Eurya emarginata	purple-black	*Photinia ×fraseri*	red
Eurya japonica	black	*Photinia glabra*	red
×Fatshedera lizei	black	*Photinia serrulata*	red
Fatsia japonica	black	*Prunus americana*	yellow to red
Feijoa sellowiana	yellow-green	*Prunus angustifolia*	yellow to red
Ficus carica	red-brown	*Prunus caroliniana*	black
Fuchsia magellanica	red-purple	*Prunus laurocerasus*	black
Gardenia jasminoides	orange-red	*Punica granatum*	red-brown, spotted
Gaylussacia ursina	black	*Pyracantha koidzumii*	red
Ilex cornuta	red	*Rhamnus carolinianus*	red to black
Ilex vomitoria	red	*Rhaphiolepis ×delacouri*	purple-black
Jasminum humile	black	*Rhaphiolepis umbellata*	purple-black
Lantana camara	metallic blue-black	*Rhus michauxii*	red
Laurus nobilis	black	*Rosa laevigata*	red-brown
Leucothoe racemosa	purple	*Rubus pentalobus*	red
Ligustrum japonicum	black, dusty wax-gray coating	*Ruscus aculeatus*	red
Ligustrum lucidum	blue-black, dusty wax-gray coating	*Sarcandra glabra*	red
		Sarcococca confusa	black
Ligustrum sinense	black, dusty wax-gray coating	*Sarcococca orientalis*	black
Lindera angustifolia	black	*Sarcococca ruscifolia*	red
Lindera erythrocarpa	red	*Sarcococca saligna*	black
Lonicera nitida	purple	*Staphylea trifolia*	green to brown, inflated showy capsule
Lonicera pileata	purple		

418

SHRUB	COLOR/COMMENTS	SHRUB	COLOR/COMMENTS
Symplocos tinctoria	orange-brown	*Viburnum japonicum*	red
Ternstroemia gymnanthera	red	*Viburnum macrocephalum* f. *keteleeri*	red
Ungnadia speciosa	brown, inflated capsule	*Viburnum nudum*	pink/rose to blue to purple-black
Vaccinium arboreum	black		
Vaccinium ashei	blue	*Viburnum obovatum*	black
Vaccinium elliottii	black	*Viburnum odoratissimum*	red
Vaccinium stamineum	white, purple	*Viburnum rafinesquianum*	blue-black
Viburnum awabuki	red	*Viburnum suspensum*	red maturing black
Viburnum ×bodnantense	red	*Viburnum tinus*	blue-black
Viburnum bracteatum	blue-black-purple	*Viburnum utile*	red to black
Viburnum cassinoides	pink/rose to blue to purple-black	*Zamia pumila*	orange to red seeds
Viburnum cinnamonifolium	blue	*Zanthoxylum americanum*	red capsules, black seeds
Viburnum davidii	metallic blue	*Ziziphus jujuba*	brown

SHRUBS: DESIGN CHARACTERISTICS
Fall Color

The following shrubs have foliage with notable fall color. For the purposes of this list, fall color has been broken down into broad categories; "red," for example, can signify anything from pinks to deep maroon tints.

YELLOW

Aesculus sylvatica
Alangium platanifolium
Edgeworthia papyrifera
Euonymus americanus
Fontanesia fortunei
Lagerstroemia hybrids
Lagerstroemia indica
Lindera erythrocarpa
Orixa japonica
Parrotiopsis jacquemontiana
Poliothyrsis sinensis
Prunus americana
Prunus angustifolia
Punica granatum
Rhamnus carolinianus
Rhododendron alabamense
Rhododendron austrinum
Rhododendron canescens

Rhododendron Confederate Azaleas
Rhododendron flammeum
Rhododendron prunifolium
×*Sinocalycalycanthus raulstonii*
Sinocalycanthus chinensis
Sinojackia rehderiana
×*Sycoparrotia semidecidua* (winter)
Viburnum bracteatum
Viburnum rafinesquianum
Zanthoxylum americanum
Zanthoxylum clava-herculis

ORANGE

Croton alabamensis
Lagerstroemia hybrids
Lagerstroemia indica

RED

Abelia ×grandiflora (winter)
Clethra barbinervis
Cyrilla racemiflora (winter)
Elliottia racemosa
Gaylussacia ursina
Lagerstroemia hybrids
Lagerstroemia indica
Leucothoe racemosa
Lindera angustifolia
Nandina domestica (winter)
Prunus americana
Prunus angustifolia
Rhododendron alabamense
Rhododendron austrinum
Rhododendron canescens
Rhododendron Confederate Azaleas

Rhododendron flammeum
Rhododendron prunifolium
Rhus michauxii
Stewartia ovata
Stewartia ovata var. *grandiflora*
Vaccinium arboreum
Vaccinium ashei
Vaccinium elliottii
Viburnum cassinoides
Viburnum cassinoides var. *angustifolium*
Viburnum nudum

PURPLE

Abelia ×grandiflora (winter)
Nandina domestica (winter)
Rhaphiolepis ×delacouri (winter)
Rhaphiolepis umbellata (winter)

Broadleaf Evergreen or Semi-Evergreen

Evergreen shrubs have foliage that remains green (alive) for at least a year and through more than one growing season; semi-evergreen implies leaf loss in winter, but this quality is variable.

Abelia ×*grandiflora*
Agave americana
Aleurites fordii
Arbutus unedo
Ardisia crenata
Ardisia japonica
Aucuba japonica
Bauhinia blakeana
Buddleia lindleyana
Buddleia loricata
Buddleia salvifolia
Buxus harlandii
Callistemon citrinus
Callistemon linearis
Callistemon rigidus
Callistemon salignus
Callistemon sieberi
Callistemon speciosus
Callistemon viminalis
Camellia japonica
Camellia oleifera
Camellia reticulata
Camellia sasanqua
Camellia sinensis
Carissa macrocarpa
Chamaerops humilis
Choisya ternata
Clethra arborea
Cleyera japonica
Cliftonia monophylla
Cocculus laurifolius
Cotoneaster lacteus
Croton alabamensis
Cycas revoluta
Cyrilla arida
Cyrilla racemiflora
Cyrtomium falcatum
Danae racemosa
Daphne odora
Daphniphyllum macropodum
Desfontainia spinosa
Distylium racemosum
Elaeagnus ×*ebbingei*

Elaeagnus macrophylla
Elaeagnus pungens
Eriobotrya japonica
Erythrina crista-gallii
Escallonia rubra
Euonymus japonicus
Eurya emarginata
Eurya japonica
×*Fatshedera lizei*
Fatsia japonica
Feijoa sellowiana
Gardenia jasminoides
Gordonia lasianthus
Grevillea rosmarinifolia
Hypericum brachyphyllum
Hypericum fasiculatum
Hypericum lissophoeus
Hypericum lloydii
Hypericum reductum
Ilex cornuta
Ilex vomitoria
Illicium anisatum
Illicium floridanum
Illicium henryi
Illicium mexicanum
Illicium parviflorum
Ixora coccinea
Jasminum floridum
Jasminum humile
Jasminum mesnyi
Jasminum parkeri
Laurus nobilis
Lavandula angustifolia
Leptospermum scoparium
Leucophyllum frutescens
Leucothoe axillaris
Leucothoe populifolia
Ligustrum japonicum
Ligustrum lucidum
Ligustrum sinense
Lindera aggregata
Livistona chinensis
Lonicera nitida

Lonicera pileata
Loropetalum chinense
Loropetalum chinense var. *rubrum*
Lyonia lucida
Mahonia bealei
Mahonia fortunei
Mahonia japonica
Mahonia ×*media*
Michelia figo
Michelia ×*foggii*
Michelia maudiae
Myrica cerifera
Myrica inodora
Myrtus communis
Nandina domestica
Nerium oleander
Osmanthus americanus
Osmanthus ×*burkwoodii*
Osmanthus delavayi
Osmanthus ×*fortunei*
Osmanthus fragrans
Osmanthus heterophyllus
Osmanthus serrulatus
Persea borbonia
Phillyrea angustifolia
Phoenix roebelinii
Photinia ×*fraseri*
Photinia glabra
Photinia serrulata
Pieris formosana var. *forrestii*
Pieris phillyreifolia
Pittosporum tenuifolium
Pittosporum tobira
Prunus caroliniana
Prunus laurocerasus
Pyracantha koidzumii
Rhaphiolepis ×*delacouri*
Rhaphiolepis umbellata
Rhapidiophyllum hystrix
Rhapis excelsa
Rhododendron chapmanii
Rhododendron Encore™ Azaleas

Rhododendron Girard Hybrids
Rhododendron Kurume Hybrids
Rhododendron Robin Hill Hybrids
Rhododendron Rutherfordiana Hybrids
Rhododendron Satsuki Hybrids
Rhododendron Southern Indica
Rosa banksiae 'Lutea'
Rosa laevigata
Rosmarinus officinalis
Rubus pentalobus
Ruscus aculeatus
Sabal etonia
Sabal mexicana
Sabal minor
Santolina chamaecyparissus
Santolina virens
Sarcandra glabra
Sarcococca confusa
Sarcococca orientalis
Sarcococca ruscifolia
Sarcococca saligna
Serenoa repens
Serissa foetida
×*Sycoparrotia semidecidua*
Sycopsis sinensis
Ternstroemia gymnanthera
Teucrium chamaedrys
Trochodendron aralioides
Vaccinium crassifolium
Viburnum awabuki
Viburnum cinnamonifolium
Viburnum davidii
Viburnum japonicum
Viburnum obovatum
Viburnum odoratissimum
Viburnum suspensum
Viburnum tinus
Viburnum utile
Zamia furfuracea
Zamia pumila

Winter Stem Color and Texture

The following shrubs have notable stem color or texture during the winter season.

Agave americana
Clethra barbinervis
Edgeworthia chrysantha
Edgeworthia papyrifera
Eriobotrya japonica
Euscaphis japonicus
Hypericum brachyphyllum
Hypericum densiflorum

Hypericum fasiculatum
Hypericum galioides
Hypericum lissophoeus
Lagerstroemia hybrids
Lagerstroemia indica
Ligustrum japonicum
Loropetalum chinense

Loropetalum chinense var. rubrum
Myrica cerifera
Myrtus communis
Osmanthus americanus
Osmanthus ×fortunei
Osmanthus fragrans
Photinia ×fraseri

Photinia serrulata
Styrax grandifolius
×Sycoparrotia semidecidua
Trochodendron aralioides
Ulmus alata 'Lace Parasol'
Vaccinium arboreum
Vaccinium elliottii

A Guide to Shrub Sizes

Note that shrubs may appear in more than one size category. This is to emphasize that, while the plant will tend to grow to within a size range, there is the possibility of attaining greater size.

SMALL (6 FT. OR LESS)

Abelia chinensis
Abelia ×grandiflora
Abutilon megapotamicum
Abutilon pictum
Agave americana
Ardisia crenata
Brunfelsia pauciflora
Buddleia lindleyana
Buddleia loricata
Buxus harlandii
Callistemon sieberi
Camellia sinensis
Carissa macrocarpa
Cassia marilandica
Ceanothus ×delilianus
Ceanothus ×pallidus
Cephalotaxus harringtonia
Chamaerops humilis
Cistus laurifolius
Cocculus laurifolius
Cycas revoluta
Cyrilla arida
Cyrtomium falcatum
Danae racemosa
Daphne odora
Duranta erecta

Edgeworthia chrysantha
Edgeworthia papyrifera
Erythrina ×bidwellii
Erythrina herbacea
Euonymus americanus
Eurya emarginata
Eurya japonica
×Fatshedera lizei
Fuchsia magellanica
Galphimia gracilis
Gardenia jasminoides
Gaylussacia ursina
Grevillea rosmarinifolia
Helianthemum nummularium
Hypericum brachyphyllum
Hypericum densiflorum
Hypericum fasiculatum
Hypericum galioides
Hypericum lissophoeus
Hypericum lloydii
Hypericum reductum
Illicium mexicanum
Indigofera amblyantha
Indigofera decora
Indigofera heteranthera
Ixora coccinea
Jasminum floridum

Jasminum humile
Jasminum mesnyi
Jasminum nudiflorum
Jasminum parkeri
Lagerstroemia 'Chickasaw'
Lagerstroemia 'Pocomoke'
Lantana camara
Lavandula angustifolia
Lespedeza thunbergii
Leucophyllum frutescens
Leucothoe axillaris
Leucothoe racemosa
Leycesteria crocothyrsos
Leycesteria formosa
Lonicera pileata
Lyonia lucida
Mahonia fortunei
Malvaviscus arboreus var.
    drummondii
Musa coccinea
Phoenix roebelinii
Pieris phillyreifolia
Plumbago auriculata
Podocarpus alpinus
Podocarpus nivalis
Prunus angustifolia
Rhaphiolepis ×delacouri

Rhaphiolepis umbellata
Rhododendron alabamense
Rhododendron Encore™ Azaleas
Rhododendron Girard Hybrids
Rhododendron Kurume Hybrids
Rhododendron Robin Hill
    Hybrids
Rhododendron Rutherfordiana
    Hybrids
Rhododendron Satsuki Hybrids
Rhododendron Southern Indica
Rhus michauxii
Rosmarinus officinalis
Rubus biflorus
Rubus cockburnianus
Rubus coreanus
Rubus idaeus 'Aureus'
Rubus koehneanus
Rubus lasiostylus var. hubeiensis
Rubus thibetanus 'Silver Fern'
Ruscus aculeatus
Santolina chamaecyparissus
Santolina virens
Sarcandra glabra
Sarcococca confusa
Sarcococca orientalis
Sarcococca ruscifolia

421

A Guide to Shrub Sizes, Small, continued

Sarcococca saligna
Serissa foetida
Sesbania punicea
Teucrium chamaedrys
Vaccinium crassifolium
Vaccinium stamineum
Viburnum davidii
Viburnum utile
Vitex rotundifolia
Zamia furfuracea
Zamia pumila

MEDIUM (6 TO 12 FT.)
Adina rubella
Aesculus sylvatica
Alangium platanifolium
Alnus serrulata
Arbutus unedo
Aucuba japonica
Baccharis halimifolia
Brugmansia ×candida
Buddleia lindleyana
Buddleia salvifolia
Callistemon citrinus
Callistemon linearis
Callistemon rigidus
Callistemon salignus
Callistemon speciosus
Callistemon viminalis
Camellia japonica
Camellia oleifera
Camellia reticulata
Camellia sasanqua
Camellia sinensis
Carissa macrocarpa
Cassia bicapsularis
Ceanothus ×delilianus
Cephalotaxus harringtonia
Choisya ternata
Clethra barbinervis
Cleyera japonica
Cliftonia monophylla
Cocculus laurifolius
Cotoneaster lacteus
Croton alabamensis
Cyrilla racemiflora
Daphniphyllum macropodum
Desfontainia spinosa
Distylium racemosum

Elaeagnus ×ebbingei
Elaeagnus macrophylla
Elaeagnus pungens
Elliottia racemosa
Escallonia rubra
Eucryphia glutinosa
Euonymus japonicus
Fatsia japonica
Feijoa sellowiana
Ficus carica
Fontanesia fortunei
Gordonia lasianthus
Hibiscus mutabilis
Hibiscus rosa-sinensis
Hypericum lissophoeus
Ilex cornuta
Ilex vomitoria
Illicium anisatum
Illicium floridanum
Illicium henryi
Illicium mexicanum
Illicium parviflorum
Lagerstroemia 'Acoma'
Lagerstroemia 'Caddo'
Lagerstroemia 'Hopi'
Lagerstroemia indica 'Cedar Red'
Lagerstroemia indica 'Cherokee'
Lagerstroemia indica 'Near East'
Lagerstroemia indica Pink
    Velour™
Lagerstroemia indica 'Pow-
    hatan'
Lagerstroemia 'Tonto'
Lagerstroemia 'Zuni'
Laurus nobilis
Leitneria floridana
Leptospermum scoparium
Lespedeza bicolor
Leucophyllum frutescens
Leucothoe populifolia
Ligustrum japonicum
Ligustrum sinense
Lindera aggregata
Lindera angustifolia
Livistona chinensis
Lonicera nitida
Loropetalum chinense
Loropetalum chinense var.
    rubrum

Magnolia liliiflora
Magnolia Little Girl Hybrids
Mahonia bealei
Mahonia japonica
Mahonia ×media
Michelia figo
Michelia ×foggii
Michelia maudiae
Musa acuminata
Musa ornata
Myrica cerifera
Myrtus communis
Nandina domestica
Nerium oleander
Orixa japonica
Osmanthus ×burkwoodii
Osmanthus delavayi
Osmanthus ×fortunei
Osmanthus fragrans
Osmanthus heterophyllus
Osmanthus serrulatus
Parkinsonia aculeata
Parrotiopsis jacquemontiana
Philadelphus inodorus
Philadelphus pubescens
Phillyrea angustifolia
Photinia ×fraseri
Photinia glabra
Pieris formosana var. forrestii
Pinckneya pubens
Pittosporum tenuifolium
Pittosporum tobira
Prunus angustifolia
Prunus laurocerasus
Punica granatum
Pyracantha koidzumii
Rhamnus carolinianus
Rhapidiophyllum hystrix
Rhapis excelsa
Rhododendron austrinum
Rhododendron canescens
Rhododendron chapmanii
Rhododendron Confederate
    Azaleas
Rhododendron flammeum
Rhododendron prunifolium
Rhododendron Southern Indica
Rosa laevigata
Sabal etonia

Sabal mexicana
Sabal minor
Serenoa repens
×Sinocalycalycanthus
    raulstonii
Sinocalycanthus chinensis
Staphylea trifolia
Stewartia malacodendron
Stewartia ovata
Styrax grandifolius
×Sycoparrotia semidecidua
Sycopsis sinensis
Taxus chinensis
Taxus floridana
Tecomaria capensis
Ternstroemia gymnanthera
Trochodendron aralioides
Ungnadia speciosa
Vaccinium ashei
Vaccinium elliottii
Vaccinium stamineum
Viburnum awabuki
Viburnum ×bodnantense
Viburnum bracteatum
Viburnum cassinoides var.
    angustifolium
Viburnum cinnamonifolium
Viburnum japonicum
Viburnum nudum
Viburnum obovatum
Viburnum odoratissimum
Viburnum rafinesquianum
Viburnum suspensum
Viburnum tinus
Zanthoxylum americanum

LARGE (12 FT. OR GREATER)
Aesculus sylvatica
Alnus serrulata
Arbutus unedo
Brugmansia ×candida
Callistemon citrinus
Callistemon linearis
Callistemon rigidus
Callistemon speciosus
Callistemon viminalis
Camellia japonica
Camellia oleifera
Camellia reticulata

Castanea pumila
Cephalotaxus fortunei
Chilopsis linearis
×Chitalpa tashkentensis
Clethra barbinervis
Cleyera japonica
Cliftonia monophylla
Cyrilla racemiflora
Daphniphyllum macropodum
Eriobotrya japonica
Eucryphia glutinosa
Feijoa sellowiana
Ficus carica
Fontanesia fortunei
Gordonia lasianthus
Hibiscus rosa-sinensis
Ilex cassine
Ilex cornuta
Ilex vomitoria
Illicium anisatum
Lagerstroemia indica 'Catawba'
Lagerstroemia indica 'Comanche'

Lagerstroemia indica 'Conestoga'
Lagerstroemia indica 'Potomac'
Lagerstroemia indica Raspberry Sundae™
Lagerstroemia indica 'Regal Red'
Lagerstroemia indica 'Seminole'
Lagerstroemia 'Lipan'
Lagerstroemia 'Osage'
Lagerstroemia 'Pecos'
Lagerstroemia 'Sioux'
Lagerstroemia 'Yuma'
Leptospermum scoparium
Ligustrum lucidum
Lindera erythrocarpa
Livistona chinensis
Magnolia ashei
Mahonia ×media
Michelia figo
Michelia ×foggii
Michelia maudiae
Musa ×paradisiaca

Myrica cerifera
Myrica inodora
Nerium oleander
Osmanthus americanus
Osmanthus ×fortunei
Osmanthus fragrans
Osmanthus heterophyllus
Parkinsonia aculeata
Persea borbonia
Photinia ×fraseri
Photinia serrulata
Pinckneya pubens
Pittosporum tenuifolium
Podocarpus macrophyllus 'Maki'
Poliothyrsis sinensis
Prunus americana
Prunus angustifolia
Prunus caroliniana
Prunus laurocerasus
Punica granatum
Pyracantha koidzumii
Rhamnus carolinianus
Rosa banksiae 'Lutea'

Sinojackia rehderiana
Sophora secundiflora
Staphylea trifolia
Stewartia malacodendron
Stewartia ovata
Styrax grandifolius
×Sycoparrotia semidecidua
Sycopsis sinensis
Symplocos tinctoria
Taxus floridana
Tecomaria capensis
Trochodendron aralioides
Ungnadia speciosa
Vaccinium arboreum
Viburnum awabuki
Viburnum ×bodnantense
Viburnum macrocephalum
Viburnum macrocephalum f. keteleeri
Viburnum odoratissimum
Zanthoxylum americanum
Zanthoxylum clava-herculis

SHRUBS: CULTURAL CHARACTERISTICS AND MAINTENANCE

Tolerance to Dry Soils

The following shrubs are good plants for dry soil conditions.

Abelia chinensis
Abelia ×grandiflora
Agave americana
Arbutus unedo
Ardisia crenata
Ardisia japonica
Aucuba japonica
Baccharis halimifolia
Buddleia lindleyana
Buddleia loricata
Buddleia salvifolia
Callistemon citrinus
Callistemon linearis
Callistemon rigidus
Callistemon salignus
Callistemon sieberi
Callistemon speciosus
Callistemon viminalis
Carissa macrocarpa
Chilopsis linearis
×Chitalpa tashkentensis

Cleyera japonica
Cotoneaster lacteus
Cycas revoluta
Cyrilla arida
Danae racemosa
Daphniphyllum macropodum
Elaeagnus ×ebbingei
Elaeagnus macrophylla
Elaeagnus pungens
Erythrina herbacea
Fontanesia fortunei
Ilex cornuta
Ilex vomitoria
Jasminum nudiflorum
Lagerstroemia hybrids
Lagerstroemia indica
Lantana camara
Lespedeza thunbergii
Leucophyllum frutescens
Ligustrum japonicum
Ligustrum lucidum

Ligustrum sinense
Loropetalum chinense
Loropetalum chinense var. rubrum
Mahonia bealei
Mahonia fortunei
Mahonia japonica
Mahonia ×media
Myrica cerifera
Myrica inodora
Nandina domestica
Nerium oleander
Osmanthus ×fortunei
Osmanthus fragrans
Osmanthus heterophyllus
Photinia ×fraseri
Photinia glabra
Photinia serrulata
Pittosporum tobira
Prunus caroliniana
Pyracantha koidzumii
Rhaphiolepis ×delacouri

Rhaphiolepis umbellata
Rhapidiophyllum hystrix
Rhapis excelsa
Rosmarinus officinalis
Santolina chamaecyparissus
Santolina virens
Sarcococca confusa
Sarcococca orientalis
Sarcococca ruscifolia
Sarcococca saligna
Sophora secundiflora
Sycopsis sinensis
Ternstroemia gymnanthera
Vaccinium arboreum
Viburnum awabuki
Viburnum bracteatum
Viburnum obovatum
Viburnum odoratissimum
Viburnum suspensum
Zamia furfuracea
Zamia pumila

Tolerance to Moist Soils

The following shrubs are tolerant of moist soil conditions.

Adina rubella
Alnus serrulata
Baccharis halimifolia
Cliftonia monophylla
Cyrilla racemiflora
Gordonia lasianthus
Ilex cassine

Ilex vomitoria
Illicium floridanum
Illicium parviflorum
Leitneria floridana
Leucothoe populifolia
Ligustrum sinense
Lyonia lucida

Myrica cerifera
Myrica inodora
Osmanthus americanus
Persea borbonia
Pieris phillyreifolia
Pinckneya pubens

Rhapidiophyllum hystrix
Sabal etonia
Sabal mexicana
Sabal minor
Sesbania punicea
Viburnum nudum

Salt Tolerance

Shrubs listed show various degrees of tolerance to aerial-
and/or soil-deposited salts.

Agave americana
Ardisia crenata
Baccharis halimifolia
Callistemon spp.
Carissa macrocarpa
Chamaerops humilis
Chilopsis linearis
Cocculus laurifolius
Cycas revoluta
Cyrtomium falcatum
Duranta erecta
Elaeagnus ×ebbingei
Elaeagnus macrophylla
Elaeagnus pungens
Eriobotrya japonica
Escallonia rubra
Euonymus japonicus

×Fatshedera lizei
Fatsia japonica
Feijoa sellowiana
Fuchsia magellanica
Ilex cornuta
Ilex vomitoria
Ixora coccinea
Leptospermum scoparium
Leucophyllum frutescens
Ligustrum japonicum
Ligustrum sinense
Livistona chinensis
Lonicera nitida
Lonicera pileata
Myrica cerifera
Myrica inodora

Myrtus communis
Nandina domestica
Nerium oleander
Persea borbonia
Phoenix roebelinii
Pittosporum tenuifolium
Pittosporum tobira
Prunus caroliniana
Pyracantha koidzumii
Rhaphiolepis ×delacouri
Rhaphiolepis umbellata
Rhapis excelsa
Rosa laevigata
Rosmarinus officinalis
Sabal etonia
Sabal mexicana

Sabal minor
Santolina chamaecyparissus
Santolina virens
Serenoa repens
Sesbania punicea
Sophora secundiflora
Tecomaria capensis
Ungnadia speciosa
Viburnum awabuki
Viburnum suspensum
Viburnum tinus
Vitex rotundifolia
Zamia furfuracea
Zamia pumila
Zanthoxylum americanum
Zanthoxylum clava-herculis

Shade Tolerance

The following shrubs are tolerant of conditions of medium shade or greater. Some plants will produce diminished flowers or fruit in shady environments.

Abelia chinensis
Abelia ×grandiflora
Adina rubella
Aesculus sylvatica
Alangium platanifolium
Arbutus unedo
Ardisia crenata
Ardisia japonica
Aucuba japonica
Buxus harlandii
Camellia japonica
Camellia oleifera
Camellia reticulata
Camellia sasanqua
Camellia sinensis
Chamaerops humilis
Choisya ternata
Clethra arborea
Clethra barbinervis
Cleyera japonica
Cotoneaster lacteus
Croton alabamensis
Cycas revoluta
Cyrtomium falcatum
Danae racemosa
Daphne odora
Desfontainia spinosa
Distylium racemosum
Edgeworthia chrysantha
Edgeworthia papyrifera
Elaeagnus ×ebbingei
Elaeagnus macrophylla
Elaeagnus pungens
Eriobotrya japonica
Euonymus americanus
Euonymus japonicus
Eurya emarginata
Eurya japonica
×Fatshedera lizei
Fatsia japonica
Gardenia jasminoides
Gordonia lasianthus

Grevillea rosmarinifolia
Ilex cassine
Ilex cornuta
Ilex vomitoria
Illicium anisatum
Illicium floridanum
Illicium henryi
Illicium mexicanum
Illicium parviflorum
Jasminum floridum
Jasminum humile
Jasminum mesnyi
Jasminum nudiflorum
Leitneria floridana
Leucothoe axillaris
Leucothoe populifolia
Leucothoe racemosa
Ligustrum japonicum
Ligustrum lucidum
Ligustrum sinense
Lindera aggregata
Lindera angustifolia
Lonicera nitida
Lonicera pileata
Loropetalum chinense
Loropetalum chinense var.
  rubrum
Lyonia lucida
Magnolia ashei
Mahonia bealei
Mahonia fortunei
Mahonia japonica
Mahonia ×media
Michelia figo
Michelia ×foggii
Michelia maudiae
Myrica cerifera
Myrica inodora
Myrtus communis
Nandina domestica
Orixa japonica

Osmanthus americanus
Osmanthus ×burkwoodii
Osmanthus delavayi
Osmanthus ×fortunei
Osmanthus fragrans
Osmanthus heterophyllus
Osmanthus serrulatus
Parrotiopsis jacquemontiana
Philadelphus inodorus
Philadelphus pubescens
Phillyrea angustifolia
Photinia ×fraseri
Photinia glabra
Photinia serrulata
Pieris formosana var. forrestii
Pieris phillyreifolia
Pittosporum tenuifolium
Pittosporum tobira
Prunus caroliniana
Prunus laurocerasus
Rhamnus carolinianus
Rhapidiophyllum hystrix
Rhapis excelsa
Rhododendron alabamense
Rhododendron austrinum
Rhododendron canescens
Rhododendron chapmanii
Rhododendron Confederate
  Azaleas
Rhododendron Encore™ Azaleas
Rhododendron flammeum
Rhododendron Girard Hybrids
Rhododendron Kurume Hybrids
Rhododendron prunifolium
Rhododendron Robin Hill
  Hybrids
Rhododendron Rutherfordiana
  Hybrids
Rhododendron Satsuki Hybrids
Rhododendron Southern Indica
Rubus pentalobus

Ruscus aculeatus
Sarcandra glabra
Sarcococca confusa
Sarcococca orientalis
Sarcococca ruscifolia
Sarcococca saligna
Serenoa repens
Serissa foetida
×Sinocalycalycanthus
  raulstonii
Sinocalycanthus chinensis
Sinojackia rehderiana
Stewartia ovata
Stewartia ovata var.
  grandiflora
Styrax grandifolius
×Sycoparrotia semidecidua
Sycopsis sinensis
Symplocos tinctoria
Ternstroemia gymnanthera
Torreya taxifolia
Trochodendron aralioides
Vaccinium arboreum
Vaccinium crassifolium
Vaccinium elliottii
Vaccinium stamineum
Viburnum awabuki
Viburnum ×bodnantense
Viburnum bracteatum
Viburnum cassinoides
Viburnum cassinoides var.
  angustifolium
Viburnum cinnamonifolium
Viburnum davidii
Viburnum japonicum
Viburnum nudum
Viburnum obovatum
Viburnum rafinesquianum
Viburnum suspensum
Viburnum tinus
Viburnum utile

Hedges and Parterres

The following shrubs are particularly amenable to pruning and are among the better choices for hedging. Pruning is a dwarfing process and often results in loss of flower buds (see following table, "Pruning Times").

Abelia ×grandiflora	Ilex cornuta	Loropetalum chinense var. rubrum	Pittosporum tenuifolium
Aucuba japonica	Ilex vomitoria	Mahonia bealei	Pittosporum tobira
Buxus harlandii	Illicium floridanum	Mahonia fortunei	Prunus caroliniana
Carissa macrocarpa	Illicium henryi	Mahonia japonica	Prunus laurocerasus
Cleyera japonica	Illicium parviflorum	Mahonia ×media	Pyracantha koidzumii
Cocculus laurifolius	Ixora coccinea	Michelia figo	Rosmarinus officinalis
Cotoneaster lacteus	Laurus nobilis	Myrica cerifera	Santolina chamaecyparissus
Elaeagnus ×ebbingei	Lavandula angustifolia	Myrica inodora	Santolina virens
Elaeagnus macrophylla	Leptospermum scoparium	Myrtus communis	Serissa foetida
Elaeagnus pungens	Leucophyllum frutescens	Nandina domestica	Ternstroemia gymnanthera
Escallonia rubra	Ligustrum japonicum	Osmanthus ×fortunei	Teucrium chamaedrys
Euonymus japonicus	Ligustrum lucidum	Osmanthus heterophyllus	Viburnum awabuki
Eurya emarginata	Ligustrum sinense	Phillyrea angustifolia	Viburnum obovatum
Eurya japonica	Lonicera nitida	Photinia ×fraseri	Viburnum odoratissimum
Feijoa sellowiana	Lonicera pileata	Photinia glabra	Viburnum suspensum
Gardenia jasminoides	Loropetalum chinense	Photinia serrulata	Viburnum tinus
Grevillea rosmarinifolia			

Pruning Times

The following table is a guide to the best time to prune shrubs. Very often people prune either too early or too late, removing flower buds or young fruit before they can develop. For plants that produce outstanding flowers and fruit, there is seldom a best time to prune. Flowers (and the fruit that follow) are formed either on the previous season's wood or on new growth of the season. Shrubs that flower on old wood should be pruned after flowering. Shrubs that flower on new growth can be pruned either before or after flowering.

SHRUB	FLOWERS ON	SHRUB	FLOWERS ON
Abelia chinensis	new growth	Aucuba japonica	old wood
Abelia ×grandiflora	new growth	Baccharis halimifolia	new growth
Abutilon megapotamicum	new growth	Brugmansia ×candida	new growth
Abutilon pictum	new growth	Brunfelsia pauciflora	old wood, some new growth
Adina rubella	new growth	Buddleia lindleyana	new growth
Aesculus sylvatica	old wood	Buddleia loricata	old wood
Agave americana	old wood	Buddleia salvifolia	old wood
Alangium platanifolium	old wood	Buxus harlandii	old wood
Alnus serrulata	old wood	Callistemon citrinus	new growth, some old wood
Arbutus unedo	old wood in fall-winter	Callistemon linearis	new growth, some old wood
Ardisia crenata	old wood	Callistemon rigidus	new growth, some old wood
Ardisia japonica	old wood, some new growth	Callistemon salignus	new growth, some old wood

SHRUB	FLOWERS ON	SHRUB	FLOWERS ON
Callistemon sieberi	new growth, some old wood	*Fatsia japonica*	old wood
Callistemon speciosus	new growth, some old wood	*Feijoa sellowiana*	old wood
Callistemon viminalis	new growth, some old wood	*Ficus carica*	old wood, some new growth
Camellia japonica	old wood	*Fontanesia fortunei*	old wood
Camellia oleifera	old wood	*Fuchsia magellanica*	new growth, some old wood
Camellia reticulata	old wood	*Galphimia gracilis*	new growth
Camellia sasanqua	old wood	*Gardenia jasminoides*	old wood, some new growth
Camellia sinensis	old wood	*Gaylussacia ursina*	old wood
Carissa macrocarpa	old wood, some new growth	*Gordonia lasianthus*	new growth
Cassia bicapsularis	new growth	*Grevillea rosmarinifolia*	new growth
Cassia marilandica	new growth	*Helianthemum nummularium*	old wood
Castanea pumila	old wood	*Hibiscus mutabilis*	new growth
Ceanothus ×delilianus	new growth, some old wood	*Hibiscus rosa-sinensis*	new growth
Ceanothus ×pallidus	old wood, new growth	*Hypericum brachyphyllum*	old wood, new growth
Chilopsis linearis	new growth	*Hypericum densiflorum*	old wood, new growth
×Chitalpa tashkentensis	new growth	*Hypericum fasiculatum*	old wood, new growth
Choisya ternata	old wood	*Hypericum galioides*	old wood, new growth
Cistus laurifolius	old wood, some new growth	*Hypericum lissophoeus*	old wood, new growth
Cistus ×purpureus	old wood, some new growth	*Hypericum lloydii*	old wood, new growth
Clethra arborea	old wood	*Hypericum reductum*	old wood, new growth
Clethra barbinervis	old wood	*Ilex cassine*	old wood
Cleyera japonica	old wood	*Ilex cornuta*	old wood
Cliftonia monophylla	old wood	*Ilex vomitoria*	old wood
Cocculus laurifolius	old wood	*Illicium anisatum*	old wood
Cotoneaster lacteus	old wood	*Illicium floridanum*	old wood, some new growth
Croton alabamensis	old wood	*Illicium henryi*	old wood
Cyrilla arida	old wood	*Illicium mexicanum*	old wood, some new growth
Cyrilla racemiflora	old wood	*Illicium parviflorum*	old wood, new growth
Danae racemosa	old wood	*Indigofera amblyantha*	new growth, some old wood
Daphne odora	old wood	*Indigofera decora*	new growth, some old wood
Daphniphyllum macropodum	old wood	*Indigofera heteranthera*	new growth, some old wood
Desfontainia spinosa	old wood	*Ixora coccinea*	old wood, some new growth
Distylium racemosum	old wood	*Jasminum floridum*	old wood, new growth
Duranta erecta	new growth	*Jasminum humile*	old wood
Edgeworthia chrysantha	old wood	*Jasminum mesnyi*	old wood
Edgeworthia papyrifera	old wood	*Jasminum nudiflorum*	old wood
Elaeagnus ×ebbingei	old wood	*Jasminum parkeri*	old wood, some new growth
Elaeagnus macrophylla	old wood	*Lagerstroemia fauriei*	old wood
Elaeagnus pungens	old wood	*Lagerstroemia* hybrids	new growth
Elliottia racemosa	old wood	*Lagerstroemia indica*	new growth
Eriobotrya japonica	old wood	*Lagerstroemia limii*	new growth
Erythrina ×bidwellii	new growth	*Lantana camara*	new growth
Erythrina herbacea	new growth	*Laurus nobilis*	old wood
Escallonia rubra	old wood, some new growth	*Lavandula angustifolia*	new growth
Eucryphia glutinosa	old wood	*Leitneria floridana*	old wood
Euonymus americanus	old wood	*Leptospermum scoparium*	old wood
Euonymus japonicus	old wood	*Lespedeza bicolor*	old wood, some new growth
Eurya emarginata	old wood	*Lespedeza thunbergii*	new growth
Eurya japonica	old wood	*Leucophyllum frutescens*	new growth
×Fatshedera lizei	old wood	*Leucothoe axillaris*	old wood

SHRUB	FLOWERS ON	SHRUB	FLOWERS ON
Leucothoe populifolia	old wood	*Philadelphus pubescens*	old wood
Leucothoe racemosa	old wood	*Phillyrea angustifolia*	old wood
Leycesteria crocothyrsos	new growth	*Photinia ×fraseri*	old wood
Leycesteria formosa	new growth	*Photinia glabra*	old wood
Ligustrum japonicum	old wood	*Photinia serrulata*	old wood
Ligustrum lucidum	old wood	*Pieris formosana* var. *forrestii*	old wood
Ligustrum sinense	old wood	*Pieris phillyreifolia*	old wood
Lindera aggregata	old wood	*Pinckneya pubens*	new growth
Lindera angustifolia	old wood	*Pittosporum tenuifolium*	old wood
Lindera erythrocarpa	old wood	*Pittosporum tobira*	old wood
Lonicera nitida	old wood	*Plumbago auriculata*	new growth
Lonicera pileata	old wood	*Poliothyrsis sinensis*	new growth
Loropetalum chinense	old wood	*Prunus americana*	old wood
Loropetalum chinense var. *rubrum*	old wood, some new growth	*Prunus angustifolia*	old wood
Lyonia lucida	old wood	*Prunus caroliniana*	old wood
Magnolia ashei	old wood	*Prunus laurocerasus*	old wood
Magnolia liliiflora	old wood, some new growth	*Punica granatum*	old wood, some new growth
Magnolia Little Girl Hybrids	old wood, some new growth	*Pyracantha koidzumii*	old wood
Mahonia bealei	old wood	*Rhamnus carolinianus*	old wood
Mahonia fortunei	new growth in August–September	*Rhaphiolepis ×delacouri*	old wood
		Rhaphiolepis umbellata	old wood
Mahonia japonica	old wood	*Rhododendron alabamense*	old wood
Mahonia ×media	old wood	*Rhododendron austrinum*	old wood
Malvaviscus arboreus var. *drummondii*	new growth	*Rhododendron canescens*	old wood
		Rhododendron chapmanii	old wood
Michelia figo	old wood	*Rhododendron* Confederate Azaleas	old wood
Michelia ×foggii	old wood	*Rhododendron* Encore™ Azaleas	old wood, new growth
Michelia maudiae	old wood	*Rhododendron flammeum*	old wood
Musa coccinea	new growth	*Rhododendron* Girard Hybrids	old wood
Musa ornata	new growth	*Rhododendron* Kurume Hybrids	old wood
Musa ×paradisiaca	new growth	*Rhododendron prunifolium*	old wood
Myrica cerifera	old wood	*Rhododendron* Robin Hill Hybrids	old wood
Myrica inodora	old wood	*Rhododendron* Rutherfordiana Hybrids	old wood
Myrtus communis	old wood		
Nandina domestica	old wood	*Rhododendron* Satsuki Hybrids	old wood
Nerium oleander	new growth	*Rhododendron* Southern Indica	old wood
Orixa japonica	old wood	*Rhus michauxii*	old wood
Osmanthus americanus	old wood	*Rosa banksiae* 'Lutea'	old wood
Osmanthus ×burkwoodii	old wood	*Rosa laevigata*	old wood
Osmanthus delavayi	old wood	*Rosmarinus officinalis*	old wood
Osmanthus ×fortunei	old wood	*Rubus biflorus*	old wood
Osmanthus fragrans	old wood, new growth	*Rubus cockburnianus*	old wood
Osmanthus heterophyllus	old wood	*Rubus coreanus*	old wood
Osmanthus serrulatus	old wood	*Rubus idaeus* 'Aureus'	old wood
Parkinsonia aculeata	new growth	*Rubus koehneanus*	old wood
Parrotiopsis jacquemontiana	old wood	*Rubus lasiostylus* var. *hubeiensis*	old wood
Persea borbonia	old wood	*Rubus thibetanus* 'Silver Fern'	old wood
Philadelphus inodorus	old wood	*Ruscus aculeatus*	old wood

SHRUB	FLOWERS ON	SHRUB	FLOWERS ON
Santolina chamaecyparissus	old wood, new growth	*Ungnadia speciosa*	old wood
Santolina virens	old wood, new growth	*Vaccinium arboreum*	old wood
Sarcandra glabra	old wood	*Vaccinium ashei*	old wood
Sarcococca confusa	old wood	*Vaccinium crassifolium*	old wood
Sarcococca orientalis	old wood	*Vaccinium elliottii*	old wood
Sarcococca ruscifolia	old wood	*Vaccinium stamineum*	old wood
Sarcococca saligna	old wood	*Viburnum awabuki*	old wood
Serissa foetida	old wood, some new growth	*Viburnum ×bodnantense*	old wood
Sesbania punicea	new growth	*Viburnum bracteatum*	old wood
×Sinocalycalycanthus raulstonii	old wood	*Viburnum cassinoides*	old wood
Sinocalycanthus chinensis	old wood	*Viburnum cinnamonifolium*	old wood
Sinojackia rehderiana	old wood	*Viburnum davidii*	old wood
Sophora secundiflora	old wood	*Viburnum japonicum*	old wood
Staphylea trifolia	old wood	*Viburnum macrocephalum*	old wood in spring and again in fall
Stewartia malacodendron	old wood	*Viburnum nudum*	old wood
Stewartia ovata	old wood	*Viburnum obovatum*	old wood
Styrax grandifolius	old wood	*Viburnum odoratissimum*	old wood
×Sycoparrotia semidecidua	old wood	*Viburnum rafinesquianum*	old wood
Sycopsis sinensis	old wood	*Viburnum suspensum*	old wood
Symplocos tinctoria	old wood	*Viburnum tinus*	old wood
Tecomaria capensis	new growth	*Viburnum utile*	old wood
Ternstroemia gymnanthera	old wood	*Vitex rotundifolia*	new growth
Teucrium chamaedrys	new growth	*Zanthoxylum americanum*	old wood
Trochodendron aralioides	old wood	*Zanthoxylum clava-herculis*	old wood

NEEDLE EVERGREENS: DESIGN AND CULTURAL CHARACTERISTICS

Single Specimens, Groupings, Screens, and Groves

In many landscapes, a grouping of three, five, seven, or more evergreens provides both visual privacy and a more aesthetically pleasing feeling than tight, boxy hedges. Be sure to provide the evergreens with ample space to spread when positioning them as single specimens or in groups, screens, or groves.

Abies firma	*Pinus elliottii*
Araucaria araucana	*Pinus glabra*
Cephalotaxus fortunei	*Pinus palustris*
Cephalotaxus harringtonia	*Pinus taeda*
Cunninghamia lanceolata	*Podocarpus macrophyllus* 'Maki'
Cupressus glabra	*Podocarpus nagi*
Cupressus macrocarpa	*Sequoia sempervirens*
Cupressus sempervirens	*Sequoiadendron giganteum*
Juniperus salicicola	*Taxus chinensis*
Pinus clausa	*Taxus floridana*
Pinus echinata	*Torreya taxifolia*

Hedges

The following needle evergreens can be used as hedges.

NEEDLE EVERGREEN	COMMENTS	NEEDLE EVERGREEN	COMMENTS
Abies firma	This species is not the best for hedges, although it and other members of its genus are often used in displays at arboreta and botanical gardens. Plants can be extremely variable, particularly in needle color, because they are grown from seed. Prune when the needles of the new spring shoots are half normal size. New buds will form behind the cuts and ensure a full, dense plant the next year.	*Cupressus glabra*	
		Cupressus macrocarpa	
		Cupressus sempervirens	
		Juniperus salicicola	
		Pinus clausa	See *Abies firma* entry.
		Pinus echinata	See *Abies firma* entry.
		Pinus elliottii	See *Abies firma* entry.
		Pinus glabra	See *Abies firma* entry.
		Pinus palustris	See *Abies firma* entry.
		Pinus taeda	See *Abies firma* entry.
		Podocarpus macrophyllus 'Maki'	
		Podocarpus nivalis	
Cephalotaxus fortunei		*Taxus chinensis*	
Cephalotaxus harringtonia		*Taxus floridana*	
Cunninghamia lanceolata	Can be pruned and will regenerate new shoots.		

Groundcovers and Massing

The following needle evergreens are good selections for groundcovers and low masses.

Cephalotaxus fortunei and cultivars
Cephalotaxus harringtonia and cultivars
Podocarpus nivalis
Taxus chinensis
Taxus floridana

Salt Tolerance

The following needle evergreens do well in saline environments.

Araucaria araucana   *Pinus echinata*
Cunninghamia lanceolata   *Pinus elliottii*
Cupressus glabra   *Pinus glabra*
Cupressus macrocarpa   *Pinus palustris*
Cupressus sempervirens   *Pinus taeda*
Juniperus salicicola   *Podocarpus macrophyllus* 'Maki'
Pinus clausa   *Podocarpus nagi*

Shade Tolerance

The following needle evergreens can tolerate shady siting. Distinctions are made here for tolerance to light, medium, or heavy shade.

NEEDLE EVERGREEN	DEGREE OF SHADE	NEEDLE EVERGREEN	DEGREE OF SHADE
Abies firma	light	Podocarpus nagi	light
Araucaria araucana	light	Podocarpus nivalis	medium
Cephalotaxus fortunei	medium to heavy	Sequoia sempervirens	light to medium
Cephalotaxus harringtonia	medium to heavy	Sequoiadendron giganteum	light
Cunninghamia lanceolata	medium	Taxus chinensis	medium to heavy
Podocarpus alpinus	medium	Taxus floridana	medium to heavy
Podocarpus macrophyllus 'Maki'	medium to heavy	Torreya taxifolia	medium to heavy

Flowers, Fruit, and Fall Color

The following vines have notably colorful or fragrant flowers, attractive fruit, and/or interesting fall color.

VINE	COMMENTS	VINE	COMMENTS
Actinidia deliciosa	fragrant white flowers, brown hairy edible fruit	Mandevilla splendens	pink flowers
		Millettia reticulata	fragrant purple flowers
Allamanda cathartica	yellow flowers	Parthenocissus henryana	red fall color, purple-black fruit
Antigonon leptopus	pink flowers	Passiflora caerulea	white, pink, blue flowers, orange fruit
Bougainvillea glabra	pink, red, purple, white, orange flowers	Passiflora coccinea	red flowers
Campsis grandiflora	orange to apricot flowers	Passiflora incarnata	blue, white flowers, yellow fruit
Cocculus carolinus	yellow-green flowers, red fruit	Pieris phillyreifolia	fragrant white flowers
Decumaria barbara	fragrant white flowers, yellow fall color	Plumbago auriculata	blue flowers
		Rosa banksiae 'Lutea'	fragrant yellow flowers
×Fatshedera lizei	white flowers, black fruit	Smilax rotundifolia	black fruit
Ficus pumila	no flowers, no fruit in juvenile state	Smilax smallii	black fruit
Gelsemium rankinii	yellow flowers	Smilax walteri	red fruit
Gelsemium sempervirens	fragrant yellow flowers	Tecomaria capensis	orange-red flowers
Hedera canariensis	no flowers, no fruit in juvenile state	Trachelospermum asiaticum	fragrant white to yellow flowers
Jasminum officinale	pink to red buds, fragrant white flowers	Trachelospermum jasminoides	fragrant white to yellow flowers
		Vitis rotundifolia	green to purple fruit
Kadsura japonica	fragrant white flowers, red fruit	Wisteria frutescens	fragrant purple flowers, yellow fall color
Lonicera caprifolium	fragrant yellow flowers, orange-red fruit		
Lonicera flava	yellow-orange flowers, orange-red fruit	Wisteria macrostachys	fragrant purple flowers, yellow fall color
Lonicera periclymenum	fragrant yellowish white flowers with a purplish pink tinge on the outside, red fruit		

True Clinging Vines

The following vines do not require support for growth.

Campsis grandiflora
Decumaria barbara
×Fatshedera lizei
Ficus pumila
Hedera canariensis

Parthenocissus henryana
Pieris phillyreifolia
Tecomaria capensis
Trachelospermum asiaticum
Trachelospermum jasminoides

VINES: DESIGN AND CULTURAL CHARACTERISTICS
Shade Tolerance

The following vines grow well in shady conditions.

Cocculus carolinus
×Fatshedera lizei
Ficus pumila
Gelsemium rankinii
Gelsemium sempervirens
Hedera canariensis
Kadsura japonica

Lonicera caprifolium
Lonicera flava
Lonicera periclymenum
Parthenocissus henryana
Pieris phillyreifolia
Smilax rotundifolia
Smilax smallii

Smilax walteri
Trachelospermum asiaticum
Trachelospermum jasminoides
Vitis rotundifolia
Wisteria frutescens
Wisteria macrostachys

Palms

The following palms are treated or discussed in this book
beginning on page 253.

Butia capitata
Chamaerops humilis
Livistona chinensis
Phoenix canariensis
Phoenix reclinata
Phoenix roebelinii

Rhapidiophyllum hystrix
Rhapis excelsa
Sabal etonia
Sabal mexicana
Sabal minor
Sabal palmetto

Serenoa repens
Syagrus romanzoffianum
Trachycarpus fortunei
Washingtonia filifera
Washingtonia robusta

Groundcovers

The following groundcovers are treated or discussed in this book.

Ardisia japonica
Epigaea repens
Hedera canariensis
Mitchella repens
Pachysandra procumbens

Rubus spp.
Trachelospermum asiaticum
Trachelospermum jasminoides
Vaccinium crassifolium

Vinca major
Vinca minor
Vitex rotundifolia
Wedelia trilobata

U.S. Department of Agriculture Hardiness Zone Map

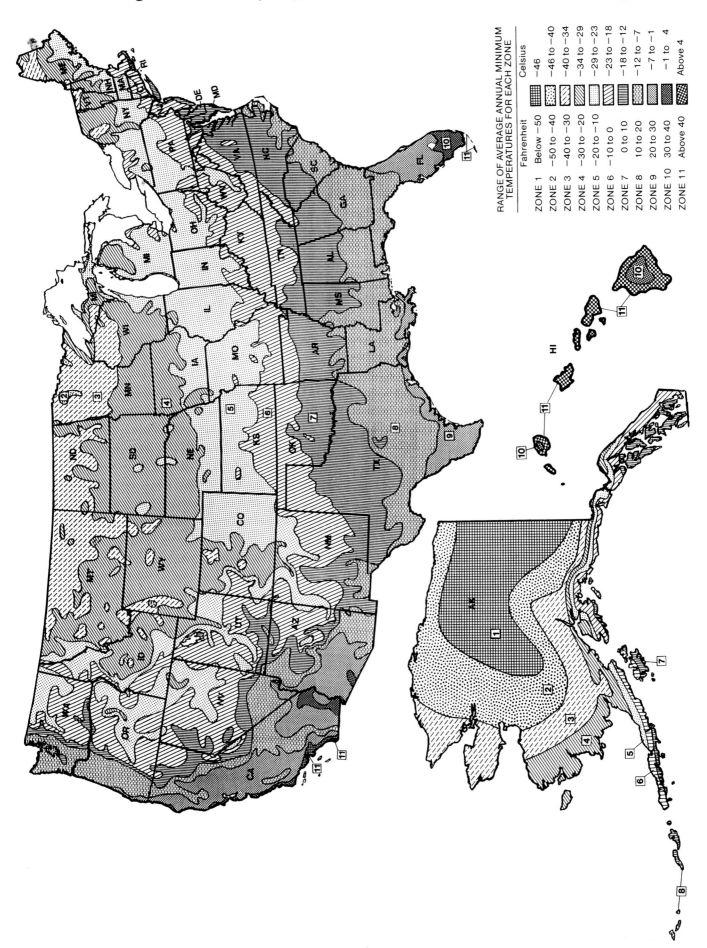

RANGE OF AVERAGE ANNUAL MINIMUM
TEMPERATURES FOR EACH ZONE

	Fahrenheit	Celsius
ZONE 1	Below −50	−46
ZONE 2	−50 to −40	−46 to −40
ZONE 3	−40 to −30	−40 to −34
ZONE 4	−30 to −20	−34 to −29
ZONE 5	−20 to −10	−29 to −23
ZONE 6	−10 to 0	−23 to −18
ZONE 7	0 to 10	−18 to −12
ZONE 8	10 to 20	−12 to −7
ZONE 9	20 to 30	−7 to −1
ZONE 10	30 to 40	−1 to 4
ZONE 11	Above 40	Above 4

Conversion Table for Metric Measurements

INCHES	CENTIMETERS	FEET	METERS
1/8	0.3	1/4	0.08
1/6	0.4	1/3	0.1
1/5	0.5	1/2	0.15
1/4	0.6	1	0.3
1/3	0.8	1 1/2	0.5
3/8	0.9	2	0.6
2/5	1.0	2 1/2	0.8
1/2	1.25	3	0.9
3/5	1.5	4	1.2
5/8	1.6	5	1.5
2/3	1.7	6	1.8
3/4	1.9	7	2.1
7/8	2.2	8	2.4
1	2.5	9	2.7
1 1/4	3.1	10	3.0
1 1/3	3.3	12	3.6
1 1/2	3.75	15	4.5
1 3/4	4.4	18	5.4
2	5.0	20	6.0
3	7.5	25	7.5
4	10	30	9.0
5	12.5	35	10.5
6	15	40	12
7	17.5	45	13.5
8	20	50	15
9	22.5	60	18
10	25	70	21
12	30	75	22.5
15	37.5	80	24
18	45	90	27
20	50	100	30
24	60	125	37.5
30	75	150	45
32	80	175	52.5
36	90	200	60

$$°C = 5/9 \times (°F - 32)$$
$$°F = (9/5 \times °C) + 32$$

434

Index of Plant Scientific Names

Page numbers in **boldface** indicate a main text entry and illustration.

435

442

Index of Plant Common Names

Page numbers in **boldface** indicate a main text entry and illustration.

443